Searching for Mary Schäffer

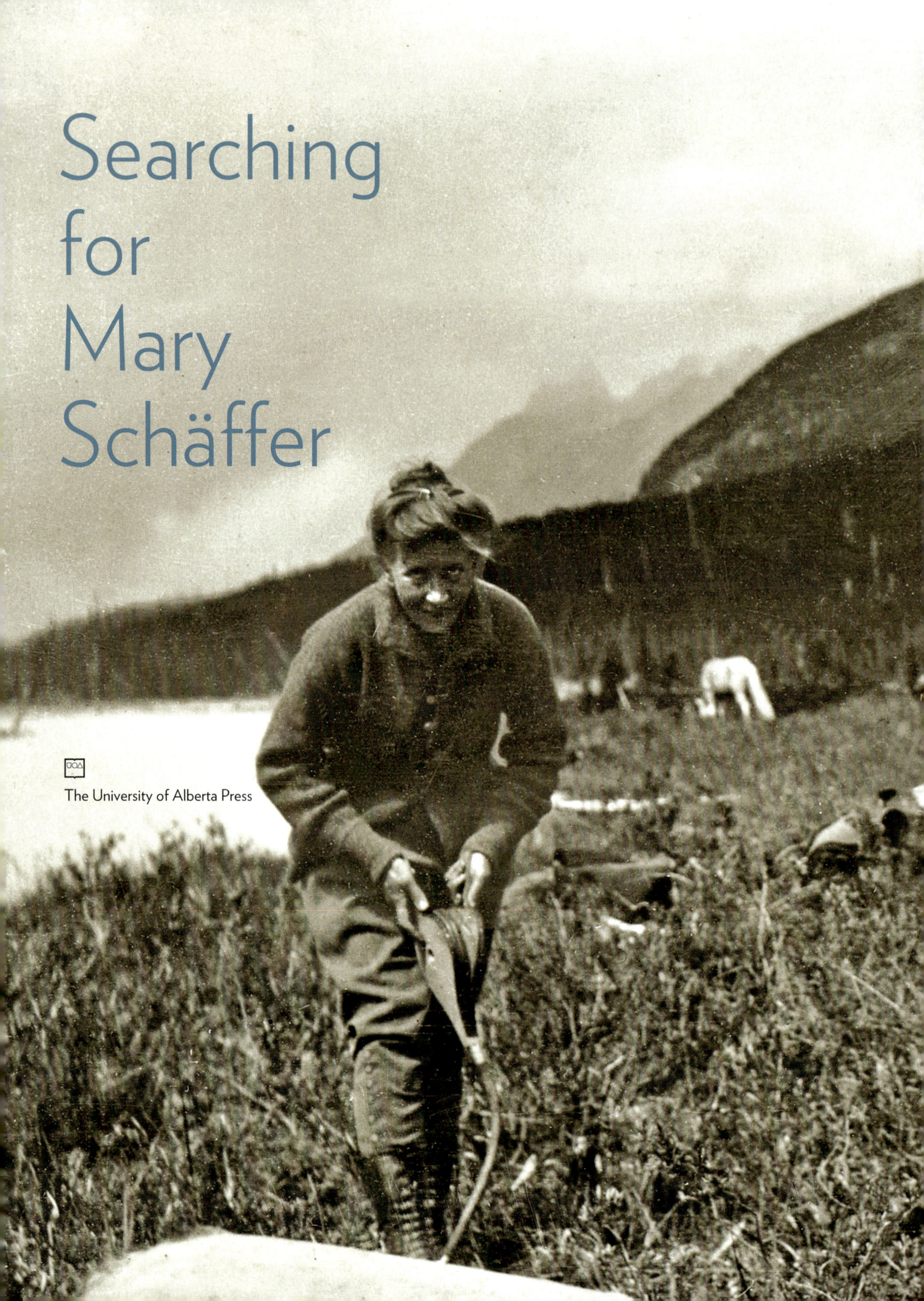
Searching
for
Mary
Schäffer
The University of Alberta Press

COLLEEN SKIDMORE

Women Wilderness Photography

Published by

The University of Alberta Press
Ring House 2
Edmonton, Alberta, Canada T6G 2E1
www.uap.ualberta.ca

LIBRARY AND ARCHIVES CANADA
CATALOGUING IN PUBLICATION

Skidmore, Colleen Marie, 1957–, author
Searching for Mary Schäffer : women wilderness photography / Colleen Skidmore.

(Mountain cairns)
Includes bibliographical references and index.
Issued in print and electronic formats.
ISBN 978-1-77212-298-5 (softcover).—
ISBN 978-1-77212-364-7 (EPUB).—
ISBN 978-1-77212-365-4 (Kindle).—
ISBN 978-1-77212-366-1 (PDF)

1. Schäffer, Mary T. S. (Mary Townsend Sharples), 1861–1939—Influence. 2. Women photographers—Rocky Mountains, Canadian (B.C. and Alta.)—Biography. I. Title. II. Series: Mountain cairns

FC218.S32S55 2017 971.1'03092 C2017-904142-8
C2017-904143-6

First edition, first printing, 2017.
First printed and bound in Canada by Friesens, Altona, Manitoba.
Copyediting and proofreading by Joanne Muzak.
Maps by Wendy Johnson.
Indexing by Judy Dunlop.

The University of Alberta Press gratefully acknowledges the support received for its publishing program from the Government of Canada, the Canada Council for the Arts, and the Government of Alberta through the Alberta Media Fund.

This book was funded in part by the Alberta Historical Resources Foundation.

This book has been published with the help of a grant from the Canadian Federation for the Humanities and Social Sciences, through the Awards to Scholarly Publications Program, using funds provided by the Social Sciences and Humanities Research Council of Canada.

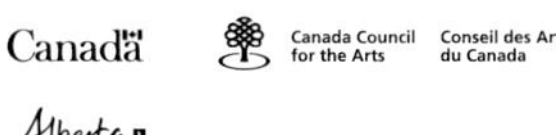

For Elizabeth

Contents

Acknowledgements

SEARCHING FOR MARY SCHÄFFER maps an intellectual, creative, and geographical journey shared and assisted by institutions and agencies, colleagues and family, friends and strangers, over many years.

Grants to support the research, writing, and publication of this book were generously provided by the Social Sciences and Humanities Research Council of Canada, the Awards to Scholarly Publications Program of the Federation for the Humanities and Social Sciences, the Alberta Historical Resources Foundation, and the Office of the Provost at the University of Alberta.

Stewards of collections at nineteen archives, libraries, and museums in Canada and the United States were unfailingly gracious and tenacious in tracking down documents, photographs, artifacts, and answers to my queries, no matter how clumsily or frequently posed. Among these, my most profound thank you is owed to staff, present and past, at the Whyte Museum of the Canadian Rockies in Banff National Park: Don Bourdon, D.L. Cameron, Edward Cavell, Nicole Ensing, Anne Ewen, Lena Goon, E.J. (Ted) Hart, Pam Knott, Elizabeth Kundert-Cameron, and Jennifer Rutkair.

Women who travelled, photographed, and wrote alongside Mary Schäffer were an important part of my search. Two of their descendants became invaluable collaborators on the historical groundwork for this book. Marjorie Adams responded to an email from a stranger—me—with enthusiasm, generosity, and a trove of documents that had been preserved by generations of family members following the death of "Aunt Molly." Susan Wilson opened her home to me, again a stranger, to study diaries, letters, and photographs made by her grandmother, Henrietta Tuzo Wilson, whom she remembers well. My life and this book are richer for encountering these two remarkable women.

Colleagues, friends, and my brother-in-law unreservedly shared their expertise in fields beyond my own, contributing much needed and deeply appreciated insight and clarity to research perplexities, tangled thinking, and muddled writing. Thank you John Coflin, Michael May, Eileen Passmore, Kel Pero, André Plourde, PearlAnn Reichwein, Joan Schwartz, Lisa Shepherd, and members of the Canadian Women Artists History Initiative (Concordia University) and the Canadian Mountain Research Initiative (University of Alberta).

The University of Alberta Press has been an important partner in this venture. In 2006, UAP published *This Wild Spirit: Women in the Rocky Mountains of Canada*, the foundational work that made this new study viable. The press then supported not only the book, now in its third printing, but also the gallery exhibitions in Edmonton, Jasper, and Banff, and the CBC Radio Alberta series that *This Wild Spirit* spawned, all the while awaiting the Schäffer manuscript as it advanced glacially among the distractions and adventures of my professorial life. It has been a privilege and a pleasure to work with these talented and dedicated professionals, from editors to publicists, and at every step in between, as they transformed *Searching for Mary Schäffer* into a book.

Finally, one day many years ago in Jasper Park Lodge, two innocent bystanders heard me utter for the first time the fateful words, "Who is Mary Schäffer?" They have been tireless, amusing—and often bemused—companions on my search ever since, from hiking at Maligne Lake to travelling by train into the heart of Philadelphia. To Joe Owens and our daughter, Elizabeth Owens Skidmore, as always, my deepest gratitude.

Author's Note on Names

ORIGINAL PUBLISHED OR HANDWRITTEN spellings and versions of Mary Schäffer's names, such as Schäffer, Schaffer, Schaeffer, and/or Warren (after 1915), have been retained.

Original published or handwritten spellings and versions of Mary W. (Molly) Adams's names have been retained with one exception: "Molly Adams" is used for letters no matter how she signed them (which generally varied between "Molly" and "M.W.A."). "Mary W. (Molly) Adams" is used for diary authorship.

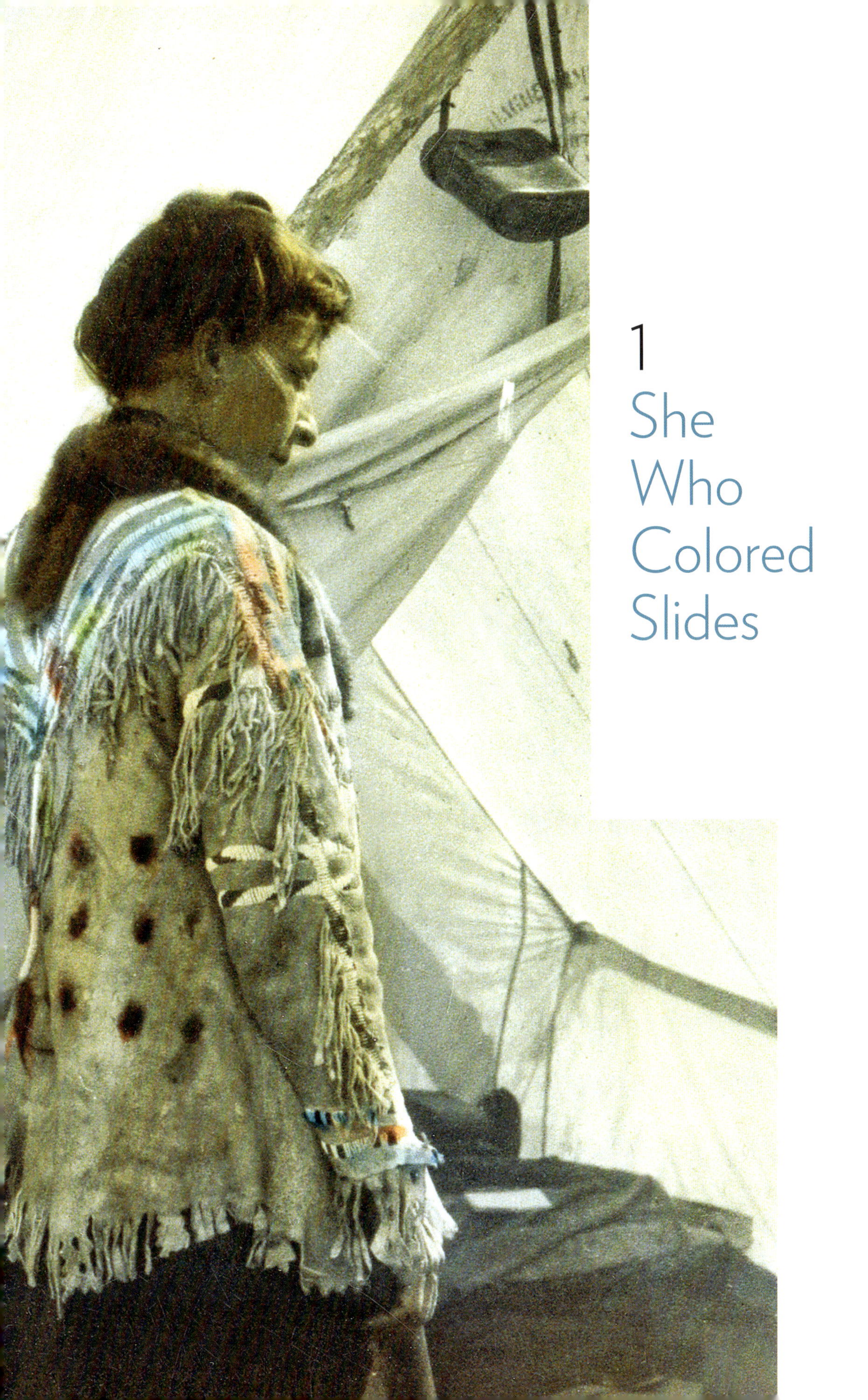

1
She Who Colored Slides

IN THE SUMMERS OF 1907 AND 1908, Philadelphian Mary T.S. Schäffer and Mary W. (Molly) Adams of New Haven, Connecticut, defied convention by setting out on four-month excursions by horseback into the Rocky Mountain range north of the Canadian Pacific Railway (CPR) line at Banff. Their aim was "to penetrate to the head waters of the Saskatchewan and Athabaska rivers"; their desire was "to delve into the heart of an untouched land."[1] These were not their first journeys along Indigenous trails in the backcountry, but they would become their most famous. Nor were the Rockies their only interest. In autumn 1908, they sailed to Japan, seeking travel beyond conventional tourist destinations and amenities to traditional Indigenous territories on Hokkaido and Formosa. By 1910, Schäffer was well known among readers in the United States and Canada for her illustrated volume on the alpine flora of the Canadian Rockies,[2] as well as photographs, journal articles, and lantern slide lectures of the trips she and Adams had made; in 1911, her fame was enhanced by publication of her story of their mountain journeys, titled *Old Indian Trails: Incidents of Camp and Trail Life, Covering Two Years' Exploration through the Rocky Mountains of Canada*, published in New York by G.P. Putnam's Sons. *Old Indian Trails* included one hundred photographs made by Schäffer and Adams, as well as a snapshot made by one of their guides, Sidney Unwin. Two maps were included: a sketch attributed to Stoney hunter Sampson Beaver and, revised in a second printing of January 1912, a topographical map made by Schäffer. The Geological Survey of Canada capitalized on Schäffer's fame in 1911 by contracting her to survey their most legendary destination, Maligne Lake.[3]

Mary Schäffer was not a lone adventurer off the beaten tracks of the railway and its tourists, either in the Rockies or Japan; she was singular, however, for the reputation that she garnered with North American and British readers as a mountain photographer, artist, and writer. A review of *Old Indian Trails* published in the Springfield, Massachusetts, *Republican* was typical, reporting that "the

FIGURE 1.1

Frontispiece and title page of Stewardson Brown and Mary Schäffer's *Alpine Flora of the Canadian Rocky Mountains* (1907).

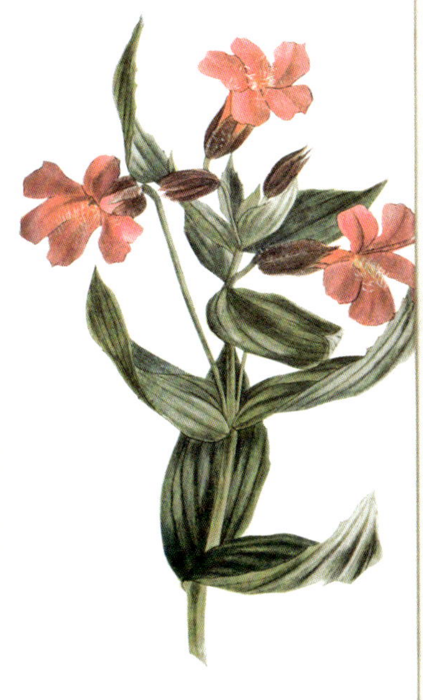

Alpine Flora

of the

Canadian Rocky Mountains

By

Stewardson Brown

Curator of Herbarium Academy of Natural Sciences
Philadelphia

Illustrated with Water-Colour Drawings and Photographs

By

Mrs. Charles Schäffer

G. P. Putnam's Sons
New York and London
The Knickerbocker Press
1907

FIGURE 1.2

Frontispiece and title page of Mary Schäffer's *Old Indian Trails* (1911).

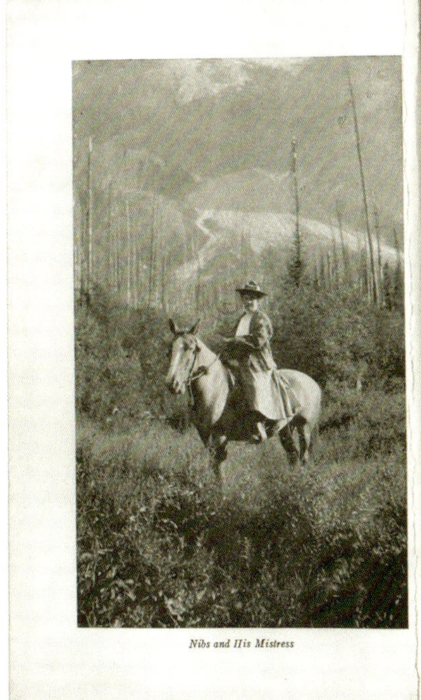

Old Indian Trails

Incidents of Camp and Trail Life, Covering Two Years' Exploration through the Rocky Mountains of Canada

By

Mary T. S. Schäffer

Author of, in Collaboration with Stewardson Brown, "Alpine Flora of the Canadian Rockies," etc.

With 100 Illustrations from Photographs by the Author and by Mary W. Adams, and a Map

Toronto: William Briggs
New York: G. P. Putnam's Sons
1911

account of the trip is modest, yet the reader cannot but marvel at the daring of the explorer."[4] Or, as the *Portland Telegram* put it, "Mrs. Schaffer is an intrepid explorer who has a heart for any hardship that she encounters in the glorious cause of exciting adventure....The dangers and discomforts she and her woman companion encountered do make a remarkable story."[5]

The impact of Schäffer's stories and photographs on readers' geographical, political, and industrial imaginings of the Rocky Mountains of Canada can be measured further by the ways in which certain British literati took up her celebrity. During Schäffer's years of backcountry exploration, Mary (Mrs. Humphry) Ward, Marion Cran, and Rudyard Kipling enjoyed Rocky Mountain sojourns as guests of the Canadian Pacific Railway, while in 1914 Arthur Conan Doyle travelled as a guest of the Dominion government along the Grand Trunk Pacific Railway to Jasper Park. These famed authors were among those who shaped the Edwardian reading public's perceptions of the Empire and its treasures. Most of them met Schäffer along the way and included stories about her in their work.[6] Schäffer was a contemporary and an acquaintance of not only these literary writers but also those of science whose work similarly shaped geographical imaginations (and whose paths she crossed on mountain trails). Such scientists included geologist and Smithsonian Institution Secretary Charles Walcott, glacier geologist and University of Toronto professor Arthur P. Coleman, whose own book, *The Canadian Rockies: New and Old Trails*,[7] was published in the same year as Schäffer's *Old Indian Trails*, and James Hector of Scotland, geologist on the Palliser expedition of 1857–1860, whom Schäffer was excited to meet and photograph when he returned to the Canadian Rockies in 1903. While Mary Schäffer's visual, literary, and scientific ambitions may seem more modest than those of her eminent acquaintances, in posterity they have proven to be no less enduring.

Exploring, Challenging, and Comprehending

Searching for Mary Schäffer: Women Wilderness Photography seeks a better understanding of how and why Mary Schäffer produced a significant number of images and texts that resonated with audiences of her day and continue to engage, more than a century later, scholars and readers whose interests range from conservation and environmentalism to Indigenous histories, women's writing and photography histories, and wilderness studies. Schäffer and Adams, and the circle of women with whom they travelled and photographed, can be counted among those "accomplished women" who, literary scholar

Carolyn G. Heilbrun writes, "were educated enough to have had a choice and brave enough to have made one."[8] This study attempts to explore how, as Heilbrun argues, "woman's selfhood, the right to her own story, depends upon her 'ability to act in the public domain'"; to challenge, as historian Carroll Smith-Rosenberg proposes, "existing gender relations and the distribution of power"; and to comprehend the courage and space needed to imagine, as Schäffer and Adams did to great success, "Why not?"[9] Along the way, analysis of Schäffer's work is extended beyond her best-known accomplishments: the two lengthy backcountry journeys in the Canadian Rockies in 1907 and 1908, publication of *Old Indian Trails* in 1911, and charting Maligne Lake that same year. Throughout, many of the details and interpretations of her biography as well as that of Molly Adams as written since 1980—including my own work in *This Wild Spirit: Women in the Rocky Mountains of Canada* of 2006—are corrected here as a result of historical materials and empirical evidence that have more recently emerged, ranging from the iconic buckskin jacket in which Schäffer was photographed by Adams in 1907 to a collection of letters and diaries written by Adams between 1893 and 1909.

The book is not the work of a biographer or a Rocky Mountain historian, nor that of a cultural studies theorist or critic. Rather, it is the work of a social historian of photography who explores how women shaped photography practices and photographic images, and how photography shaped ideas of women in late nineteenth- and early twentieth-century North America. It is written for those interested in women photographers and artists, as well as those with a special interest in Mary Schäffer and her experiences with Molly Adams and others in the Canadian Rockies. My focus is archives of women's photographs or photographs of women, and the archives of Schäffer's work, as well as that of Adams, are rich in content, meaning, and impact. My questions and analyses are grounded in a view and an argument that photography, cartography, and travel writing are creative endeavours, however much each is informed by facts and experience. This does not make such work any less truthful than non-fiction. It is, however, neither literal nor documentary. Nevertheless, most of the work on Schäffer, both popular and academic, has taken her photography and writing to be biographically factual. Schäffer's work is charismatic for many and it is challenging not to be drawn in by her writing and photography, as well as by the images and personas of Schäffer that have been created by those who have written about her.

It is striking to me that the vast majority of contemporary sources that I have found and draw upon are written by women. This is a significant shift from earlier periods, as recent as 1980, in which women scholars, like scholars of women, were rare; women's imagery and writing had fallen from sight and interest in histories or knowledge of past times; and men's depictions of women, where they existed at all, were the main sources for facts and analysis, rather than women's own depictions of themselves. This latter phenomenon was noted by Smith-Rosenberg, who corrected it in her own work by seeking out women's private writing in diaries and letters. Such materials, she argues, "provide us with a unique opportunity to hear women's own words directly, not filtered through a male record."[10] Nonetheless, women's words and images, like those of men, must be read and considered with an eye to their own socialized views of the world as a place in which people, their activities and opportunities, are organized by gender. Expectations of themselves and others, women and men as well as children, more often than not fall along gendered lines. As letters and diaries in public and private archives show, Schäffer and Adams were perfectly aware of this; many of those writing about their lives and work nearly a century later are much less so.

Furthermore, when considering Schäffer's unpublished work and personal papers, as well as Adams's private correspondence and diaries, it is important to recognize that neither deposited any of their photographic or written work, published or unpublished, public or private, in a public archive. Friends, acquaintances, and a descendant supplied most of the Schäffer materials that have entered archives over the decades since her death in 1939, while Adams's family descendants held her materials privately. Neither explicitly gave permission to share these materials publicly, an issue with considerable ethical implications. At the same time, the value of the materials for contributing to new or expanded knowledge and understanding of a historic time and place is indisputable, and not using such materials in the absence of permission many decades after their deaths is equally an ethical concern.[11] Materials unpublished at the time of death, whether remaining unpublished or now in public circulation by virtue of having been posthumously published, need to be considered with care and respect. When read in comparison to her published work, for example, Schäffer's unpublished manuscripts are clearly not of the same quality and had not been subject to the revision and editing that made the published works so successful. And in correspondence with family and friends, both women express opinions about their own and others' actions and behaviours that they did not originally intend to share with a broader audience. Still, Adams's diaries and correspondence offer a wealth of detail about other women with whom she and Schäffer met and interacted in the Rocky Mountains, and often corroborate or contrast Schäffer's narrative about activities or events.

Mary Schäffer became a public person through her publications, while Molly Adams became one only after her death in 1909, with the publication of *Old Indian Trails* and the equal credit she received on the title page as one of the book's photographers. Schäffer deliberately constructed a public role and reputation, and she kept financial papers, business correspondence, photographs, and family heirlooms in good order, but without any written directions for their disposal following her death or that of her surviving husband, who inherited her estate. Subsequently, most of the early Schäffer collection came into the possession of the Whyte Museum of the Canadian Rockies when the family that acquired Schäffer's Banff house and its contents from her husband, William Warren, after Schäffer's death sold it decades later. In addition, family descendants of Schäffer's friend and attorney, George Vaux Jr., donated to the Whyte Museum extensive collections of correspondence and legal papers related to Schäffer's affairs. In contrast, Adams was known as a woman of few words in private life. She allowed some of her photographs to be published in articles written by friends, but most of her surviving photographic work is found in two albums among Mary Schäffer's possessions, and one in the possession of her family. A typed transcription of Adams's 1908 diary of their trip to Maligne Lake is also among Schäffer's papers, the only extant written material from Adams in a public archive while this book was being written. Molly Adams's sister, Catherine Adams Elkin, however, retained and transcribed her abundant correspondence, written over nearly two decades; neither woman had children, but their brother Roger Adams's descendants have cared for the papers since their great aunt Catherine Adams Elkin's death. (See Appendix 2 for an overview of Molly Adams's family.) The nieces who shared this material with me a little over a century after Adams's death offered its full use at my discretion, a tremendous responsibility.[12] So too did the granddaughters of another travel companion of Schäffer and Adams, Henrietta L. Tuzo, who retain diaries, photographs, letters, and other materials from that time. I have proceeded with the questions of privacy, permission, and public knowledge always in mind, attempting to integrate and recognize the push and pull of the individuals and the social contexts in which they were living, travelling, photographing, and writing.

Women

Old Indian Trails is first and foremost a story of exploring women. Introducing their tale, Schäffer draws a captivating picture of how and why she and Molly Adams undertook their journeys:

> *With willing ears we listened to the tales brought in by the hunters and trappers, those men of this land who are the true pioneers of the country in spite of the fact that they have written nothing and are but little known. With hearts not entirely on pelts, they had seen and now told us of valleys of great beauty, of high unknown peaks, of little-known rivers, of un-named lakes, lying to the north and north-west of the country we knew so well,—a fairyland yet a land girt about with hardships, a land whose highway was a difficult trail or no trail at all. We fretted for the strength of man, for the way was long and hard, and only the tried and stalwart might venture where cold and heat, starvation and privation stalked ever at the explorer's heels. In meek despair we bowed our heads to the inevitable, to the cutting knowledge of the superiority of the endurance of man and the years slipped by.*
>
> *From the States came Allen and Wilcox, (men of course), gathered their outfits together and left us sitting on the railroad track following them with hungry eyes as they plunged into the distant hills; to listen just as hungrily to the camp-fire tales on their return, of all the wonders of the more northern Rockies; came Stuttfield, Collie, Woolley, Outram (names so well known in the alpine world to-day), to tell again to our eager-listening ears of the vast, glorious, unexplored country beyond; came Fay, Thompson, and Coleman—all men!*[13]

In 1979, in her study *Reinventing Womanhood*, Heilbrun observed a certain pattern of behaviour in women: "Men have monopolized human experience, leaving women unable to imagine themselves as both ambitious and female. If I imagine myself (woman has always asked) whole, active, a self, will I not cease, in some profound way, to be a woman?"[14] Schäffer and Adams are portrayed as struggling with this very issue:

> *There are few women who do not know their privileges and how to use them, yet there are times when the horizon seems restricted, and we seemed to have reached that horizon, and the limit of all endurance,—to sit with folded hands and listen calmly to the stories of the hills we so longed to see, the hills which*

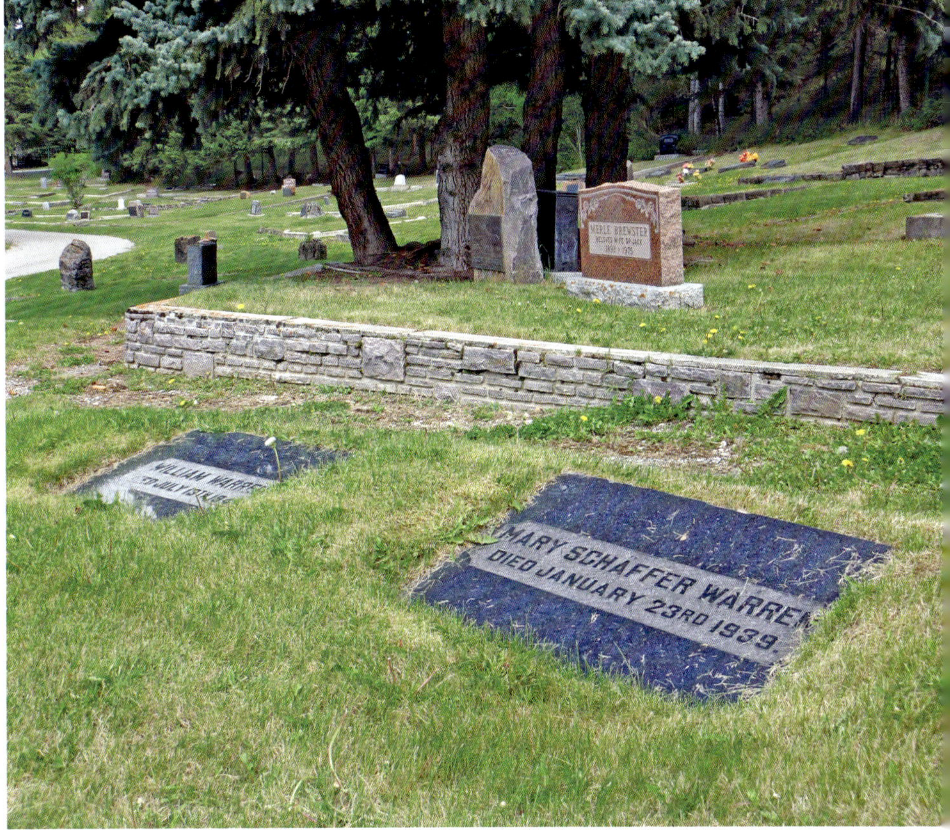

FIGURE 1.3

Mary Schäffer and William Warren gravestones, Old Banff Cemetery, 2009.

[Photo: Colleen Skidmore]

> *had lured and beckoned us for years before this long list of men had ever set foot in the country. Our cups splashed over. Then we looked into each other's eyes and said: "Why not?"*[15]

"Why not?" indeed. Or, as Heilbrun observed of women's responses, "The answer must be: imagine, and the old idea of womanhood be damned."[16]

Mary Townsend Sharples Schäffer was born in West Chester, Pennsylvania, on 4 October 1861, six months after the Civil War began in the United States.[17] (See Appendix 1 for an outline of Schäffer's family histories and spellings of her surnames.) She grew up during the postwar era of reconstruction, rapid industrialization, and capitalist expansion, when suffrage and other rights were sought for women in North America, Western Europe, and Australia. In 1889, she was twenty-seven years old, newly married to Charles Schäffer, and living in Philadelphia as intensified debate over social, political, and economic reform marked the emergence of what became known as the Progressive Era in US history. When she was widowed in 1903, she was forty-two, and was forty-nine when *Old Indian Trails* was published in late May 1911. In 1912, Schäffer moved permanently to Banff, Alberta. In 1915, in Vancouver, British Columbia, she married William Warren (whom she called Will),[18] a British

> FIGURE 1.4
"She Who Colored Slides," Mary W. Adams photograph, 1907.
Mary Schäffer hand-tinted lantern slide [WMCR V527/PS1-1]

immigrant, outfitter, and chief guide on her Rocky Mountain journeys from 1904 to 1908.[19] She was fifty-nine years old when the Nineteenth Amendment granted women suffrage in the United States in 1920, two years after most (but not all) women in Canada had been granted the right to vote federally and, in 1919, to stand for election to the House of Commons.[20] Nine years later, when the British Privy Council ruled that Canadian women were persons under the British North America Act and thereby eligible to be appointed to the Senate of Canada, Schäffer had been a Canadian resident for seventeen years and a British subject, by marriage, for fourteen years. She died in Banff at seventy-seven years of age on 23 January 1939, and was buried in the Banff cemetery across the road from her home.[21]

Studying women's lives and their creative work, individually and collectively, in concert with the times and places in which they lived and travelled, worked and played allows us to explore and know more about the complexities, diversities, possibilities, and contradictions of women's experiences in times, places, and events of the past, in histories and in societies in which gender is fundamental to the distribution of power.[22] In her introduction to *Old Indian Trails*, Schäffer deliberately placed the journeys that she and Adams made in the context of the politics and power of gender and the impact of those factors on their decisions and actions. Gender politics also followed Schäffer to her grave and perform a central role in posthumous re-creations of her life and work. Although as historian Joan Wallach Scott argues, "the creation of women as subjects in history places them temporally in the contexts of their action, and explains the possibility of such action in terms of those contexts,"[23] the politics of the eras in which biographers, historians, journalists, novelists, playwrights, and others contemplate a woman's life inevitably, and often usefully, inform the ways in which they read and imagine their subject's life.

The touchstone image for this reflection on women, wilderness, and photography is a lantern slide, made of glass, hand-tinted, and 3.25 x 4 inches in size—but potentially life-size or larger when projected. It is an image that Schäffer did not publish in her lifetime, although it is likely one that she displayed publicly in one or more of her lantern slide lectures. In March 1911, for example, three months before the release of *Old Indian Trails*, Schäffer presented a lecture on "Explorations in the Canadian Rockies" to an erudite audience of women and men in the rooms of the Geographical Society of Philadelphia. A newspaper article following her lecture stated, "All the slides were beautifully colored and illustrated some of the grandest mountain scenery

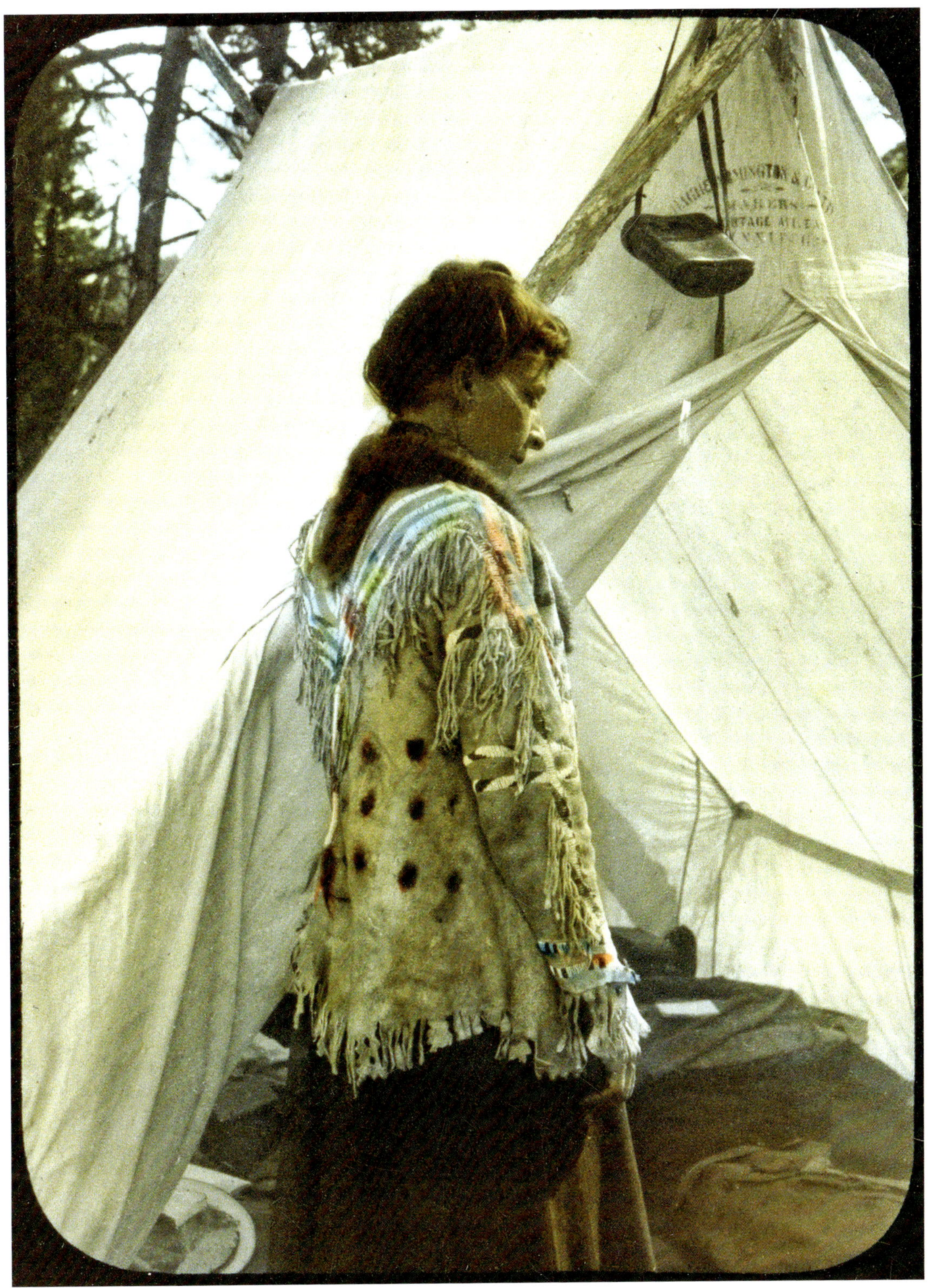

in the world."[24] This image would have fit well the theme of the lecture and the manner of its illustrated presentation.

> FIGURE 1.5
Suzette Chalifoux Swift and her children, Mary Schäffer photograph, 1908.
[WMCR V527/PD-1-116 and V527/PD-4]

Molly Adams made this photograph during the 1907 journey, their third together into the Rockies and off the tourist tracks. The woman whose back is turned to Adams, the camera, and, ultimately, the learned urban audience in Philadelphia viewing the projected slide, is Mary Schäffer. With her face turned away, the viewer is led to focus on her jacket as the centre of attention. Yet the title that Schäffer pasted on the glass plate, "She Who Colored Slides," casts her, rather than the garment, as the subject of the image. It was she, the accomplished and published botanical photographer, painter, and writer, who tinted this slide (among hundreds of others), showing to great effect the masterful beaded, ochred, and fringed details of the fine buckskin jacket that fits her so well. The jacket is displayed in the time and place in which it had been acquired, and in which she wore it as the most comfortable and practical garment for her activities. Schäffer poses in front of an open white canvas tent pitched against a forest background. A binocular case hangs from the tent, while a mound of snow lodged against the tent's base gives a sense of the cold air, reminding the viewer of the context and activities of exploration in which Schäffer was engaged. Such exploration included not only scanning and traversing the environment but also collecting samples of it for study, including alpine flowers, geological specimens, and Indigenous handcrafts. It was, in fact, the exquisitely designed, cut, and decorated buckskin jacket, rather than the wearer, that was the original subject of the photograph when Adams exposed the negative, documenting the beauty of the garment in the wilderness environment in which it was worn. The monographic print that Schäffer preserved in an album, and which is cropped in the lantern slide, does not create the same visual or documentary impact.

This jacket and its provenance are a significant example of how access to historical materials has a bearing on understanding Schäffer's work and its influence. Although this image does not appear in *Old Indian Trails*, past writers, myself included, have attributed the jacket, through what is taken as narrative inference by Schäffer and Adams rather than material evidence, to the well-known and respected Métis artisan and Jasper homesteader, Suzette Chalifoux Swift.[25] Schäffer writes in *Old Indian Trails* about meeting Swift and admiring her handwork:

> *Then Mrs. Swift (oh, we women are all alike!) unearthed a box from beneath her bed and showed us a half dozen gowns made by herself, most of them her*

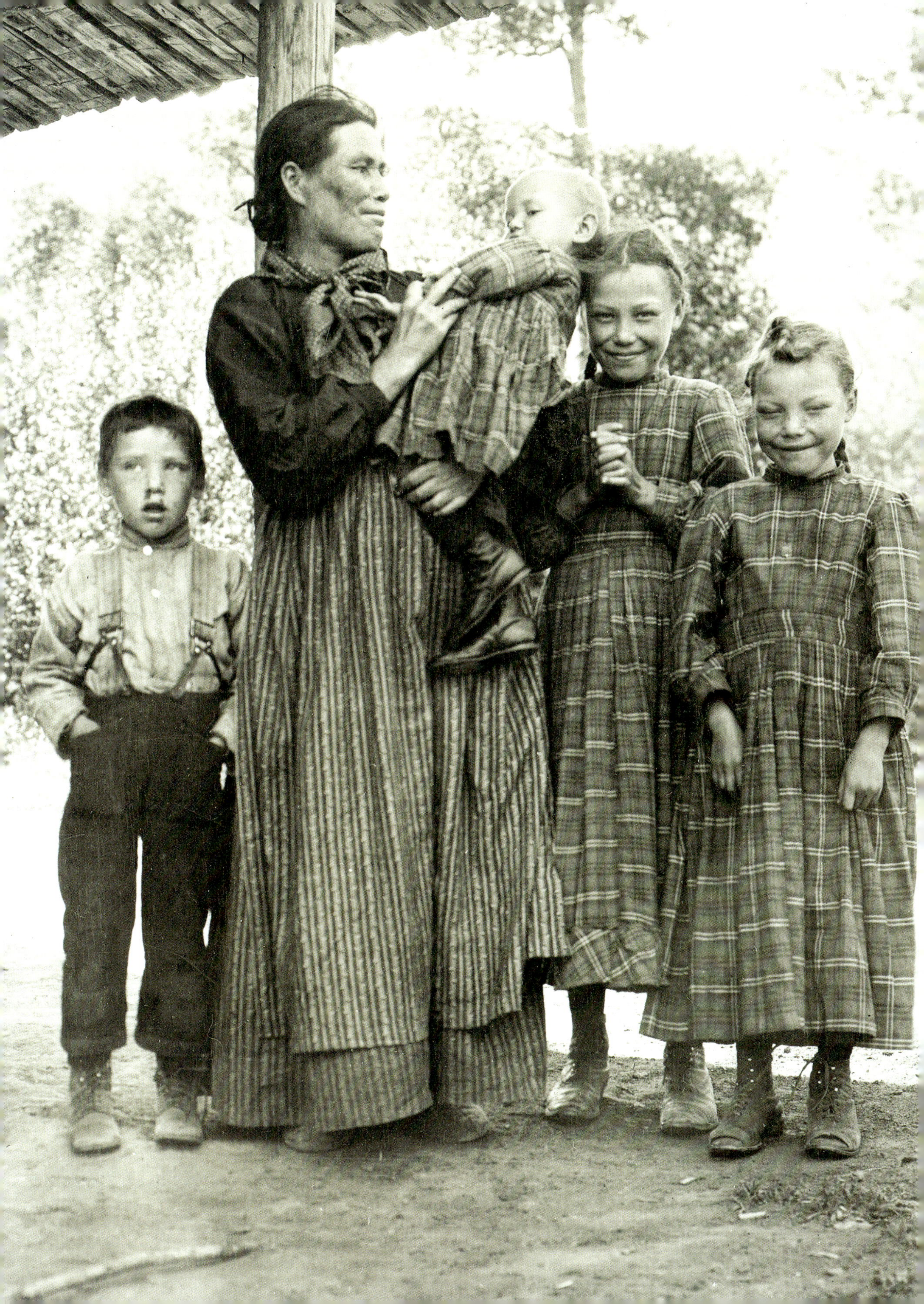

FIGURE 1.6

Mary Schäffer's buckskin jacket worn on 1907 and 1908 journeys, maker unknown.

[WMCR Heritage Collection]

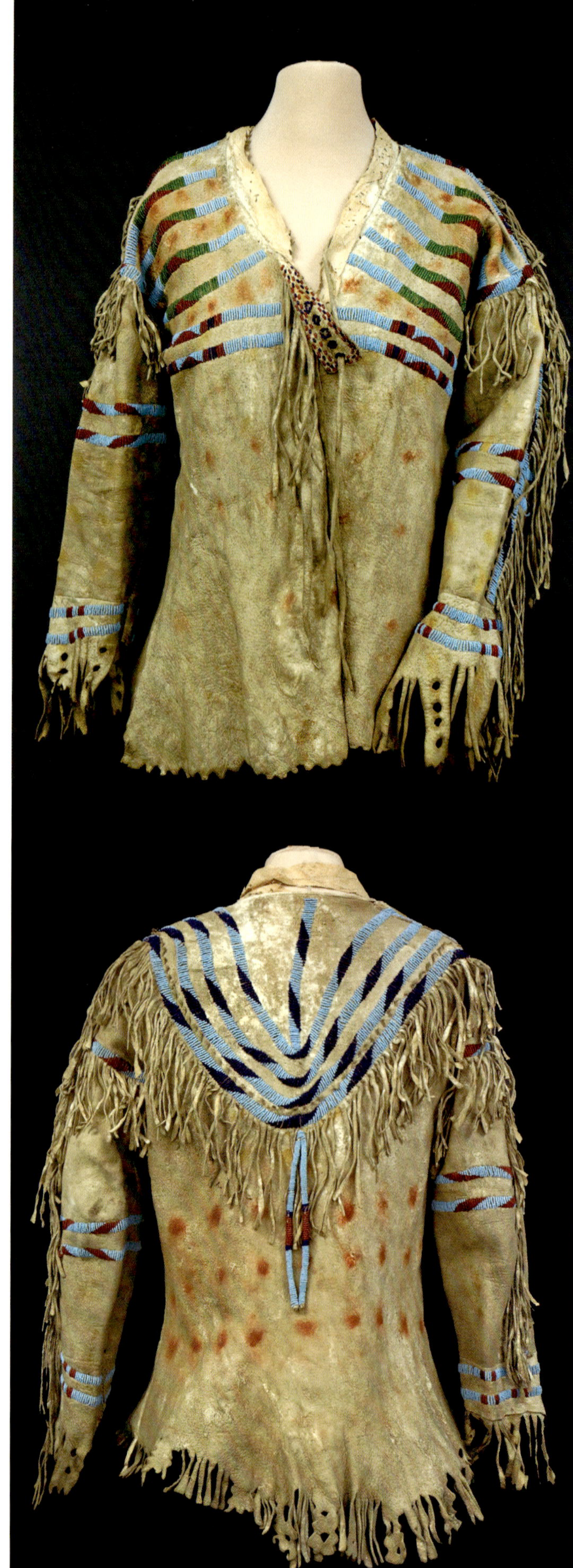

> *bridal finery, and, as we looked on the carefully treasured garments, I realized—be it mansion or shack—there is sure to be stowed away just such a precious horde [sic] around which a woman's heart must always cling. Then came her fancy-work which she did in the short winter days and the long evenings by candle-light and we began taking a deep interest. She had quantities of silk embroidery on the softest buckskin I have yet seen. Her silks she dyed herself, and her patterns were her own designing. There was a most delicious odour to the skins which she said was through their being tanned by poplar smoke. Gloves, moccasins, and beautiful coats, we took everything and wished she had more; it was a grand afternoon's shopping for us all, for the lonely Athabaska woman and the two white women who had seen none of their kind for many a long day.*[26]

On Monday, 31 August 1908, Molly Adams recorded in her trip diary that Schäffer had purchased a coat that Swift tailored to Schäffer's body: "M. and I ambled back and forth between our house and the Swift shack, as Mrs. S. was finishing a buckskin coat embroidered with silk work for M., and it had to be tried on a good many times."[27] The elaborately decorated and well-fitted jacket appears to match the anecdotal inferences of both the story and the diary; however, new evidence, and a more careful reading of *Old Indian Trails*, proves that this is not the case.

In 2009, the jacket itself came to light when Schäffer's grandnephew, Eric Sharpless, donated it to the Whyte Museum of the Canadian Rockies. It was his understanding that Schäffer gave the jacket, along with a second, smaller woman's jacket decorated with silk thread floral embroidery (which he also donated) to his father, Paul, who had travelled as a young boy to Maligne Lake with his aunt, Mary Schäffer, and his mother, Caroline Sharpless, in 1911.[28] The jacket is made of buckskin decorated with ochre smudges on the front and back bodice, which is shaped at the waist so it flares over the hips, and yellow smudges on the sleeves. It is fringed across the back yoke and along the sleeves, cuffs, and bottom edge of the garment. The details that are not clear in either the black-and-white or hand-tinted positive are that the jacket does not have a collar (the fur collar that Schäffer has on in the photograph lies on top of the jacket), the front is closed with a tie, and the decoration is done not in silk embroidery but in fine glass beadwork on thread. The Whyte Museum accessioned the jacket with the notation that it appears to be a Stoney garment, an assessment based on the colour of the beadwork, two shades of blue and ochre, and the lazy stitch that is employed, a beadwork technique in which the thread is drawn through the top layer of the skin, rather than all the way through.

The comparison of the material details of the jacket in the image with Schäffer's and Adams's written descriptions reduces the likelihood that the jacket we see in the image was made by Suzette Chalifoux Swift. Nevertheless, Swift's beadwork was legendary, and so more evidence was needed to suggest otherwise firmly. Two additional photographs of Schäffer in the jacket, the chronological location of the black-and-white print in an album made by Schäffer and of one of the prints in *Old Indian Trails*, and a descriptive passage in the book that aligns with the details in the other two images place the jacket in the 1907 expedition. Schäffer, Adams, and Swift did not meet until late August 1908, and therefore it becomes clear that this jacket cannot be the one made by Swift.

While attribution of the jacket in the image remains elusive, as does the Swift jacket about which Adams writes, more than a century later "She Who Colored Slides" offers manifold possibilities for thinking, reading, writing, and curating exhibitions about intellectual and creative women's lives and practices. Margaret Atwood's meditation on the writer's double in *Negotiating with the Dead* is helpful here: "Can an 'author' exist," Atwood asks, "apart from the work and the name attached to it? The authorial part—the part that is out there in the world, the only part that may survive death—is not flesh and blood, not a real human being. And who is the writing 'I'?"[29] Who was "She Who Colored Slides"? Do two of the three "authors" of this collaborative image, she who exposed the negative and she who made the jacket, disappear with the formal titling of this image? Laying bare the complexity of the matter, Atwood questions, "Which half of the equation, if either, may be said to be authentic?"[30]

As Atwood implies, there seems little to be gained by seeking the "authentic" historical person of Mary Schäffer, "the writing 'I,'" the "she" who coloured slides. Nevertheless, the persona of a historical figure, one who seems to have pursued an especially interesting life, captures the imaginations of readers and writers of biography, and many have sought the persona of Mary Schäffer. As Smith-Rosenberg urges, they have done so by seeking Schäffer's own voice, using her private correspondence in later life, unpublished fiction and non-fiction manuscripts, as well as secondary accounts of her life, "the authorial part" of her existence, as material from which to reconstruct the historical figure. Smith-Rosenberg cautions, however, that an analytical framework is essential to writing histories that take women's own work and words as their most significant primary sources.[31] Herein lies both challenge and opportunity for reconsidering the practice and impact of Schäffer's writing and photography. Taking up the challenge of rethinking the documentary view and use of Schäffer's texts and photographs, both private and public, published and unpublished, that serves as the foundation of Schäffer studies, this book approaches her texts as crafted narrative and her photography as a fluid, collaborative, and creative gaze. The persona of Mary Schäffer is not sought, although one does emerge. What is sought is twofold: a multifaceted understanding of her work in its time and places, and the significance of both her work and its interest to others. All of this is considered within an analytical framework of the role and impact of gender in Schäffer's time, place, and practices.

Atwood argues, "We assume too easily that a text exists to act as a communication between the writer and the reader. But doesn't it also act as a disguise, even a shield—a protection?"[32] Seeking to recreate the historic person and character, biographers, historians, journalists, playwrights, anthropologists, and literary critics, like the original reviewers of Schäffer's work, have done what Atwood, who is attuned to the vagaries of gender in life, literature, career, ambition, and success, warns will happen, eventually, to all women writers: "Writers are fond of saying that writers are androgynous as to their capabilities, and that is no doubt true, though it is telling that most of those who make this claim are women. But they are not gender-neutral in their interests. Most importantly, they are treated differently, especially by reviewers, however that difference in treatment may manifest itself; and sooner or later that will affect them."[33]

The fulcrum of the problem identified by Atwood, Heilbrun, and Smith-Rosenberg as well as Schäffer herself is the politics of gender, a society's rules, written and implied, about expected and accepted roles and behaviours for women and men, and how those rules are enforced, obeyed, and defied. Heilbrun identifies one way that women of Schäffer's generation, women "who died before the middle of the twentieth century," interrupted the trajectory of gender: "by committing a social, usually a sexual sin."[34]

What was Schäffer's sin? That would be a matter of perspective. In our time, for some, Schäffer's social, sexual "sin" was her marriages—first to a man more than twenty years her senior, then to one twenty years her junior.[35] For others, it was an imagined or hoped-for sexual liaison with a like-minded female travelling companion or with one of their wilderness guides, or both.[36] For many,

> FIGURE 1.7
"Criticisms of 'Old Indian Trails' 1911," Mary Schäffer's scrapbook. [WMCR M79/9B]

Schäffer's sin was the social class into which she was born and in which she was educated and lived as an adult, a complex and shifting part of her identity through which she has been colourfully, if mistakenly, described as a socialite.[37] Some art and photography historians have been struck by the sense of modernity and contemporaneity of the sitters evident in her photographs of Stoney-Nakoda people she met on their traditional territory of the Kootenay Plains.[38] In contrast, a pernicious sin lately perceived by literary scholars was Schäffer's failure to transcend turn-of-the-twentieth-century colonial racism.[39] Schäffer's views on wilderness and her seemingly contradictory relationship with and understanding of it has caused other scholars to find her guilty of being in the forefront of the intrusion of industrial development, resource exploitation, and tourism in the Canadian Rockies.[40]

In her own time, some found Schäffer's sin to be naming geographical sites and asserting her claim to Maligne Lake and its surrounding topography, something normally left to official government surveyors, and thereby declaring her authority in a role understood to be the preserve of serious men: explorer. According to Schäffer, in the eyes of her contemporary Arthur O. Wheeler, a Dominion land surveyor, "My chief piece of wickedness had been in giving the lake the name of the outflow which was 'Maligne,'"[41] which he futilely protested to both the CPR and the Geographic Board of Canada: "He has always been enraged that a mere woman could find her way in—and—survey that glorious lake."[42] For Schäffer's most famous observer, Rudyard Kipling, the audacity of saying "Why not?" to exploring, photographing, mapping, and writing into the public imagination uncharted Rockies wilderness, and in the process to be at times unwashed, rationally dressed, and mounted astride a horse, proved a startling and entertaining transgression of gender and racial boundaries.[43]

Between 1904 and 1927, Schäffer published at least two dozen articles in scientific journals in the United States and the United Kingdom, and popular American and Canadian newspapers and outdoors magazines. Most of these articles were illustrated with photographs made by Schäffer and others. Furthermore, she contributed photographs to others' publications, including a book published in 1905 by her later nemesis, Arthur O. Wheeler.[44] She also published two substantial and richly illustrated books: one was to have been a first of its kind and definitive scientific contribution, a botanical accounting of the alpine flora in the Canadian Rockies (while the first aspiration was thwarted, the latter was realized); the other is a narrative in the grand tradition

Criticisms of "Old Indian Trails" 1911

N.Y. City Times — 7-16-'11

TWO WOMEN IN AN UNTROD LAND

Exploring in the Canadian Rockies, They Add a New Lake to the Map

IN reading "Old Indian Trails,"* by Mary Schäffer, it is difficult to decide just what impresses us most: the excellence of the writing, the picturesqueness of the country described, or the personality of the author herself. All three elements, indeed, work together in making this a most enjoyable outdoor book, but without doubt the average lover of the wilds will dwell longest upon the personality. For always the wildernesses have belonged to the male. Physiological facts and teperamental tendencies have seemingly ordained that it should be so.

The ordinary woman travels much better in a Pullman than with a pack train, and is much more efficient in parlor adventures than on long hard trails; for a trail appears much more flowery and poetic in print and picture than in reality. A wild country is an inhospitable country, and tries the intruder's mettle in a thousand unexpected ways. While only a small percentage of seemingly sturdy men are fit for wild places, there are a hundred men to one woman who could possibly "make good" in wilderness expeditions. With men, the fault is in "the yellow streak" which civilized life does not readily betray; with women, it is the natural timidity, fastidiousness and love of ease.

Now the trails described in this book are hard ones, and the traveler-author is a woman; wherefor, any trail-wise man who does not figuratively remove his hat as he reads, is no sportsman and wouldn't "split fair" with a comrade.

"The section of the country which had so long been our dream," writes the author, "lies in the Canadian Rockies, directly north of that portion which is penetrated by the Canadian Pacific Railway. Our chief aim was to penetrate to the headwaters of the Saskatchewan and Athabaska Rivers." Still, the author states, this was but an excuse; for her real object was "to delve into the heart of an untouched land, to tread where no human foot had trod before"; to go to a place where hatpins are not the mode and the lingerie waist a dream."

From the beginning, the author realized that the virgin country was a man's country. She had studied all available writings bearing upon that region and the writers were all men. Were women always to be barred from this shut-in Paradise of strange streams, green silences, soaring peaks, unmapped lakes? "To sit with folded hands and listen calmly to the stories of the hills we so longed to see, the hills which had lured and beckoned us for years before this long list of men had ever set foot in the country?"—that was the sting. And here speaks a very fine spirit: "Why not go? We could starve as well as they; the muskeg woulc be no so ter for us than for them; the ground no harder to sleep upon; the waters no deeper to swim."

So the author and a friend, also a woman, boldly planned the matter. And, in spite of the undeniable courage displayed, the feminine explorers placed at the head of their list of necessities guides—men, of course! But if the gentle and inexperienced reader imagines that this provision suppplied all the necessary nerve, let him try it.

The result was the expeditions of 1907 and 1908 so entertainingly described in the volume before us. The country explored lies between latitudes 51.30 and 52.30, and between longitudes 116 and 118. The region was quite thoroughly covered and some valuable facts were added to the geographical knowledge of that section of the Rockies. Mrs. Schäffer, among other things, may lay claim to the distinction of having placed a new lake upon the map, which fact in itself should commend her book to all amateur explorers.

Although there was much picturesque scenery along the various trails, there are no verbal flights of sentimental ecstasy to be endured, nor is there any attempt on the part of the author to prove to the reader what a rarely sympathetic soul she has. She is sincere, as all good travelers should be. One sees it all and longs to go there too. A genuine, quiet love of beauty, considerable descriptive ability, and an active sense of humor join to make the book worth reading. The hundred photographs taken by the author are remarkably fine.

Mrs. Schäffer is the wife of the late Dr. Charles Schäffer, the eminent Philadelphia scientist, who made an exhaustive study of the flora of the Canadian Rockies.

Crag & Canyon — 9-2-11

Anyone who has not read "Old Indian Trails," by Mrs Mary Schaffer, has missed something that can be bought only in this one volume. Those who know Mrs Schaffer will readily understand why this book has an individuality all its own. For twenty years Mrs Schaffer has been coming to these Canadian mountains and she has got closer to them in every sense of the word than any author, newspaper editor, descriptive writer or the special man ever will if he lives a thousand years. From mountain to mountain, across valleys, through rivers and around lakes Mrs Schaffer carries her reader with such vivid descriptive powers that the guides and party are lost sight of and the wonders of nature become as real living creatures as her own packhorses. A few copies of this book are on sale at Luxton's Curio Store.

Mrs. Murphy in Winnipeg Telegram

"Old Indian Trails" by Mary T. S. Schaffer. G. P. Putam's Sons, New York.

While passing through Edmonton on her usual trip to the mountains, I had the pleasure of meeting the author of this volume, Mrs. Charles Schaffer of Philadephia. She was leaving the next day with a party for the Yellow Head Pass. She has discovered more valleys, lakes and mountains than almost any traveler in the west, her latest discovery "Lake Maligne" being embodied in Mrs. Humphrey Ward's "Lady Merton, Colonist" under the name of Lake Louise.

"Were I" she said while here, "to spend a hundred years exploring the mountains, I believe I should explose a new valley every year. That is what the charm of mountaineering is to me—to keep from the beaten path and to go where no one has ever gone before."

To the Indians, Mrs. Schaffer has become "Yahewta," the woman of the mountains, and so completely has she won th[eir] confidence that they are her consta[nt] friends and helpers. In her book M[rs.] Schaffer tells of her start in the B[ow] Valley; her search of Fortress Lake; h[er] journey through the Brazean country a[nd] numerous other places.

Before me is another recent volume which covers much the same route, "The New Garden of Canada" (Cassell and Co. Toronto) and I have found it of much interest to compare the impressions and experiences of the two travelers. Both of them visited Swift, the frontiersman, one of the most celebrated characters between Edmonton and the Pacific. Mr. Talbot talks of Swift's journeys to Edmonton, his manufacture of a flour mill and other items of especial interest to men. Mrs. Schaffer tells of Swift's family and of how their domestic affairs are conducted — what Mrs. Swift keeps hidden in a box underneath the bed and of what she (the traveler) purchased therefrom. In a word, Mrs. Schaffer shows how a book may have all the useful qualities of a guide and at the same time all the delightful qualities of an essay, when it is written by one as familiar with the charm of the places she visits and who is as capable of describing it.

of the seasoned traveller about her pursuit to find peace in the wake of deep personal loss, as well as a physical quest to find a legendary and uncharted lake.

By means of her literary and visual work, Schäffer crafted two identities. The first was for herself—a respected and credible public persona that aligned with the popular profile of the British and North American woman travel writer as an educated, civil, spiritual, adventurous, artistically talented, modest woman with a self-deprecatory sense of humour and pragmatic ways. This was a persona welcomed and embellished by reviewers' portrayals of her in their unanimously positive responses to *Old Indian Trails*, published in at least twenty-nine newspapers across the United States, which Schäffer collected in a scrapbook, as well as by many of her contemporaries, women and men alike, and women of succeeding generations who followed her into the Rockies. The second identity was not for herself but instead one for the wilderness and culture of the Rocky Mountains, particularly by means of the newly charted Maligne Lake. This was a popular identity for a legendary lake, reportedly known to Stoney people as Chaba Imne, that evolved through Schäffer's narratives and images to be understood as a symbol of the sublime beauty of the Rocky Mountains as wilderness in which humans had an ancient presence, and a future as a place on which human politics and economic structures would have a profound impact.

Schäffer's reputation remained widespread during her lifetime and has continued among those who live or travel often in the Canadian Rockies. During her lifetime, *Old Indian Trails* became a trusted reference work of early written descriptions, photographs, and a map of the Rockies. From comments made occasionally in her private correspondence, it seems that readers contacted Schäffer from time to time over the years, seeking a copy of the book.[45] In 1948, nearly a decade after her death, Dan McCowan included Schäffer in his book *Hill-Top Tales*, placing her among the "men and women drawn from all quarters of the globe" to the Rockies, and noting that her *Alpine Flora of the Canadian Rocky Mountains*, "now long out of print...is still considered an outstanding work."[46] In 1949, Mabel B. Williams retold Schäffer's story about her first trip to the lake she named Maligne in *Jasper National Park: A Descriptive Guide*, a book written to lure tourists to the northern Rocky Mountains park.[47] Then in 1957, Elsie Park Gowan published the first detailed posthumous article to appear on Mary Schäffer.[48]

Gowan, like those who have followed her, "went searching for Mary Schaffer, in her own book, in Alpine journals, in geographic records and in the memory of old timers."[49] "It seems to me," she decided,

> *that the phrase "sacred soil" is the clue to Mrs. Schaffer's attitude to the wilderness. You may read her book through without knowing that she belonged to the "Society of Quakers," the Friendly Persuasion. But Quakerism is not a creed or a ritual; it is a philosophy, a manner of life and attitude of mind. This philosophy I find implicit in her attitude, first to the country, and second to the people she met. In the unspoiled wilderness she felt herself, happily, in a sacred place, in the presence of the Creator's handiwork. And she approached the men and women of the wild land, white or red, as truly her friends, in the Quaker sense, with respect for common dignity and humanity.*[50]

Seeking the authorial "I," Gowan found a woman of spiritual sensibilities and egalitarian ethics that aligned with Quaker testimonies.

In 1980, Mary Schäffer was reintroduced to a new generation and an international audience of readers. E.J. (Ted) Hart and the Whyte Museum of the Canadian Rockies in Banff, Alberta, established the foundation of Schäffer studies with the publication of *A Hunter of Peace*. This book was published during Alberta's seventy-fifth anniversary, when the province invested in the celebration of its literary heritage, and is distinguished by the fact that it was the work of a woman writer and photographer that the Whyte Museum selected to honour. Although published during a time in which there was growing interest in admitting women to North American and European histories as part of second-wave feminist activism, it was still an extraordinary choice for a cultural institution to recognize and celebrate a woman artist or author in 1980. Not so for the Whyte Museum, however, whose imaginative and inspirational co-founder was a woman. Catharine Robb Whyte, a painter, collector, philanthropist, and long-time and beloved member of the Banff community who had known Schäffer, had died just the previous year.[51] The book has remained in print ever since, updated by a second edition in 2014—a testimony to its tremendous appeal as well as that of Schäffer's life and work. *A Hunter of Peace* encompasses Hart's biographical introduction of Schäffer, an edited and annotated republication of the text of her 1911 book *Old Indian Trails*, numerous photographs from Schäffer's collection (published for the first time), and a previously unpublished draft manuscript of Schäffer's second visit to Maligne Lake in 1911 under the auspices of the Geological Survey of Canada. The Whyte Museum of the Canadian Rockies is the repository of Schäffer's photographic, literary, and personal estate. Schäffer's glass negatives, lantern slides, prints, unpublished manuscripts and private papers, including a transcribed copy of sister in law Caroline Sharpless's diary of the trip to survey

Maligne Lake in 1911, personal photograph albums, and letters to friends and acquaintances are in the Whyte collection. Other items ranging from a camera and lantern slide projector to embroidery samplers and Schäffer's bed are also there.

Hart's biographical essay, "Yahe-Weha—Mountain Woman: The Life and Travels of Mary Schäffer Warren, 1861–1939," epitomizes the respect and appreciation that most who have studied her work share. He presents her as "this remarkable woman" who has become "a source of wonder and inspiration" for those who study her work, distinguished by her reverence for the wilderness, its natural elements and its inhabitants both, and "by her spirit and pluck in venturing into that wilderness to discover them."[52] Schäffer's work strikes a chord in the late twentieth and early twenty-first centuries as the politics and well-being of the environment as well as the dismantling of the colonization of Indigenous people in Canada have grown to be primary social concerns. Furthermore, the politics of gender underscore both Hart's reading and his readers' interests in 1980 and beyond. While publishing a book about Schäffer and her work at that time was a daring choice, the ways in which she and her work were presented were conventional for their time.

Hart crafts a life story that frames the complexity and personal growth of a lifespan informed by education, travel, scientific collection and recording, creative work, economic opportunity and loss, and historical happenstance. His brief introductory biography is based on the Schäffer archives of private letters and diaries, unpublished manuscripts, and published works that were available in 1980 (the collection continues to grow as new materials continue to be acquired), as well as, it would seem, undocumented oral histories of some who had known her or her second husband. Hart casts Schäffer in her private life as an indulged child, the pampered bride of a man "much older," a dependent wife, and a needy widow who ultimately achieved financial independence. Finally, she becomes a devoted and increasingly dependent older wife married for a second time, an arrangement that he characterizes as "the answer to her prayers," although "the details are not known." Nevertheless, Hart opines that because of the age difference in her second marriage, "it seems likely it was a match of mutual admiration and convenience" and that the much younger William Warren used Schäffer's "considerable funds" to finance new business interests in Banff. No material evidence has emerged in the vast archives of Schäffer's correspondence with her lawyer and financial advisor in Philadelphia to show that this was so, although it would perhaps not be surprising if it were. There is no evidence that Schäffer spent the years of her second marriage seeking ways to make her life "meaningful"; nor is there any information about the intimate details of her marriage to Warren, although Hart states that Warren kept busy with "other matters" that "included several lady friends whom Mary certainly knew about but never made an issue of, understanding the needs of her much younger husband on this score."[53]

Focusing on the private details of a woman's life was standard and expected in 1980. New ways of thinking about and assessing a woman's life were just beginning to emerge beyond circles of feminist scholars, and Hart's work is a good example of the gap between subject matter and approaches to it. This type of assessment of Schäffer's marriage patterns says more about stereotyped ideas of women and their roles in marriage in 1980 than about norms and deviations of age difference in spouses at the different times and places and in the specific socioeconomic strata in which Schäffer married. In 1890, for example, the year after Mary Sharples and Charles Schäffer married, the median age of first marriage for women in the United States was twenty-two years, for men twenty-six.[54] Sharples was twenty-seven. In contrast, this was Charles Schäffer's third marriage, undertaken in middle age. While nothing is yet known about his first wife's education or pursuits (she was three years his elder), his second wife (three years his junior) was a physician; his third wife, Mary Sharples, was also a woman of mind. There was likely more to her decisions to marry, and those of her husbands, than has been implied or speculated in later commentary.

Whether Schäffer or either of her husbands experienced any public or private censure about age differences, and if so, what the implications of such social views at the time might have been, is a compelling question. While American data about marriage between partners with age differences of twenty years in the late nineteenth and early twentieth centuries has proven elusive, a study of those numbers in the early twenty-first century shows that 1.5 per cent of men and 0.3 per cent of women married a spouse twenty years their junior.[55] Extrapolating this data to one hundred years earlier is impossible, but if such marriages were even many times more common, they would still have been rare enough to be notable. Schäffer and Warren's marriage certificate suggests that something was at play. The document notes his age as thirty-five, which is accurate, while hers is recorded as thirty-eight. (The marriage certificate asked for age, rather than birthdate.) In June 1915, Schäffer was fifty-three. If family, friends, or society at large disapproved of the match because of the age difference, or if Schäffer or Warren were uneasy about others' responses to their decision to marry—had their relationship been the subject of gossip in 1915, as it was in 1980?—no documentary evidence of any such concern has appeared. Other explanations may be valid: perhaps Schäffer considered her age a private matter, as so many women "of a certain age" did in the twentieth century, well aware of the diminishing social value that aging creates for women. Or perhaps the age recorded was simply an error on the part of the scribe. Whether or not the record of age was indeed a matter of discretion for unknown reasons of public or private concern, the marriage was nevertheless heralded with a round of cheers in Banff's local newspaper.[56]

In contrast to the personal identity, Hart casts the core of Schäffer's public identity as that of "Mountain Woman," a descriptor and an identity both derived from and authenticated by the Stoney name Yahe-Weha, which Schäffer wrote was bestowed upon her.[57] He underscores Schäffer's emotional motivation for her two major Rocky Mountain journeys—rather than her intellectual and creative interests in that space and place—with the title of his book, taken from one of Schäffer's letters: "No one may know I went among those hills with a broken heart and only on the high places could I learn that I and mine were very close together. We dare not tell those beautiful thoughts, they like to say 'explorer' of me, no, only a hunter of peace. I found it."[58]

Hart's essay has been treated as historical fact and formed the biographical framework of virtually every subsequent study of Schäffer since 1980. Furthermore, the edited republication of *Old Indian Trails* in *A Hunter of Peace*, which excluded most of the original photographs and inserted others, has served as the primary source text for most scholars and other writers since that time. As a result, mistaken conclusions have been drawn and significant aspects of Schäffer's work missed because of the abridged nature of the 1980 version of her work and its integration with other materials.

Twenty years after Hart's work was published, Mary Schäffer's first (and to date sole) book-length biographer, Janice Sanford Beck, published *No Ordinary Woman: The Story of Mary Schäffer Warren*.[59] Beck has filled in the gaps between published historical documents, both written and visual, with material from Schäffer's private correspondence and unpublished manuscripts, memoir and fiction both, as well as her own literary imagination, to write an engaging story of a woman she deeply admires. Beck's biography charts a lifecycle that begins with an adventurous young girl and ends with an opinionated old woman, building it on the traditional touchstones of significance that are believed to shape a North American woman's life: her emotional relationships, especially with men, including the special relationship with and foundational influence of her father; her first husband's impact on the shape and values of her life; the role of children; struggles with grief as Schäffer's parents, first husband, and her friend Molly Adams died; and finally, in this rare case, a happy ending with a second, enduring marriage to "her handsome young guide Billy Warren."[60] (Warren is always referred to as "Billy" by Hart and then Beck, but never by Schäffer or in any primary documents that have so far come to light.) Following Hart's lead, Beck's book also includes formerly unpublished manuscripts and photographs. The Mary Schäffer of Beck's biography is bold, determined, brave, and zealous; that is, no ordinary woman.[61] Like Hart's *A Hunter of Peace*, Beck's *No Ordinary Woman* remains in print, with a second edition, years after publication. The popularity of the book represents the abiding interest of readers in Schäffer's life story and the engaging account that Beck wrote based on Schäffer's own stories, both published and unpublished fiction and non-fiction texts.

The dramatic climax of Schäffer's life, as presented by Beck, is the period of Rocky Mountain journeys that Schäffer undertook during her widowhood in the early 1900s. It would seem that this was a moment Schäffer was fated to meet from childhood, as at the age of eighteen, "She was a bright, enthusiastic young woman searching for a mission....Little did Mary Sharpless know that her future awaited her amidst the splendour of the Canadian Rockies."[62] Two dominant themes emerge as Beck strives to create an authentic portrayal of a complex character. In counterpoint to the adventurous personality that she invokes as the driver of Schäffer's experiences, Beck's Schäffer often appears physically and psychologically weak; that is, she appears conventionally feminine. Whenever Schäffer failed, in Beck's view, to be bold, daring, or strong, her behaviour is accounted for by either illness or regression to the dependent conduct of women of her perceived social class, that of a "Philadelphia lady."[63] Seeking to account for the absence of grand exploratory journeys following 1908, for example, a period that included not just the successful pursuit of Maligne Lake and the return to chart it for the Geological Survey of Canada in 1911, but also a three-and-a-half month journey to Japan with Molly Adams, who died on that journey, Beck surmises that after 1908, "bereft of her travelling companion and all the more conscious of her own poor health and the dangers of adventurous travel, Mary never again set out on an expedition akin to those of 1907 and 1908."[64] And yet, Schäffer did attempt to do so, setting

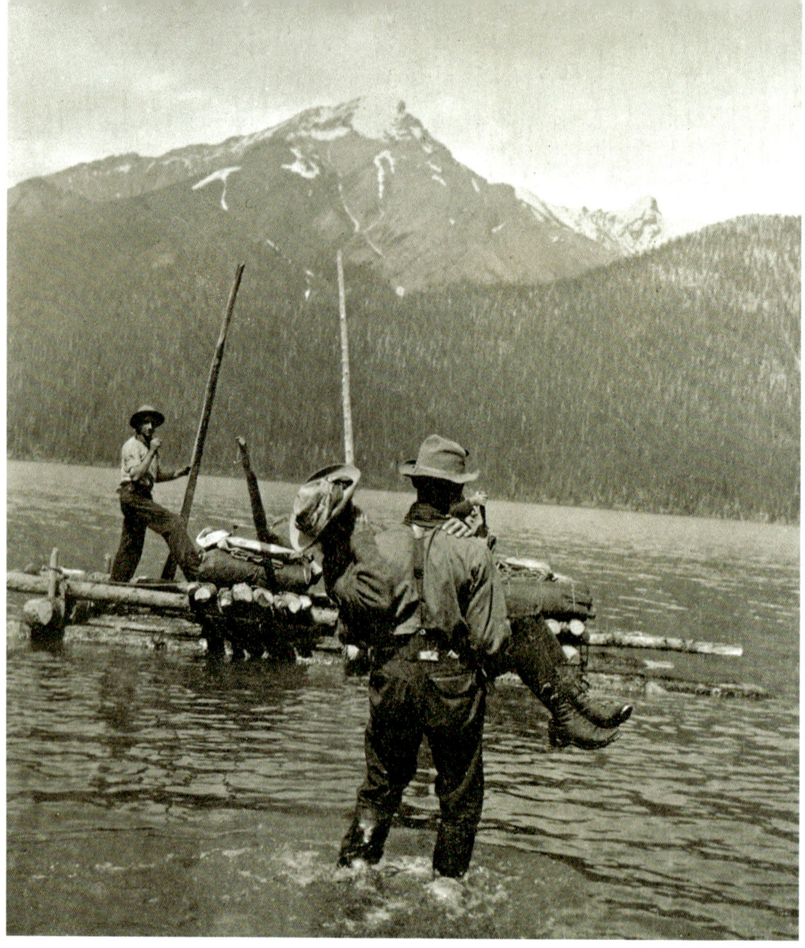

FIGURE 1.8
Raft on Maligne Lake, [Mary Schäffer or Mary W. Adams photograph], 1908.
[WMCR V527/NA-66-1405]

her sights on a voyage along the Mackenzie River in 1912. Her plans were thwarted first by the cancellation of an unnamed woman companion, and then by financial constraints.[65] Furthermore, while Schäffer suffered occasional bouts of illness over the years, and Adams coped with chronic heart problems and an eye injury, serious health issues are not mentioned in *Old Indian Trails* or any published articles, nor more than in passing in Adams's diaries and other private materials that have been located since Beck published her biography. Although such physical challenges might have been cited as further evidence of Schäffer's and Adams's physical and psychological determination and discipline—the trip to Asia that began just two and half weeks after completing the four-month Maligne Lake journey, and without returning home to Pennsylvania and Connecticut in between, included rigorous travel beyond tourist destinations—such challenges are instead attributed as the cause of what is perceived to be Schäffer's withdrawal from adventure in life.

A 1908 photograph of one of the women being carried over water to the raft that their guides had built to travel the length of Maligne Lake, which was included in Hart's edition but not in Schäffer's book, is used to illustrate one example of the sin of class that Schäffer committed.[66] Schäffer writes in *Old Indian Trails* that she was not convinced that the raft built with materials scavenged on-site was sturdy enough to carry all of the passengers—six adults and a dog—as well as all of their camping gear. She suggested that they lighten the load and instead rough it in the bush while they were away from the main camp. "Faced with an unfamiliar challenge," Beck writes, "some of Mary's earlier timidity resurfaced...In her insecurity, Mary fell into the role of a Philadelphia lady. The guides had to carry first the gear, then her and Mollie out to the raft."[67] Schäffer's own explanation was different and highly entertaining, grounded in experience, humour, and a seemingly healthy will to survive: "Personally my sensations towards large bodies of water are similar to those of a cat, and though I begged to rough it, it was not so much to do something uncomfortable as to keep from drowning on an overtaxed raft."[68]

Schäffer and Adams could well have waded through the water to the raft. Adams wrote that "M. and I were ignomously [*sic*] picked up and dumped on too, as H.M.S. 'Chaba' drew too much water to be brought quite up to shore, or even near enough for a long jump."[69] As they themselves were well aware, when compared to men's experiences and abilities, "the waters [would be] no deeper to swim, nor the bath colder if we fall in."[70] The guides were the ones being paid to get wet; perhaps they were also paid to keep their customers dry, or perhaps good-natured chivalry or friendship determined that it was not necessary for everyone who boarded the raft to spend the day with sodden boots. All such extrapolations may have merit, but like Beck's, all are imaginary; while derived from Schäffer's travel narrative, none is based on documentary evidence. The informed imagination of the biographer who pieces together a life from the scattered remains of literary, visual, journalistic, and private materials can become the voice of fact. The complex (and entertaining) person of a moment in history, one who claimed to prefer roughing it in the bush to drowning, for example, is reduced to a persona who, despite the evidence of her accomplishments and the Quaker foundation of her values, and the biographer's straightforward admiration of those things, was found to have failed to rise above "the sin" of her social class—the well-educated, professional and academic, travelling urban class of the northeastern United States—and to remain at heart a dependent, insecure "lady." This makes for a vivid rendering, however, and one that has coursed with ease through most subsequent writing on Schäffer and her work.

Wilderness

Another major theme woven by both popular and academic writers through the trajectory of Schäffer's life, from her childhood through 1908, is her interaction with Indigenous people in both North America and Asia. Seeming inconsistencies in Schäffer's writing and published portraits of Indigenous people, with certain photographs widely considered to be among the most compelling of the time, have led some of those writing about Schäffer in the early twenty-first century, such as literature scholar Lisa MacFarlane, to find her guilty of "voyeuristic and colonizing activities."[71] "She Who Colored Slides" is the provocative cover image on *Trading Gazes: Euro-American Women Photographers and Native North Americans, 1880–1940*. It is a sign of the visual sophistication and impact of Schäffer's Rocky Mountain images and practice that this lantern slide was chosen to introduce readers to a collection of essays that sought to reveal Euro-American women photographers' colonizing engagement with Indigenous people and to explore how these women's photographs could be used at the turn of the twenty-first century to read history in ways that are "different and more complex" than common narratives.[72] Used in this context, the reader, before even opening the book, is directed to perceive the image in a sharply reductive manner, representing white women's intractable racism rather than some individual women photographers' multifaceted, interactive, and at times resistant visual practices. In her contribution, MacFarlane describes her impression of the image this way: "It is significant that not only do we not see Swift, the coat's maker, but also we do not see very much of Schäffer, the coat's owner, either beaming or smug with the pride of possession."[73] The photographer looms as the subject of analysis in this collection of essays, displacing the photographs themselves. Nevertheless, MacFarlane ultimately corroborates what art critic and curator Lucy Lippard, a decade earlier, had posited and struggled to understand in a manner fair to the photographer and her Indigenous acquaintances alike: that Schäffer's photographs and practice were complex and compelling, complicit yet in conflict with imperialist thought.[74]

Lippard contemplated the question of the relationship between the photographer and sitters in Schäffer's portrait of the Beaver family. "I am examining my deep attraction to this quiet little picture," Lippard writes. "Good photography can *embody* what has been seen," Lippard believes, and she attributes the impact of the image to its "crisp 'presentness,'" and the sense of a moment of interaction between the sitters and photographer.[75] Lippard's own work

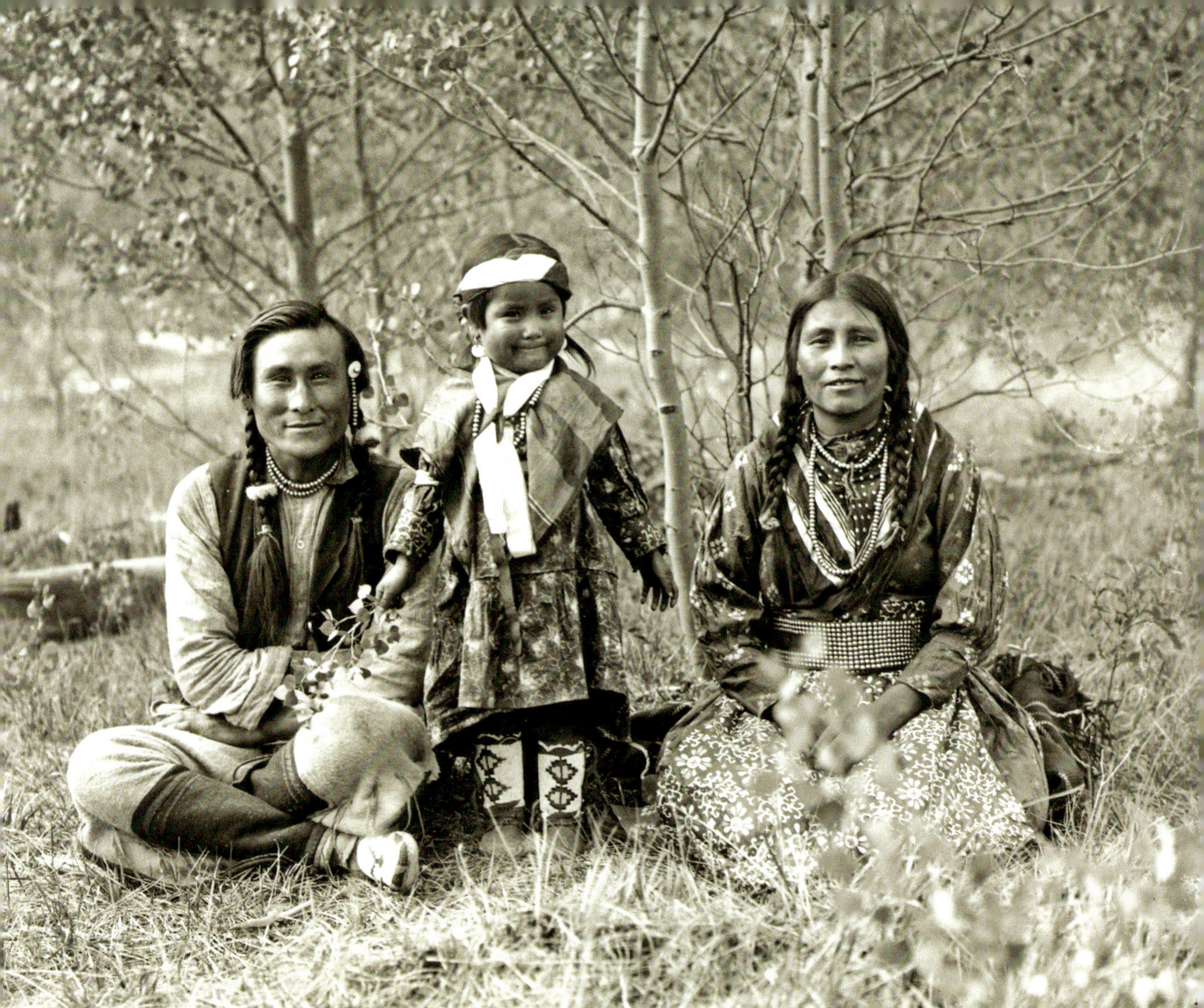

FIGURE 1.9
Sampson, Frances Louise, and Leah Beaver. Mary Schäffer photograph, 1906.
[WMCR V527/PD-1 and V527/PD-4]
Reproduced from original glass negative
[WMCR V527/NG-124]

resonates with readers through its contemplative and spare prose, and the space left open alongside Lippard for readers to look and think about the image with her. She admits early on that she is "looking at this triple portrait cut loose from all knowledge of the people involved—an aspect that normally would have informed much of my own position. With only the postcard's caption to go on, my response is not neutral, but wholly subjective."[76]

In contrast, MacFarlane presumes knowledge of at least one person involved, Mary Schäffer, whom she describes as a "co-conspirator" with Rudyard Kipling "in the construction and dissemination of the Canadian Rocky Mountain West and of Euro-American views of its Native peoples."[77] With no more empirical evidence than Lippard had at hand, MacFarlane creates a historical caricature "by looking both at her published travelogues and photographs and at the unpublished materials she chose to exclude,"[78] not only taking such material as documentary fact rather than literary narrative, but also implying that Schäffer was a cunning, deliberately misleading author. MacFarlane claims, "Schäffer used Indians, and especially Indian women, as a vehicle for living out her own aspirations and for reworking a lifelong fascination with the 'primitive.'"[79] This despite MacFarlane's own experience of finding the sitters in the "stunning family portrait" of Sampson, Leah, and Frances Louise Beaver, "remarkably familiar, even now" and concluding that the sitters and photographer alike resisted the "pictorial conventions" of Euro-American photography of Indigenous people in Canada and the United States.[80] To make her argument, MacFarlane relies on the stereotype of women that she believes Schäffer represents: "the straitlaced Victorian lady, at home in the tea parlor and concert hall, and the wild and free mountain woman, friend to Indians, homesteaders, trappers,"[81] an amalgam of Hart and Beck's Mary Schäffers.

In the end, however, MacFarlane, like Lippard and others, concedes that Schäffer was finding, and working at times in, an alternate way that defies expectations of how resistant imagery should look, but nevertheless serves in a powerful way to show another kind of human and cultural contact, one of mutual respect and even warmth. MacFarlane grants that for those thinking about the traumatic history of Indigenous and Euro-North American interaction, there is a "place where we might suspend final positions in favor of fluid and contingent readings."[82] This is an important point. That Schäffer's visual and written work creates such a place is what makes it so compelling and worthy of study and debate a century later.

As with her relationship to Indigenous people, Schäffer's relationship with the environment also appears to have been "fluid and contingent," that is, of its time with all of its contradictions, paradoxes, and inconsistent positions and behaviours. Historian Ian MacLaren is skeptical and critical of what he reads as a sin of the "enigmatic" Schäffer,[83] her conception of her relationship with Rocky Mountain wilderness: "Schäffer and the generation of alpinists that she represented would find themselves adopting a conflicted and essentially contradictory regard for the past. Like most early travellers, Schäffer dissociated herself from 'civilization's march' but although she herself would have been repulsed by the thought, she was in fact in its vanguard."[84]

Was Schäffer so naïve? On the contrary, her work suggests that she was fully aware that she was in the Rockies at a liminal moment, cognizant of the potential of her work both to attract tourists and to persuade the public of the value of conserving wilderness areas. It also demonstrates her intellectual and emotional grasp of the complicated position she and her contemporaries (men and women, tourists, scientists, and surveyors alike) occupied in a historical moment of unprecedented human intervention and intrusion into this place. MacLaren writes that although Schäffer was an advocate of national parks, particularly Jasper Park, her "attitude of regret for development of the wilderness in her time…typifies many tourists': it celebrates past human presence and activity romantically and uncritically, while it demonizes their present-day counterparts."[85]

In Schäffer's time, as today, to be labelled a tourist is disparaging to those who travel for more than pleasure and leisure, with intent to engage in an environment on their own and in a deeper and more sustained manner than the common tourist. Schäffer dissociated herself from the type of tourist of her place and time who "flitted across the country as bees across a flower garden, and were gone."[86] She lived in the mountains for periods stretching from a few weeks to four months each year from 1889 until 1912, and then year-round until her death in 1939; that is, she spent extended periods of time there in one way or another every year for fifty years, a far deeper engagement and more complicated relationship than tourists normally have with a place. Like most visitors at the turn of the twentieth century, she entered the Rockies by train and relied at first on the railway's amenities. She, along with other women she met in the Rockies such as Molly Adams, aspired to range much farther from the railway than tourists could, to experience the mountains as some men of her generation and acquaintance were doing, by foot and on horseback, relying on immigrant outfitters rather than Indigenous guides to explore, document, and chart wilderness. In *Old Indian Trails*, she casts their travels as the knowing rear guard of a generation, and characterized their experiences as "the beginning of the end….As we crossed the Athabaska, we realized that next time we came that way…the hideous march of progress, so awful to those who love the real wilderness,…would wipe out all trail troubles."[87] In contrast to MacLaren, naturalist and Canadian Rockies expert Ben Gadd observes that Schäffer's book "was a hit; she wrote humorously and well about roughing it in the remote Canadian mountains…The book captures the feeling of that age: ladies and gentlemen enjoying the Rockies area for its wilderness and beauty. Schäffer's work helped to establish the value of the region as a place for wilderness journeys and scientific study—right in line with the objectives of the growing national park system."[88]

The historical and cultural meaning of wilderness shifts with time and place. William Cronon's thinking on this, especially in "The Trouble with Wilderness; or, Getting Back to the Wrong Nature," has informed and encouraged nuanced understandings of such meanings and their significance.[89] Cronon writes that "the trouble with wilderness is that it quietly expresses and reproduces the very values its devotees seek to reject," that is,

> *if by definition wilderness leaves no place for human beings, save perhaps as contemplative sojourners enjoying their leisurely reverie in God's natural cathedral—then also by definition it can offer no solution to the environmental and other problems that confront us. To the extent that we celebrate wilderness as the measure with which we judge civilization, we reproduce the dualism that sets humanity and nature at opposite poles. We thereby leave ourselves little hope of discovering what an ethical, sustainable, honorable human place in nature might actually look like.*[90]

This is the context in which MacLaren is assessing and critiquing the thinking about the seeming dualities of "civilization" and "wilderness" that Schäffer's work appears to represent, and he leaves little room for conflicting or emerging ways of thinking about those concepts among those testing the boundaries, both literally and figuratively. While Schäffer made use of the concept of wilderness in ways that ignore the intellectual paradox that Cronon and MacLaren lay bare, she also challenged such binary concepts of wilderness and civilization and defied the prevailing idea of wilderness as a space and place for men alone. She did this by focusing her powers of written and visual persuasion on disproving the notion of wilderness exploration as a masculine domain, while tourism contained the feminine. In so doing, she proposed new ways of thinking about wilderness exploration and tourist travel, striking a chord with some while unsettling others, both in her time and a century later.

Photography

Crucial to Mary Schäffer's work was the role that the visual played in travel and travel writing, as well as powerful shifts in social relations in North America at the time. These factors in turn played a role in the production and reception of Schäffer's published writing and public lectures. This is why at the core of this study rests the visual, and especially photography. Schäffer articulated and shared many of the experiences and much of the knowledge she had accrued through a variety of visual media in which she was trained to work, primarily painting and photography, as well as cartography, along with the literary, journalistic, and scientific texts that accompanied the images.

Schäffer's purpose and accomplishments as a photographer were both veiled and illuminated when the text of *Old Indian Trails* was republished in *A Hunter of Peace*. In 1980, the photographic elements of the original book were set aside. Many photographs in the original text were not included in the republication while many that were not in the original edition were printed in the new version. Most significantly, numerous colour reproductions of lantern slides that Schäffer had tinted for lectures that she presented, such as "She Who Colored Slides," were reproduced in *A Hunter of Peace*. The change in photographic elements was an important and effective editorial choice that took advantage of colour reproduction technology that was not available in 1911 to publish for the first time samples of Schäffer's lantern slides. Doing so also broadened the appeal of the book to more readers than might otherwise have been attracted by black-and-white photographs alone. Since 1980, however, most writers and scholars, as well as readers with an abiding interest in Rocky Mountain history and culture in general or Mary Schäffer in particular, have overlooked this important and clearly stated point in *A Hunter of Peace*, and based their impressions, analyses, and arguments about Schäffer's work on this significantly revised and expanded, yet incomplete, edition. Also missing from it are the original list of illustrations, the table of contents and the index, as well as Schäffer's dedication of the book to travel companion and co-photographer Molly Adams and the preface in which she lays out the premise—the "Why and Wherefore"—of her book.[91]

The omission of one of Schäffer's primary modes of communication—the visual, the one in which she trained and specialized—and its role in her published work, particularly in *Old Indian Trails*, is further heralded by an unrelated 2007 republication of *Old Indian Trails* from which all visual materials have been omitted, with no disclaimer or explanation. Furthermore, Schäffer's preface is again absent, suggesting that this version was based on the 1980 Hart publication, rather than Schäffer's own 1911 volume.[92] And yet in a 2007 edition of the book, Schäffer's biographer Janice Sanford Beck claims that "with a format that makes it more accessible to travellers and scholars alike, this reprint gives *Old Indian Trails of the Canadian Rockies* its rightful place among the classics of Canadian Rocky Mountain literature."[93] While the book is smaller in size than *A Hunter of Peace* and so perhaps easier to pack, travellers and scholars are treated to just a fraction of Schäffer's classic volume of literary, photographic, and cartographic work. In 2011, on the centenary of the publication of *Old Indian Trails*, the 2007 book was repackaged in cloth binding mimicking the cover design of Schäffer's original publication and marketed as a limited edition. Three sets of colour photographs organized in a manner unrelated to the original edition are inserted without explanation in the volume.[94]

The editing or absence of Schäffer's photographs is all the more perplexing given that she almost always published photographs as primary materials alongside her texts. The visual was fundamental to knowing, understanding, and sharing knowledge for Schäffer, who was trained as a painter and practiced as a photographer before she began to publish her writing. She spent nearly a decade working on visual imagery for scientific purposes in support of her first husband's work in botany before publishing her first article in 1904. Consequently, the visual was not merely decorative or illustrative. Photographs, like text, are an integral part of the narrative of Schäffer's travels, essential to her case about gender and wilderness travel, and crucial to her credibility in 1907 and 1911 (the years in which her books were published) as a commentator in spaces normally the preserve of men: wilderness, botany, toponymy, travel writing, and publication.

Most work on Mary Schäffer focuses on her Rocky Mountain activities, especially between 1906 and 1911—understandably, as the bulk of her published work was completed during those years. The skill Schäffer displayed in her publications, however, was years in the making. While married and resident in Philadelphia, Schäffer was not only an active member of the Geographical Society and the Academy of Natural Sciences of Philadelphia, both she and her husband were active in the photography circles of Philadelphia, with their work known to friends and colleagues who were members of the Photographic Society of Philadelphia, of which they were members as well. In 1899, Mary Schäffer organized a summer field trip to the Canadian Rockies for Photographic Society members.[95] In 1900, an exhibition juror for the Photographic Society of Philadelphia brought Schäffer's work to the attention of Frances Benjamin Johnston, the well-known Washington-based photographer and curator of an exhibition of the work of American women photographers in Paris that same year, in which Schäffer's work was then included. The 1890s and early 1900s were years of urban, educational, creative, and cultural engagement and productivity for Schäffer, complemented by summers of travel and botanical work in the Rocky Mountains—significant and profound years in Schäffer's life. Photography and painting were the common elements, the vocation, and they laid the foundation for the professional success that was to follow.

While Schäffer's work, along with that of most other important or accomplished women practitioners of photography, is not prominent in twentieth-century photography histories, it is there. Like most of her generation of women in North America (especially in the northeastern United States) who exhibited in photography salons, ran commercial galleries, or made careers in photojournalism, she is entirely absent from the general surveys and canonical modernist histories of male lineage, such as Beaumont Newhall's *The History of Photography: From 1839 to the Present Day*, which was first published in 1964 and remains in print in revised editions. Schäffer's work does, however, garner attention in histories of women in photography written after 1990, such as Naomi Rosenblum's *A History of Women Photographers* and Martin Sandler's *Against the Odds: Women Pioneers in the First Hundred Years of Photography*.[96] These later writers have relied on the work of specialist curators and scholars who continue both to recover and critically examine women's practices in photography through focused and rigorous inquiries that insist on assessment of women's considerable presence in the medium's founding and history since its official introduction as a new invention in France and England in 1839.

Bronwyn A.E. Griffith's 2001 salutary exhibition catalogue, *Ambassadors of Progress: American Women Photographers in Paris 1900–1901*, reproduces a group of nine platinum prints submitted by Schäffer, three of which were selected for inclusion in the exhibition at the World Fair in Paris, which travelled to St. Petersburg and Moscow as well.[97] Griffith examines the exhibition and its genesis, finding that in 1900 the women were seen as "examples of both social and photographic advancement: the accomplished techniques were proof of their photographic expertise and the fact that so many of them were professionals proof of the independent 'new woman.'"[98] *Ambassadors of Progress* makes it clear that in 1900, American women positioned themselves on the world stage of Paris not to compare themselves to men but to ensure that "an example of the modern woman or the 'new woman,' as part of the American national identity, was represented as a symbol of social progress."[99] Mary Schäffer stood among those women.

This group of photographers was working at the pinnacle of what C. Jane Gover calls the golden age of photography. In her groundbreaking 1988 examination of the period and American women's photographic practices—groundbreaking because she approached the subject and time period as cultural history and in the then-liminal area of women's presence in a critical intellectual contrast to the traditional stylistic history of Newhall—Gover concisely summarizes the times:

> *This was at once an era of technological and aesthetic development. The dry plate, rolled film, and the hand held camera were among the many mechanical advances that created modern photography. At the same time, Alfred Stieglitz, Edward Steichen, Clarence White, Gertrude Käsebier, and others demonstrated that photography was indeed an art form. Always a popular undertaking, George Eastman and his Kodak company in the 1880s made photography once and for all accessible to everyone. In that process, photography lost its status as a novelty. It emerged both as a legitimate art form, as a professional endeavor, and as an everyday technique that virtually anyone could master.*[100]

Gover's work was important when published and remains so today because she identified women photographers of the time as "significant transitional figures in the history of women in American artistic and professional life."[101] She accounted for women's contributions to the field and profession of photography, and studied their work in the turn-of-the-century social and cultural contexts of the "rise of the professional woman, the impulse toward organization (as seen for example in the camera club and women's networks), the gentility and complexity of Victorian home life, the connections of women photographers to the aesthetics of nineteenth and early twentieth century photographers (especially in the person of Alfred Stieglitz), and indeed, the very perceptions of women themselves."[102]

Gover found that this generation of American women photographers "honored expectations" of their society and time regarding their choices of photographic subjects, but also took the "occasional swipe at prevailing ideology,"[103] an apt description of Schäffer's work and actions. Gover also argued that since most women photographers worked with subject matter that is associated with the feminine, mainly portraits of children and women or genre studies of private life, they were excluded from Newhall's and others' surveys of the history of photography because of a prevailing belief that "the imagery they produced linked them to the domestic and…eroded the judgment of their artistic contribution."[104] This mid-twentieth-century view stands in contrast to the assessment of critics in 1900, who viewed the collection of work of American women photographers and found it to be representative of both the quality and range of artistic and technical practices in photography at the time in the United States. Despite their aesthetic lineages and technical merits, let alone their sheer numbers, women's camera work was invisible to those who were focused on tracing the history and legacy of male practitioners. Gover noted also that in women's work, "only an occasional male portrait or a rare landscape could be found among the many representations of women."[105] This is where Schäffer's work is distinguished, as her oeuvre in 1900 is notable for the absence of subject matter associated with the feminine and domestic, and for its focus instead on the natural world, from intimate alpine flora studies to monumental mountain landscapes; indeed, there is even one male portrait to be found.

Rethinking Mary Schäffer Studies

One of the objectives of *Searching for Mary Schäffer: Women Wilderness Photography* is to demonstrate the role and significance of the visual in Mary Schäffer's work. Photographic historian Joan Schwartz argues that historical methodology must move away from interrogating photographs for facts, that is, "what they show us"; instead, "we need to be more imaginative about the questions we pose to them and we need to be more receptive to the questions they pose to us."[106] To offer a rigorous and insightful assessment of the aesthetic and artistic places, practices, and legacies of Schäffer's work, it is essential to consider two things. The first is the ideas and values of her day, upon which she drew in various, sometimes contradictory, ways. The second is the genre of what she created: cultural artifacts produced with visual, literary, and aesthetic skill meant to entertain as much as to inform, depending on where they were published or viewed. To achieve all this, the photographs must, as Schwartz maintains, be "embraced not as illustrations but as primary sources, and employed as a means to ponder human relations with and shifting attitudes toward nature."[107]

In the case of Schäffer's writing and photography, when combined in her published articles and books, fact and fiction often merge and thereby challenge biographers and historians to analyze her practice in diverse ways. Writer, scholar, and filmmaker Trinh T. Minh-ha observed in 1989, "Literature and history once were/still are stories: this does not necessarily mean that the space they form is undifferentiated, but that this space can articulate on a different set of principles, one which may be said to stand outside the hierarchical realm of facts."[108] Two decades later, historian Jill Lepore teased out the question of "two kinds of historical writing: history based in fact (whose truth is founded in documentary evidence), and history based in fiction (whose truth is founded in human nature.)"[109] Lepore sees that fiction "can do what history doesn't but should: it can tell the story of ordinary people"—people she describes as obscure and often identifies ("a lot of them") as women.[110] Novels were originally written about women, read by women, and meant in great part for women, while history emerged as a discipline about men, written and read mainly by men.[111] Lepore notes that in the eighteenth century, when these genres appeared, history and fiction were not distinguished as truth versus invention, but as one kind of story (history) that was of interest to men, and another kind of story (novels) that was of interest to women.[112] She also observes that academic histories from the 1970s on, the so-called "social histories," take up ordinary people, those who populate novels. These social histories have failed to capture large numbers of women readers, however, who still account for the majority of fiction readers, while most readers of non-fiction or history are men. Lepore concludes that historians have something to learn from novelists, for whom storytelling is paramount.[113]

How does this relate to Schäffer? She was a woman, her topic was of interest to women, and her style of writing resonated with the genre of women travel writers. While based on experience and her own personal history, and informed by her reading of male predecessors' accounts of their own travels in the Rockies, *Old Indian Trails of the Canadian Rockies* nevertheless reads as a quest; the narrative tension and arc, the atmosphere of adventure and uncertainty, take on the qualities of drama, comedy, and mystery. Schäffer's signature volume is a visual and textual work shaped by an able, educated, reading, and thinking woman. It is a book that defies the binary categories of fact and fiction, and is best categorized today as creative or literary non-fiction, whereby the facts of Schäffer and Adams's journeys are portrayed through photographs and text in an entertaining style so as to engage and hold the interest of a diverse audience of women and men both. As such, any reading that historians or biographers take from *Old Indian Trails* must recognize and take into consideration the imaginative, literary aspects that are mobilized to convey something of the truth of the experience that a reporting of facts or data cannot do. For example, did Schäffer and Adams literally sit with folded hands and listen to men's stories of their adventures in the Rocky Mountains until they looked each other in the eye and asked "Why not?" as Schäffer wrote? Perhaps, although empirical evidence indicates that they did not. Instead, this description is better analyzed and understood as a vivid narrative device that succinctly creates, in a way that a straightforward accounting would not, a provocative image of the story's main characters as socially proper women, properly comported, who finally just reached the ends of their ropes.

Stephen Jay Gould, a geologist and biologist, also contemplated the role of storytelling, or what he called "literary bias," in the construction of a scientific understanding of evolution.[114] Gould's attention was fixed on another classic Canadian Rockies story, that of Charles Doolittle Walcott (1850–1927), who is credited with discovering the celebrated fossil field known as the Burgess Shale, west of Banff near Field, British Columbia, in 1909. Walcott was an acquaintance of Mary Schäffer and, later, the husband of Mary M. Vaux, Schäffer's long-time colleague in Philadelphia and the Rockies, who was a botanical painter, photographer, and glaciologist. Gould concluded that "words and images have enormous power and can easily displace actual experience over the years," creating what he called "the power of legend" as truth.[115] What concerned Gould was not so much how scientific truth and accuracy might be jeopardized because of "literary bias"; he was, instead, interested in the way in which "literary bias" is as significant as cultural or social bias in scientific study and reporting. The "web of tales" that emerges over years of communicating experience through the framework and cannon of storytelling does not follow the pattern of life so much as it does the conventions of narrative, within which something is always happening. Gould's point is that the Burgess Shale revealed a frenzy of activity on earth 500 million years ago, and that nothing much else has happened since, with the exception of the emergence of "self-conscious intelligence" on the planet—that is, human beings; as humans communicate primarily through language, the world and our broad knowledge of it is primarily framed through stories that change in time with memory and transmission to others.

Gould's meditations on narrative and knowledge resonate for this study for two reasons. The first is related to the various caricatures of the historical persona of Mary Schäffer that seem so different from the figure one can glimpse from time to time through bits and pieces of archival sources. These do not form a whole greater than the sum of its parts; they cannot be dissected to find the real person and practice, and cannot be ascribed as definitive—indeed, most must be taken as partial and mostly fictive, glued together by an author's imagination or based upon the imagination of previous writers. The second reason for Gould's reflection is to emphasize that Schäffer's narratives—both her published books, articles, images, and private correspondence and her unpublished photographs and manuscripts, as well as those of her peers and colleagues of her time and place—should therefore not be taken as pure fact or historical truth. They were as much memoir as journalism, subject to the vagaries and invention of human recall and imagination ("Memory is a fascinating trickster," Gould observes),[116] and consequently rife with contradictions, anomalies, and pastiches of truths and events. This, in fact, is their strength. Gould does not suggest that truth can be found by untangling this web; rather, he is willing to "accept this limit of mentality upon knowledge, for we receive in trade both the joys of literature and the core of our being."[117] This premise, coupled with Lepore's views on history and fiction, is central to my rethinking of Schäffer's creative practices.

A comparison of *Old Indian Trails* with Molly Adams's diaries and letters from their journeys shows that Schäffer did craft a story as her narrative sweep grew, invoking in her readers her own feelings of impatience, curiosity, lack of knowledge, surprise, pleasure, and self-conscious ineptness. Schäffer's account conveys emotions of a moment and desires for the future or outcome of each journey, whereas Adams's diary and letters are very much accounts, selective and without embellishment, but with personal views and impressions, of events of interest to the chronicler at the time. Much that is in Adams's 1908 diary appears quite differently in Schäffer's final story. The same holds true for Adams's diaries and letters, as it turns out. And much of what happened on the trail did not find its way into either Adams's diary or Schäffer's story at all. Glimpses of the interpersonal relationships that are sprinkled throughout the book in text and photographs—the reader learns more of the personalities and idiosyncrasies of the pack ponies than of "M.," "K.," and "Chief"—as well as the final fates of the four central travellers (Adams died in Japan in January 1909; guide and cook Sidney "K." Unwin died in Britain in June 1917 from injuries sustained two months earlier at Vimy Ridge during the First World War; Schäffer and Warren married in 1915) have sparked speculation and inspired not only biographical interpretations but also fictional portrayals of Schäffer.[118]

Where Mary Schäffer appears most vividly in fiction today is not as a woman of romantic interest or an extraordinary woman adventurer but as a ghostly irate spiritualist, disturbed seventy years after death in the Old Banff cemetery, where the real Schäffer is buried, by the protagonist in Todd Babiak's novel, *The Book of Stanley*.[119] This Mary Schäffer is cast as having arrived in Banff posing as a botanist while in fact "looking for something else. Proof of something. And, by all accounts, she found it."[120] The persona of the hunter of peace endures in the fictive afterlife, and is not amused by the bumbling intrusion on her uncanny existence. Also unique to this fictional rendering is the fact that William Warren, Schäffer's second husband, whose ashes are buried next to her, does not play a role.

Women's personas, however—and certainly that of Mary Schäffer—are rarely reconstructed without attention being paid to the woman's intimate relationships, especially marriage (or lack of it), and any behaviour outside of sanctioned later twentieth-century traditions of heterosexual propriety. Heilbrun argues, "Marriage is the most persistent of myths imprisoning women, and misleading those who write of women's lives."[121] Such relationships are scrutinized and analyzed, often in pursuit of a glimmer of the woman's private anima. In Schäffer's time, through conventions of naming, marital status was the first thing sought and known about a woman. Schäffer's status is signalled throughout her publication history as her surname changes with her changing status in accord with the social conventions of the day: from Mrs. Chas. Schäffer while married, to Mrs. Mary Schäffer and her monogram of MTSS on works while widowed, to Mrs. William Warren and Mary Warren during her second marriage, or, on occasions when her past travels and publications were of interest to correspondents, to Mary Schäffer Warren. It is also telling that most writers of Schäffer's life refer to her by her first name only.[122] Such informality and familiarity, however, is jarring and presumptuous; it reduces the interpersonal distance between the subject and her biographer and, in turn, readers. Such intimacy implies special knowledge of the subject and her private life, an insider's view that is being shared with readers. It also focuses attention most strongly on the private life rather than on the activities and accomplishments of the subject in public life and the broader significance of those matters. Such intimacy is rarely presumed with historical male subjects.

Heilbrun suggests three alternative approaches to the issue of the personal in considering a woman's biography, and her reasoning informs some of the approach of this study. One is to look "at that marriage in middle age that is remarriage; we must look for its conversations…for its qualities of friendship, above all for its equality and the equality of the man's and woman's quests."[123] While Heilbrun is thinking of a long-term marriage that is recast in mid-life as the partners mature, it is a useful formulation for the second marriage of a mature widow, one who is an "accomplished woman" of independent means.[124] Contemplating or at least acknowledging a different kind of imperative, such as the equality and value of the woman's quests, opens space for matters such as Schäffer's ongoing engagement with photography, writing, investment management, travel, and living in the Rocky Mountains.

A second alternative approach is directed at other relationships in a woman's life, especially those with other women: "The sign of female friendship is not whether friends are homosexual or heterosexual, lovers or not, but whether they share the wonderful energy of work in the public sphere. These, some of them hidden, are the friends whom biographers of women must seek out."[125] Mary Schäffer's close relationships extended beyond those with parents and husbands, as she tended an extensive network of family, friends, acquaintances, and colleagues throughout her life. She continued to add new people to her circle as she aged, including family such as twin grandnieces born in 1907 in New York State who moved to Banff in 1931,[126] and those who had learned of her through her books, especially *Old Indian Trails*, and sought her out. These admirers included Humphrey Toms (also a correspondent of painters Georgia O'Keeffe and Emily Carr, Schäffer's slightly younger contemporaries),[127] Lillian Gest, Raymond Zillmer, and Minnie Nickell. Missing from the biographical imaginings of Schäffer's persona are the numerous other women who were travelling in the Rockies at the turn of the twentieth century. These of course include Molly Adams, but also Henrietta Tuzo, Zephine Humphrey, Edith Farr, Ida Ogilvie, and Julia Henshaw, as well as family and friends such as Mary Morris Vaux (later Walcott), Mary James Vaux (wife of George Vaux Jr., Mary M.'s brother),[128] and Caroline Sharpless and Jeannette Sharpless, the wives of Schäffer's brothers.

As a third alternative, Heilbrun argues, "We must recognize what the past suggests: women are well beyond youth when they begin, often unconsciously, to create another story. Not even then do they recognize it as another story. Usually they believe that the obvious reasons for what they are doing are the only ones; only in hindsight, or through a biographer's imaginative eyes, can the concealed story be surmised."[129] In Schäffer's case, one astute book reviewer took note as early as 1911. The unnamed critic for the *Brooklyn Eagle* observed that Schäffer's "incentive to so radically change the course of her life from one which offered every advantage and opportunity for social and home pleasure or popular travel, was the desire to continue and complete the work of her brilliant and scholarly husband, Dr. Charles Schaffer, who died before he could finish" his alpine botany study.[130]

Privately, in later correspondence, Schäffer declined reviewers' assertions that she was an explorer, the persona that they found in her book.[131] In later life, she recalled the journeys that began in 1904 and continued through 1911 as an extension of the life she had led before those years, rather than a break with that time, having spent fifteen summers working in the Rockies with her husband prior to his death. When she returned to the mountains in mourning, what she was seeking, she wrote, was solace in her grief, and she ultimately found peace. The public story that began when Schäffer and Adams are said to have asked "Why not?" portrays a decisive moment in these women's lives, and solicits different kinds of questions in response. These questions weigh the political, economic, and social moments and places in which Schäffer lived, moved, and worked as a photographer, painter, writer, cartographer, traveller, and trail rider, as well as a woman: east and west, American and Canadian, metropolitan, small town, and wilderness. Heeding Schwartz's point about examining photographs, more imaginative questioning of Schäffer's and Adams's photographic images and careful attention to the responses those questions elicit are essential to a complex understanding of Schäffer's story and work.

Heilbrun suggests that a woman may write under a pseudonym to create "an alter ego as she writes, another possibility of female destiny,"[132] and that "women have long searched, and continue to search, for an identity 'other' than their own. Caught in the conventions of their sex, they have sought an escape from gender."[133] Women such as Schäffer and Adams, as well as other travel writers of their day, were certainly doing or seeking as much; subsequently, their work served as "a disguise," as Atwood suggests texts do for some novelists, "concealing from view the person who has concocted" a book's stories.[134] Heilbrun believed that she herself wrote fiction under cover of a pseudonym "to create a space" for herself. While Schäffer may not have perceived or deliberately undertaken her journeys, photography, or writing for such a reason, her published work did in fact create a space for Schäffer alone, both in history and posterity, but also during life. Until she published, she was identified only as bride, wife, and widow—that is, in relation to another, Charles Schäffer. Her 1902 portrait, however, attributed to Mary M. Vaux, offers a hint that she was

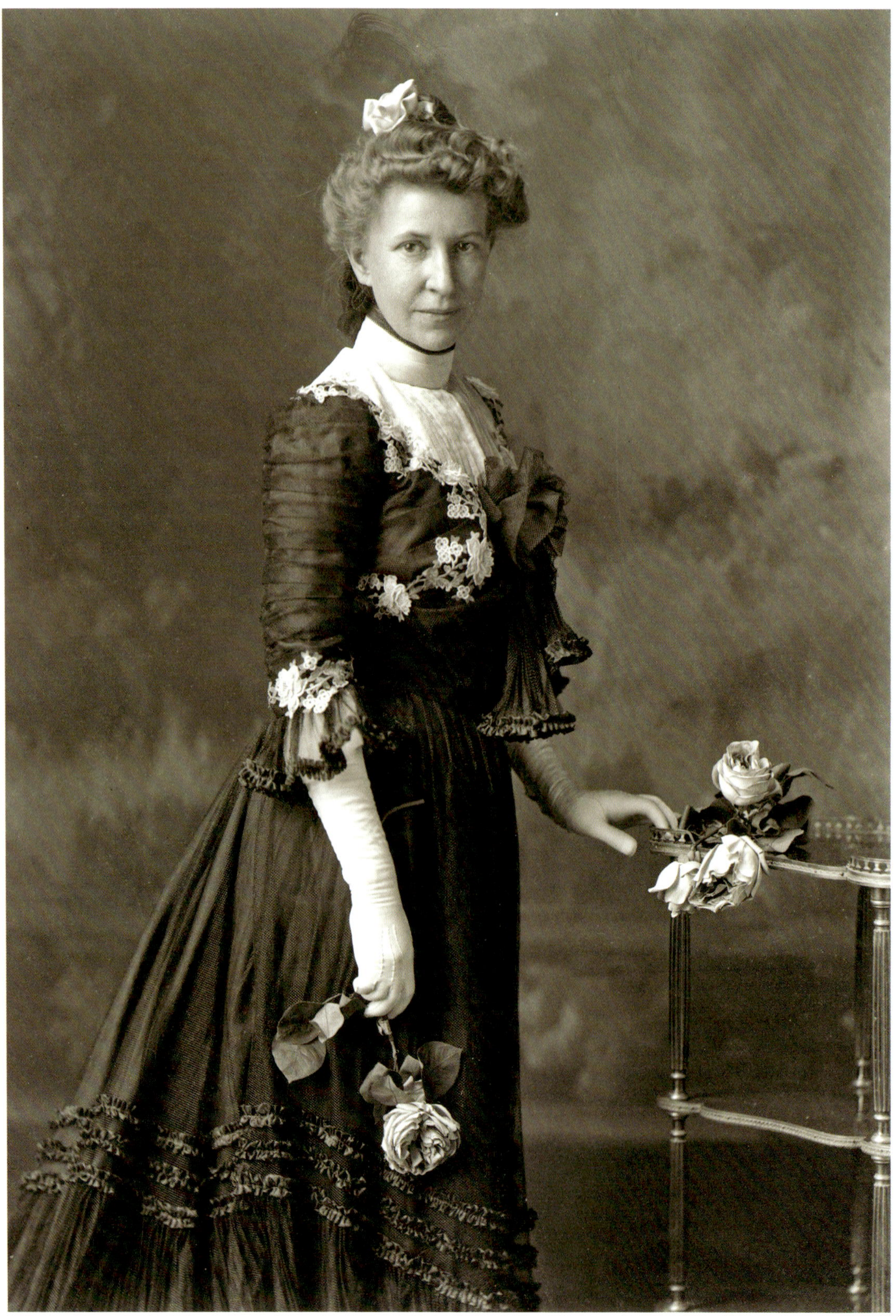

distinguished in private life for her botanical work. The luscious roses in her hair and hand, and on the table, as well as the floral crochet decoration on her dress, emphasize this trait. With her published work and public name she became, as well, an autonomous—and independent—photographer, painter, explorer, traveller, rider, camper, cartographer, and author in and of the Canadian Rockies especially, but also briefly Japan.

‹FIGURE 1.10

Mary T.S. Schäffer, Mary M. Vaux photograph, 1902.

[WMCR V653/NG4-959]

Searching for Mary Schäffer: Women Wilderness Photography proceeds from Schäffer's visual practices, particularly photography. It does not aspire to recover or restore Schäffer to mainstream photography histories—although it does that to some extent (recovery of women's histories continues, as it must). Nor does it simply report new facts; rather, it aspires to ask new questions and to tell new stories with new or more fully formed characters (at least, in the Schäffer literature) and new viewpoints.[135] American and women's studies scholar Laura Wexler talks about what we need to ask beyond the questions of recovery and recuperation:

> *But it is not enough to look at what turn-of-the-century American women photographers were doing in terms of their numbers or their own individual achievement. Nor is it enough to look even in terms of the collective success as a group unless at the same time the "cultural work" of this success itself is also exhumed and interrogated.... It is crucial to ask not simply why these highly successful women disappeared from history but, even more fundamentally, why these women were able to have such careers in the first place.*[136]

As with "She Who Colored Slides," in this study women are both subjects and agents, both portrayed in photographs and the makers of photographic images. A single image can both connote historical individuals and denote the work itself that they did, whether it was making photographs, crafting buckskin jackets, or painting images. The visually layered "She Who Colored Slides" serves as documentary evidence of a Stoney woman's powerful textile skills and Molly Adams's presence as photographer, traveller, and diarist who is also the embodiment of Schäffer's audience. It is also, and ultimately, a portrait of Mary Schäffer as the agent of these adventures, as well as a photographer, artist, and writer weaving the web of the story. The story is collaborative, as in this image, but also in many ways unspoken, interwoven with ambiguity and gaps for readers and viewers to question. Such are the questions that *Searching for Mary Schäffer* sets out to explore.

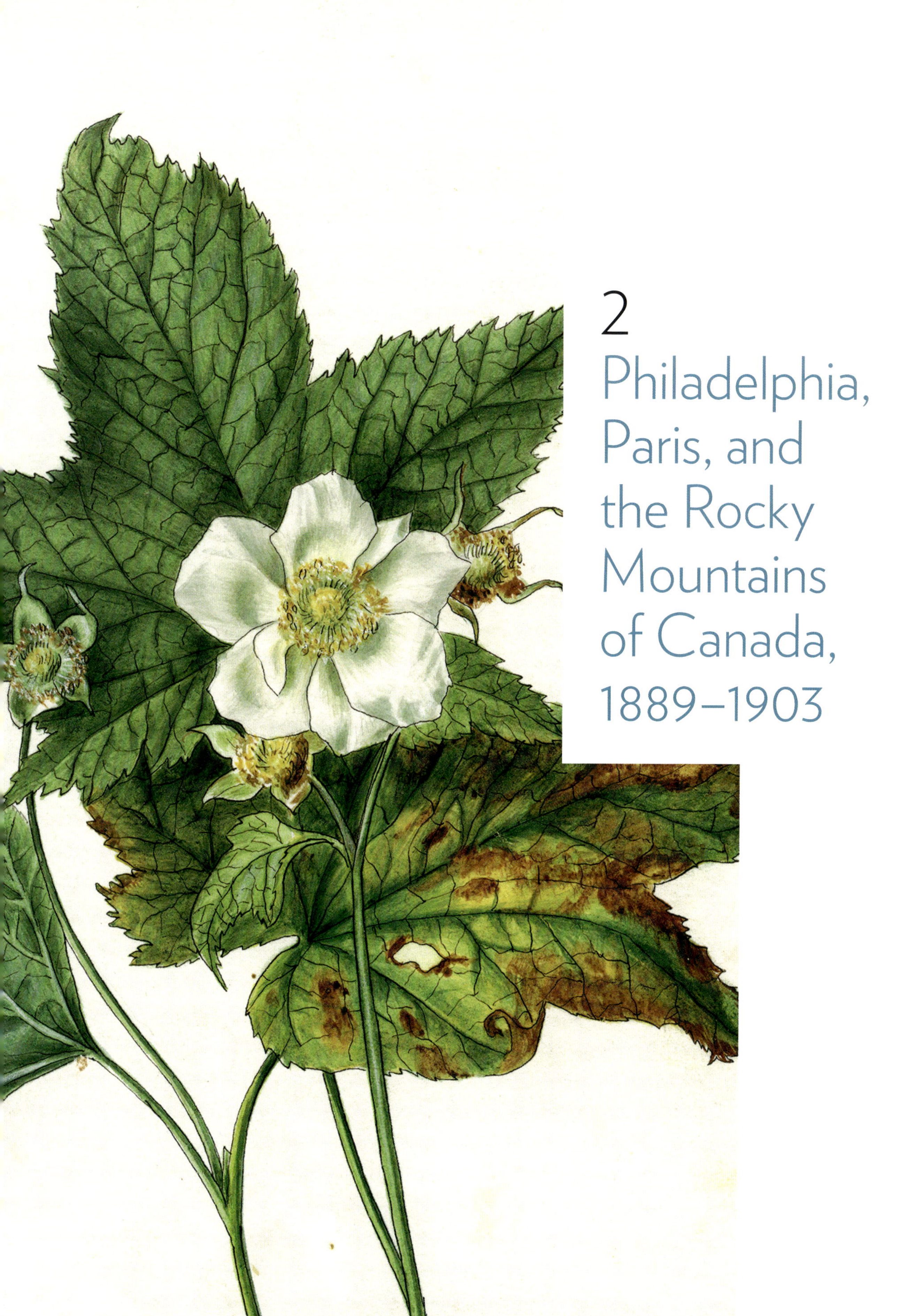

2
Philadelphia, Paris, and the Rocky Mountains of Canada, 1889–1903

AT HOME ON ARCH STREET in the heart of old Philadelphia on 12 June 1900, Mary Schäffer received in the morning post an unexpected summons from Washington, DC. Her correspondent was none other than Frances Benjamin Johnston, a photographer and writer of considerable reputation. Schäffer read,

> *I have just been named by the U.S. Commission, a delegate to the International Photographic Congress, to be held in Paris, July 23–28, with the request to prepare a paper on the work of American women photographers. The commission recognizes this work as unique, and it is their desire that the wonderful achievement of American women in Photography should be adequately and worthily represented at this Congress.*
>
> *It is to this end that I hope to receive your hearty co-operation and support.*[1]

Schäffer knew Johnston's work well, and admired it. Reproductions and articles about Johnston's work had appeared over the past decade in books and magazines, such as the *Ladies' Home Journal*, *Harper's Weekly*, *Demorest's Family Magazine*, *Frank Leslie's Magazine*, and *Cosmopolitan*. Furthermore, their paths had crossed more than once at the Photographic Society of Philadelphia, most recently in 1899. The Board of Directors reported, for example, that

> *at the Visitors' Meeting, May 3, Mrs. Charles Schäffer exhibited a choice collection of slides illustrating most admirably the photographic beauties and grandeur of the Canadian Rockies.*
>
> *The wall display for the month is the work of Miss Frances B. Johnston, of Washington, D.C.*[2]

In 1900, Mary Schäffer was especially well situated to be included in Johnston's call for submissions to the American exhibition that was taking place during the Paris Universal and International Exposition. Philadelphia was the birthplace and cultural centre of American photography from 1839 through the close of the century, and Mary Schäffer was typical of women and photographers in that milieu in 1900.

Schäffer had been born in West Chester, Pennsylvania, and spent her early childhood in Philadelphia until age eight, when her parents moved first to East Bradford and then back to West Chester.[3] In 1889, she married and returned to Philadelphia, settling into 1309 Arch Street, a home that had been owned by her husband's family since 1844.[4] The census of 1900 counted a population of almost 1.3 million in Philadelphia that included 16,000 Quakers, among them Mary Townsend Sharples and Charles Schäffer, whose mother's family was of British Quaker descent and whose father's ancestors were German Quakers.[5] Nathaniel Burt writes that "a sort of strict Quaker ghetto occupied Arch Street" where the Schäffers made their home.[6] They lived not only in the historical heart of the United States and Philadelphia—Betsy Ross House is further east on Arch Street, as is the historical Quaker's Friends meeting house and the cemetery that holds Benjamin Franklin's grave, and Independence Hall, the home of the Liberty Bell, is in the same area two blocks south of Arch—but also in the geographical and intellectual heart of photography in the United States at the time.

Rallying her peers in 1900, Frances Benjamin Johnston's exhibition in Paris would be representative of the vibrant photography, publishing, and science environment from which Schäffer emerged fully in her own right in 1907 with the publication of *Alpine Flora of the Canadian Rocky Mountains*, followed in 1911 by her travel book, *Old Indian Trails: Incidents of Camp and Trail Life, Covering Two Years' Exploration through the Rocky Mountains of Canada*. At the turn of the century, the photography environment was especially lively, marked by a large proportion of active women and by strong thinking by both women and men about the content of photographs and the aesthetics of photography. Also in contention were photography's relationship to American nationalism, imperialism, optimism, and ambition, and women's rights and roles in democratic societies. Schäffer's intellectual and aesthetic pursuits in photography were rooted in and fostered by the dynamic thinking, debating, and exhibiting activities of the large and vigorous organizations of professional and amateur photographers and critics that thrived in later nineteenth-century Philadelphia. These were complemented by groups of botanists and geographers and their institutionally based societies. Those interests and activities reached into the Rocky Mountains of Canada with the opening of passenger service on the Canadian Pacific Railway in 1886 and the first visits of tourists from Philadelphia, including Mary M. Vaux and her family in 1887 and Schäffer herself in 1889.

Photography in Philadelphia

Mary Schäffer received with enthusiasm the invitation from Frances Benjamin Johnston; in fact, she wrote in reply that very afternoon. Others who received invitations wrote back immediately as well.[7] Their responses ranged from excitement to dismay, from modesty to pride at having been invited or at having to write about their own work. There were also some polite refusals due to previous commitments of prints to other exhibitions, or due to family holiday commitments that took precedence over short notice in early summer. Schäffer's response and the biographical sketch that she later sent portray the vigour, defensiveness, and intense interest in the world around her that characterized her extensive correspondence throughout her life. Schäffer was a dedicated writer, who honed and often deployed her skills in letters written in a large, flowing, and energetic script.

> *1309 Arch Street*
> *Philadelphia*
>
> *My dear Miss Johnston,*
>
> *Your request rec'd in this a.m. mail. I am going to try to accede to to* [sic] *your request. If not satisfactory, throw my work to one side. I am at present just recovering from a year's illness, & cannot do the later & more artistic finishing to my prints. I am also determinedly old-fashioned & will not see the artistic in some of the work which is being shown in the last year. I enclose a test print. The other negative is the same except the focusing glass was set the other way, giving at the lower portion a prettier reflection & a sketchy foreground of grasses. I had it enlarged to 18x22, a greyish sepia tone.—I think it my best. Is it too large for your purposes? It is rather expensive, & unless I was sure of your using it, wd. not care to send it.*
>
> *Allow me to add that I am delighted, from what I have seen of your work, that you are to represent the American women abroad. Several Phila & N.Y.*

women have gone so outrageously into impressionism that, to the more conservative it has become farcical. I enclose sta[...] regarding the 18x22. It is rather Horsley Hinton in its effect, which may give you some hint as to its merits.

I am sincerely,

MARY T.S. SCHÄFFER
1309 Arch St.
Phila

June 12, 19__[8]

Exuding energy and opinion, Schäffer's letter introduces much about her thoughts on photography and the informed aesthetic choices on which her photographic practice was based. It is clear that she was well-versed in current photography debates and practices in Philadelphia, and did not hesitate to express her critical position. Schäffer also situated herself as a fully contemporary and knowledgeable photographic artist by comparing her own work to that of British photographer Alfred Horsley Hinton, whose expressive landscapes had attracted exceptionally favourable critical reception at the acrimonious Philadelphia salons of 1898 and 1899.[9] The juries of the Philadelphia Photographic Salons of those years, which included Frances Benjamin Johnston in 1899, had championed new pictorialist aesthetics at the expense of all other photographic work, including that of accomplished realists (as Schäffer was) who had submitted prints for adjudication, and sparked a divisive dispute among members of the Photographic Society of Philadelphia.

Photography in the late nineteenth century was an established locus of practice and invention in a city with a proud heritage at the centre of American history and culture. Founded in 1682 by English Quaker William Penn, the city emerged as one of wealth and influence during the eighteenth and nineteenth centuries as industry and education were established and nurtured. Political power was also concentrated there during the Revolutionary War, when it served as capital of the American Colonies, and it was in Philadelphia that both the Declaration of Independence and the Constitution of the United States were signed. The intellectual and fine arts communities' histories were equally long. In 1900, Philadelphia was home to the University of Pennsylvania, founded in 1740; the American Philosophical Society, established in 1743 by Philadelphia resident Benjamin Franklin and friends; the Library Company of Philadelphia, a lending library made up of dues-paying members who could borrow the books purchased by the dues, established by Benjamin Franklin in 1751; the Pennsylvania Academy of the Fine Arts, the first art school in the United States, established in 1805; and the Franklin Institute, focused on the promotion and support of science education, established in 1827. Philadelphia was also home to three prominent associations of which Mary Schäffer was a member. The first was the Academy of Natural Sciences of Philadelphia, established in 1812 and to which Schäffer was elected in 1896. The second was the Photographic Society of Philadelphia, established in 1862 by a group of thirty-three Philadelphia men with a serious interest in photography whose activities ranged from technical experimentation to those with commercial interests, and of which Mary Schäffer was a member from the early 1890s until 1906.[10] The third association was the Geographical Society of Philadelphia, a division of the Academy of Natural Sciences established in 1891 with fifty-one members, including twenty-one women. Charles Schäffer was among the founders of the Geographical Society,[11] and Mary Schäffer was an active member, publishing three articles in the *Bulletin of the Geographical Society* between 1907 and 1909.[12]

Schäffer and her husband were members of the Photographic Society of Philadelphia during its most contentious, lively, and important years in the history of photography in the United States. Members of the Photographic Society of Philadelphia experimented and achieved recognition for technical advancements in areas such as platinum paper printing, hand-coloured lantern slide projection, and animation.[13] The Society also received and examined photographs from elsewhere, and in 1872 members began presenting lantern slide lectures "in the Lecture room of the Franklin Institute,"[14] an activity that would continue into the twentieth century, and to which Mary Schäffer would contribute both at the Photographic Society of Philadelphia in 1899[15] and at the Geographical Society in 1911.[16] In 1876, when Philadelphia hosted the World's Fair to mark the centenary of the United States, an entire pavilion was devoted solely to photography.

After 1879, when invention of the gelatin dry-plate negative greatly simplified photographic processes, the membership of the Photographic Society of Philadelphia grew more rapidly, although until at least 1884 there were no women members.[17] In 1889, the *Photographic Times* of New York reported that the Photographic Society of Philadelphia included "skillful amateurs, who find in photography pleasant and healthful recreation; scientists who study the art experimentally; artists to whom the camera is a helpful tool; travelers who [make] pictorial records in all parts of the world, and professional photographers of the highest ability."[18] During their period of membership, Mary and Charles Schäffer could be counted among those described as skillful amateurs and travellers. In her study of naturalistic photography in Philadelphia at this time, Mary Panzer describes amateur photographers as those who made images that "were meant for public view. Whether as informative documents, demonstrations of expertise, or records of a particular experience, the amateur photographer intended to present his images before an audience. Amateurs worked for exhibition, finding reward through recognition from colleagues."[19] Schäffer's correspondence with Johnston shows that recognition from peers was very much on her mind when Johnston's invitation arrived.

Furthermore, by the 1890s, amateur photographers were not exclusively male. A text titled "Some Salon Statistics" was appended to Joseph T. Keiley's lengthy article on the "origin and influence" of the Philadelphia Photographic Salon and its autumn 1898 exhibition that was published in the January 1899 issue of *Camera Notes*. The statistics showed that "[a] remarkably strong showing was made by the women, both in quality and numbers. Of the hundred exhibitors, seventeen were women, sixteen of whom were American and one European." Six of these women contributed 37 prints, and 11 contributed one each, for a total of 47 photographs, or 18 per cent of the 259 photographs exhibited.[20] That this rate was considered remarkable or relevant enough, and of sufficient interest to readers, to be included in the statistical overview hints at the wider social interest in women's growing participation in public activities like commercial, amateur, and artistic photography.

The interest in women's participation rates was not confined to the photography salon. Women's roles and economic activity in the United States were of sufficient interest that the census of 1900 assembled and published a separate 392-page volume of statistics on women at work.[21] In 1900, of the 26,941 people who claimed employment as photographers in the continental United States, 3,514 (or 13 per cent) were women.[22] The growth of women's participation in paid photography activity was a phenomenon shared across the professions and was sufficiently marked to incite comment from the census reporters: "While the percentages are in most cases still small, a comparison with the earlier censuses indicates clearly the general movement among females toward professions which until recently have been filled almost exclusively by men."[23] The statisticians reported not only the numbers, but attempted to illuminate underlying sociological forces for why the number of women earning a living outside the home was rising proportionately in the population. They argued, for example, "The extent to which women in different classes of population engage in breadwinning pursuits is no doubt determined largely by differences in economic welfare. Probably few women take up a remunerative occupation who are so situated that they can live comfortably without."[24] This did not explain to the statisticians' satisfaction, however, the move into the workplace of women who were "removed from the necessity of earning a living."[25] Despite the fact that those in this class of women "are not at present numerous enough to affect materially the percentages shown," they nevertheless opined that

> *Doubtless a considerable number of the women who engage in such pursuits as teaching, literary work, or some other of the so-called liberal professions, are not constrained thereto by any necessity of earning a living, but are actuated by the motives that do not differ materially from those which appeal to men in similar circumstances, such as some form of ambition, a love of activity, or a desire for social usefulness. But it is safe to say that while women of this class may be increasing in numbers, they make up only a very small fraction of the total number of women returned by the census as breadwinners.*[26]

In Philadelphia in 1900, 14 per cent of commercial photographers were women: 87 women and 544 men reported photography as a paid occupation.[27] The social profile of those in occupations in Philadelphia was also broken down and reported according to ethnicity, marital status, and age. Among women photographers, two-thirds were of Euro-American origins; 40 per cent were aged 16 to 24 years; 46 per cent were aged 25 to 44 years; 90 per cent (78/87) were single; 5 per cent (4/87) were married; and 6 per cent were widowed (4/87) or divorced (1/87).[28] These proportions were in keeping with the general occupational distributions in which census summaries showed 5.6 per cent (1 in 18) of married women as employed, but were strikingly different from the general distribution of 45.6 per cent (9 in 20) of single women being employed.[29] What does this suggest? That for those who had come of age after the introduction of gelatin dry-plate technology, which by 1880 had fuelled a huge expansion of the uses of photography and those employed in it, photography seems to have been especially attractive as an occupation for young women and those who needed or chose to work for income.

Photographers and commentators had been debating women's involvement in photography since its invention. In its early days, opinions were mixed, and the debate was closely intertwined with the larger questions of women's social role. In 1873, British photographer and writer Jabez Hughes, a self-proclaimed "well-wisher to the women's movement," argued for the greater participation of women in the photography workforce. He wished to make it clear to "those interested in spreading the domain of female labor"[30] that "in photography there *is* room for a larger amount of female labor, that it *is* a field exactly suited to even the conventional notions of women's capacity, and further, that it is a field unsurrounded with traditional rules, with apprenticeship, with vested rights, and it is one in which there is no sexual hostility to their employment. It is a business easily learnt, moderately well paid, and affording scope for all gradations of skills and ability."[31]

Although, Hughes wrote, "it is admitted that women can do everything photographic,"[32] his article "Photography as an Industrial Occupation for Women," published in New York's *Anthony's Photographic Bulletin*, was focused on the employment of women as photography assistants in photography portrait studios (or galleries, as they were then called).[33] In 1873, Hughes was not concerned with advancing the cause of women photographers per se, although he noted that "there are portrait establishments in town and country, on the Continent, and in America, that women have successfully conducted, and even gained reputation, for their ability. These, however, are exceptions."[34] He did not pursue the issues that he raised, such as the art and "intellectual aspect" of photography, noting that they would "lead from the main idea of this paper"; he did, however, point out that in London, "this art has a valuable and interesting literature of its own" as well as "many societies in London and the provinces expressly devoted to its cultivation and advancement…and that on the Continent and in America its literature is equally well cared for."[35] By 1880, however, as American census figures show, women photographers began to move from being an exception, and the first critical mass of women took up the camera as a serious pursuit, both commercially and as committed amateurs.

In 1897, Frances Benjamin Johnston framed the topic "What a Woman Can Do with a Camera" in a businesslike manner for her audience of women readers of the *Ladies' Home Journal*, describing the traits a successful commercial photographer needed and outlining the facilities and investment required. At no time did she lean on stereotypes or platitudes to make her case. The information and advice she presented was gender-neutral.

> *Photography as a profession should appeal particularly to women, and in it there are great opportunities for a good-paying business—but only under very well-defined conditions. The prime requisites—as summed up in my mind after long experience and thought [Johnston first started studying photography in 1885 and opened a studio in Washington, DC in 1890]—are these: The woman who makes photography profitable must have, as personal qualities, good common sense, unlimited patience to carry her through endless failures, equally unlimited tact, good taste, a quick eye, a talent for detail, and a genius for hard work. In addition, she needs training, experience, some capital and a field to exploit....To an energetic, ambitious woman with even ordinary opportunities, success is always possible, and hard; intelligent and conscientious work seldom fails to develop small beginnings into large results.*[36]

For those who aimed for "distinction and originality" in their photographic work, Johnston recommended fine art training first, followed by photography training, which, given the very few photography schools in the United States, especially outside of large cities, would need to be obtained through "an apprenticeship in the establishment of some professional photographer, who has a good knowledge of his profession" and through membership in a progressive camera club—the educational and training trajectory that Johnston herself followed.[37] Although she cautions, "Even if a woman finds such an opportunity it is most important that she learn to think for herself, and to keep her own ideas and individuality in her work."[38] This is advice that Schäffer lived.

Photography Aesthetics and the Photographic Society of Philadelphia

Both in Philadelphia and internationally, the fault line of debate toward the end of the century emerged not around women's participation in photography, but rather between two views on photography. One was that photographs should be created and consumed as fine art objects in themselves, achieving aesthetic merit based on originality of concept and individuality of expression. Such photographs were to be considered fine art, and were distinguished by the term "pictorial photography." The contrary view held that photography was necessarily bound to the physical, material world external to human beings, and as such did not or should not need to construct itself self-consciously as fine art or be limited to a particular visual style; nor was it a less-valuable activity or object for that. While the membership and executive of the Photographic Society of Philadelphia accepted that some photographic practices ranked as fine art, a move to limit the Society's exhibition to such photographic work alone would have disenfranchised a significant portion of its membership.

The salon jury of 1898, which included Alfred Stieglitz, who had been lobbying for an American photography salon dedicated solely to displaying juried pictorial photographs, in fact excluded the majority of submissions, including all that did not fall within the bounds of pictorialism. Among the images excluded were those in the long and widely practiced realist genres of descriptive (as opposed to expressive or impressionistic) landscape and botanical photography, the genres in which Mary Schäffer worked.

In Philadelphia, the practice of landscape and botanical photography had deep roots in a society whose founders and subsequent generations of citizens and leaders had profound interests in science and the natural world. By the late nineteenth century, these Philadelphians—descendants of William Penn's Quakers and Benjamin Franklin's scientists—had a long tradition of discovery and invention in the sciences, making contributions to mathematics, optics, astronomy, biology, and botany, and a deep commitment to study of the natural world and its minerals, plants, and animals.[39] Quakerism had been founded on the principle that a person comes to know God not through formal doctrines of scripture or rite, but through experience from within—that is, by personal, physical experience of God, an experience that came through or of nature, God's creation. Science in the age of Enlightenment was valued as the study of empirical reality; the observation, examination, description, and depiction of natural phenomena was a study of "the manifestation, by means of this empirical reality, of God's majesty and beauty."[40] Simplicity of lifestyle and dress, absence of institutional clerical hierarchy, and valuing of education also distinguished Quakerism. Educational reform was among the accomplishments of seventeenth-century Quakers, who turned the focus of their education to the study of nature and to that to which such study could be applied and deemed useful, especially medicine; this stood in explicit opposition to the fine arts. The study of nature was not viewed as the purview of professional scientists or physicians alone, but a worthwhile leisure activity for all, men, women, and children alike. For Philadelphians with such a heritage, including Mary and Charles Schäffer and the Vaux family, the Canadian Rockies proved a rich field for photography and research in the natural sciences, especially botany, geology, and glaciology.

It is not known whether Schäffer submitted work for adjudication to the salons of 1898 to 1900, as no documentation to that effect remains. Two letters that Schäffer wrote to Johnston resonate with a tone of exclusion—whether effected through elimination by a jury or through Schäffer's self-exclusion because even competing for a place seemed futile—and the generally bitter feeling of the majority of Society members. In light of the narrowed pictorial aesthetics that had come to dominate the decisions of the adjudication committees of the Philadelphia salon by 1900, and Schäffer's absence from those shows, for her to have been invited to participate in an international exhibition of the best of American women photographers' work was an experience both extraordinary and, from the tenor of Schäffer's response, perhaps vindicating. It was an opportunity she would not pass up.

Exhibition of American Women Photographers

It was on 12 April 1900, only three days prior to the opening of the Universal Exposition in Paris, that Frances Benjamin Johnston was invited to serve as a US delegate. Her role was to speak about the accomplishments of American women photographers at the International Congress of Photography, convening 23 to 28 July in conjunction with the fair. The request was sent by Mrs. Ellen M. Henrotin, secretary to Mrs. Potter (Berthe Honoré) Palmer of Chicago, a member of the United States National Commission for the Paris Exposition. Henrotin was charged with recruiting twenty-five women delegates to represent an array of fields in which American women's endeavours were making a mark. There was a good reason why Johnston received this invitation so late, necessitating the urgent tone regarding the time constraint as she in turn issued her own invitations: women had not originally been included in the United States' ambitious plans for Paris. Palmer had served as Head of the Board of Lady Managers for the 1893 World's Columbian Exposition in Chicago, at which American women's interests and concerns had been prominently showcased in the Women's Building and had effectively presented American women as the most progressive in the world. When no women were appointed to the US Commission for the Exposition in Paris, American women who had been active in Chicago were both surprised and displeased—and they mobilized, demanding a seat.

In response, the editor of the Philadelphia-based *Ladies' Home Journal*, Edward Bok, argued against a separate building for women, calling the Chicago pavilion "a hen's house" and asserting that many women preferred their presence to be integrated and their work included on the basis of merit, rather than gender.[41] Taking a different tack, but the same position, Commissioner General Ferdinand W. Peck, in a *New York Times* article, claimed that no women had been appointed to the commission because Congress had not mandated their participation, nor had the French government advised him that "such appointments are desirable." The astute and well-connected Palmer, thoroughly versed on World's Exposition policy, procedure, and politics, dismissed Peck's equivocation, stating that the French "exposition management leaves us free to form our own committees without dictation or suggestion, but it has a Woman's committee, and of course we are at liberty also to appoint women, as other countries have done. If we do not choose to do so, the fault is our own." Furthermore, Palmer had encountered women who were serving on the Paris Exposition's women's committee: a Woman's Pavilion, the Palais de la Femme, was being organized. She found those women to be "much surprised that no women have a place on the United States Commission, but I feel sure that when the management of the exposition of 1900 is thoroughly organized there will be proper recognition of women in some way, either through President McKinley, or Mr. Peck, or the proper official."[42]

Berthe Palmer prevailed, obtaining appointment to the commission in late 1899 through the intervention of the president of the United States. While a crucial victory, it was also a partial one. In *Ambassadors of Progress: American Women Photographers in Paris, 1900–1901*, Bronwyn A.E. Griffith makes clear that because of the intervention of Palmer and her supporters, "Women participated in each of the fields to a certain extent, but without an independent voice. For the Exposition in France, the United States reverted to the Old World conception of a woman's role in society—one to be strictly defined by men."[43] Photography was meant to be a case in point. While presented in a variety of exhibition venues as either documentary—Frances Benjamin Johnston's series of photographs of African American students at the Hampton Institute displayed in the Palace of Congress and Social Economy, as part of the "American Negro Exhibit," is a notable example—or a domestic hobby displayed in the Women's Palace, photography was not presented as a profession for women or displayed by organizers as fine art.

Alfred Stieglitz had failed in his campaign to have photography included with painting and sculpture in the fine arts exhibition hall rather than in the Palace of Letters, Arts, and Sciences where the American women photographers' show was to appear briefly.[44] As a result of exclusion from the fine art venue, photography groups in the United States as well as Britain, Germany, Belgium, and Australia refused to contribute work.[45] Johnston had no such qualms. In fact, Johnston was charged with subverting this monocular view at the International Congress of Photography, which had been expressly organized to meet in Paris during the Exposition, by being engaged to demonstrate American women's leading accomplishments in the fields of professional and serious amateur photography. Mary Schäffer's work ranked among these accomplishments.

Explaining her mission to Frances Benjamin Johnston, Henrotin wrote, "We are endeavoring to secure women who are specialists in their line of work. Women photographers, in this country, have accomplished such unique work that I am endeavoring to ascertain who among them will be in Paris this summer and would take part as a delegate in that congress. Are you to visit Paris during the coming summer and would you be willing to serve as a delegate? Do you speak or write French and could you give a short address on the work of women in Photography and their specialties?"[46] Johnston was familiar with Paris, having studied drawing and painting there at the Académie Julian for two years starting in 1883, and subsequently travelling to Europe, including Paris, frequently over the intervening fifteen years.[47] Correspondence exchanged during May shows that Johnston agreed to serve as one of "about twenty-five women specialists" recruited, after inquiring about funds "to defray the expenses of a collection" and "pecuniary recompense" for the delegate, neither of which was forthcoming.[48] Johnston is recognized today for her entrepreneurial, if somewhat chaotic, approach to the business side of her practice.[49] The Paris exhibition is a good example: she recognized an unusual opportunity to enhance not only her own career but women's lot in the field in general, and cast her net broadly to gather a long list of American women working in photography—women whose work was admired by other photographers, women and men both, whether or not as well-known as her own. She also expected and planned for a positive response and for more requests for commentary on women's work by seeking reproduction rights in advance.

Once she had agreed to terms with Henrotin, Johnston began to prepare her presentation.

On 2 June, she sent letters and a draft list of women photographers to a half-dozen male colleagues in the photography field (fine art, commercial, and amateur photographers, and journal editors), seeking their opinions on those she had listed and soliciting additional nominations. Correspondents included photographers Alfred Stieglitz of New York and Henry Troth, a photographer and salon juror in Philadelphia. Replying on 8 June from his home at Lake George, to which he had retired from New York for the summer, Stieglitz wrote—"somewhat sanctimoniously," in the well-considered opinion of Judith Fryer Davidov,[50]

> *My dear Miss Johnston*
>
> *Pardon the delay in acknowledging the receipt of your letter before this. Winding up my affairs in the city before leaving for the summer necessitated my neglecting all my correspondence, even the most important. The list of women photographers you sent me is complete, & I can think of no one that you may have over looked.*
>
> *I'd certainly ask them all.*
>
> *The women in this country are certainly doing great photographic work & deserve much commendation for their efforts.*
>
> *I have been overworked & am pretty well used up physically & mentally & need a rest. You have no idea how I am overrun with requests in one way or another, & my position is not an enviable one, as it is nearly impossible for me to get a chance to do any work for myself.*
>
> *With kind regards,*
> *Yours very truly,*
> ALFRED STIEGLITZ[51]

Stieglitz was not a champion of Johnston, who practiced both the realism of the studio portraiture tradition and the pictorialism of turn-of-the-century fine art photography, nor of Henry Troth. He confided his position in a letter to pictorial photographer F. Holland Day, who was seeking Stieglitz's perspective on the invitation Day had received from the Photographic Society of Philadelphia to serve on the jury of the Philadelphia Photographic Salon in

1899: "I like you as a juror but Miss Johnston! And even Troth. Why not Day to represent the East, Käsebier the Middle States and White the West. Of course that would leave Philadelphia out, which would be a good thing for obvious reasons....Nevertheless, it may be a good thing for you to accept so as to prevent the thing from being mediocre."[52] Stieglitz's response to Johnston's request for nominations for her Paris exhibition, with its tone of ennui and social courtesy and lack of real assistance or support for the project, takes on clearer meaning when viewed in this light. And so, while Stieglitz pursued his rest, Johnston seized opportunity and persevered in the heat and humidity of a Washington summer until, in just a few short weeks, she had collected and presented a representative sample of the best of the American School of photography as practiced by women from across the country in 1900.

Henry Troth proved infinitely more helpful. Writing on 7 June, he endorsed Johnston's list as "undoubtedly the best and most artistic women workers, but I will give you a list of others who have done more or less good work."[53] This is how Schäffer's name came to Johnston's attention, as she was listed among the additional ten women photographers recommended by Troth, six of whom Johnston subsequently and successfully recruited: "Mrs. Charles Schaffer [*sic*], 1309 Arch St Philadelphia, has been photographing wild flowers for several years," he wrote in his recommendation.[54] Troth shared similar interests in subject matter with Mary Schäffer, as well as a documentary aesthetic. For both reasons, Schäffer's name would lie outside the list of "artistic women workers," as Troth described Johnston's initial list. Troth offered no critical comment on Schäffer's work or its reputation, but listing her name among the others was sufficient endorsement for Johnston to solicit work from Schäffer.

"I hope to receive your hearty co-operation and support," Johnston wrote to Schäffer,

> *by the preparation of a brief biographical sketch, and the loan of a few prints, showing your most individual and distinctive work. In regard to the personal sketch, I would like a short but comprehensive account of how you happened to adopt photography as an art or profession, what your training—technical and artistic—has been, and what special lines you have developed; something of the methods and conditions under which you work, and any other details which you consider of interest and as bearing upon the subject. If you can accompany this text with your own portrait, it will be highly acceptable.*[55]

On 24 June, Mary Schäffer wrote in greater detail than most of Frances Benjamin Johnston's correspondents in response to the request for a biographical sketch explaining how she came to photography.

> *Asked why I turned from the brush to the camera, I can say mostly through chance. Health would not tolerate close confinement to the brush, & that seemed the end of flower study.*
>
> *One of the household being confined with a long attack of illness, my mind constantly in the sick room, the blues spreading from day to day, an idea suddenly developed, why not try some form of amusement which would entertain both sick and well? To photograph some of the invalid's beautiful flowers,* [sic] *appealed to my long training with the brush. I knew no more about lenses, stops, shutters, plates, or any other part of the instrument, than what I had heard from daily conversation & that not from close listening, & as the instrument was an exceeding fine one, you can rest assured I kept my aspirations to myself, or I fear the object of amusing the invalid would have been lost. So with books & quiet, with lovely flowers, & plenty of fear I set out to work. Disappointments were numerous, but they were all saved for records & the first success was hailed by the household with delight, especially the invalid who was too polite to hint at the many accidents which* <u>*might*</u> *have occurred to his beautiful camera.*
>
> *There started a new field for an old study & afterward becoming very valuable in connection with botanical work.*[56]

Illness is an occasionally recurring theme in Schäffer correspondence. Her biographers have stated that she suffered throughout her life from neuralgia, a painful condition affecting nerve fibres, although Schäffer herself rarely explicitly names any malady or its treatment in surviving correspondence.[57] Her husband Charles also reportedly suffered poor health throughout adulthood, and this is credited with his greater focus on medical and science studies rather than medical practice. After a serious illness in 1895, he retired altogether from practicing medicine and spent the remaining years of his life on serious amateur science studies, especially in botany and geology.[58] He was the invalid who inspired Schäffer to turn to photography that year. His serious interest in photography supported his botanical studies. By the time he married Mary Townsend Sharples in 1889, he was well into a long-term study of botany. Mary Schäffer was already a skilled painter when she married. "Having had," she wrote to Johnston, "a year with G.C. Lamdin, the greatest idealizer of roses in the art world, the mind naturally turned to flowers in all their natural beauty, leaving much of their grouping to themselves, & considering that nature knew her own business much better than man."[59] Taking up photography in addition to botanical painting, she became responsible for the illustrative aspect of the foundational work on the flora of the Rocky Mountains of Canada that she and her husband pursued together during annual summer field trips until his death in 1903. It was this work that Troth knew and recommended.

In her letter of invitation, Johnston also asked Schäffer for exhibition prints:

> *In regard to examples of your work, I should like a few prints,—not more than ten—of what you consider your highest and best product, showing as much diversity as possible, and perhaps covering different periods of your progress. These prints should be lightly and compactly mounted, but unframed, and should reach me not later than the 25th of June. I shall use them solely as an exhibition in connection with the paper I am preparing, and will hold them subject to your disposition on my return. In this connection, I will say that I am certain to have many requests, both from foreign and home publications, for the use of these pictures, and I shall be glad to have you mark any of them which you might be willing for me to publish, at my discretion. I will, of course, employ my best efforts to protect your interests.*
>
> *Trust that you will grant me an immediate reply—and the time is so limited—and thank you in advance for your favor,*
>
> *I am, Very sincerely,*[60]
> *[FRANCES BENJAMIN JOHNSTON]*

On 24 June, Schäffer wrote to Johnston advising, "we will mail you to-morrow the prints asked for. There are 11 instead of 10," as Johnston had requested,

> *to deal with as you see fit. I often feel like turning it to some money value but never have as I am usually working up something for my husband's scientific friends. It isn't lucrative but very fascinating. I wish I might hear from you personally & hope we can arrange to have a talk from you before the Phila Photo Society next winter.*
>
> *Wishing you a pleasant trip and success in your work.*[61]

Schäffer was one of 31 women, excluding Johnston herself, whose work—142 photos in all—Johnston carried to Paris.[62] Her photographs travelled in distinguished company with the works of Frances and Mary Allen, Alice Austin, Mary Bartlett, Zaida Ben-Yusuf, Elizabeth Brownell, Rose Clark, Annie Crowell, Fannie Elton, Sarah Jane Eddy, Emma Farnsworth, Floride Green, Gertrude Käsebier, Edith Lounsbery, Emily Mew, Anne Pilsbury, Mary Paschall, Virginia Prall, Addie Robinson, Alta Belle Sniff, Virginia Sharp (whose daughter would later travel with Schäffer in the Rocky Mountains), Sarah Sears, Ellen and Lillian Selby, Amelia Van Buren, Myra Wiggins, Eva Watson, Mabel Wright, Eva Walborn, and Mathilde Weil.

Genre studies and portraiture dominated the collection solicited and curated by Johnston. Technical excellence distinguished it. A few still lifes, fewer botanical photographs, and equally few landscapes were included. Of the eleven photographs offered by Schäffer, Johnston chose three for the Congress in Paris: two intimate flora studies and a landscape. Schäffer's oeuvre is distinctive as that of the only photographer in the exhibition who included no human or animal figures, but focused exclusively on botanical and landscape subject matter. Only Mary Paschall of Doylestown, Pennsylvania, also exhibited sharply focused botanical prints, along with genre and urban landscape images. Today, only nine Schäffer prints, all mounted on 8 x 10 inch mats and including the two flora studies chosen for the exhibition (Figs. 2.13 and 2.15), remain in the Smithsonian collection in Washington. The fate of the remaining two of the eleven submitted to Johnston is unknown. The landscape chosen for exhibition is one of the missing prints, and there is no record of the name of its view.

The display of 1900 in Paris (and later, Moscow) was the only time that Mary Schäffer is documented as having participated in an exhibition in which her photographs were primarily viewed as expressive works, rather than images of descriptive interest for their content—that is, as art rather than document. Schäffer was aware of the shift of attitude toward photographic imagery that was taking place, at least among dedicated photography amateurs and in Philadelphia. Describing her images to Johnston, she wrote that

> *These pictures were made mostly in 1899 or previously, with the old fashioned idea that a good photo was to be as near an absolute representation of the object as possible, clear & clean & sharp, & all study of light & shade was but to enhance this condition....In the last year or so, & in all the mad rush of*

> *change I am fane [sic] to believe that Nature knows nothing about it, & to make a perfect picture, I must learn new tricks in developing, printing etc.*[63]

Schäffer's frustration represents much more than it articulates. Contemplating women's camera work during this era, Judith Fryer Davidov notes that "the premises of the fine-art movement in photography conceived of the history of the medium as a history of styles....'Artists' thus insulated themselves from the work of 'documentary' photographers....*Art* and *document* turn out to be terms that have to do more with institutions of power—of exhibition and distribution—than with the content or form of a given picture."[64] Mary Schäffer had learned this the hard way in practice at the Photographic Society of Philadelphia as factions clashed over adjudication for the Photographic Salon in the late 1890s. Her frustration was well founded. Those like herself who were committed to the pursuit of scientific knowledge as well as aesthetic beauty—a hard-fought battle in nineteenth-century art and photography debates—were summarily displaced in the either/or onslaught of the turn-of-the-century modernist vanguard.

Nevertheless, despite the "mad rush of change" if not because of it, Schäffer's work held its own visually among the best of American photographers represented in Paris, not only technically and aesthetically, but scientifically and socially. She knew the science of botany and the art of botanical imagery, as well as how to meet the standards of botanical documentation through lighting and exposure techniques, and the effect of various photographic papers, such as albumen or platinum paper, on the impact of the print. Describing for Johnston the range, purpose, and value of her photographic practice, Schäffer explains that

> *we now have flower studies up in the hundreds, flowers from the Atlantic to the Pacific.*
>
> *Though flowers are a special hobby, they cannot but open the eye to any beauty surrounding us, & for their use in the study, we turned to mushrooms. The camera helps materially to classify them, & through it, we have brought much valuable material from our summer haunts in the Canadian Rockies.*[65]

Two of Schäffer's botanical photographs not exhibited in Paris, *La France Rose, Sprinkled with Water* and *La France Rose, Indoor Study*, are intimate studies of the first hybrid tea rose, a fragrant single pink flower on a long stem,

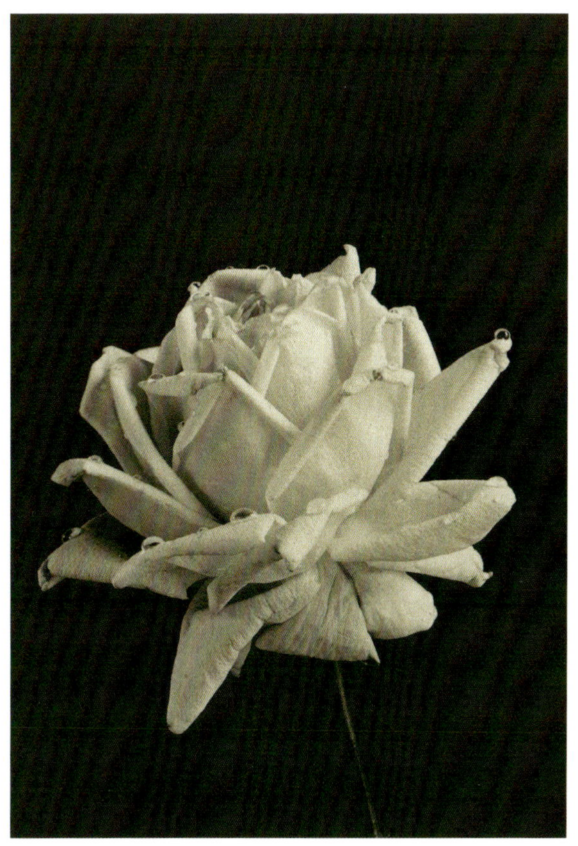

FIGURE 2.1

Mrs. Chas. [Mary T.S.] Schäffer, *La France Rose, Sprinkled with Water*, ca. 1899, platinum, 6 x 4 inches. [NMAH-C-77.92.30]

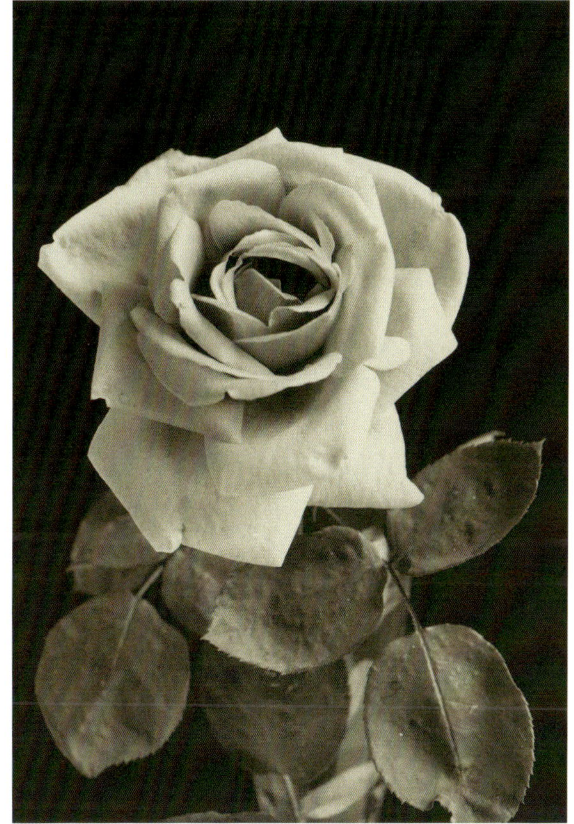

FIGURE 2.2

Mrs. Chas. [Mary T.S.] Schäffer, *La France Rose, Indoor Study*, ca. 1899, platinum, 6.7 x 4.6 inches. [NMAH-C-77.92.32]

cultivated in 1867 in France and popular in the late nineteenth century. Set against a deep black background, the texture of the petals was emphasized in contrast to the transparency of water drops in the one and leaves in the other, showing off skilled lighting technique. The platinum paper on which the images are printed offered a tonal range that allowed for greater subtlety and variation in monochromatic printing than the more common albumen paper. One of the shortcomings of platinum was a lighter tone in shadow areas, but this Schäffer used to effect to sculpt three-dimensionality in the two-dimensional print as well as to present the kind of detail that was essential to the scientific merit of botanical studies, whether painted or photographed, in both of which Schäffer was accomplished.

Botany

Mary and Charles Schäffer and their contemporaries in Rocky Mountain botany pursuits, such as Mary M. Vaux and Julia Henshaw, were part of the natural history movement in North America that grew exponentially through the nineteenth century, but especially in post–Civil War America. By the 1900 Paris Exposition, where the United States claimed the vanguard as the world's most progressive culture—economically, scientifically, industrially, and even socially—natural history was a component of the nation's identity. Hundreds of scientific societies had been established across the United States in the nineteenth century, and in greatest numbers in the post–Civil War decades.[66] The by-laws of the Academy of Natural Sciences, instituted in 1812 in Philadelphia, represent the movement well, stating that its "exclusive" purpose "shall be the cultivation and study of the natural sciences and the encouragement thereof—by the publication of discoveries, by collecting natural objects and a library, by extending and making useful a knowledge of nature through the agency of lectures, and by other means of instruction."[67] Mary Schäffer joined her husband Charles, who was elected to the Academy in 1861,[68] as an elected member on 31 March 1896.[69] George Vaux Jr. and Edward J. Nolan, a physician as well as librarian and recording secretary of the Academy, had nominated her, but it would seem that success was not a given, although details are vague. In a note to Nolan, Schäffer thanks him for "getting me so safely thru., [*sic*] despite the pocketful of black balls which Dr. Sharp threatened to carry to the meeting." To ensure that her membership would not be easily revoked, Schäffer enclosed a cheque for a lifetime membership.[70] Together the Schäffers took the collecting mission to heart in two fields, botany and ethnography; following her husband's death in 1903, Schäffer donated to the Academy more than sixty Indigenous objects, ranging from snowshoes to dishes, clothing and carved wood pieces.[71] These they had collected in the Rocky Mountains while also gathering and documenting alpine flora.

Progress was the American theme at the 1900 Paris Universal Exposition, and from botany to photography, participants rallied around it. Mary Schäffer's participation can be seen as layered: her photographic work was recruited for exhibition because she was a woman whose technical and aesthetic expertise were recognized for their quality, while the botanical subject matter of much of the work she presented for exhibition also functioned in a field that was reinventing itself as a rigorous, progressive, and modernized scientific endeavour, one with an approach to classification and nomenclature that broke with European tradition. As in photography, in which women's independent amateur and commercial practices as photographers had gained a foothold but women's roles continued to be debated, botany practices remained predominantly organized by gendered codes of labour in which women were viewed as assistants to male botanists, and the role of botanical illustrator (as documentarian rather than artist in such instances) was predominantly women's. Art historian Ann Birmingham notes, "The beauty of flower painting was that it allowed women the freedom to embrace the dominant cultural stereotypes of femininity—that overdetermined relationship of women to flowers—while, if they wished, using this relationship to pursue art in a professional way as artists, teachers, authors, and exhibitors."[72]

Schäffer's own engagement with botany is a classic case. In 1911, she credited Mary M. Vaux with inspiring her to take up and complete the botanical work that she and her husband had pursued.[73] Trained first in the art of flower painting, and later self-trained in the craft of botanical photography, she was left at her husband's death in 1903 with a massive collection of plants and images but without the scientific credentials or depth of knowledge to complete the project on her own. To that end, she contracted Stewardson Brown, curator of the herbarium section of the Academy of Natural Sciences to which Charles Schäffer had devoted considerable time, interest, and specimens, to complete the work of collecting, organizing (in sixty-one families), and describing the hundreds of specimens gathered in preparation for publication. In 1905, Brown had published, as second author with I.A. Keller, *Handbook of the Flora of Philadelphia and Vicinity*.

In April 1906, a formal agreement was drawn up between Mary Schäffer and Stewardson Brown outlining their responsibilities and contributions. While the contract stipulated that Schäffer retained creative, editorial, and financial control of the project, Brown agreed to produce within a year a botanical manuscript "suitable to give to a printer for publication."[74] The descriptions that Brown was to produce, while "scientifically accurate…are to be prepared in such a style as to be understandable by and attractive to the general public." Brown, who had not been to the Canadian Rockies before, agreed to spend two months travelling in the region of the Rockies and Selkirks that encompassed the range of the Schäffers' collecting legacy. Mary Schäffer would share "all of the notes and other information which she may have on the subject which may be useful in connection with the undertaking," pay the costs of the travel, and retain ownership of the resulting manuscript. Finally, it was agreed that the intention was to publish the results "in an illustrated volume," with the illustrations supplied by Schäffer and "due credit" given to Brown for his contributions. Schäffer also retained the right to choose the publisher and determine the form of the book. In 1907, under the joint authorship of Stewardson Brown and Mrs. Charles Schäffer, *Alpine Flora of the Canadian Rocky Mountains* was published.[75] The book was dedicated to Dr. Charles Schäffer.

Brown and Schäffer's manual, which they characterized as a guide—perhaps to encourage a range of readers wider than that of the dedicated scientist seeking a reference manual—was very much a product of its time. A century of botanical exploration of the Rocky Mountains by American and Canadian collectors preceded publication of the Schäffers' work in 1907.[76] The approach to the botanical listing used by Brown and Schäffer drew upon and benefitted from the direction that American botany took towards a rigorous scientific practice and system in which collectors were no longer admired for the pursuit and capture of rare or new species alone but instead were expected to contribute to an emerging picture of the complexity and diversity of plant life within a particular geographic environment.[77] Differences emerged between those serious amateurs who pushed the edges of the field's growing discipline and hobbyists collecting for the sake of doing so. John Coulter described the change in botanical collecting and analysis practice between 1885 and 1909 as having "merged into more or less intensive studies," when his popular 1885 *Manual of the Botany of the Rocky Mountain Region* was extensively updated as the *New Manual of Botany of the Central Rocky Mountains (Vascular Plants)*; this not only featured plants newly known to Euro-American collectors,[78] but also organized and described the material so as "to represent current knowledge in reference to the flora for the benefit of the ordinary user of a manual."[79]

Like Coulter's manual, Brown and Schäffer's work carried the weight and authority of being rooted in their own fieldwork and that of Charles Schäffer undertaken over more than two decades. Brown travelled with Schäffer in the Rockies in June and July 1906, collecting over four thousand specimens, and again in 1908 after publication of the volume.[80] Schäffer identified him as "The Botanist" in *Old Indian Trails*, and he was with Schäffer, Adams, and their guides when they finally found their way to Maligne Lake. This original research in the field was important because such activity now signalled work that was professional and credible, in contrast to the botanical collection and identification that had been an armchair pursuit earlier in the century, when specimens were identified in isolation and without reference to their place of origin or relation to other flora in the area. By the turn of the twentieth century, as part of their records, botanists were expected to locate their specimens within their geographic range, as Coulter's revised manual did, and Brown and Schäffer did as well. The latter two took this farther, however, also including altitude.[81] Furthermore, Brown and Schäffer contrasted their findings with similar specimens known in European alpine regions, establishing both the breadth of the knowledge underlying their manual and the specificity of their study. They also employed both American common English and European Latin-based nomenclatures and, again like Coulter, they gathered and presented their specimens by family. They differed from Coulter and convention, however, in two significant aspects: their plant descriptions were written in a spare narrative form that contrasts acutely with the terse, dense listings of descriptive terms that pack Coulter's manual, and their work was illustrated. One hundred of Mary Schäffer's watercolour and photographic illustrations of a selection of plants were featured. Together, this approach of narrative text and descriptive image established the rigour and scope of the book's botanical content, while appearing accessible as a reference volume for the less-knowledgeable reader, new either to the Rocky Mountains of Canada or to botany itself. It also established Mary Schäffer's publication style of writing an entertaining narrative complemented by equally engaging imagery.

Alpine Flora is illustrated with both watercolour drawings reproduced in colour and black-and-white photographs. The drawings are lively renderings that offer the reader and viewer not only the colour and structural details of the plant, but also a sense of the textures, weight, and fragility of the

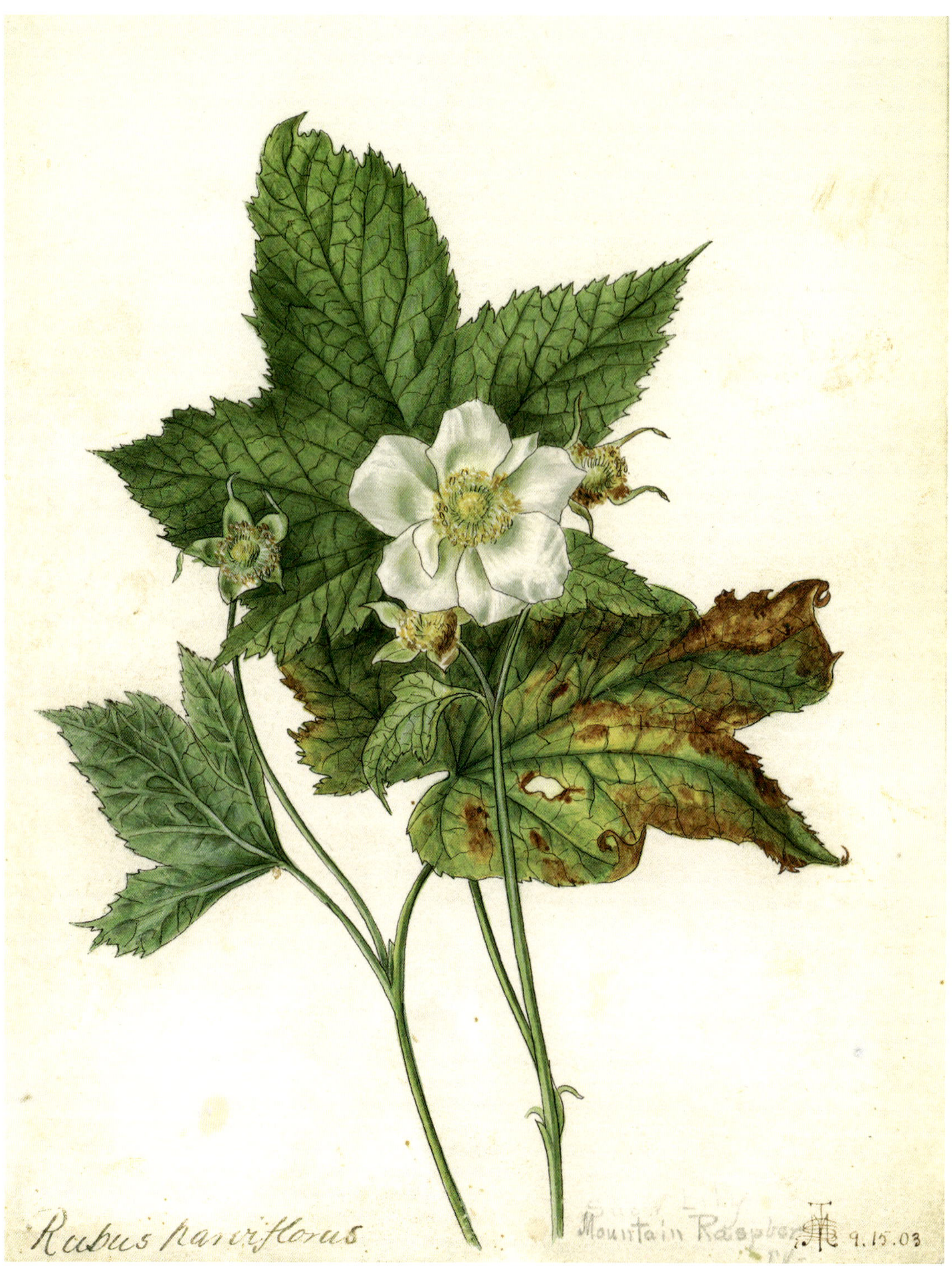
Rubus parviflorus
Mountain
9.15.03

‹FIGURE 2.3

Mary Schäffer, *Rubus parviflorus / Mountain Raspberry*, 1903, watercolour on paper, 10 x 6.9 inches. Published in Stewardson Brown and Mary Schäffer's *Alpine Flora of the Canadian Rocky Mountains* (1907) as *Rubus parviflorus Nutt. (2/3 Nat.) Salmon-Berry*, opposite page 156.

[WMCR Art Collection ScM.05.16]

›FIGURE 2.4

Mary Schäffer, *Lonicera involucrate (Richards.) Banks. (2/3 Nat.) Involucred Fly Honeysuckle*, n.d., watercolour on paper, 10 x 6.9 inches. Published in Stewardson Brown and Mary Schäffer's *Alpine Flora of the Canadian Rocky Mountains* (1907), opposite page 270.

[WMCR Art Collection ScM.05.30]

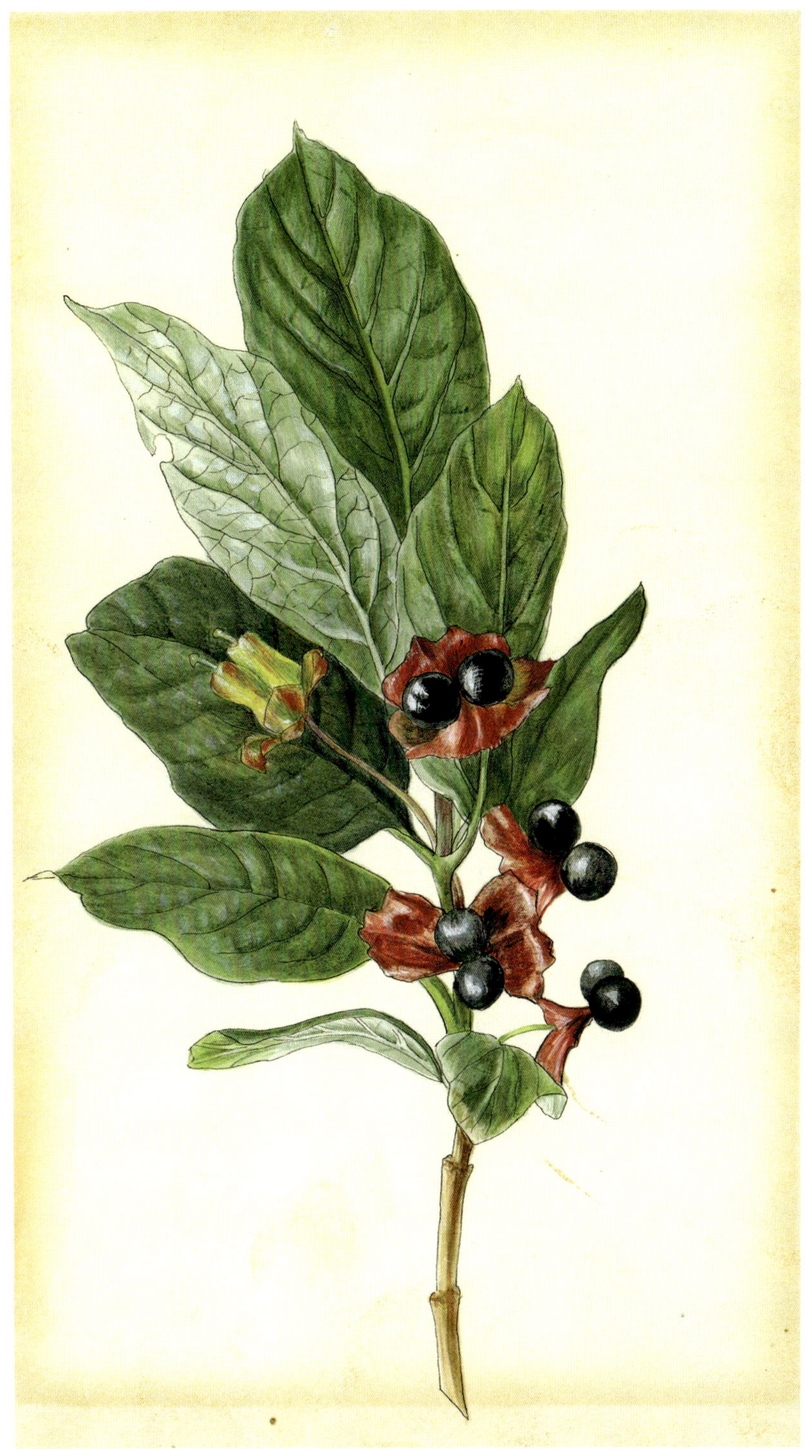

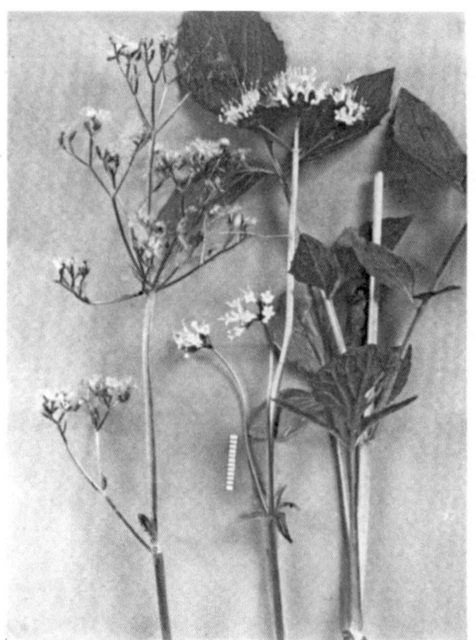

Valeriana sitchensis Bong. (⅓ Nat.)
Wild Heliotrope.

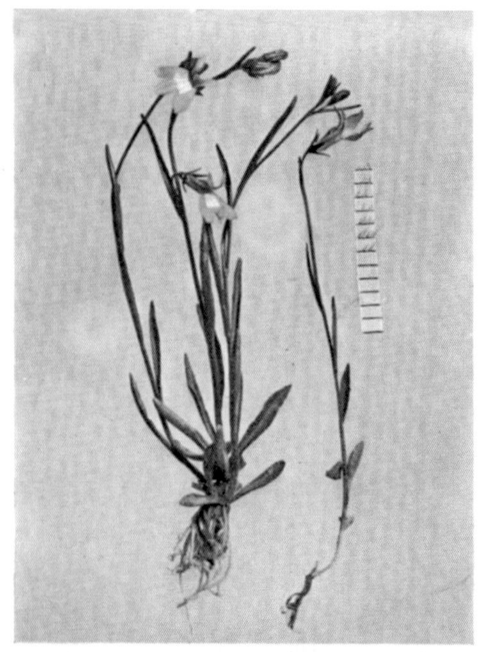

Lobelia Kalmii strictiflora Rydb. (Nat.)
Brook Lobelia.

FIGURE 2.5
Valeriana sitchensis Bong. (1/3 Nat.) Wild Heliotrope / Lobelia Kalmii strictiflora Rydb. (Nat.) Brook Lobelia, Mary Schäffer photographs. Published in Stewardson Brown and Mary Schäffer's *Alpine Flora of the Canadian Rocky Mountains* (1907), opposite page 272.

specimens.[82] These images are documents that trigger the senses in a way that the monochromatic photographs do not. The photographs present the plants against either a very light grey or black background, against which the details of petals, stem, and leaf shapes, with a stick measure alongside, are seen with ease. Like a mug shot, they convey in a clear and comparatively stark manner the physical facts of the plant.

Demand for "a botany" of the alpine region through which Canadian Pacific Railway passenger trains passed grew with the numbers of tourists who undertook the journey after the route opened to tourist traffic in 1886. The Schäffers were just two of the many from Philadelphia alone who sought relief from the humid heat of summer in the mild, drier air of the Rockies. Hundreds of others from central Canada, the northeastern United States, and England also made the journey, many returning each year. In an article called "Haunts of the Wild Flowers of the Canadian Rockies (Within reach of the Canadian Pacific Railroad)," published in 1911 in the *Canadian Alpine Journal*, Schäffer's lengthy introduction set the stage through a story of her own experience with the popularity of wildflower viewing among tourists, something that was at times a problem for serious practitioners:

> *Few are those who climb through the Canadian mountains to whom the flowers of the region do not appeal. When twenty years ago there was one botanist [Charles Schäffer] searching hills and valleys, to-day there are fifty.*
>
> *Twenty years ago there was little known of a large number of the varieties, there was no Botany published to cover the ground, to-day one may study with a fair amount of information to hand to do it intelligently.*
>
> *But what the Botanies do not do is to tell the visitor to our great Rocky Mountain garden of the special haunts and the special times of blooming of these children of the hills. There is a good reason for this apparent lack of valuable information, which all true lovers of flowers recognize without comment on my part, for there are thousands who gather only to throw away, those who in gathering, ruthlessly destroy the roots, and those who are collecting, who pluck till the last rare speciment [sic] is in their vasculum. To illustrate: There was a small bed of epilobium at Glacier—whose location in a moment of weakness (ignorance really), I betrayed, and as it was about to bloom I would then be able to find out which one it was. In three or four days I went to look for my treasure only to behold the party to whom I had confided my new friend returning with every specimen of the plant in his hand.*
>
> *I never got a photograph of it, I never found out what one it was, but I learned to keep the haunts of rare plants to myself. If now I break to some extent my hard learned rule and mention some of the localities which contain the rarer blossoms, I trust that those who read will respect the rights of the flowers and not slaughter them.*[83]

Schäffer's professional exasperation was especially tested when a Rocky Mountain acquaintance, Julia Henshaw, a journalist from Vancouver with no specialized training in botany or illustration, published a book on Rockies flora a year in advance of Schäffer's own work. Schäffer's collaboration with Stewardson Brown, based on the many years of fieldwork undertaken by the Schäffers, was intended to be a scientifically sound, groundbreaking introduction to the flora of that alpine region. It was a volume invested with significant intellectual, physical, aesthetic, and financial resources. Henshaw's *Mountain Wild Flowers of Canada: A Simple and Popular Guide to the Names and Descriptions of the Flowers That Bloom Above the Clouds* (which was released at the same time in the United States under the title *Mountain Wild Flowers of America*), published in 1906, stood in contrast.[84] A glossary of plant terms and nearly one hundred black-and-white photographs supported the more

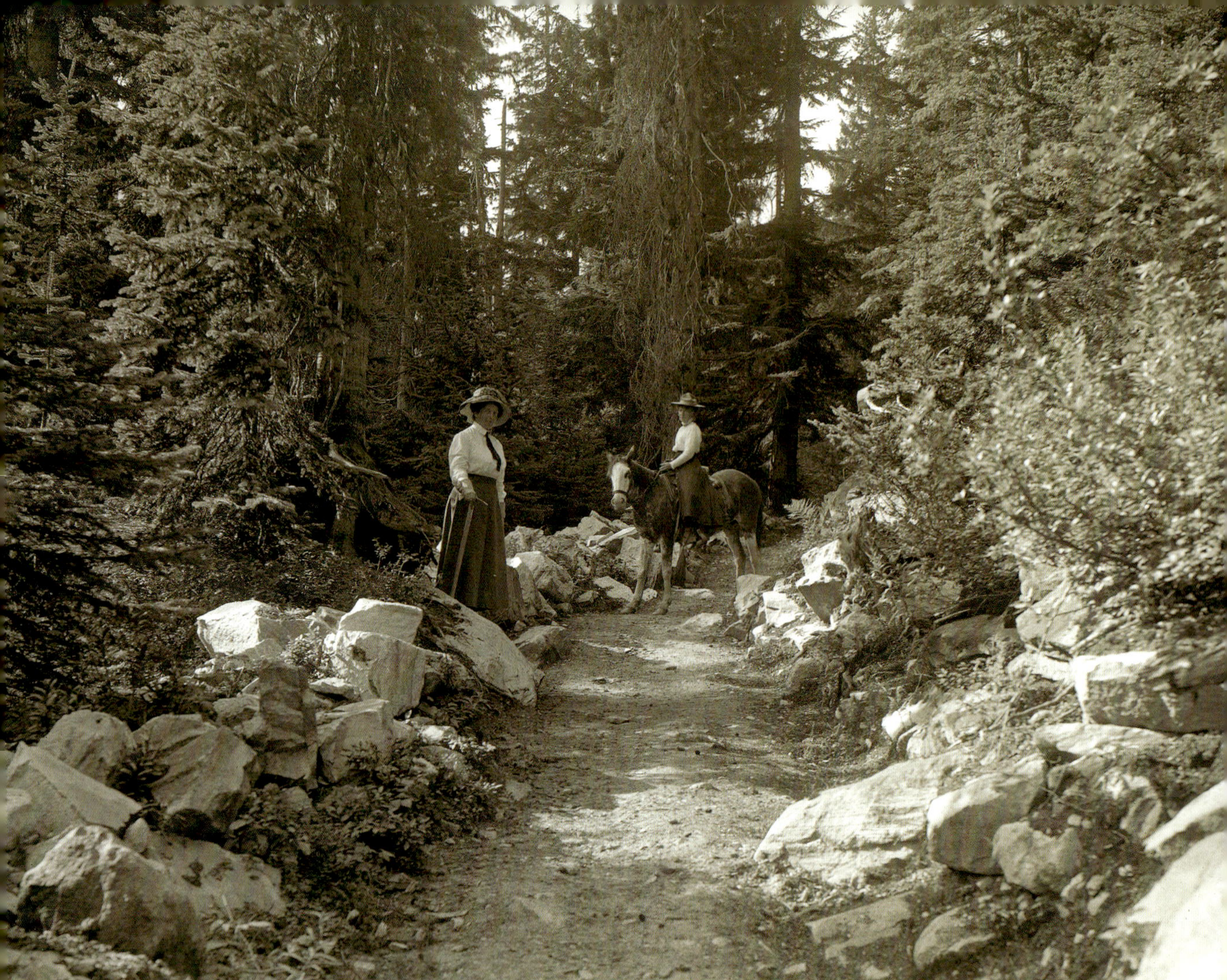

FIGURE 2.6
Mrs. Julia Henshaw and Mary Schäffer near Glacier House, BC, Mary M. Vaux photograph, 1910. [WMCR V653/NG4-908]

numerous text entries in Henshaw's volume. In contrast, Brown and Schäffer's manual included a glossary and a key to plant families, along with eighty plates of illustrations, including ninety-eight black-and-white photographs published two to a page, and thirty watercolour drawings, some with more than one plant in the image, published in colour. The size of the image relative to that of the plant in nature is also noted.

Henshaw's preface sets a tone that could hardly be more antithetical to Brown and Schäffer's when she writes that

> *"when the book of life falls open at the page of spring," who does not long to enter the kingdom of Nature and wander therein, with bright-hued flowers abloom about his feet and the silent scintillating peaks standing circlewise above his head?*

> *High up where the snow-crowned mountain monarchs rule over an enchanting land of foliage, ferns, and fungi, outspanned in sunshine beneath the broad blue tent of the western sky, the alpine meadows are ablaze with starry blossoms.*[85]

She also appealed to a wide range of readers by describing the book as "intended more for the use of the general public than for botanists[;] the flowers herein described are classified according to colour, and without special reference to their scientific relationship."[86] One can only imagine the outrage, still simmering thirty years later, of a long-working amateur practitioner like Schäffer who understood her responsibility not only to further the boundaries of knowledge but also to assist lay readers in becoming more knowledgeable about the physical world. As Schäffer recalled the matter in a private letter following Henshaw's death in 1937, "We were at it at least three years and just about the time it was to come from the press, I learned Julia had brought out the edition of which you must have seen many copies. Knowing this, I wrote her as kindly a letter as I could, told her I was glad hers had come first for mine was only meant in memory of a great botanist and I trusted it would not interfere with her work. No reply."[87]

Schäffer's alpine flowers were classified by family, Henshaw's by colour. Therefore, while the Western Anemone is to be found in Brown and Schäffer's book under "Ranunculaceæ/The Crowfoot Family," it is classified in Henshaw's book in the section "White to Green Flowers" (Figs. 2.7 and 2.8). Henshaw reasoned that "the first attribute of a plant that attracts the traveller's eye is invariably its colour, his first question usually being, What is that red flower? (or blue flower or yellow flower, as the case may be). Of order, genus, and species he probably knows nothing." Nevertheless, she took pains to establish scientific credibility for her work, stating in her preface that "The nomenclature followed throughout this work is strictly in accordance with that endorsed by Professor John Macoun, botanist to the Federal Government of Canada."[88]

Henshaw received assistance from both the CPR and the Geological Society of Canada, although she acknowledges not the institutions but instead senior individuals with those organizations whose names would have been recognized by many readers and perhaps perceived as contributors to or endorsement of Henshaw's work.[89] Henshaw names David McNicoll, who was a vice-president of the CPR (and father of Canadian painter Helen McNicoll), Passenger Traffic Manager Robert Kerr, and Richard Marpole, general superintendent of the

94 Ranunculaceæ

hairy outside, receptacle oblong, in fruit densely woolly.

The most abundant anemone through the Rockies in the low open valleys, and, occasionally on the slopes, presenting the greatest variety of colouring from deep rosy pink to pure white and occasionally blue; flowering in early June.

Pulsatilla hirsutissima (Pursh.) Britton. *Pasque Flower.*

Villous, 6–18 inches high. Leaves much divided into narrow, linear, acute lobes, the basal on slender petioles, those of the involucre sessile and erect or ascending. Flowers bluish purple, sometimes nearly white inside; sepals 5–7 ovate-oblong 1–1½ inches long, forming a cup; fruit a head of long silky achenes 2 inches or more in diameter.

This is one of the earliest and most beautiful of all the spring flowers, in the open meadows and mountain sides, blossoming through May and June according to the situation. Probably its most common local

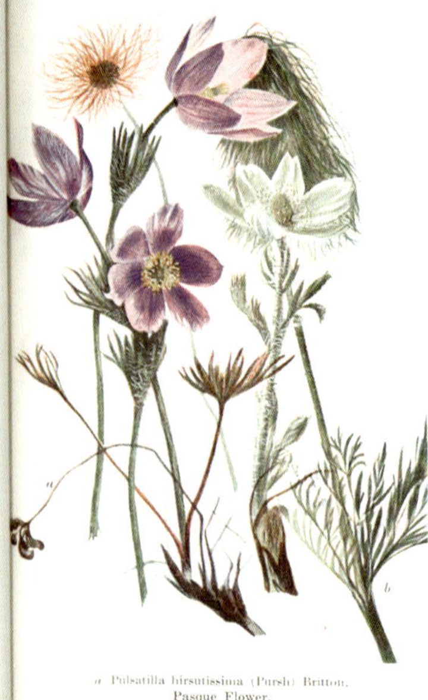

a Pulsatilla hirsutissima (Pursh) Britton.
Pasque Flower.
b Pulsatilla occidentalis (S. Wats.) Freyn. (⅔ Nat.)
Western Anemone.

FIGURE 2.7

Mary Schäffer, *Pasque Flower (a) and Western Anemone (b)*, n.d., watercolour on paper. Reproduced in Stewardson Brown and Mary Schäffer's *Alpine Flora of the Canadian Rocky Mountains* (1907), opposite page 94.

4 WHITE TO GREEN

WESTERN ANEMONE

Anemone occidentalis. Crowfoot Family

Stems: erect, six to eighteen inches high. **Leaves**: large, long-petioled, biternate and pinnate. **Flowers**: large, solitary; petals none; sepals five to seven. **Fruit**: carpels with long filiform styles that become plumose tails to the achenes.

The Western Anemone is one of the most beautiful of the early spring mountain flowers. Its handsome white cups, purple-shaded on the outside, may be found growing close to the retreating line of snow during the months of May and June, and later on in the season its big fluffy seed-heads are eagerly gathered by those who delight in artistic things. This plant, like many others of the Crowfoot Family, has no petals, only a lovely calyx fashioned into about six sepals, which do duty instead.

WIND-FLOWER

Anemone multifida. Crowfoot Family

Stems: villous with long silky hairs. **Leaves**: long-petioled, nearly semicircular in outline, ternate, stem-leaves smaller, nearly sessile. **Flowers**: of five to eight sepals. **Fruit**: globular to oblong; achenes densely woolly.

The Wind-flower, as this delicate little Anemone is usually called, appears on the dry meadows in the spring time in a vast variety of hues, with many blossoms and much fruit. Its colours range from white to red, with many intermediate shades of yellow, pink, and purple-blue. It is to Pliny, the famous ancient philosopher, that it owes its name, for he declared that only the wind would cause Anemones to open; while a later poet has sung how Venus in her grief over the death of Adonis "poured out tears amain," and how "gentle flowers" were born to bloom at every drop that fell from her lovely eyes:

> "Where streams his blood, there blushing springs the rose,
> And where a tear has dropped, a wind-flower blows."

PLATE I

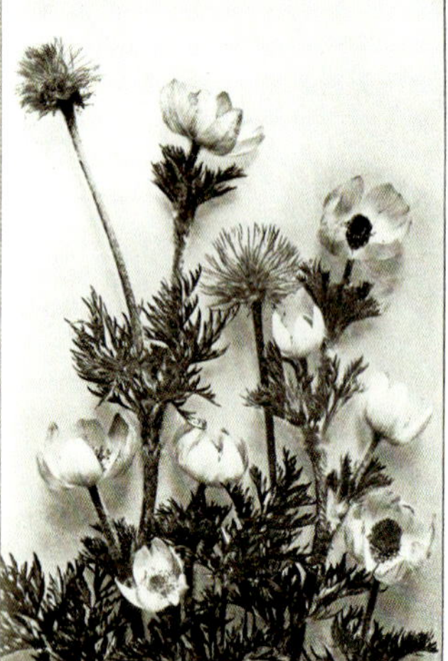

WESTERN ANEMONE
(*Anemone occidentalis*)
5

FIGURE 2.8

Western Anemone, Julia Henshaw photograph, in her book *Mountain Wild Flowers of Canada* (1906) and *Mountain Wild Flowers of America* (1906), Plate I, page 5.

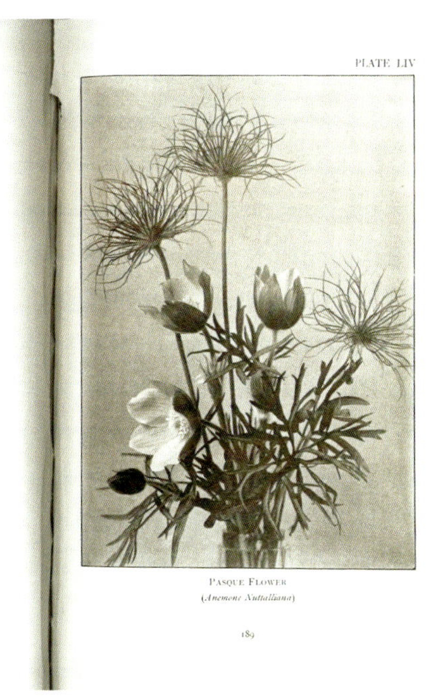

FIGURE 2.9

Pasque Flower, Julia Henshaw photograph, in her book *Mountain Wild Flowers of Canada* (1906) and *Mountain Wild Flowers of America* (1906), Plate LIV, page 189.

CPR's Pacific Division. Stewardson Brown also acknowledges McNicoll and Kerr, as well as the CPR itself, in the preface to *Alpine Flora of the Canadian Rocky Mountains*.[90] Henshaw further names James Fletcher, Dominion entomologist and botanist who founded the National Herbarium of Canada, as well John Macoun and his son James, both of whom held positions with the Geological Society of Canada and who contributed more than 100,000 specimens to the National Herbarium's collection (which now serves as a significant historical legacy for the collection in the Canadian Museum of Nature).[91] Henshaw thanked these men "for valuable scientific advice and for their interest in my work."[92] Macoun was an old-school amateur naturalist and botanist, not unlike Charles Schäffer in this way (although he parlayed his avocation into remunerative appointments while Schäffer did not), whose interest lay in collecting masses of specimens from the field, but who, unlike Schäffer, was not interested in undertaking the analysis and orderly documentation of specimens in their environmental context and botanical families. His method and purpose aligned well with those of Henshaw, and stood in contrast to the method and purpose of the Brown and Schäffer volume, which fell in line with the increasingly specialized, disciplined, and formalized collection and analysis practices of the field of botany.

Early in 1907, Henshaw published an article called "The Mountain Wildflowers of Western Canada," in the first issue of the new *Canadian Alpine Journal*. An "Editorial Note" appended to the end of the article drew readers' attention to her book, which had been published the previous year: "No visitor to the Canadian Rockies should come without Mrs. Henshaw's book. Written in a most delightful and artistic manner, it furnishes a text that, while appealing to the layman in the simplicity of its language, does not neglect the scientific aspect of the subject. It is designed with the purpose of enabling the traveller to identify the various species seen and it fulfills its mission well."[93]

Although colour was the driving force of organization rather than botany's established classification systems, illustrations in Henshaw's *Mountain Wildflowers* are exclusively black-and-white photographs.[94] The debt to Schäffer's "vertical photography" process is clear: the isolated specimens, removed from their natural environment, are represented in a bare manner, with a plain background and lighting that sculpts their three-dimensionality. They are portrayed as standing upright on their own, as if standing alive and strong in nature rather than lying preserved and displayed on a horizontal surface for examination. The detail and textures of the petals, stems, and leaves are suggested but not especially clear, much like the plates in Schäffer's book, and a function of the publishing technologies of the day. The glass vase in which the Pasque Flower specimen is arranged offers a hint of the method. What is missing is a sense of the size and scale of the specimens.

In comparison, Schäffer presents the same two specimens in a single watercolour drawing. While photographs offer a seemingly accurate and reliable image for readers to work with, their verisimilitude is compromised by the absence of colour and a sense of texture that the reproduced watercolours relay. Drawn or painted images, of course, are subject to the choices made by the artist in representing the specimens. What is left out and what an artist especially emphasizes is something that viewers of the time thought would not have a role in the making of the photographs. As Oliver Wendell Holmes had famously declared in 1859, "photographic delineation" offered much to be seen that the naked eye could not fully comprehend in nature or that could not be fully included by an artist in a painting; repeated viewing of a photograph allows the viewer to pick out or notice new details, he claimed.[95] Both mediums, however, were credible and respected means for the scientific purposes of descriptive illustration in botany, as the perceived strengths and weaknesses of each were well understood by informed botany readers. In the same way, both mediums lent themselves equally well to expressive purposes. It all depended on the uses to which the image was put and the context in which it was viewed. The floral studies that Schäffer sent to Frances Benjamin Johnston to consider for inclusion in the Paris exhibition can be read not only for the descriptive detail and accuracy, but also for the beauty as perceived by the human eye and mind.

Schäffer's aesthetic sense and conception of the photograph intersect at their most considered and finished in these works. The photographs of flora convey the sense of intense focus on perceiving and examining the details of the specimen. Evident in these photographs is the debt to Schäffer's skills of observation honed by watercolour drawing and painting. *La France Rose, Sprinkled with Water* (Fig. 2.1) is a perfect specimen, isolated and tightly embraced by a framing that eliminates any visual distraction; every petal, as well as the pistol and stamen, are a pleasure to the eye in the delicate, intricate, and almost tangibly soft presentation. The water drop, poised on the petal and vulnerable to gravity, infuses the image with immediacy and a sense of reality. In comparison, or perhaps contrast, Schäffer's watercolours portray specimens within a range of beauty and states of decay. One example of the latter is *Rubus parviflorus / Mountain Raspberry* (Fig. 2.3). The specimen is shown in four stages of maturity, including a state of advancing decay; only one blossom remains, shown just at its peak against a full and finely rendered leaf at maturity, along with three heads that have lost their petals and at least one leaf curling and brown with decay; a small, newly unfurled leaf, and one somewhat larger and more mature, rendered in detail, complete the cycle. In comparison, Brown describes the plant, labelled in the book as *Rubus parviflorus Nutt. Salmon-berry*, as "Stems shrubby, 3–8 feet high, smooth or more or less glandular-hairy. Leaves round-cordate in outline, palmately 3–5 lobed, the lobes acute or acutish, rarely acuminate, coarsely and unequally serrate. Flowers few, 1–2 inches broad, white, in corymbose, terminal heads, calyx lobes tipped with a long slender appendage. Borders of woods, and in thickets among rocks, throughout the region, but most abundant in the Selkirks; flowering in June and July."[96]

Schäffer's visual style of sharp focus and documentary description in painting and photography stood in contrast to the rising tide of soft-focus, tonally dark, atmospheric photographs of pictorialism in photography that in the late 1890s temporarily usurped the annual salons of the Photographic Society of Philadelphia. In response to Johnston's request to explain her photographic approach, Schäffer identifies her photographs as "clear & clean & sharp," not unlike her watercolour drawings.[97] It was work rooted in this kind of aesthetic principle that fell out of favour with Salon committees of the late 1890s.[98] This is the context that drove Schäffer's clear if not caustic explanation of her photographs, and her stake in the debate, as observed by Schäffer in her letter to Johnston: "As my work lies in realism, rather than idealism, it seems scarce fair to call them pictures, but records of objects & places, two seperate [*sic*] schools. Will the modern photographers blend the two, or must one go to the wall & disappear utterly? Let there be a happy tempering of both, & then we may have reached art in photography."[99]

Beauty, Realism, and Mountain Landscapes

Schäffer's commitment to realism did not negate an equal commitment to beauty. The aesthetic of beauty was something with which she struggled and to which she eventually conceded defeat in her attempts at landscape photography: "Noble mountains, snow clad, or fir clad, are seldom artistic, in the general use of the term. They have a beauty and fascination all their own, to those who love them, but as a work of art, they are more or less a failure—they are too massive, too pronounced."[100]

Nevertheless, she included landscape photographs in the portfolio of work that she submitted for consideration, and Johnston in fact chose one of these for the Paris exhibition. Sensitivity to light, shadow, detail, and composition are equally apparent in exterior landscape studies such as *Lake Marion in the Canadian Rockies* and *Mount Sir Donald*. Both images were exposed on a 5 x 7 inch glass plate and contact printed to meet Johnston's need for small, easily packaged and transported photographs. While the subject matter would seem to demand a much larger print to convey its real physical impact on a visitor to the area, *Lake Marion* nevertheless conveys the monumental beauty and deep stillness of a mountain lake. The photograph is carefully composed around the horizontal line of the far shore, intersected by the strong verticals of the forest and its reflection. Light picks out the detail of the mountains with some snow behind the trees, and the exposure and printing are sensitive to detail and texture in water, sky, rock, and foliage. Equally impressive is the grandeur rendered in the elusive *Mount Sir Donald*, which was first ascended in 1890 and was a popular destination for climbers based at Glacier House. On the back of the mount in Schäffer's hand is written, "Mount Sir Donald. The Matterhorn

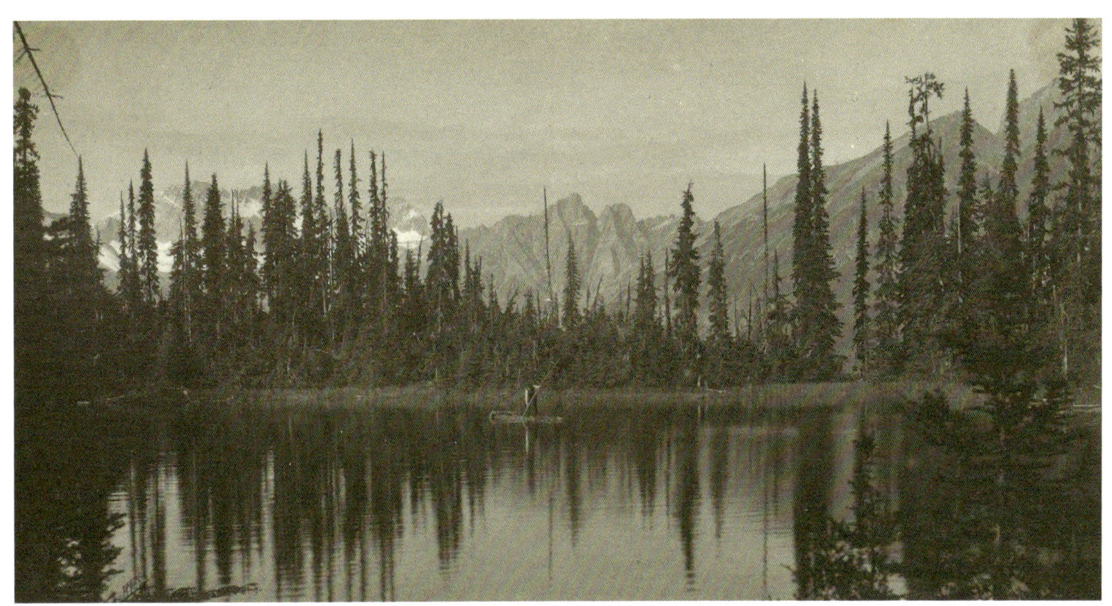

^FIGURE 2.10

Mrs. Chas. [Mary T.S.] Schäffer, *Lake Marion in the Canadian Rockies*, ca. 1899, platinum, 3.4 x 6.6 inches. Verso in ink: "Lake Marion in the Canadian Rockies. 5000 ft above the sea." [NMAH-C-77.92.35]

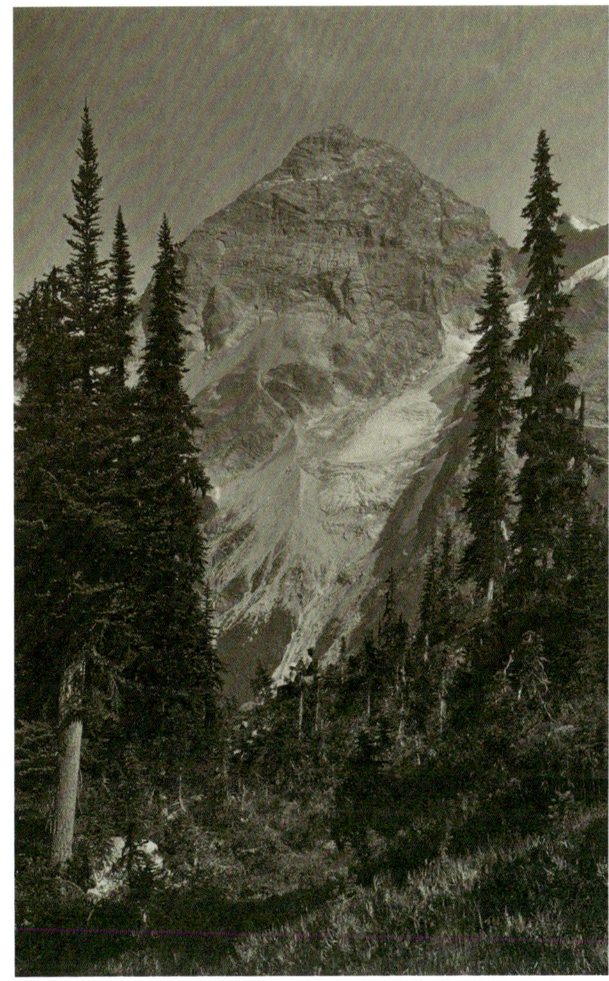

>FIGURE 2.11

Mrs. Chas. [Mary T.S.] Schäffer, *Mount Sir Donald*, ca. 1899, platinum, 6.4 x 4 inches. Verso in ink: "Mount Sir Donald. The Matterhorn of America, in the Canadian Rockies, Height 10646 ft. Taken from an elevation of 6000 ft." [NMAH-C-77.92.34]

of America, in the Canadian Rockies. Height 10646 ft. Taken from an elevation of 6000 ft."[101] In Schäffer's small image, a sense of the immensity of the mountain is created by means of framing by trees that tower in comparison to human height, but that are themselves diminished by the magnitude and mass of the mountain. The strong dark verticals of the trees emphasize the rise of the mountain in the background, and their airy texture stands in contrast to the solid bulk of granite and glacier.

›FIGURE 2.12
Mrs. Chas. [Mary T.S.] Schäffer, *Epigaea Refiens—Trailing Arbutus, Botanical Study*, ca. 1899, platinum, 4.6 x 6 inches. [NMAH-C-77.92.29]

›FIGURE 2.13
Mrs. Chas. [Mary T.S.] Schäffer, *Sedum Latifolium*, ca. 1899, platinum, 4.3 x 6.6 inches. Verso in ink: "'Sedum Latifolium' Taken for botanical study in the Rocky Mountains of Canada." Frances Benjamin Johnston label: 88. [NMAH-C-77.92.33]

The detail in the titles of Schäffer's photographs or noted on the back of the images, such as the altitude of Rocky Mountain landscape photographs, both Latin and English nomenclature of botanical specimens, and the geographic location of the chalk mushrooms speaks to the significance of precise description in progressive scientific practice among naturalists to which Schäffer subscribed. This kind of detail alongside carefully composed images that are impressive for their aesthetic strength and sensitivity also speaks to what American photographer and writer Catharine Weed Barnes had identified in 1890 as part of the appeal of photography for women at that time: "the exactness of scientific truth with the keen pleasure of artistic effort."[102]

Schäffer's view that scientific study and the perception of beauty were not mutually exclusive may have been influenced by her Quaker heritage, instilled in her childhood and infusing her adult social and intellectual milieu in Philadelphia; there is, however, no direct textual evidence in her published writing or private correspondence of any such connection. In comparison, in her 2005 study "Quakers in Nature: The Vaux Family's Photographs of Mountains and Glaciers," Katherine Milliken traces through published writing and photographs the connection of Quaker belief with a reverence for nature, specifically mountain nature, in the photographic work of Schäffer's Philadelphia and Rocky Mountain colleagues Mary M. Vaux and her brothers George Vaux Jr. and William Vaux in the Canadian Rockies.[103] Milliken argues that for the Vauxes, who used photography in their founding study of glacier recession at the turn of the twentieth century,[104] "the Quaker culture of benevolence engendered a sense of wonder about the environment which encouraged their perception, and in turn, photographic depiction of nature as a place of spirit."[105] William Vaux, the youngest sibling, was an engineer and architect in Philadelphia who drove the observational side of the studies and published the Vaux family glacier study findings until his death at age thirty-six in 1908. In one article, he described his profound sense of the "littleness of man and the omnipotence of the Creator" that being in the mountains

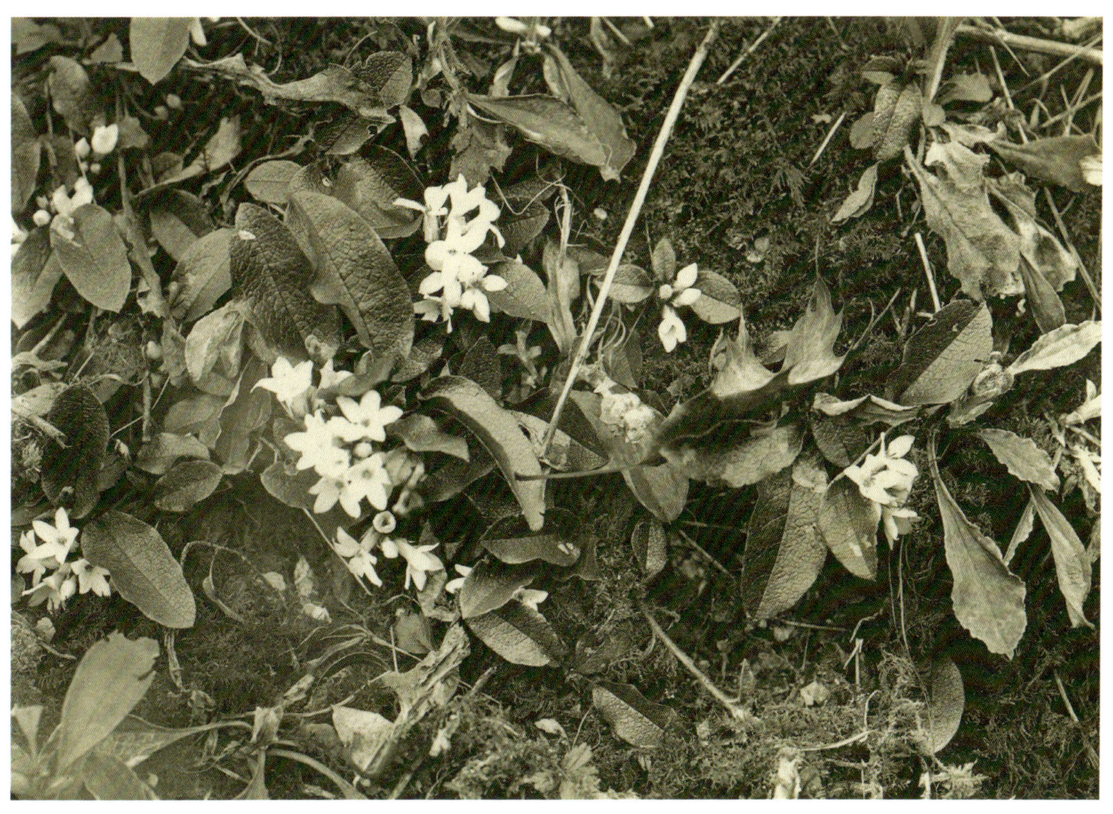

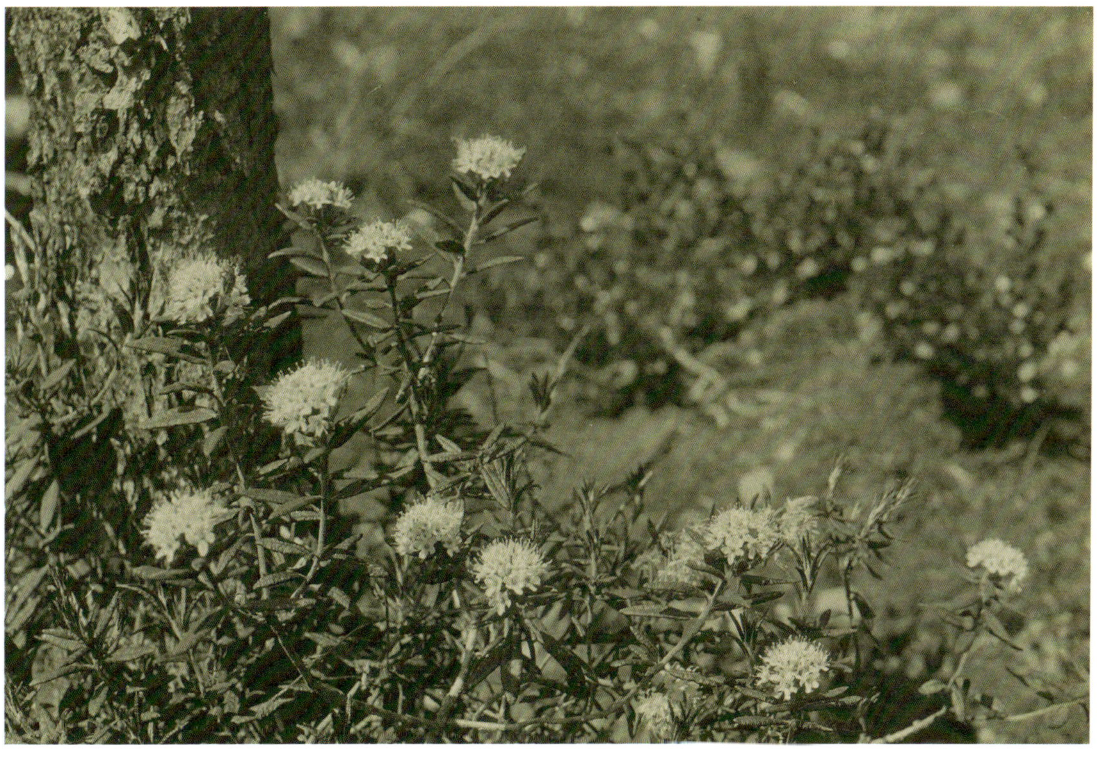

›FIGURE 2.14

Mrs. Chas. [Mary T.S.] Schäffer, *Cornus Florida*, ca. 1899, platinum, 6.3 x 4.5 inches. Verso in ink: "Cornus Florida 'dog-wood tree.' Botanical study." [NMAH-C-77.92.36]

˅FIGURE 2.15

Mrs. Chas. [Mary T.S.] Schäffer, *Chalk Mushroom from the Selkirk Mountains of Canada*, ca. 1899, platinum, 4.5 x 6.5 inches. Frances Benjamin Johnston label: 87. [NMAH-C-77.92.31]

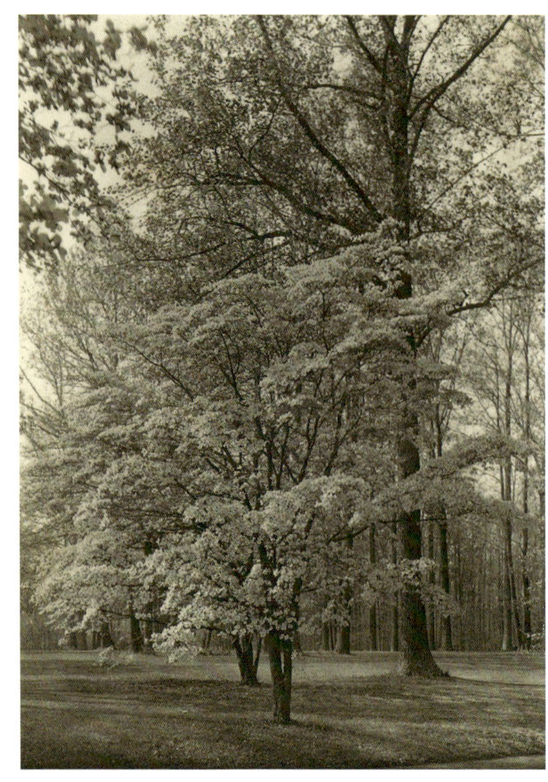

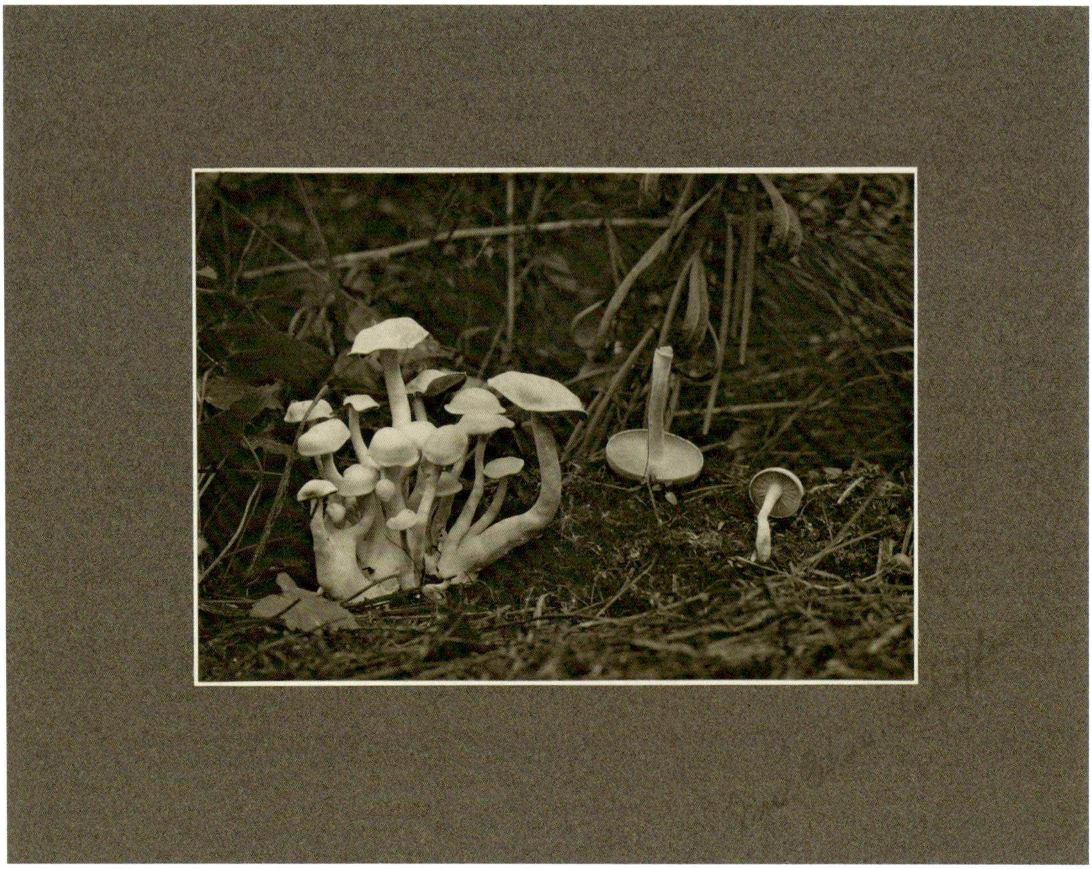

FIGURE 2.16

Mt. Sir Donald in Cloud from Glacier House Porch, Glacier trip 1898 (No. 86), Mary M. Vaux photograph, 1898. [WMCR V653/NG4-507]

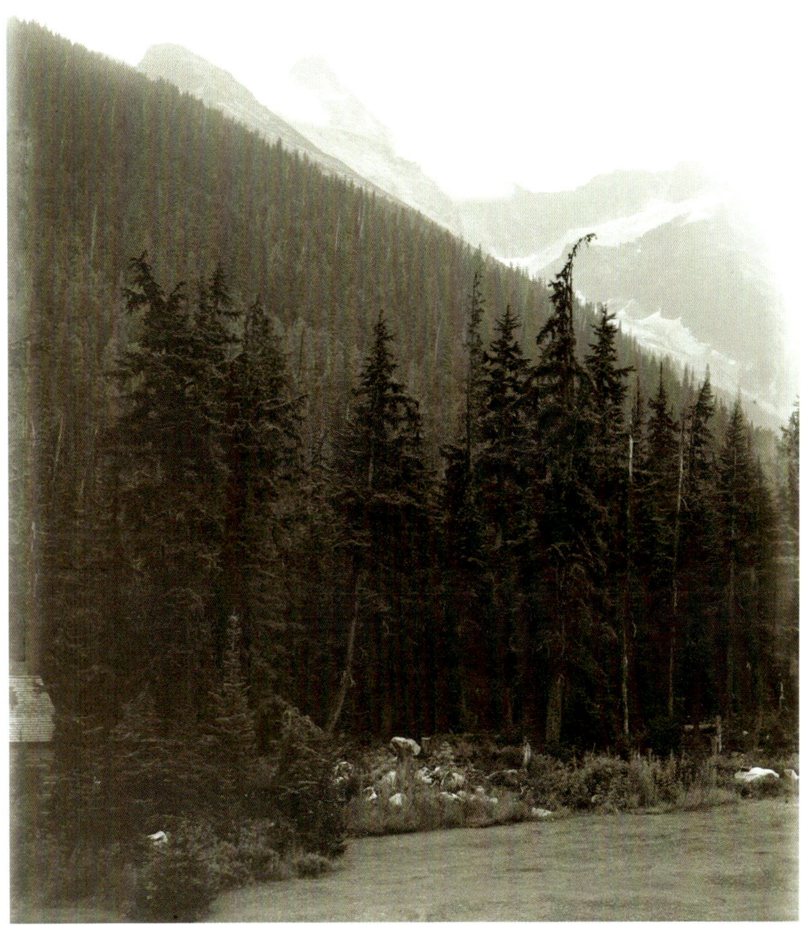

induced.[106] In contrast to William Vaux's focus on observation and recording of physical phenomena, Edward Cavell writes that George Vaux Jr., an attorney by profession as well as an amateur mineralogist and photographer, "was more likely to wander off with sister Mary in search of high places and scenic wonder."[107]

The Vaux photographic archive is extensive and any one of scores of its images may be chosen to illustrate this point.[108] While little critical commentary on the Vauxes' work in exhibition has been published, Mary M. Vaux earned a brief critique in a review of the Annual Members' Exhibition of the Photographic Society of Philadelphia held in late autumn of 1898. Herbert A.

North stated that "Miss Vaux, I am sorry to say, only sends one picture, No. 192—'Mt. Sir Donald in the Clouds.' This is a happy conception—full of atmosphere and artistic feeling."[109] Only one photograph in the Vauxes' carefully indexed collection of photographs is similarly titled, and is likely the photograph exhibited (Fig. 2.16).

Whereas Mary M. Vaux's mountain photography was met with some positive response, Mary Schäffer's was not. Despite her conviction that mountains did not lend themselves to photography, in late 1900, Schäffer exhibited a photograph (which has not come to light) in the Photographic Society of Philadelphia's members' exhibition. The reviewer of that exhibition, whose commentary was published in the Society's *Journal*, found that

> *Mrs. Shaffer, in No. 96a, "Vermillion [sic] Lake at Banff," shows a print that challenges criticism by something more than its mere size. It is fine as a study of clouds and reflections, and is probably a good reproduction of the scene, but considered as a picture is unsatisfactory because of its lack of balance. The dark mass of the mountain and its reflection seems floating in space, and the reeds in the foreground do not give sufficient support. I feel that there is too much of both foreground and sky, and that the panel shape is not suited to the subject.*[110]

The reviewer's comments suggest that, at least in his opinion, it might have been Schäffer's technique rather than the mountains themselves that led her to reach the conclusion she did. Either way, she struggled with the monumental subject matter. In his foundational study of the Vaux family's photography, *Legacy in Ice: The Vaux Family and the Canadian Alps*, Edward Cavell makes the important point that Quaker faith would have been uneasy with the emerging philosophy of art for art's sake that drove pictorialism's champions, even if the art were born of science, as photography is at times seen to have been.[111] Scientific study and photography of the natural world may have aligned for the Vauxes and for Mary Schaffer in the way in which both could be employed to reveal to the human eye and mind invisible or physically imperceptible facts and truths about both the physical world and the human experience of it, including responses of awe or wonder at perceived beauty or at the grandeur of natural phenomena.

Schäffer's mix of realism and wonder permeates and is exemplified by the finely composed and finished botanical and landscape photographs that she

FIGURE 2.17

Mrs. Chas. [Mary T.S.] Schäffer, *Calla lilies. Easter Morning*, ca. 1899, platinum, 5.7 x 4 inches. Verso in ink: "Calla lilies. Easter Morning." [NMAH-C-77.92.37]

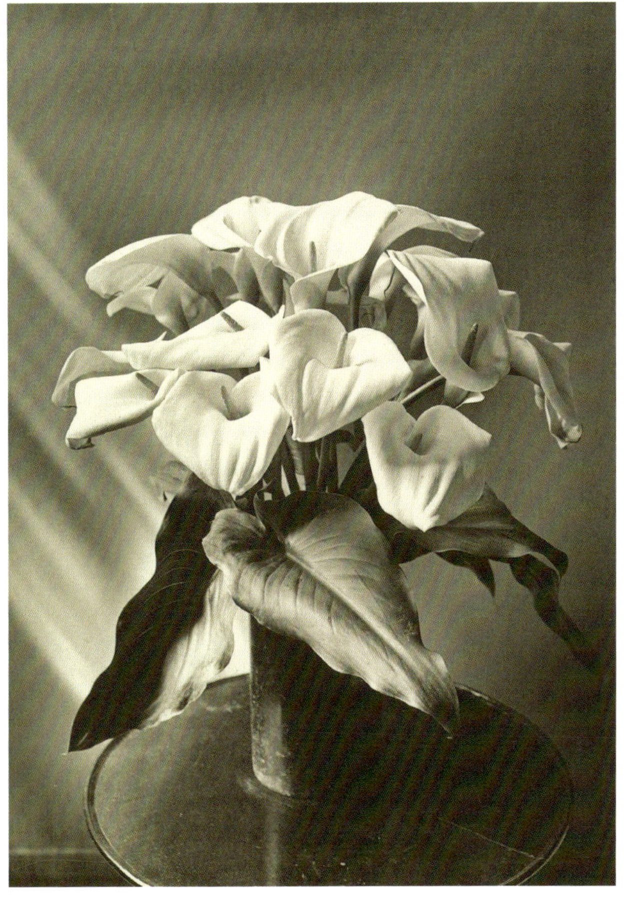

sent to Frances Benjamin Johnston. Only one photograph of the nine extant in the Johnston collection at the National Museum of American History reads as a study of form for the sake of photographic beauty rather than science. "Calla lilies. Easter Morning," as the image was labelled by Schäffer, is a closely framed still life of cut flowers arranged in a vase and set on a table against a stream of sunlight. The lighting creates a sense of atmosphere that is absent from the rose studies; here, light itself is an element of the subject matter, evoking the spirituality associated with Easter morning. This photograph is not one made to serve as representation or for study of a particular specimen. It does serve to show that Schäffer also understood and explored an interest in visual aesthetics and expression of meaning, a trait that was noted in the work of the American women photographers by those reviewing the collection in Paris.[112]

Mary Schäffer is typical of the women, especially the accomplished amateurs, who found a place in the field of photography in the United States in the late nineteenth century. Her social, economic, and educational backgrounds and environments were quite representative of this group, and of both their opportunities and constraints, financial, social, and otherwise. She did not use photography to make money during these years, citing the demands of her husband's and his colleagues' scientific projects to explain to Johnston why she did not do so.[113] It was not until after her husband's sudden death three years after the Paris exhibition that Schäffer began to push the boundaries of expectations for women's behaviour.

Nowhere in the archives of Schäffer's correspondence and the unpublished manuscripts that remain does she mention the 1900 Paris exhibition or her interaction with other photographers—women like herself, or men such as Troth—in Philadelphia in the years prior. She in fact cancelled her membership in the Photographic Society of Philadelphia in 1906 while retaining membership in the Academy of Natural Sciences of Philadelphia and its Geographical Society. Only one more time did she participate in a photography exhibition when she contributed a set of her signature hand-tinted lantern slides to be shown as part of the Alpine Club of Canada's presentation at the Congress of Alpinism in Monaco in May 1920.[114] Instead, she turned her attention to completing the grand project that she and her husband had pursued in Canadian alpine botany and to rebuilding an independent financial foundation for herself.

In time, Schäffer took pleasure and satisfaction in making her own way, becoming and remaining monetarily independent. She did this partly through investments made in the wake of managing assets as executor of Charles Schäffer's severely diminished estate, and partly by means of her writing and photography. This sense comes through succinctly in 1912 in one of her many letters to her friend, attorney, and fellow photographer George Vaux Jr. regarding the mortgages, rents, bonds, dividends, securities, and savings that she held and nurtured. She tells him, "I have earned the money to fence in the lot, and am as proud as a peacock over it—some writing."[115]

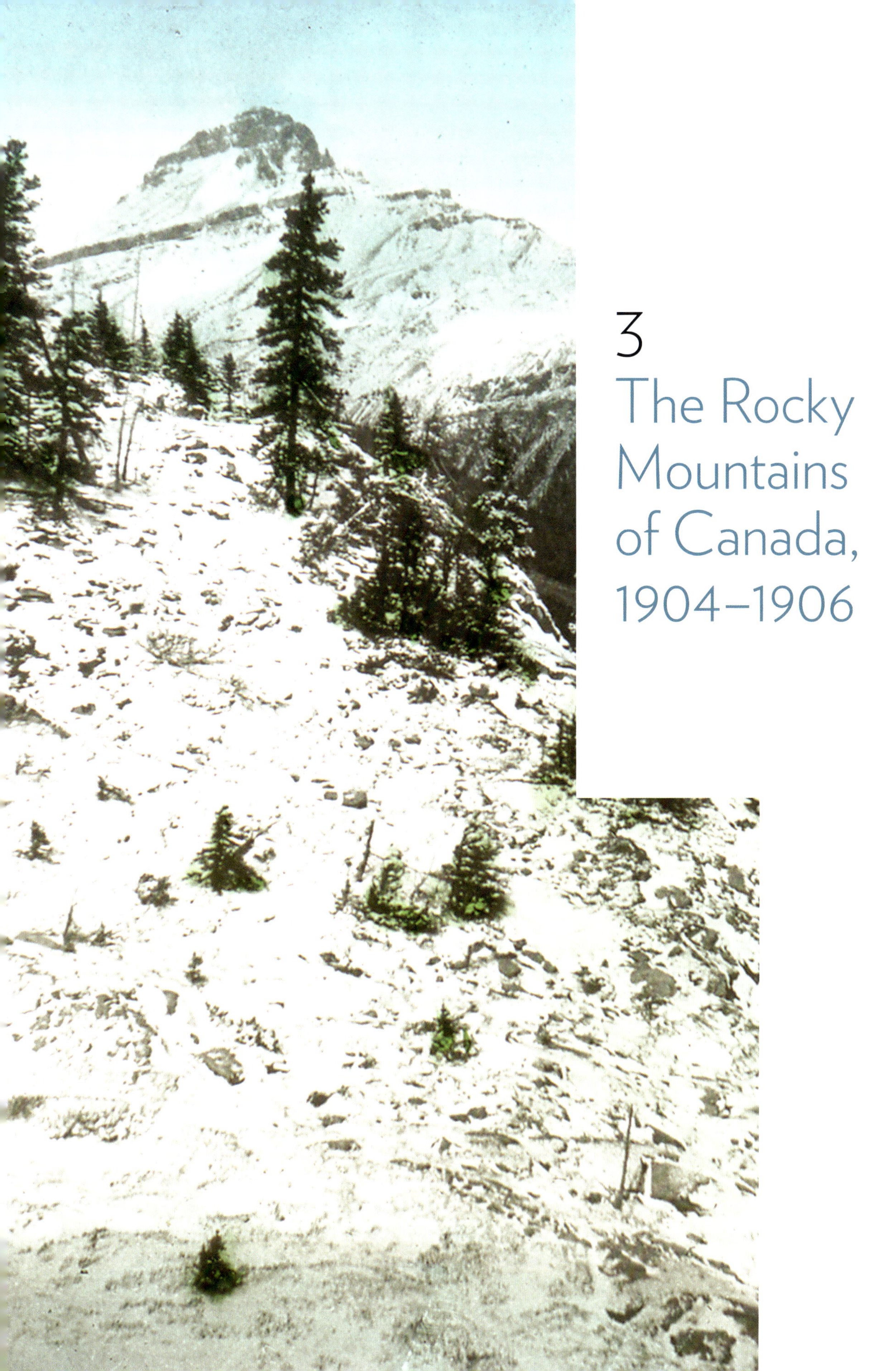

3 The Rocky Mountains of Canada, 1904–1906

ON 16 MAY 1904, six months after her husband's death, Mary Schäffer wrote to her estate attorney George Vaux Jr.

Dear George,

Thank thee for all thy thoughtful kindness. Saying "goodbye" to thee & Mary was like shutting the door. You are so associated with what was happiest & saddest, that I was glad to be through with it. Do appreciate a home & family while thee has one, (I think thee does) for this utter adriftness is something awful.

MARY[1]

Divested of her late husband's collections, home, and debts, and mourning deeply, Schäffer had departed Philadelphia in April to spend the next six months in the Rocky Mountains of Canada. She had first travelled to the Rockies in 1889, following her marriage to Charles Schäffer.[2]

I saw the first sketch of Louise in 1889 in Toronto where there was meeting a huge scientific convention of British and Americans. I cannot remember where the wonderful pictures were on display, except that it was some university hall and that I was taken to see them.

Having had at least what was called a pretty good general education, I stood dumbfounded at these various pictures, each and all contributing glaciers or winding bits of railway in high places and all I could think or say, was: "I did not know we had anything like that on this continent." I had not been a stay-at-home by any means, traveling across the U.S. continent, up and down since I was fourteen, so I frankly thought those pictures a figment of a fine, imaginary brain.

> *A few days later I was given the opportunity to go and see for myself if those pictures were true. It was tremendously exciting.*[3]

Part of Schäffer's purpose in returning to the mountains in 1904 was to continue the fieldwork needed to complete the project that she and her husband had imagined during their fifteen years together collecting alpine botanical specimens: producing the definitive guide to the flora of the Canadian Rocky and Selkirk Mountains adjacent to the tracks of the Canadian Pacific Railway. Her work on the book continued into late 1907, when *Alpine Flora of the Canadian Rocky Mountains* was published.[4] In December 1937, at age seventy-six, Schäffer reminisced a bit about why and how she had published *Alpine Flora*: "When my first husband died I simply had to dash into anything I could to avoid the loneliness and that is how I managed to get out my botany. Gathering plants, painting and photographing did an enormous amt. for me."[5] Finding relief and making peace with her grief is the best-known outcome of Schäffer's immediate and ongoing return to the Rockies after 1903. She wrote of this in private letters, while only alluding to it in published work such as in the preface to her best-known work, *Old Indian Trails: Incidents of Camp and Trail Life, Covering Two Years' Exploration through the Rocky Mountains of Canada*. Nevertheless, her biographers have developed their stories of her life around this theme, following the lead of E.J. Hart's foundational publication, *A Hunter of Peace*.[6]

Travelling to the Rockies in 1904 and in each of the four years thereafter led to much more than peace, however. Returning to the Rockies without a family travel companion, male or female, opened both need and opportunity for Schäffer to circulate in the community of Rocky Mountain travellers on new social terms and in a different relationship to gender mores of the time and place. Her widowed status led to new dependence on other women to join her—or allow her to join them—on the trail and in camp. It also opened opportunity for her to reinvent herself with a new, public, literary persona, which she crafted over time through her published work. This in turn led to a changed social stature that derived not from her husband's status, or from her widowhood, but from her new vocation. She never declared an occupation on a census or other government documents, but between 1904 and 1912 she did develop a reputation and body of work as a writer, photographer, botanical artist, surveyor, mapper, and public speaker, telling stories, projecting hand-coloured glass slides, and sharing knowledge based on her experiences in articles, books, and lectures.

The preface to her 1911 book *Old Indian Trails*, titled "Why and Wherefore," set an intimate and personal tone that continues to captivate readers today:

> *During the two summers of the herein described little journeys among the Canadian Rocky Mountains, there had never been a thought that the daily happenings of our ordinary camp-life would ever be heard of beyond the diary, the family, the few partial friends.*
>
> *However, when the cold breath of the mountaintops blew down upon us, and warned us that the early winters were not far away, that the camping days were almost done for the year, when we reluctantly turned our backs upon the sweet mountain air, the camp-fire, the freedom, discarded the much loved buckskins and hob-nailed shoes for the trappings dictated by the Delineator, we emerged into the world—the better known world—sure of the envy of all listeners.*
>
> *Did they listen? No, scarce one. With all the pigments we might use, the numbers were few who "enthused." Those who needed "enthusing," they with aches and pains, with sorrows and troubles, listened the least, or looked upon our mountain world as but a place of privation and petty annoyances.*
>
> *For them I have written the following pages, tried to bring to them the fresh air and sunshine, the snowy mountains, the softly flowing rivers,—the healers for every ill. Will they close their eyes and shake their heads? Not all, I trust.*
>
> *To you who are weary both in body and soul, I write the message: "Go! I hand you the key to one of the fairest of all God's many gardens. Go! Peace and health are there, and happiness for him who will search."*[7]

The preface not only sets the tone for the book, it also establishes Schäffer's central theme of gender and social roles from which her literary and historical personas have subsequently grown. Clothing, accommodation, and civilization, ever-popular concerns in women's international travel literature at the turn of the twentieth century, forewarn of the tension between adventure and convention that underpins the narrative. Casting the journeys as a personal quest rather than professional expedition, for the purpose of seeking peace rather than an uncharted lake, also serves the literary leaning of the narrative. *Old Indian Trails* is a story told after the fact and, along with her portrait of Sampson, Leah, and Frances Louise Beaver that is included in the book, is the most famous and influential legacy of Schäffer's life and work.

As a result of her literary work, and despite the seemingly modest claims about her pastime as a woman traveller seeking peace on mountain trails long established by Indigenous people, the historical persona of Mary Schäffer, crafted by biographers, journalists, playwrights, and historians, has become one of an extraordinary woman doing extraordinary things. This Mary Schäffer can be an inspiring woman to spend time with through her biographers' work and their use of her published work, as well as her letters, photographs, house, furniture, garments, needlework, and other ephemera preserved in the Whyte Museum of the Canadian Rockies in Banff. She is a public character originally crafted by Schäffer herself in her published work and then elaborated upon by others—based on the actual person and her experiences, but shaped to inform, entertain, and motivate audiences. Autobiography and memoir scholar Julie Rak has shown that "the attempt to write oneself into a narrative results in the creation of oneself as 'other,' a person who exists in a book as a character, in order to turn one's life into a story for others' enjoyment, provocation, and education."[8] The literary persona of Schäffer is a blend of fact and fiction, fashioned by a combination of description and invention, constructed with photographs, maps, and geographical details, and written with imagination and literary licence.

The private Mary Schäffer who created the original public literary persona did not travel, photograph, paint, and write in isolation, however. Other women and men were part of her experience, and their stories are traceable in archival records. These diaries, letters, photos, and published articles enhance Schäffer's narrative and make it possible to construct a rich, nuanced, and complicated context for Schäffer's public persona and her published works. They also illuminate the gendered persona that is of much interest to travellers, especially women travellers, in the Rocky Mountains of Canada today.

1903: Wealth and Widowhood

More than grief drove Mary Schäffer's travel, writing, and photography in the years immediately following her husband's and parents' deaths in 1903. Financial loss, and loss of the security of inherited wealth or a male family member's professional income, played a part as well. Looking back in 1935, she wrote, "The Dr. really died of a broken heart when one of the world's crashes came and I was left to stare the future in the face with very little. All this taught me such a bitter lesson, to count the pennies, to lean on no one and make the best of the crumbling fortunes.... Things were really growing desperate at the time my parents and the Dr. died."[9] While in later years Schäffer wrote that she was shocked by the triple blow of the deaths of her parents and husband in 1903 and by what she recalled as the severely diminished state of her family finances, an examination of her financial state in early widowhood demonstrates that while she was no longer wealthy, neither was she destitute. As much as the balance may have been much smaller than she might have imagined (and needed), the final account paid to her from her husband's estate, coupled with an inheritance of an unknown amount from her parents, was sufficient to allow her to rebuild a secure financial position.[10]

Charles Schäffer and Alfred and Elizabeth Sharpless, alongside other families with inherited wealth, suffered significant and cumulative financial losses during an intermittent series of recessions in the 1890s and early 1900s. In Mary Schäffer's retrospective view, however, her husband's and parents' diminished status was also a result of indiscriminate spending:

> *I lived my earlier life among the dreamers of my world. They were dear people but absolutely the most impractical ones you could conceive. My father, a scientist of high order; lots of money to-day, all spent on poor relations the next. My mother a little dark-eyed heiress many times over and her impractical husband spending it for gay horses or whatever came into his mind, tho the poor relations were forever to the front. Later I married the most wonderful scientist of my acquaintance. He could never resist giving me anything money would buy and tho his mind was so remarkably keen for science, he had no business acumen. Again I had to stand by and see this and that inconsequential [family member] getting solid lumps of money for the mere making of a poor mouth.*[11]

Schäffer attributed her husband's sudden and unexpected death to the stress of severe investment losses incurred during the recession that began in 1902. By November 1903, the Dow Industrial Average had dropped 40 per cent. In early December, however, just two weeks after his death, a sustained recovery began.[12] The Schäffer losses were exacerbated by obligations her husband had maintained towards family members, including those of his two deceased wives (he had no children; see Appendix 1), compounded by the loss of a significant amount of money that left the extended family when an elderly spinster aunt, Elizabeth Schäffer, died in about 1898: according to Mary Schäffer, she bequeathed her entire estate, estimated at one million dollars, to her church and the Pennsylvania Hospital rather than distributing the bulk of it among family members, as was a common expectation among moneyed families.[13] In 1916, Schäffer wrote to George Vaux Jr., "The want of money killed Dr. Schaffer. Had I known as much in those days as I know to-day, I firmly believe we would have broken that will, but Dr. had no business ability." She also advised Vaux that the cemetery in Philadelphia was prodding the family to erect a headstone, which she believed to be the hospital's responsibility given the nature of the donation.[14] It appears that a headstone was never installed and today the Laurel Hill Cemetery gravestone records do not include Elizabeth Schäffer.

Charles Schäffer's will of 1895 had listed various sums to be disbursed to domestic staff, to Mary Schäffer's two brothers, to obligations owing to the families of Charles's first two wives (alongside both of whom he is buried in the North Laurel Hill Cemetery in Philadelphia),[15] and to the Franklin Institute, the Historical Society of Pennsylvania, the University of Pennsylvania, and the Academy of Natural Sciences of Philadelphia. These were institutions that the Schäffers had supported as members or patrons. A codicil attached in 1897 revoked the 1895 dispositions, however, and bequeathed all property to his wife Mary Schäffer, "on account of the great diminution in value of my estate, which I believe to be temporary; and on account of certain financial operations in which I am interested and which I want my wife to fully control in accordance with her best judgment."[16] The will was filed on 2 December 1903 and a final statement of value recorded in February 1905. A total of $94,544.37 was disbursed to Schäffer's widow, the equivalent of approximately $2.6 million in 2015.[17] This included $10,566.94 in cash, nearly $40,000 in investments, and the Schäffer family residence at 1309 Arch Street in Philadelphia, valued at $44,000.[18] The cash balance Mary Schäffer was left to re-establish her independence was comparatively small and the investment portfolio had been severely affected by losses at the time of death. In addition, the aging house may have been perceived as a burden to maintain without a guaranteed income. On those terms, the future of a newly widowed forty-two-year-old could have indeed appeared bleak. Steps taken to deal with the estate, as well as an improving investment climate, however, stabilized Mary Schäffer's financial situation.

In early 1904, Mary Schäffer donated her husband's collections to the Academy of Natural Sciences of Philadelphia, of which Charles Schäffer had been a long-time and active member and to which she had been elected in

1896.[19] These included a herbarium of one thousand plants from British Columbia,[20] a set of mahogany cases from his library,[21] and a large number of Indigenous artifacts,[22] as well as a mounted human skeleton, "a collection of mounted heads of mammals and two skins," a "collection of mounted birds," three insects ("Coleoptera [beetles], Texas"), a "collection of microscopical slides," and "collections of minerals and rocks."[23] The Academy of Natural Sciences also accepted the donation of the Schäffers' Arch Street residence; in return Mary Schäffer received an annual payment of $1,800 from the Academy that continued until her death.[24] Relying on a lifelong pension as a long-term financial base rather than selling real estate and buying new property or reinvesting the income from such a sale was a conservative choice, but one that could have been appealing and prudent for the sense of security it may have evoked.

Furthermore, however stark her financial state appeared to be in late 1903, in spring 1904 Schäffer had sufficient means to return to the Rocky Mountains for six months, which she did again in 1905 and 1906. On 4 June 1904, the Banff newspaper *Crag and Canyon* reported that "Mrs. Dr. Schaffer, of Philadelphia, arrived here several days ago with Miss Farr, of the University of Pennsylvania, Miss Day, of the Philadelphia High School and Miss James of the same place. Mrs. Schaffer is well known throughout the Canadian Northwest, having for years travelled with her late husband, Dr. Schaffer. The lady is continuing the writing of Dr. Schaffer's book on Flowers of the Rockies, and already has added some 40 new varieties to the collection. Mrs. Schaffer and party will stay in this vicinity until October."[25]

On 22 April 1905, the *Crag and Canyon* noted "Mrs. Schaffer and Miss James will arrive in Banff at an early date this year, as it is the intention of Mrs. Schaffer to try to close her book 'The Flowers of the Rocky Mountains,' next winter."[26] Seven weeks later, Banffites were updated on Schäffer's progress:

> *Mrs. Schaffer and Miss Farr, who were collaborating last summer on an exhaustive work on the botany of the Rocky Mountains, have returned to the West. They have done about three weeks' work round Glacier, and are making their headquarters in Banff during June. On Wednesday Mrs. Schaffer and Miss Farr were in Field, returning to Banff in the evening. Miss Day, who is assistant to Miss Farr in the descriptive work, is expected next week. The ladies hope to be able to have their book ready for publication next spring, when there is sure to be a wide demand for their able descriptions and delineations of the botanical glories of the Rocky Mountains.*[27]

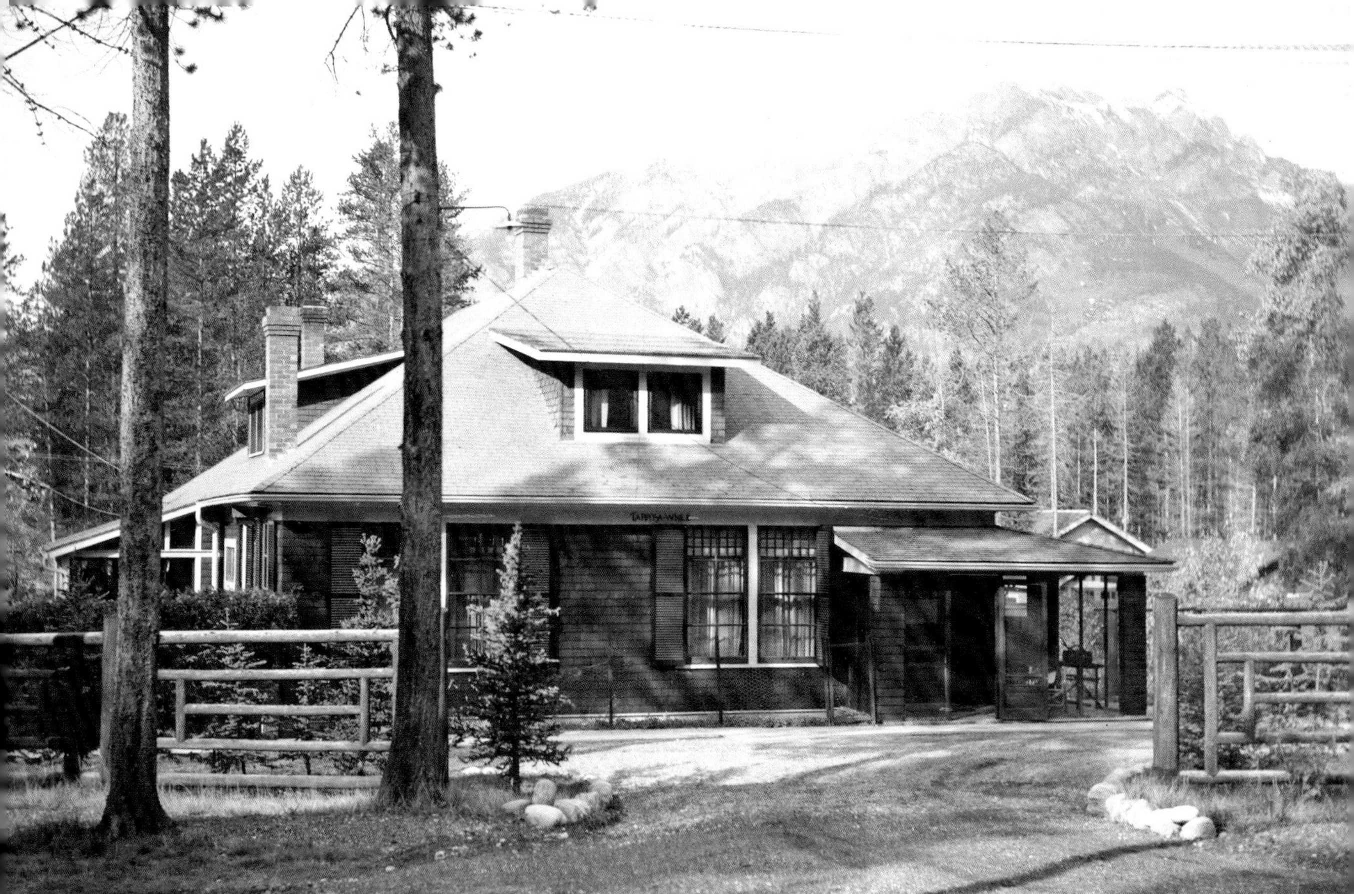

FIGURE 3.1
Tarry-a-while, Banff, photographer unknown, 1937. [WMCR ALR V488, Block 27, Lots 23-24-25]

By 1906, Schäffer was able to cover the expenses of Stewardson Brown, credited with authorship of *Alpine Flora*, to travel to the Rockies to undertake research as well as pay for the publication of the botany manual; in 1911, she also underwrote the publication of *Old Indian Trails*. During the decade following her husband's death, Schäffer recovered to a level of financial sufficiency that allowed her to spend four to six months each summer living at hotels in the Rocky Mountains and to travel for weeks and then months at a time on guided pack horse trips into the back country; to spend almost four months travelling in Japan between October 1908 and late January 1909; to travel to California; and to build her own house in Banff to which she moved permanently in 1912. Between 1904 and 1912, she boarded during winters with a variety of family members in the northeastern United States, particularly in West Chester, near Philadelphia. This arrangement appears to have been as much a matter of financial necessity as it was conventional for unmarried women to reside with extended family throughout their lives, rather than live alone in their own homes, as Schäffer ventured to do in 1912 when she moved into the house built on Grizzly Street across from the Old Cemetery in Banff that she named "Tarry-a-while."

In September 1911, when Schäffer first made the decision to build her own home, she wrote about it to George Vaux Jr.:

> *Dear George,*
> *I think in every woman's heart (perhaps man's too) is a dim longing for even a small spot to call "home."*
> *It's been eight years since I felt I could not afford one & do all the other things I want to do. I'm far from being certain I can afford it now.*
> *A year ago Mary J. [Vaux] said "why doesn't thee have a shack at Banff?" That question from her, was like Mary V's remark which really inspired me to finish the botany. Mary J's remark has hung in my brain a long time. Was there a possibility of having a home? The way has opened for me to use a small cottage here for a couple of months & see how I like it....*
> *I've longed for a log shack all my life. What does thee say to it?...*
> *Keep in mind that I've been restive for three years for a home in the west where I could go out, saddle my pony & ride among the hills I love better than smoke-stacks.*[28]

Although Mary Schäffer is described as a "pampered and charming socialite," "wealthy," "well-heeled," and "white and wealthy, a 'lady'" in later twentieth-century biographical descriptions,[29] it is not actually clear how wealthy the Sharpless and Schäffer families had been in prior decades. The origins of this view of Schäffer may be a description of both Schäffer and Adams as "society women of Philadelphia" published in 1908 in a Vancouver newspaper and clipped and saved by Schäffer in her scrapbook of reviews of *Old Indian Trails*.[30] In 1985, Schäffer's great-nephew Eric Cope Sharpless (b. ca. 1934), following publication of E.J. Hart's *A Hunter of Peace* in 1980, cautioned that "I would question the amount of money that Alfred & Elizabeth [Sharpless, Schäffer's parents] actually had." His grandfather, Schäffer's youngest brother Frederick, had "for all intents & purposes worked his way through" his studies at the University of Michigan from which he graduated in 1888.[31] This understanding is corroborated by an article published in the West Chester *Local Daily News* in 1921 that stated, "Columbia and Tech. were beyond his means, but the generosity of Michigan rendered possible the study of chemistry at Ann Arbor."[32] Furthermore, Schäffer was not entirely left on her own to sort out and then direct her finances; she employed George Vaux Jr. to assist in managing her affairs. Later on, William Warren advised as well. She wrote to Vaux in 1917,

> *Thy letter with its enclosure of check received this morning and I have gone carefully over figures and shaken them into shape. Fortunately Will's training was that of books and accounts, so when I get in a muddle I can always depend on him to unravel me....I am afraid thee will think me a lot of nuisance but Will makes me keep my books very strictly now and show details of all transactions. I do not complain over it. I was not brought up to business, Father never knew any more about it than I did and Dr. was scientific, as thee knows. I have learned the value of hard headed accounts, of books which I can open and know at a glance every detail, and of a husband who eliminates sentiment when it comes to business. He is one of the kindest, most generous men, but when its [sic] business with him, it is plain business, and I often think if others had kept to that line I might have had a really respectable bank account by this time.*[33]

Despite her displeasure with what she perceived as constraints in her circumstances in 1917, Schäffer remained financially independent and comfortable for the remainder of her life.

Schäffer's 1914 US income tax return is one indicator of her financial position. That year, she reported an income from US investments and mortgages of $8,812.87,[34] including the $1,800 payment "from a gift to a scientific institution reserving a quarterly payment during life," plus net income of $2,748.00 from Canadian investments.[35] Her total income was equal to about $273,000 in 2015. Correspondence over the years with George Vaux Jr., who continued to represent her interests in Philadelphia until his death in 1927, contain details of Schäffer's financial activities and investments, and demonstrate her growing expertise. A mortgage loan of $3,000 from Charles Schäffer to the well-known Philadelphia photographer William Rau, for example, continued to be carried by Mary Schäffer. Rau had been paying 4 per cent interest at a time when Schäffer was receiving 9 to 10 per cent on other mortgage loans, and she was, in her words, "seething" over Rau's refusal to pay back the principal.[36] In 1912, Rau was forced to comply when she called in the entire loan to divert the funds to industrial rather than mortgage investments.[37] In spring of 1913, she called in all of her remaining mortgage loans in Philadelphia.

Her correspondence with Vaux also details Schäffer's decisions about spending, such as her considerable investment in publication of the two books that she authored and in her new home in Banff. The cost of *Alpine Flora* is not documented in Schäffer's papers, but would have been at least comparable to

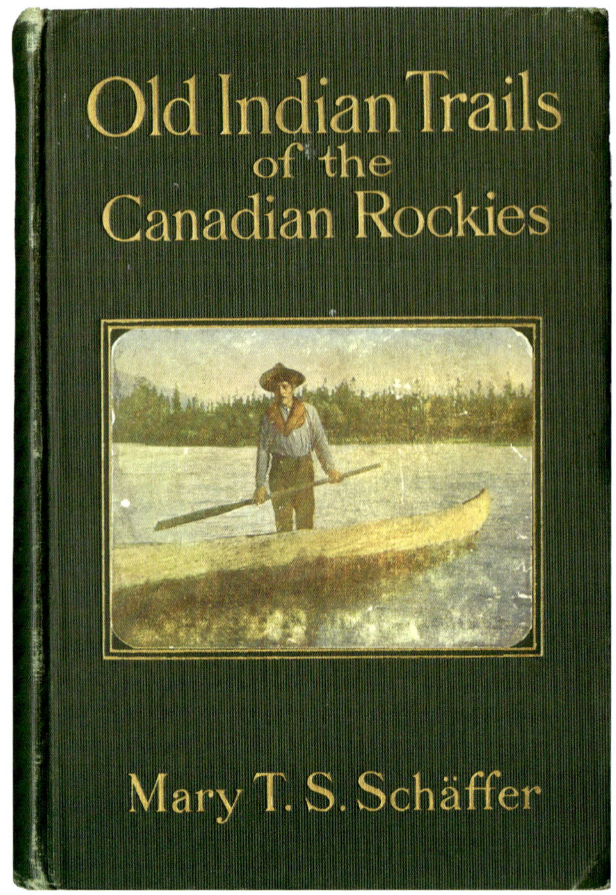

FIGURE 3.2
Cover of Mary Schäffer's *Old Indian Trails of the Canadian Rockies* (1911). 5.75 x 8.25 inches. [WMCR Archives and Library Collection 02.6.Sch1]

that of *Old Indian Trails* if not higher, given its greater length and the larger number of colour images. *Old Indian Trails* had just one colour image, a photo pasted on the cover, as well as a foldout map with colour. After a deposit of $462 she was billed $1,018.98 by her publishers for *Old Indian Trails*.[38] As for her new home in Banff, when the project began in 1911 she had hoped to build Tarry-a-while for $2,000, but by 8 April 1912 she had spent $5,338.16 on construction and related expenses.[39]

Schäffer lived in Banff for twenty-seven years. When she died there in 1939, her estate was valued at $4,019.10 for personal property including clothes, jewelry, investments, and cash.[40] No property, mortgages, or other real investments remained in her name at death. In her will of 29 December 1927, Schäffer bequeathed her entire estate, "whatsoever and wheresoever found to my beloved husband William Warren," with nothing designated for other family members. William Warren died five years later with an estate valued at $165,000 that included investment securities, cash, debts, real estate, and personal property.[41] The estate included the value of four properties in Banff that were mortgaged to friends and whose loans were forgiven upon Warren's death. The estate did not include Schäffer's home in Banff. Warren had transferred the land lease for the Tarry-a-while property to Philip A. Moore, a family friend in Banff, a year-and-a-half after Schäffer's death, at which time he moved to Vancouver. The house and its contents were transferred to Moore as well.[42]

Mary Schäffer's transition from the traditional position of middle- and upper-class women, no matter their marital status, as financial dependents of male family members to one of independence occurred during a time in which women were moving in increasing numbers into the work force, as the 1900 US census demonstrates.[43] She was among the privileged of this change, building her financial independence on the diminished remains of her husband's and parents' estates, supplemented by income earned through writing and publishing, rather than through waged employment. And just as she was not alone in building her financial security, neither was she a woman travelling alone when she arrived as a widow in the Canadian Rockies in 1904.

1904: Meeting Molly Adams

That summer and in the years following, the mountains were well-populated with women travelling on their own or together in small groups of friends or with family companions. There were those camping under the comfortable touring auspices of the CPR hotels, those who did so independently at camping locations established at short distances from Banff, Laggan, and other stops along the rail line, and those who went out some distance and at length with the assistance of immigrant guides and packers. Some of the women were tourists; others were amateur scientists, while some were professional scientists pursuing fieldwork and assisted by other women. Some were single, some married, some partnered with female companions, some widowed. The vast majority were white, and North American or British. Vancouver-based writer Julia Henshaw was there, collecting specimens for the alpine botanical guides that she subsequently published in 1906. British mountaineer and traveller Gertrude Benham, who had already climbed more than 130 peaks in the Alps, including Mont Blanc and the Matterhorn, was there climbing in the Rockies and Selkirks during her first and only visit to the Canadian ranges. One of the first articles that Schäffer published was about Benham's climbs of Mount Lefroy and Mount Victoria.[44] Benham climbed other Rocky Mountain peaks that summer, including Mounts Assiniboine, Balfour, and Stephen, and made the first summit of Fay. In 1909, Benham would climb Mount Kilimanjaro in Tanzania. After her death at sea in 1938 following a solo trip to Africa, she was recognized as the most travelled woman in history.[45] Schäffer's friend and colleague Mary Morris Vaux also arrived in the Rockies from Philadelphia that summer, photographing and measuring the movement of glaciers, along with her brothers William and George Jr., Schäffer's attorney and friend.[46]

Schäffer travelled in the Rockies in 1904 with three other women: Edith M. Farr (1864–1956) of Philadelphia who was collecting botanical specimens as part of a study for the University of Pennsylvania; Farr's assistant, Olive S. Day (1870–1940), from New Haven, Connecticut, but living in Philadelphia; and a Miss James. While camped at Lake Agnes on 3 August, Schäffer and her group crossed paths with another group of three northeastern American women who were climbing in the area that day from their nearby camp above Lake Louise. This proved to be an important meeting.[47] These three women had particular interests in mountain geology and botany and were visiting the Canadian Rockies and ranges west for ten weeks from 23 July to 13 October. They stayed occasionally at CPR hotels in Banff, Laggan, and Field, but camped most of the time at Lake Louise, Moraine Lake, Emerald Lake, and the Yoho Valley between 28 July and 7 September. They then went on to Golden, Glacier, North Bend, and Sicamous, Vancouver, and finally Victoria en route to Seattle.

The professional scientist of the group was Ida Helen Ogilvie (1874–1963), newly graduated with a PHD in geology from Bryn Mawr College near Philadelphia. Ogilvie had been hired immediately by Columbia University in New York City to teach geology in the women's undergraduate program at Barnard College. Ogilvie also wanted to teach graduate students at Columbia, however, and so she shifted her research focus to glacial geology, a field in which Columbia lacked a specialist. Her 1904 trip to the Rockies was the beginning of fieldwork in her new specialty, and she reported results in two published articles in the *Journal of Geology* that same year.[48] Ogilvie was accompanied on this trip by her domestic partner (in an arrangement known as a "Boston marriage" in that time and place) Käthchen I. Cook (b. 1869), and Cook's friend and cousin Mary W. (Molly) Adams (1868–1909) of New Haven, Connecticut.[49] Ogilvie, Cook, and Adams were seasoned travellers and campers. In 1901, they had spent a number of weeks together in the Adirondack Mountains in northern New York State while Ogilvie undertook fieldwork during her doctoral studies.[50] Their 1904 journey to launch Ogilvie's new research program was the first trip for the three to the Rocky Mountains of Canada.[51]

On 3 August, Adams noted in her diary that she "met some ladies while waiting at Lake Agnes who are doing botany for the U. of P.—one a Miss Day from New Haven," Adams's hometown.[52] In 1904, Adams was especially interested in botany. Just prior to leaving New York for the Rockies, she had purchased an unnamed botany guide, but found it inaccurate when she first put it to use in the Rockies.[53] Nevertheless, on 28 September she wrote to her sister,

> *My botany [guide] by this time looks as if it had been through the wars. It has been the most satisfactory botanizing I ever did somehow….I am thinking of offering myself as an assistant to Miss Farr, the lady who is writing the botany. I think they need one who can climb higher than any of them have. It must be awfully interesting work. This year there were four of them. Two did the scientific part, one pressed specimens and one painted and photographed and illustrated. Just think how useful I could have been to them, a regular jack of all trades.*[54]

The one who painted and photographed and illustrated was Mary Schäffer.

Like Schäffer's group, Ogilvie, Cook, and Adams encountered other women in the Rockies and Selkirks that year: there was "an English lady, Mrs. Bernard Smith…going around the world alone" and another "Englishwoman, 65 years old, with guide and cook. She left this morning with pack train of 7 horses."[55] Mary Schäffer is first mentioned by name in Adams's 1904 trip diary on Thursday, 22 September while at Glacier, BC: "Mrs. Schäffer talked to us all evening." Over the next week Adams makes two more references to Schäffer in her diary: On Friday, 30 September, "Miss B[enham] and I went up Glacier Crest to look for my sweater a.m. Found it—all chewed up. Developed rest of my films p.m. K. and Ida went to measure Asulkan Glacier. Mrs. Schaeffer and Miss James came back."[56] The following Sunday, Adams again recorded spending her day with "Mrs. Schaeffer," who showed her botanical paintings she had done, and time spent printing her own photographs along with Gertrude Benham.[57] The following day, she left with Ogilvie and Cook for Sicamous, and then North Bend, British Columbia. Gertrude Benham joined them in North Bend, and again in Vancouver and Victoria. On 14 October, Benham left Victoria for New Zealand, a day after the other three carried on by ship to Seattle, en route to California for a few weeks in late autumn, and then winter in New Mexico and Mexico as Ogilvie continued geological fieldwork.[58]

Adams's friendship with Benham grew enough that Benham invited Adams to join her on a trip in the future. Adams expressed her excitement with the prospect: "Miss Benham is here which is very pleasant. She and I are going to meet in Switzerland some time. Perhaps summer after next. Next summer she will be in Japan. You can imagine how set up I feel to have her ask me to do it. She is really a celebrity in the climbing line."[59]

Adams does not appear to have secured a place as a botany assistant with Farr. Instead, she was pressed into service as a geology assistant to Ogilvie. In late February 1905 from Dolores, New Mexico, Adams wrote that "just within the last week I have been promoted from a mere tagger-on of Ida's to assistant geologist, and you would laugh to see me start forth as proud as Punch with my hammer and compass and rucksack to carry home rocks in."[60] Nevertheless, Adams expressed some skepticism about the quality of Ogilvie's published work. While in North Bend in early October, she observed

> *We might just as well have gone to Vancouver with Miss Benham this morning, for it is raining and Ida has not stirred out of the house to measure her terraces, and we are going tomorrow without having measured them. Ida does not seem to mind at all running hastily around and casting her eye over the country, casually taking a few notes with aneroid and compass, and then publishing a learned article in a solemn geol. magazine. Some day she will be discovered in some fatal mistake, I am sure. Sometimes too she does not even read over once what she has written, it bores her so, but sends it right off to be printed, just hot from the pen, as it were.*[61]

Over the course of her 1904–1905 travels, Adams expressed a developing sense of herself as a practicing scientist. Writing on 13 March, about two weeks after being "promoted" to geological assistant, she reflected, "I don't feel, however, that I am even as much of a professional geologist as I am botanist. Paleobotany is my specialty! We have found some dandy fossil ferns and a few leaves, but more creatures."[62]

Like Schäffer, Molly Adams was a dedicated and entertaining letter writer who expressed joy and frustration with her companions, as well as her love for travel, and especially mountains. She created vivid portraits of Cook and Ogilvie, whom she dubbed "the catamounts,"[63] through her descriptions of their day-to-day activities and actions, and her frustrations with some of their habits. While travelling, she corresponded regularly with family members, especially her sister Catherine (whom she called Katy) and their cousin Alice. She wrote from Europe in 1891; between 1893 and 1903 she wrote from summer stays in the Adirondacks and Vermont; from the Caribbean with ports of call in Chile and Venezuela in February 1904; from the Canadian Rockies and west coast, and the southwestern United States from summer 1904 to early spring 1905; and from the Rockies again each summer between 1906 and 1908. Adams wrote her last letters from Japan between October 1908 and her death there in January 1909.[64] She was also a dedicated diarist when travelling. Her letters and diaries from her trips, preserved by her sister Catherine and brother Roger and his descendants, offer a strong sense of the pleasure she took in being outdoors and outside of cities, as well as a trace of her wide network of women friends and family, and her capacity for developing friendships with new women acquaintances in the Rockies, such as Gertrude Benham and Mary Schäffer.

Adams was moreover a photographer who developed and printed her own work when in the Rockies (where some hotels such as Glacier House and Mount Stephen House had facilities), which she maintained in albums. She mentions occasionally in correspondence with her sister the names of women friends who ask for prints to include in articles they were publishing. Adams would refer her sister to albums where the prints were placed.[65] At least two of these albums survive: one of her 1904 travels to the Canadian Rockies, followed by Oregon, California, New Mexico, and Mexico,[66] and a collaborative album of the 1906 and 1907 trips with Schäffer in the Rockies.[67] Landscape photographs of mountains are her best work. Like Schäffer, she also made the occasional photo of activities with others, such as one of riders ahead of her on the trail during the 1906 trip, which she took with four other women including Schäffer—their first trip together.[68]

In Adams's letters and diary of 1904, there are far fewer references to Mary Schäffer than to Benham, or to Ogilvie and Cook, and those few references have a different tone, one that is more formal and less personal. In contrast to Schäffer's succinct and poignant description of her relationship with Adams in later years, on which biographers have built a story of a deep and abiding friendship that they claim was carried on winter and summer,[69] Adams's own comments between 1904 and 1908 show both a greater reserve and a growing ease. They also render a sense of Schäffer as someone with a larger, more commanding personality than the "quiet, little eastern woman," as Schäffer in retrospect portrayed Adams, who has become her best-known, if still largely

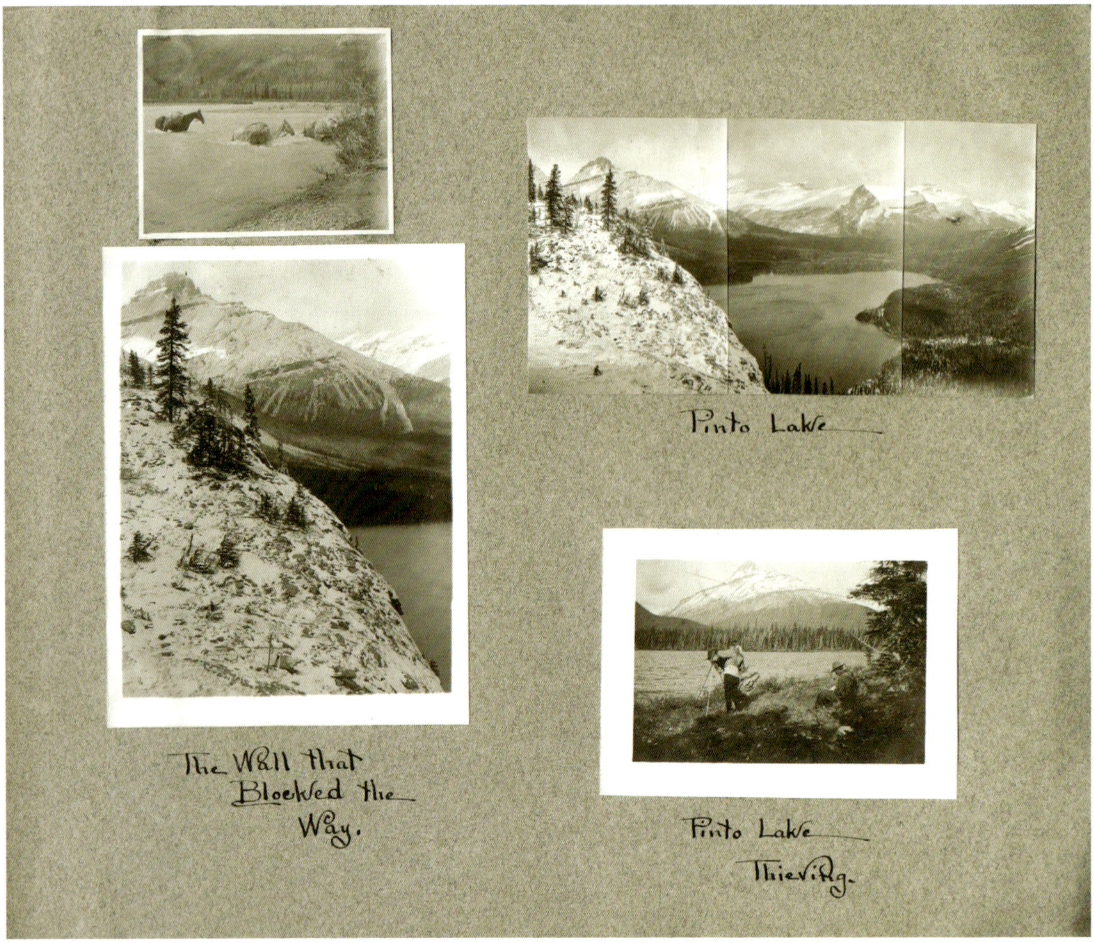

Pinto Lake

The Wall that Blocked the Way.

Pinto Lake Thieving.

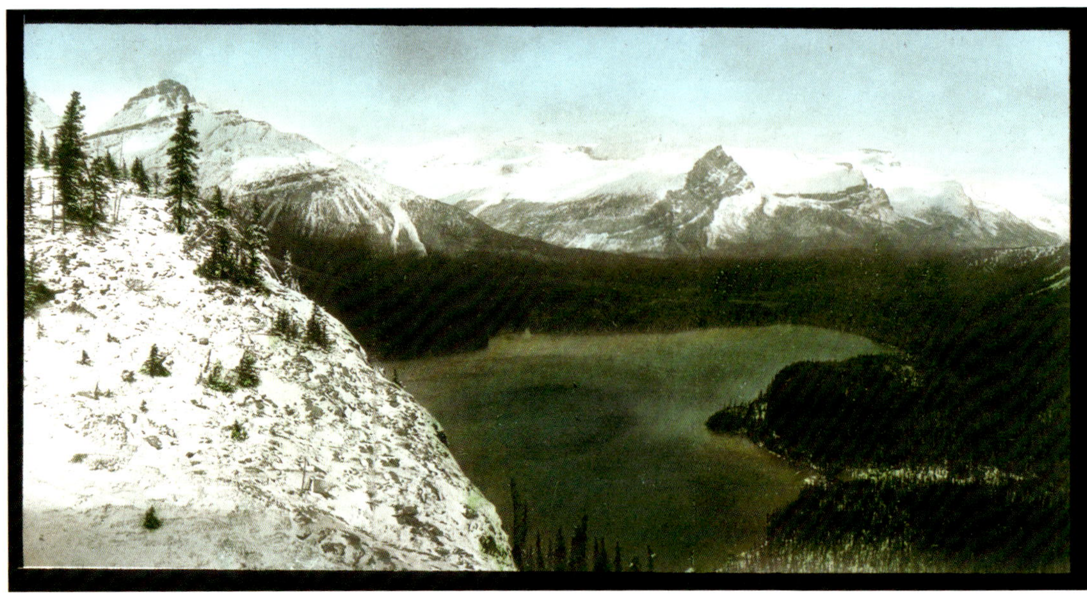

opaque, travelling companion.[70] On 23 October 1904, Adams first wrote at length about Schäffer in a letter to her sister from Berkeley, California:

‹FIGURE 3.3

Album page with "Pinto Lake" and "The Wall that Blocked the Way," Mary W. Adams photographs, 1906. [WMCR V527/PD-4]

‹FIGURE 3.4

"Solitude in the Rocky Mountains," Mary W. Adams photograph, 1906, as captioned in *Outing Magazine* 54 (1909), 197. Labelled "Pinto Lake" in Mary W. Adams and Mary Schäffer photograph album, 1906. See Fig. 3.3. [WMCR V527/PD-4] [Mary Schäffer] hand-tinted lantern slide [WMCR V439/PS1-76]

> *I was quite in earnest when I offered my services to Mrs. Schäffer as a humble botanical assistant, although of course I did it in a flippant manner. I never quite found out who was the boss of the outfit, did not like to ask too many pointed questions. I heard third hand that Mrs. Schäffer's husband had begun this botany before he died and she was carrying it on. I also heard, at North Bend, that there was a lady who lives in Vancouver who is also getting up a Rocky Mt botany, and that Mrs. Schäffer is very meanly cutting her out especially in the photographic illustrations she is making. Mrs. Schäffer is the kind of lady who likes to manage things, and is awfully nice to you when she likes you, but I have a suspicion that she would throw you over without thinking twice if she found some one else she liked better.*[71]

The "outfit" was the group Schäffer was with: Farr, Day, and James. The Vancouver woman was Julia Henshaw, the writer and journalist who published *Mountain Wild Flowers of Canada* a year in advance of Brown and Schäffer's *Alpine Flora of the Canadian Rocky Mountains*.

Schäffer's competition with Henshaw, while a matter of conversation in their Rocky Mountain botanical community, was not one Schäffer commented on in any extant correspondence or manuscripts from this period. Upon learning of Henshaw's death in 1937, however, she did so in a private letter. Her recollection casts matters differently:

> *When Dr. S. was working among the plants at Glacier, those long gone years, I began to note Julia's interest in his work. She asked so many inane questions regarding his form of work, then she annoyed me by insisting that she watch my painting. She had no art drill and of course it was quite useless. Then she got interested in my part of photographing plants. That is an art in itself and I gladly showed her what is called vertical photography. But it never entered my head what had already gone into her own.*[72]

Neither account can be taken as authoritative: Adams's account was, by her own admission, "third hand," and Schäffer's was in remembrance thirty years later; neither is verified by others nor offset by Henshaw's own view. That the incident is recounted in letters both at the time and in retrospect nevertheless demands attention, as it demonstrates that the women working in botany and other sciences in the Rockies were friendly and collaborative at times, but were also competitive and ambitious. "Firsts" were a point of rivalry and pride between and among both women and men in the Canadian Rockies. In 1900, for example, Mary M. Vaux was the first woman to ascend the peak of Mount Stephen, which was also the first climb over ten thousand feet made by a woman in the Rockies. In 1904, Gertrude Benham, along with Swiss guide Christian Kaufmann, attained the first ascent of Mount Fay—angering the man after whom it was named, who then had to settle for second place when his own first attempt, made on the same day Benham summited, failed.[73] In 1905, Vaux and Schäffer were the first white women to enter the Nakimu Caves in Glacier National Park, British Columbia, with miner Charles Deutschman who had found the cave system a year earlier. In one of her earliest published accounts, Schäffer expressed pleasure in having "seen it still fresh and undimmed from the years of silence."[74] She expressed the same sentiment in *Old Indian Trails* about the journeys that she and Molly Adams undertook in 1907 and 1908: "Our chief aim was to penetrate to the head waters of the Saskatchewan and Athabaska rivers. To be quite truthful, it was but an aim, an excuse, for our real object was to delve into the heart of an untouched land, to tread where no human foot had trod before, to turn the unthumbed pages of an unread book, and to learn daily those secrets which dear Mother Nature is so willing to tell those who seek."[75] And of course, Schäffer had aspired to publish the first botanical guide to the alpine flowers of the Canadian Rockies and Selkirks, a first she lost—with some bitterness, it would seem—to Julia Henshaw.

As well as ambitious and competitive, these women were also highly accomplished in their chosen interests, or on the way to becoming so. They were neither socialites nor dilettantes. Their work and reputations, and the income they generated from their writing or fieldwork to support themselves in whole or in part, mattered to them. They were sufficiently educated and had sufficient professional or family income to undertake serious botanical and geological studies, travel (in greater or lesser degrees of comfort), make photographs, spend long periods of time writing, and fund the related costs of publishing.

These women were also varied in their personalities and temperaments. In her letter of 23 October 1904, Adams revealed to her sister something of both her own more reticent personality and her impression of Schäffer in the first months of their acquaintance:

We exchanged addresses and she was most cordial, invited me to go with her next July on a four weeks packing trip into almost unknown regions north of the C.P.R., and said that if I ever thought of coming out to the Rockies again to let her know. She spends every summer there. I think she probably liked me because I admired her photos and water colors for illustrations so much and told her so. You would not like her at all probably, but I always get on with that kind of person with a slightly sporty tendency, and a way of making all the men stand around. Perhaps because they see with one blow of the eye that I will never be a rival.[76]

Adams evokes the legendary notion of female competitiveness for men's attention, but also her own view of herself. In a humorous, succinct, and self-deprecatory manner, she conveys much about the differences between her personality and that of Schäffer. Despite their differences, Adams too displayed a somewhat sporty tendency—a preference for the outdoors and physical activity—between 1904 and 1908. Both her activities and photos made by her and of her in the Rockies attest to this. Through the concept of sportiness, Adams articulates a type of femininity that pushed and defined the boundaries of urban women, in this case specifically those who travelled in the Canadian mountains as climbers and hikers, and worked there as scientists (professional and amateur), writers, and photographers at the turn of the twentieth century. The boundaries of the urban rubbed up against those of wilderness, and in that liminal space, ideas of gender, race, and class were tested and traversed for the duration of these women's time beyond the bounds of urban and professional life and the places and activities that were thought of as the heart of civilization.

Civilization and Wilderness

In early twentieth-century North America, the concepts of civilization and wilderness—and the tension between them—were important literary devices. Travel writers in particular, including Mary Schäffer, leveraged these concepts in their work. Historian Phoebe Kropp describes the idea of wilderness at the time as "less a physical description than a social marker indicating a place beyond civilization."[77] The two concepts—wilderness and civilization—served complementary and integrated roles in turn-of-the-century urban, educated, literate American and Canadian society. Spending time in wilderness meant camping, an activity that, Kropp argues, "defined, disciplined, and ultimately

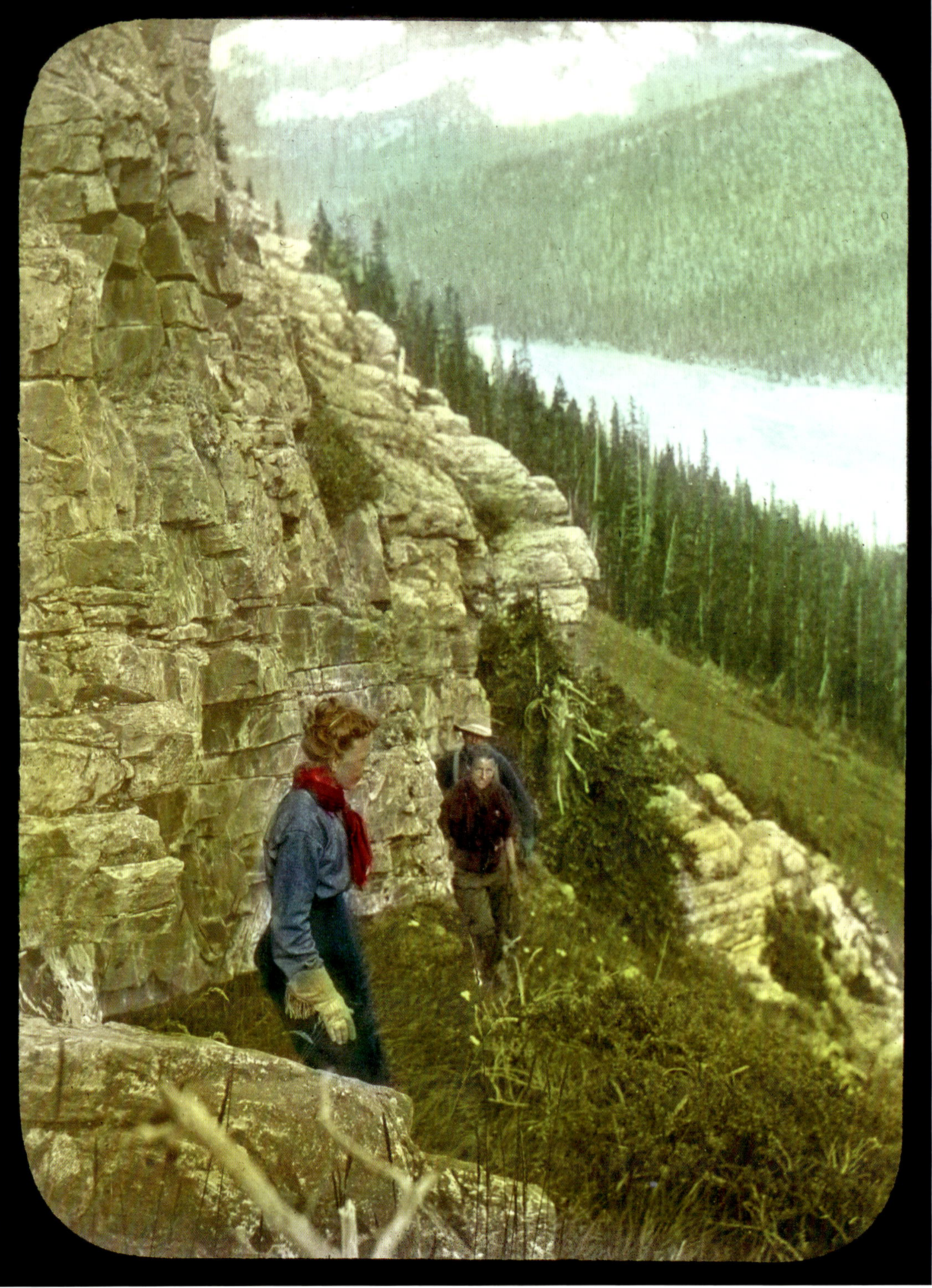

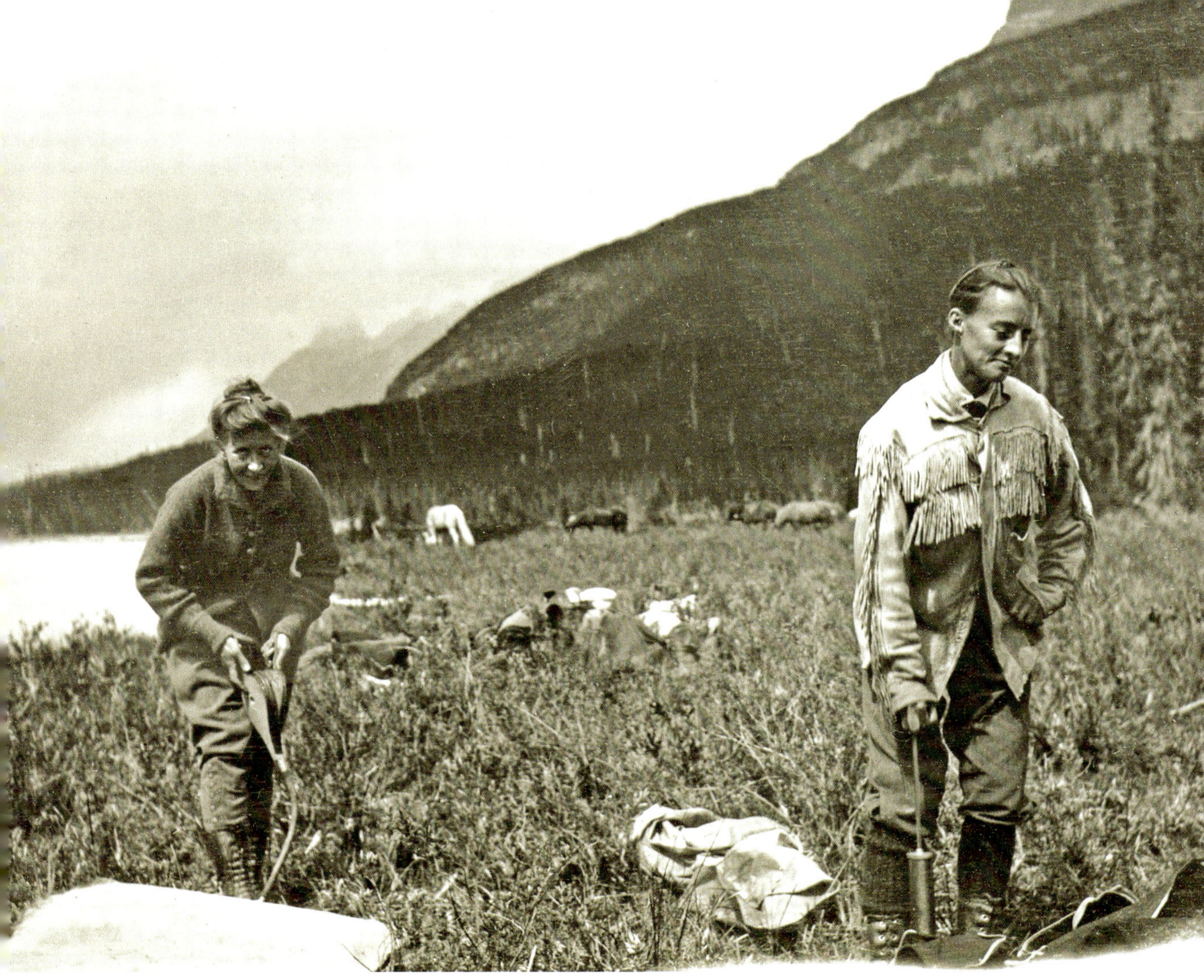

<FIGURE 3.5

Mary Schäffer and Molly Adams "Climbing the 'Bump,'" photographer unknown, 1907. [WMCR V527/PD-1 and V527/PD-4] [Mary Schäffer] hand-tinted lantern slide [WMCR V439/PS1-4]

^FIGURE 3.6

Mary Schäffer and Molly Adams "Pumping Air Beds," photographer unknown, 1907. [WMCR V527/PD-1 and V527/PD-4] Reproduced from V527/NA-102

tamed wilderness—at least rhetorically—as [a] key component of modern civilization."[78]

Leisure camping was growing in popularity in North America, and opening the Canadian mountains to tourist traffic in the latter half of the 1880s contributed to its growth. Outfitters set up businesses to equip and guide tourists, men and women alike, in mixed- and single-sex groups, to spend one or more nights around campfires and in tents a short ride away from the hotels along the railway, such as at Lake Louise where Mary Schäffer first experienced camping in 1893.[79] When Adams, Ogilvie, and Cook arrived in the Rockies for Ogilvie's fieldwork, Adams reported to her sister Catherine, "We had a guide come up to see us this evening to find out about going into camp. He was a nice boy but did not seem to think there was anything out of the way of our being in camp alone."[80] Expecting social disapproval of unchaperoned activity, an anticipated barrier instead fell away.

More and more "sporty" women hiked, climbed, rode, and camped in the mountains, often without male family members but with Euro-Canadian male outfitters and guides. Along the way, they adapted their clothing, responsibilities, and expectations to account for the conditions in which they travelled, and the social structures in which these travels took place and that such travels challenged and upended. Camping offered the chance to move temporarily into nature and away from a built environment and, often, the gendered social roles of that environment: the guides were men, and they did the packing, the cooking, and the cleaning up. Furthermore, the balance between comfort and austerity in camping was a fine one, evoked by "tenderfoots" and veterans alike to assess a camper's credentials. Warmth, dry feet, comfortable sleeping arrangements, hygiene and grooming, food quality, quantity, and those responsible for its preparation, as well as appeals for understanding about discomfort or scorn for those unduly concerned, are both markers of success and recurring matters of attention, if not obsession, in women's accounts. At the same time, it was impossible to "bring camp home."[81] Schäffer expressed this sentiment in *Old Indian Trails*, as Adams did in her letters and diaries. Like others, they returned from their journeys with mixed feelings over the loss of the social liberty experienced on the trail and renewed acquaintance with the creature comforts of hotels and home.

Schäffer famously underscored the significance of the contrast in clothing and behaviour between society and camp life as a literary device playing on contemporary concerns about both gender and race in her description of tourists along the road near Field, British Columbia. She and Adams emerged in early October 1907 from a full sixteen weeks of camping in the mountains to encounter Rudyard and Caroline Kipling, exact contemporaries of Schäffer's from Britain. Both Schäffer and Rudyard Kipling mobilized current notions of gender and race to underscore the mix and clash of wilderness and civilization in this meeting as representative of early twentieth-century modernity. It should be noted that both women and Indigenous people in the Canadian Rockies were active participants in the tourist economy that emerged with the arrival of passenger service on the Canadian Pacific Railway.

In April 1908, Kipling recounted their meeting this way:

> *As we drove along the narrow hill-road a piebald pack-pony with a china-blue eye came round a bend, followed by two women, black-haired, bare-headed,*

wearing beadwork squaw-jackets, and riding straddle. A string of pack-ponies trotted through the pines behind them.

"Indians on the move?" said I. "How characteristic!"

As the women jolted by, one of them very slightly turned her eyes, and they were, past any doubt, the comprehending equal eyes of the civilized white woman which moved in that berry-brown face!

"Yes," said our driver, when the cavalcade had navigated the next curve, "that'll be Mrs. So-and-So and Miss So-and-So. They mostly camp hereabout for three months every year. I reckon they're coming in to the railroad before snow falls."

"And whereabouts do they go?" I asked.

"Oh, all about anywhere. If you mean where they come from just now—that's the trail yonder."

He pointed to a hair-crack across the face of a mountain, and I took his word for it that it was a safe pony-trail.

The same evening, at a hotel of all the luxuries, a slight woman in a very pretty evening frock was turning over photographs, and the eyes beneath the strictly arranged hair were the eyes of the woman in the beadwork jacket who had quirted the piebald pack-pony past our buggy.[82]

Schäffer's friends and acquaintances ensured that his commentary was brought to her attention. An excerpt of the relevant portion of the full article is pasted in Schäffer's scrapbook along with copies of reviews of *Old Indian Trails*.[83] When she wrote *Old Indian Trails*, she crafted the encounter from her own literary point of view. She did not name the Kiplings, but she could be assured that his published letters had been widely read and the reference understood by her own readers:

And then we struck the highway and on it a carriage with people in it! Oh! The tragedy of the comparison! The woman's gown was blue. I think her hat contained a white wing. I only saw it all in one awful flash from the corner of my right eye, and I remember distinctly that she had gloves on….It was then that I wanted my wild free life back again; yet step by step I was leaving it behind.

We entered the little mountain town of Field…and fled from the eyes of the curious tourist to that civilized but perfect luxury—the bath-tub.[84]

›FIGURE 3.7
"Nibs and His Mistress," photographer unknown, n.d. The photograph is printed in reverse from the negative as the frontispiece of *Old Indian Trails* (1911). [WMCR V527/NG-112]

Schäffer appears in only four of the one hundred photos published in *Old Indian Trails*. One is the frontispiece in which she sits astride her horse, Nibs (Fig. 1.2). The others include one in which she is bent over a campfire tending a pot in a buckskin jacket and skirt, and another in which she is standing in a lake washing blankets (Figs. 3.8 and 3.9). Molly Adams probably made these photographs. Adams herself appears in just one in the book and it too has overtones of wilderness domesticity: a group portrait of the two women, along with guides William Warren and Joe Barker, labelled "One of our summer homes." Although its presence in *Old Indian Trails* implies that this particular gathering took place in the course of the stories being told, this photograph was in fact made in 1906 during a different, late-summer trip to the Kootenay Plains. Barker was not employed for the 1907 or 1908 journeys. Adams labelled it "The Last Camp" in the 1906 photo album (Fig. 3.10).[85]

The women's eyes are on the dog that is entertaining them with its master, Joe Barker, while Warren stares at the camera. Smoke from a campfire, a defence against mosquitoes, billows thickly. The group is at ease, informally posed and dressed for travel, and a sense of the rugged and simple conditions of the tent and environment are clearly conveyed. Both the men's and women's clothing attract attention, but it is the women's that is of greatest interest because of its specificity to the environment. The buckskin jacket is exotic compared to Euro-North American wear, and is one signal of the disruption of gender and race expectations in the meaning of wilderness as a defining element of early twentieth-century modernity. Adams's jacket is especially notable, as she had purchased it in Banff along with some buckskin gloves as a warmer option to the fabric coat she had travelled in earlier that summer in her first pack train excursion with Schäffer and three other women.[86] She regretted that it had only one pocket, however.[87] Where this photo was made, and who else was in camp that day and operated the camera to expose the negative, are both unknown. The photograph was later hand-coloured by Schäffer and, given the generic title attached to it, likely used in a lantern slide lecture about her Rocky Mountain journeys.

Like most tourists with cameras, the women made photographs of each other both active and posing in their travel environment. Gender, inextricably tied to class and race, was a defining category for identification, assessment, and judgement in Rocky Mountain travel and its literature. Schäffer's and Adams's experiences were no exception, nor was Schäffer's story of their quest, built on these contemporary social interests among her readership. Adams

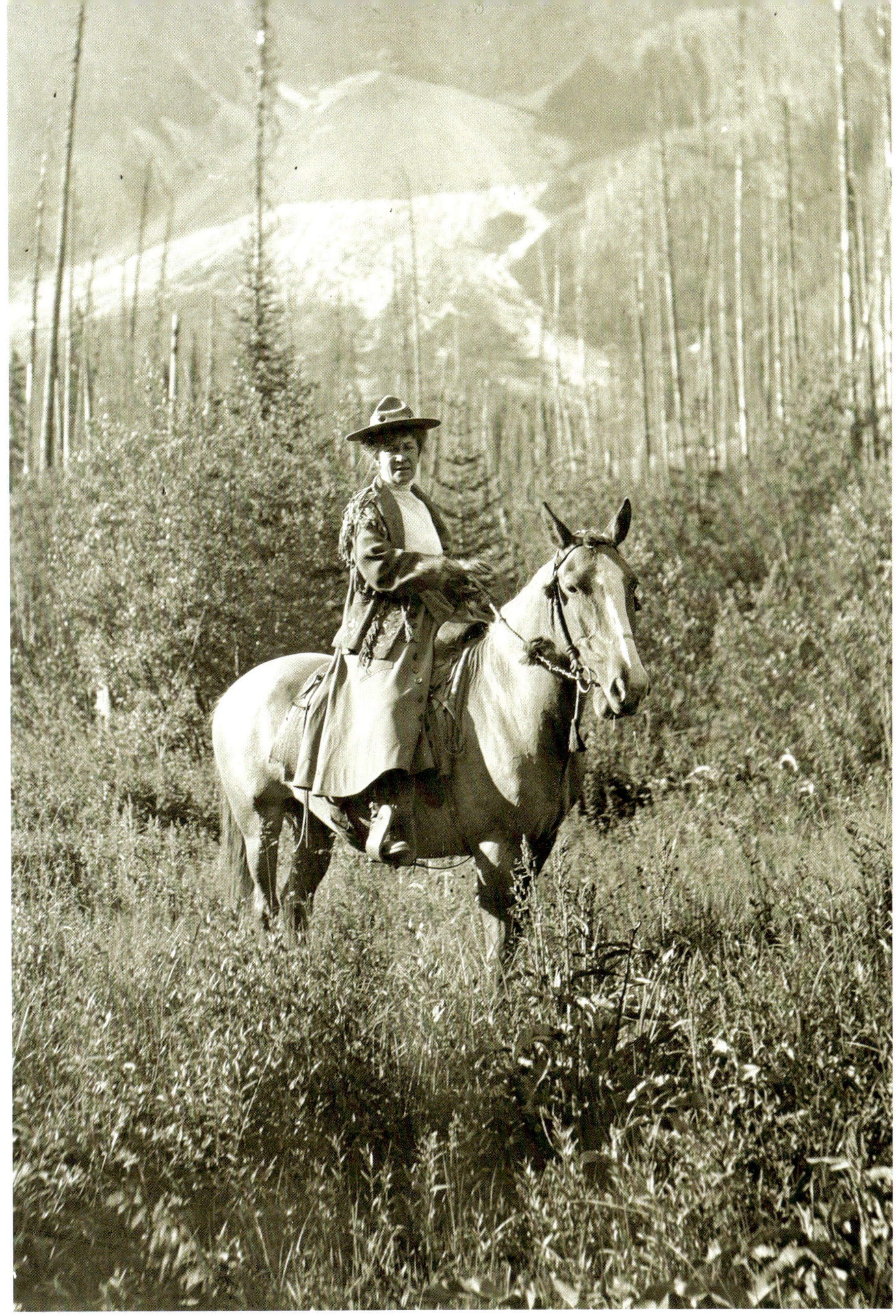

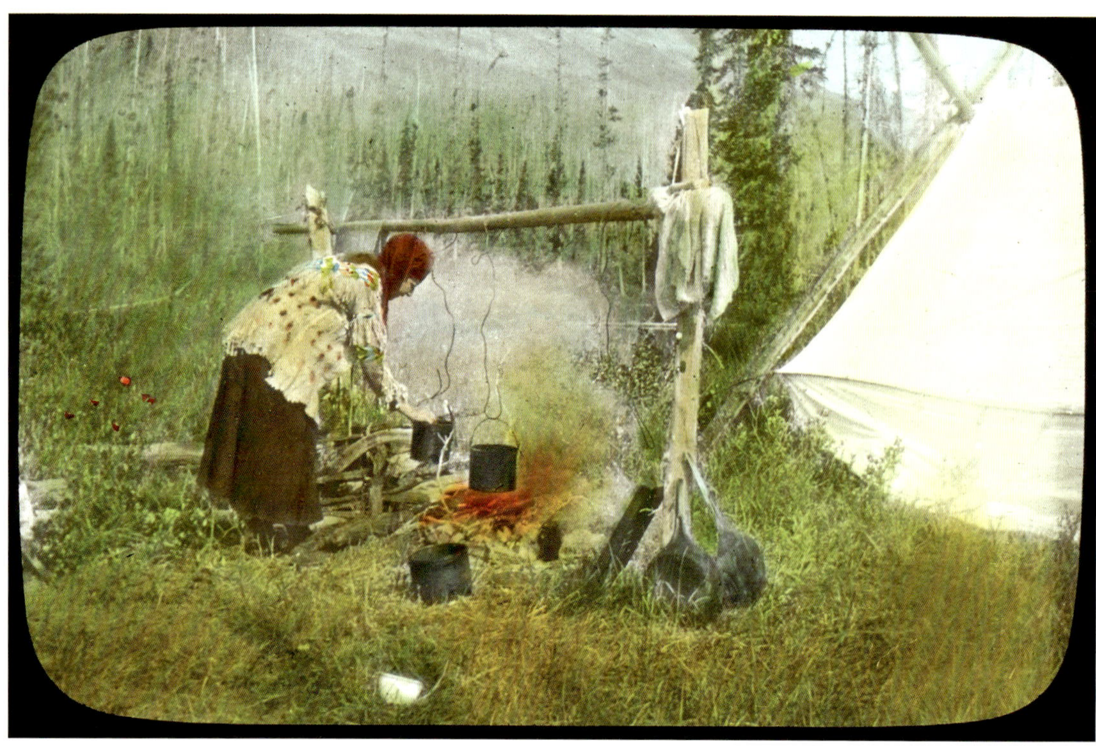

^FIGURE 3.8

"A Camp Dinner," [Mary W. Adams photograph], ca. 1907, in *Old Indian Trails* (1911), 253.

[WMCR V527/PD-1]

Mary Schäffer hand-tinted lantern slide

[WMCR V527/PS1-27]

>FIGURE 3.9

"When I saw the last of those four men I knew what was going to happen," [Mary W. Adams photograph], ca. 1907, in *Old Indian Trails* (1911), 279.

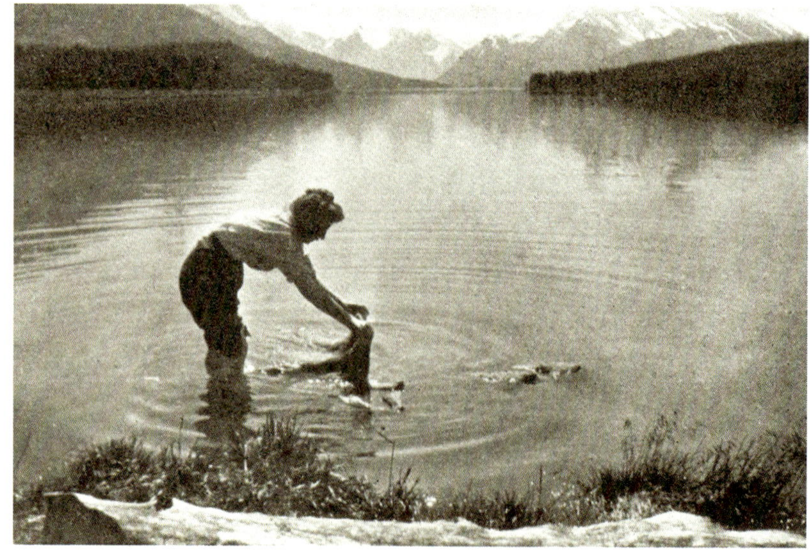

"When I saw the last of those four men I knew what was going to happen"

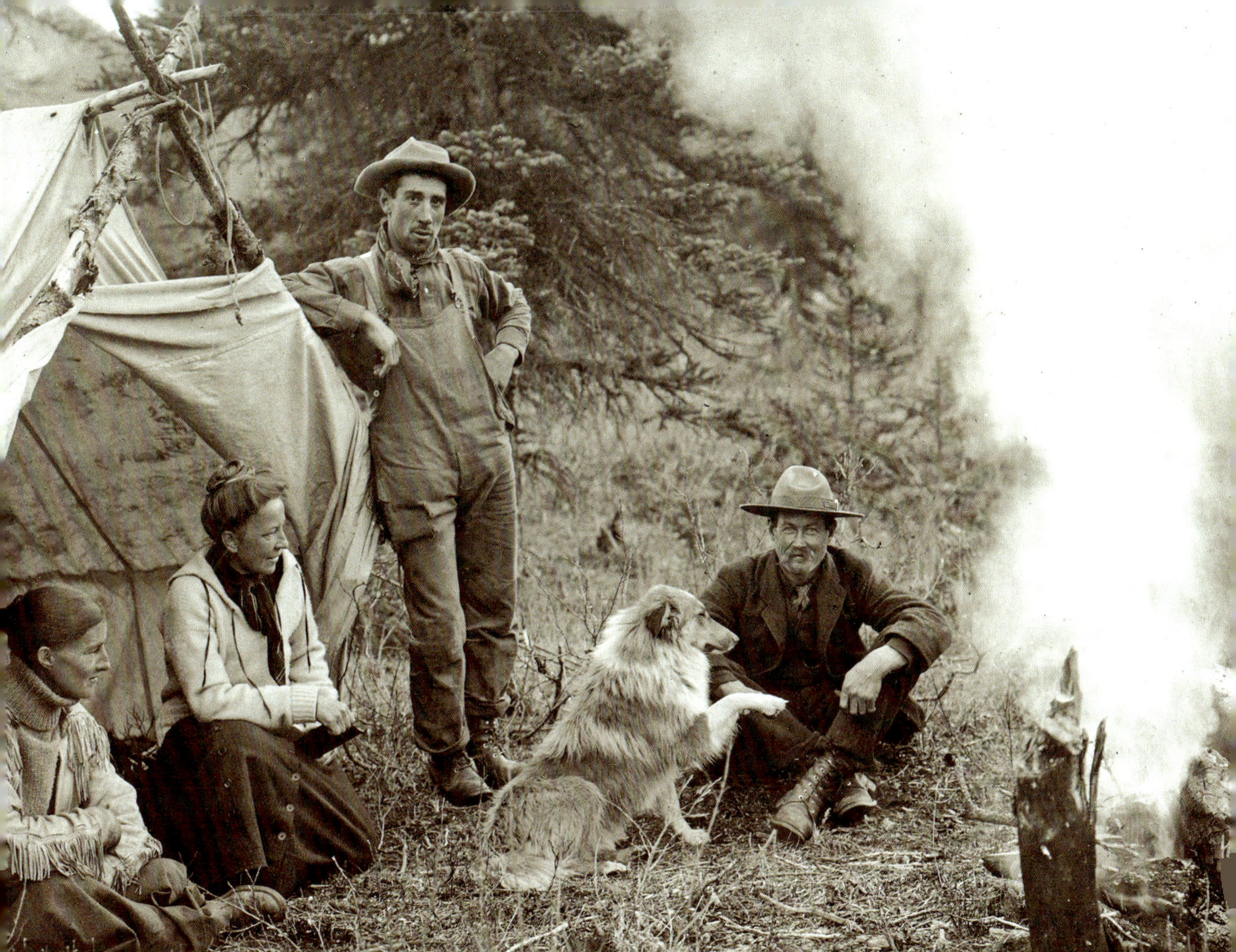

FIGURE 3.10

"One of our summer homes," photographer unknown, 1906, in *Old Indian Trails* (1911), 259. Labelled "Last Camp" in album WMCR V527/PD-1 and "The Last Camp" in album WMCR V527/PD-4. (Also Mary Schäffer hand-tinted lantern slide [WMCR V439/PS1-1])

commented in her 1908 diary, for example, that "M. and I went fossil hunting after lunch. Mosquitoes pretty chewy. When we got back to camp M. wanted her picture taken as a martyr to science. She was a handsome sight with her head tied up in her red cotton neckerchief to protect her from the bugs, every pocket in breeches, and sweater bulging and hanging down with the weight of fossils, and carrying a great wad of specimens for Mr. B."[88]

Among the hundreds of photographs in the Whyte Museum archives in Banff, there are a number of images of both Schäffer and Adams riding horses, scrambling along mountains, setting up, reading, writing, and resting in camp, and otherwise engaged in the day-to-day activities of their journeys, few of which appeared in *Old Indian Trails*, where the visual focus remains on the landscape through which they travelled. In all of these, they are dressed for physical activity in wilderness in split skirts or trousers, buckskin jackets, gloves, and bandanas, occasionally with bug nets protecting their heads, and

FIGURE 3.11

Mary Schäffer sewing and Molly Adams writing in camp, photographer unknown, ca. 1907.

[WMCR V527/PD-4]

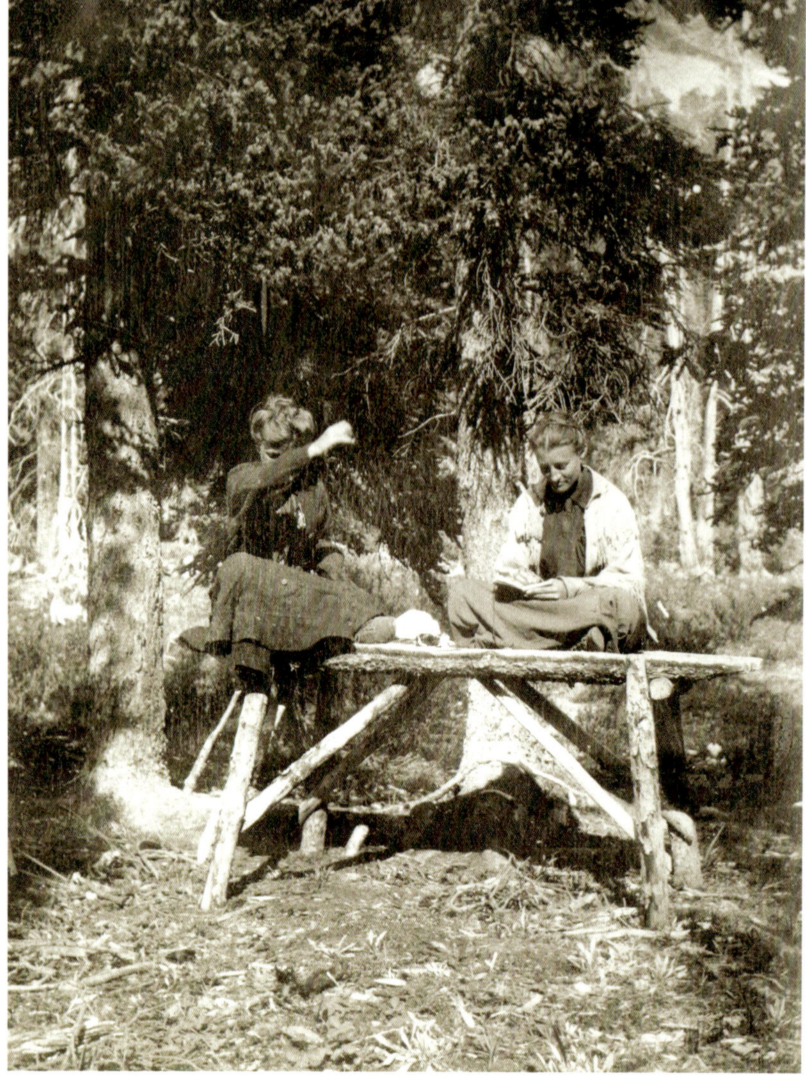

always in sturdy boots. Adams needed some time to adjust to such masculine attire, especially wearing it in front of strangers, but her discomfort passed. On first arriving in Banff, she wrote to her sister from the Banff Springs Hotel on 25 July 1904, "I was so shy of my divided skirt that I did not wear it to breakfast, but changed afterward and hopped into the runabout with great agility." Five days later, in her camp diary, she noted, "Put on skirt to pass men's camp." But by 9 September she wrote home that in camp whenever other campers came by they would find her, Ogilvie, and Cook "of course dressed in our little trousers. Käthchen always had a skirt ready to leap into at the slightest strange sound, but Ida and I grew very hardened."[89]

The most formal and deliberate of these photographs is a pair of portraits made in 1907. These portraits, which they made of each other, were not included in *Old Indian Trails*; nor were they published elsewhere in Schäffer

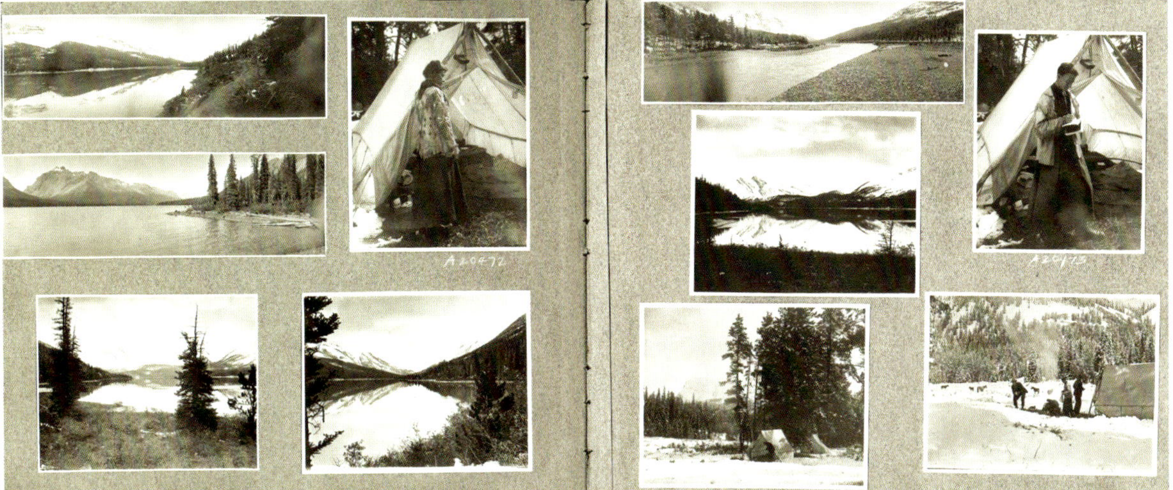

FIGURE 3.12

Facing album pages with photographs Mary Schäffer and Molly Adams made of each other in camp wearing buckskin jackets, 1907. [WMCR V527/PD-1]

and Adams's lifetimes. Rather, 4.5 x 3.5 inch black-and-white prints were mounted, untitled and on facing pages, in the photograph album that Schäffer kept of their time in the Rocky Mountains. The setting for both portraits is a large white canvas tent, big enough for two, pitched over poles made from tree branches. The front flaps are pulled back to reveal the daytime environment, with cups and plates in the foreground and sleeping bags arranged further inside along opposite walls of the tent. A binocular case hangs above, and snow on the ground at the corner of the tent indicates a cold day. Both women are dressed for cool weather in buckskin jackets, long, heavy skirts (Adams's clearly split), and heavy boots.

Schäffer is facing away from the camera in her portrait, in a three-quarter profile that hides her face and privileges the back and side of the jacket, instead of its wearer, as the point of focus. The viewer's eye rests mainly on the jacket, but also follows the direction that Schäffer is facing, effectively drawing interest to the inside of the tent pitched among the trees while setting the jacket solidly in its wilderness context. The jacket is fitted well to Schäffer's form, shaped to the waist. The edges are pinked, and the sleeves are fringed at the cuff, the shoulder, and along their lengths. Fringe also falls from the back yoke. The back of the jacket is decorated, as is the sleeve that is visible. It is a very fine garment that Schäffer is displaying for the camera and a future audience. It is not on display merely as a collector's item, however, but as a working coat. She is seen in photos wearing it while at work over a campfire, and with it tied around her waist as she hikes a mountain trail, with Warren following behind.

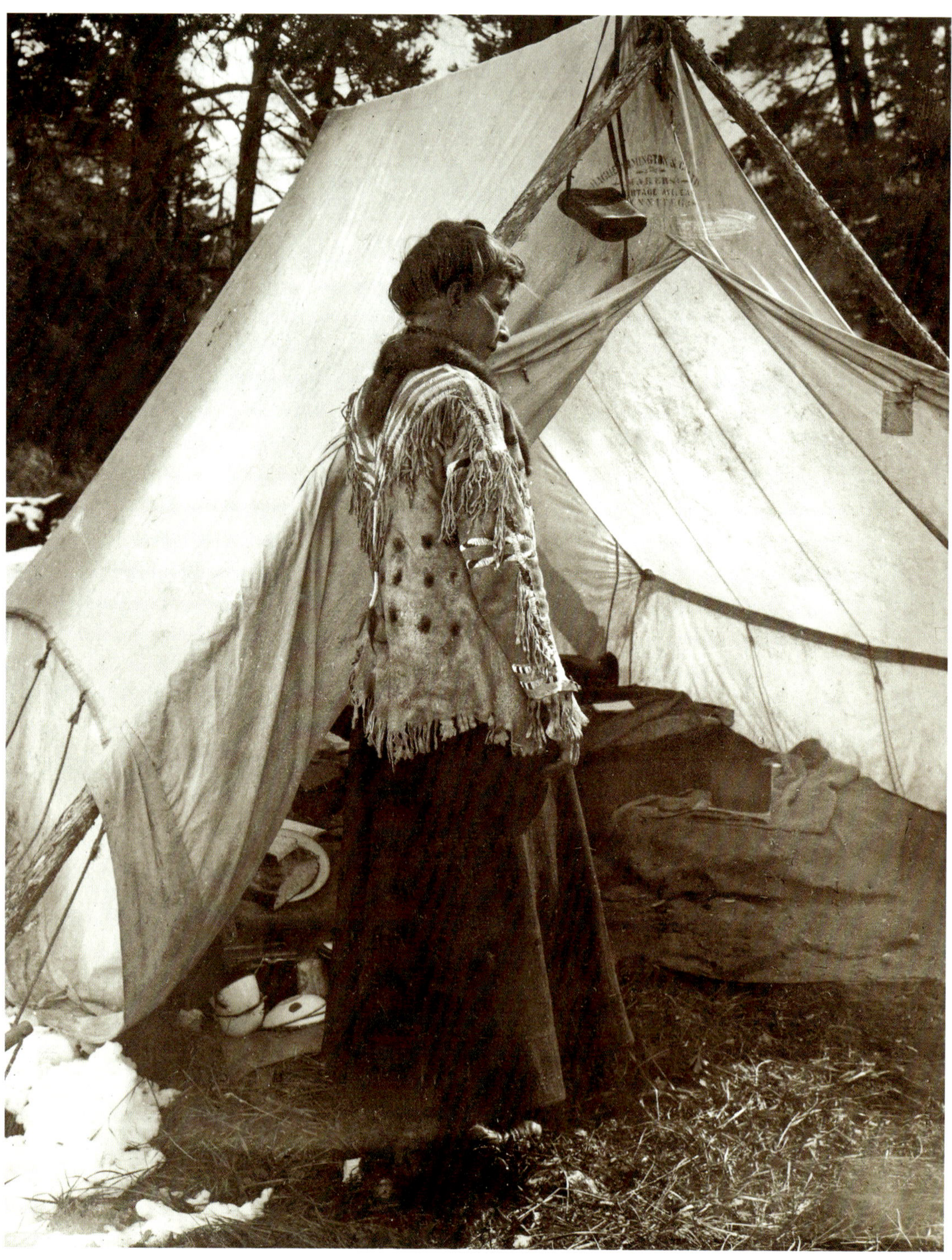

FIGURE 3.13

Mary Schäffer in buckskin jacket,

Mary W. Adams photograph, 1907.

[WMCR V527/PD-1]

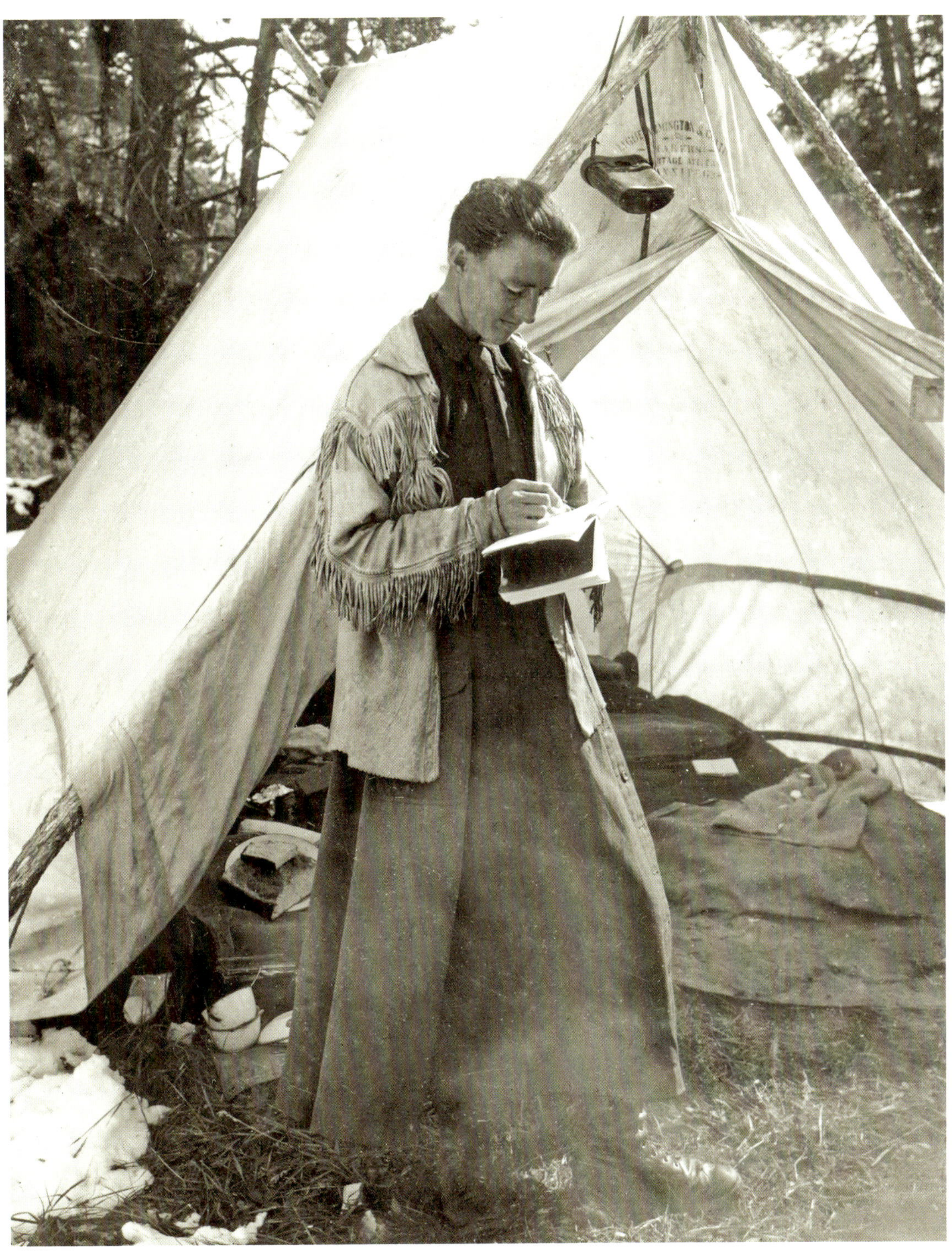

FIGURE 3.14

Molly Adams in buckskin jacket, Mary Schäffer photograph, 1907.

[WMCR V527/PD-1]

In contrast to Schäffer's portrait, Adams appears facing forward in three-quarter profile, not looking at the camera but instead writing in a book, as if adding another entry to her trip diary, which is placed on a sleeping bag in the middle ground of Schäffer's portrait. Her buckskin jacket is different from the first one she acquired in 1906, seen in the group portrait from that year. Only the sleeve fringe is especially visible here. The casual manner in which the jacket is worn makes it at best secondary to the diary as the centre of attention—the viewer's eyes follow Adams's to the point of focus—suggesting comfort in her clothing, ease in her environment, and diary writing as a defining activity. Embroidered details on the shoulder yokes are lost to the wide angle and monochromatic print.

›FIGURE 3.15
Mary Schäffer and William Warren, [Mary W. Adams photograph], 1907.
Mary Schäffer hand-tinted lantern slide [WMCR V439/PS1-6]

A second print of Adams's portrait is preserved in the collection of Adams's brother's descendants. As for Schäffer's portrait, two hand-tinted glass lantern slides were made. One was cropped and titled by Schäffer "She Who Colored Slides" (Fig. 1.4). No lantern slide was made of Adams's portrait. In the cropped Schäffer image, the emphasis moves away from showcasing Schäffer's very fine jacket, and the skill of the woman who made it in its original context and environment. The focus instead is on Schäffer's activities and considerable skill as a painter and storyteller back in day-to-day life—civilization—in Philadelphia and West Chester. These posed photographs of Schäffer and Adams, despite their limited public circulation in the early twentieth century, are of tremendous interest today as tangible traces of the women and how they chose to portray themselves in the wilderness space of modern North American civilization.

1906: Imagination, Literary Licence, and Five Women on the Trail

On 24 September 1908, Adams observed, "I think we were more awful sights than ever when we came in this time, & by the way I have never read that Kipling letter myself, M.S. only told me about it & she always gets things twisted, when she comes to the point of a story. She sent him her article in the Phila. Geog. magazine & found a note waiting for her just now from Mrs. Kipling, a very nice note."[90]

The roles of imagination and literary licence, and the risks of taking Schäffer's narrative work and photography (whether published or unpublished) as pure and intentional historical documentary, may be demonstrated by a comparison of four accounts of a trip to the Kootenay Plains on the North

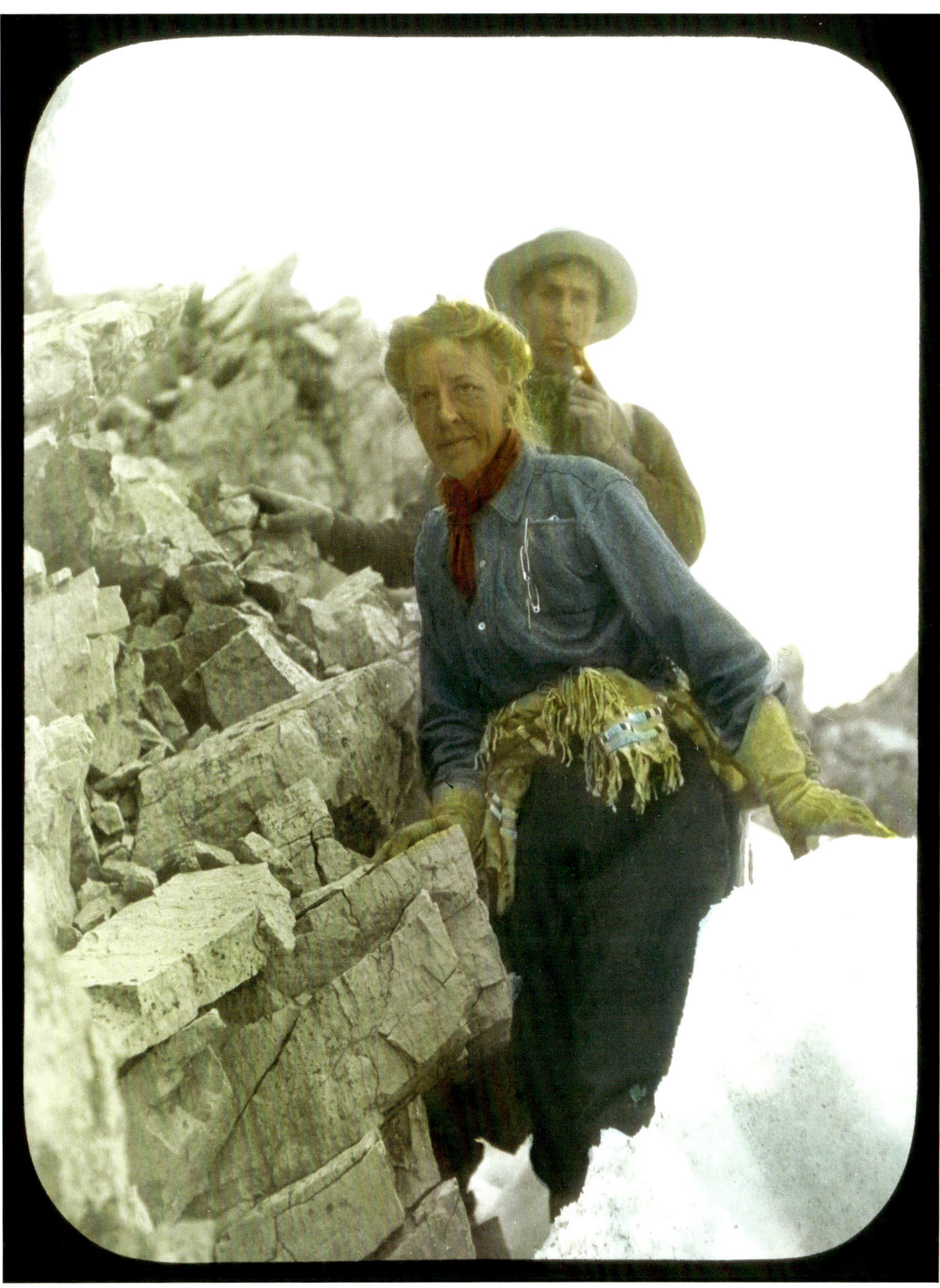

Saskatchewan River that Schäffer and four other women, accompanied by two guides, undertook in 1906. One account is Schäffer's, written almost thirty years later, in 1924, and included in a lengthy, unedited manuscript of anecdotes titled "Tepee Life in the Northern Hills." This account, which Schäffer did not publish, has become a heavily mined primary source for Schäffer biographers and other researchers seeking to reconstruct Schäffer's life.[91] A second account was written by Zephine Humphrey and published in three installments in the American leisure sport magazine *Outing* in 1909; it is called "Five Women on the Trail."[92] This series of articles is illustrated with fourteen photographs credited to Mary W. Adams. Molly Adams wrote the third account, a letter to her sister Catherine from Lake Louise shortly after returning from the trip in July 1906. (Adams wrote that she "took seven dozen pictures. There ought to be some good ones of fording streams etc.")[93] A fourth is Henrietta Tuzo's description, written in her diary from the summer of 1906. Tuzo also wrote by hand two drafts of a manuscript, "A Glimpse of the Saskatchewan,"[94] published in two parts during September 1906 in the Banff *Crag and Canyon* and a second article, "Lady Explorers on the Trail, Through the Pipestone Pass to the Saskatchewan River," published in *Rod and Gun and Motor Sports in Canada* later that year.[95] Both publications were illustrated with photographs made by Tuzo (at least one of which remains in her family's collection). The fifth woman, as Adams describes in a letter, was "Mrs. Schäffer's young friend Dorothy Sharp."[96] Any written record Dorothy Sharp may have made, whether a diary or letters, has yet to be found. She did make photographs, however, and sent prints to Tuzo.[97]

Schäffer's story is a short and entertaining tale about poorly matched trail companions. She did not name names. At first, she wrote, she was setting out to accompany "a charming Boston girl" to the Saskatchewan River. This was twenty-three-year-old Dorothy Sharp (b. 1883), the daughter of Schäffer's photographer colleague in Philadelphia, Virginia May Guild Sharp, and Dr. Benjamin Sharp (who had threatened to thwart Schäffer's admission to membership in the Academy of Natural Sciences in 1896).[98] In 1906, Sharp lived with her parents in Brookline, Massachusetts, near Boston.[99] Then Schäffer added, "A quiet, little eastern woman asked if she and a companion might join our small party." This was Molly Adams from New Haven, Connecticut. Adams's companion was her friend Zephine Humphrey (1874–1956), a fiction and short essay writer who lived in Dorset, Vermont, with her husband and children. "Then another party," Henrietta L. Tuzo (1873–1957), born in Victoria, British Columbia, but who had spent much of her life in England, "asked if she might join us." By her account, Schäffer welcomed the women who asked to join the group, but later came to regret doing so.

By 1906, Schäffer had spent almost eighteen summers in the Rockies. In contrast, it was Humphrey's first trip to the Canadian Rockies, and first time on horseback. She was the only newcomer, however. Falling between these extremes of experience were Sharp and Tuzo, both seasoned mountaineers, and Molly Adams.[100] Tuzo was a founding member of the Alpine Club of Canada and, in May of 1906, Schäffer had nominated Sharp as a graduating member of that same group.[101] On 21 July that year, Tuzo made a first ascent of Peak Seven in the Valley of the Ten Peaks, later named Mount Tuzo in her honour. Tuzo and Sharp had returned from that climbing expedition just two days before setting out with Schäffer, Adams, and Humphrey on what Tuzo called their "long trip."[102] When she joined the group at Schäffer's invitation, Adams was an experienced outdoorswoman, having hiked and camped in the Alps, Adirondacks, and Canadian Rockies.[103] In her manuscript, Schäffer refers to Adams two or three times as her "little new friend," implying that she and Adams first met on this trip, although they had in fact met in 1904, as Adams's correspondence shows.

Written with customary wit, Schäffer described a group that "had separated as oil and water figuratively," although no "unkind words" were ever exchanged.[104] While Schäffer and her "new friend" "loved every moment of the day, every mile of the trail," the two "knew the others were beginning to think the whole jaunt a perfect bore."[105] The worst of it, Schäffer wrote, was when the three "strangers," as she called them, wanted to end the two-week trip three days early so as to return to a much longed-for bathtub. Schäffer intervened, salvaging the time by claiming that she never travelled on Sundays, just as the group of three had claimed they never would either, and as the next day was Sunday, the group remained in camp.[106] This led to a guilty conscience, Schäffer confessed in her manuscript, as she and "the little new friend" had, in fact, whispered to each other about not wasting Sundays by staying in camp rather than travelling the trail as they normally would.[107] Did Schäffer really do this and feel this way, or did she simply add it to a tale based on experience and then embellished, rather in the spirit of a campfire gathering?

The novice trail rider Zephine Humphrey, the only member of the group who may not have been an acquaintance of Schäffer's prior to the trip, not only wrote about the journey but also published her account of it in "Five Women

›FIGURE 3.16

Tepee and sweat lodge frameworks, [Mary W. Adams and/or Mary Schäffer photograph], 1906.

Mary Schäffer hand-tinted lantern slide [WMCR V439/PS1-308]

on the Trail." Adams's photographs that illustrate the article encompass mainly landscapes, often populated with pack horses, a row of women on horseback riding ahead of the photographer, and one featuring an Indigenous marker in the wilderness—the frame of a sweat lodge seen near one of their tents at Dustheap Camp. (Similar photographs also appeared in Tuzo's illustrated *Rod and Gun* article.) Prints of a few of the published Adams photographs are in Schäffer and Adams's albums in the Whyte Museum archives (Figs. 3.3 and 3.4), as well as others from the journey that were not published. Schäffer produced hand-tinted lantern slides of some of the photographs, as well, such as one of tepee and sweat lodge frameworks.

Humphrey's version of events both corroborates and contradicts aspects of Schäffer's story, suggesting that both authors employed a mix of fact and fiction, memory and imagination to craft their travel narratives for the entertainment of their readers. Like Schäffer, Humphrey does not name names. Unlike Schäffer, she does use pseudonyms, and these are easily unveiled: Schäffer became "Mrs. Selwin"; Adams was "Doe"; Sharp was "Gypsy"; and Tuzo was "Britannia." Guides William Warren (called "Chief" in Schäffer's *Old Indian Trails*) and Dan ("Danny") Campbell became Weston and Cobell.[108] Campbell's dog was called Lulu. Photographer Elliott Barnes, whom they encountered on the Kootenay Plains where he homesteaded from 1905 to 1908, was named Mr. Bradley.[109]

For Zephine Humphrey, the adventure began months earlier:

> *I had never had the least belief in the whole experience from the time Doe had said to me, in the spring, in New York: "Why don't you come to the Canadian Rockies with me this summer?" and I, opening my mouth to deprecate the impossible suggestion, had surprised myself by replying: "Why not!"*[110]

Upon arrival in the Rockies in early July, they visited Lake Louise and then Glacier National Park to climb Mount Afton.

> *But better still than the climbing of mountains was the rare opportunity which came to us presently. Mrs. Selwin, a friend of Doe's, had been a frequenter of the Canadian Rockies for some fifteen years. All the usual short trips she had taken, some of them several times. Now at last her ambition was shaping itself for an enterprise hitherto untried by the feminine tourist. She was going north to the Kootenay Plains, over the Pipestone Pass. Two friends had agreed to*

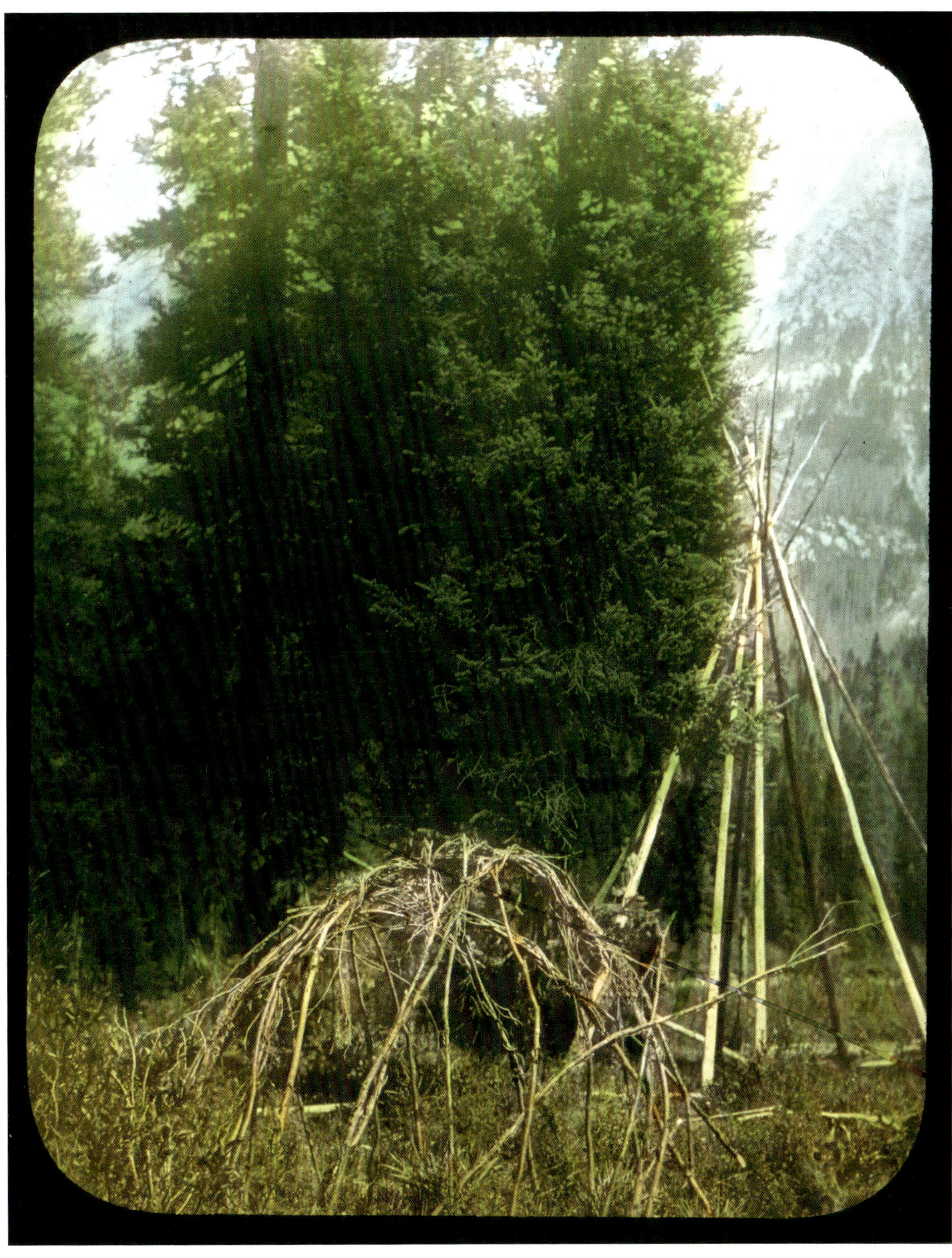

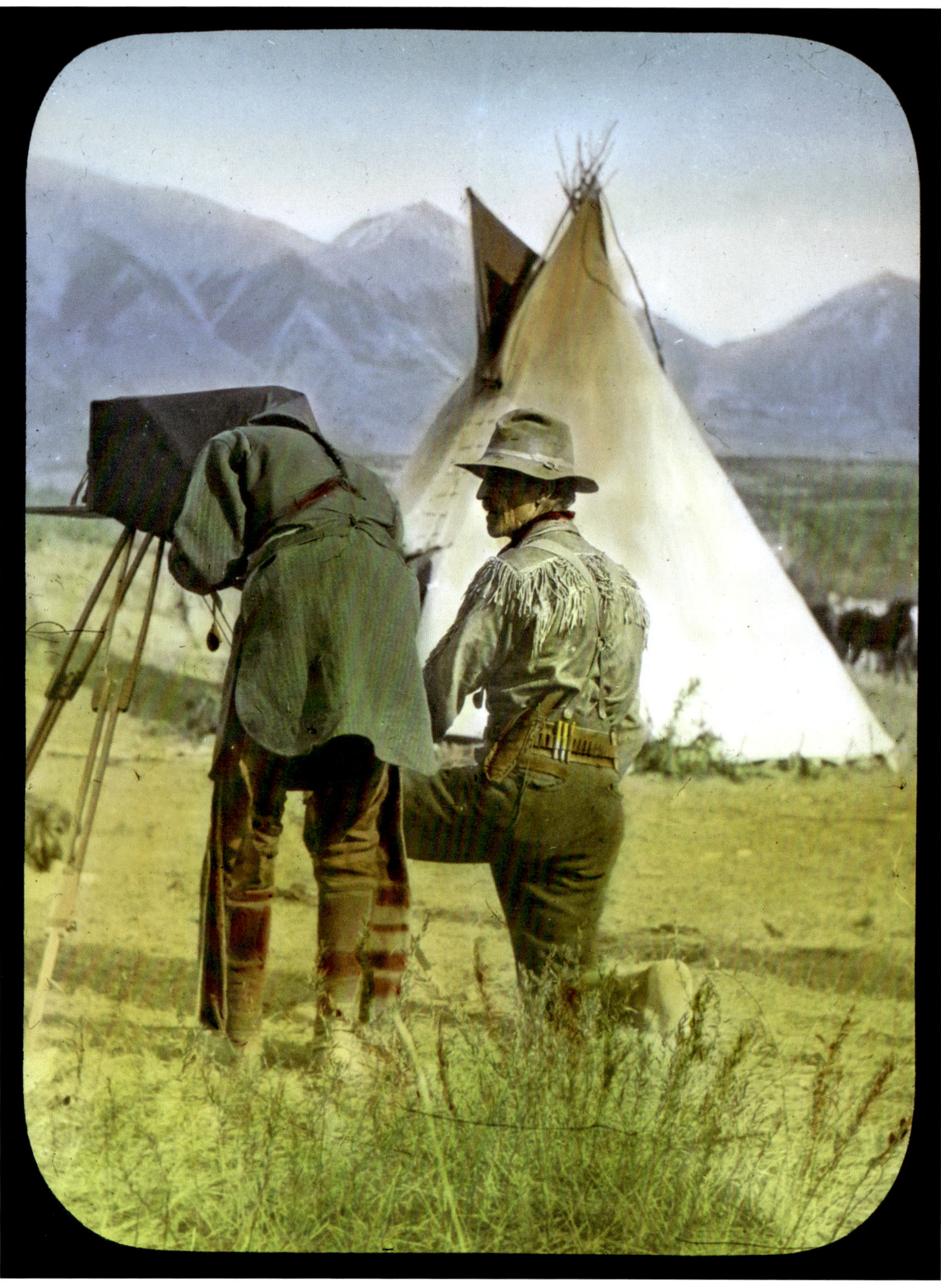

accompany her; would Doe and I also come along and share the fine adventure? Would we! Doe's eyes sparkled, as she turned away from the telephone, having received the exciting message. But I—what a doubtful tenderfoot! She shook her head over me for two hours before I could persuade her of my sufficient prowess, and even then she consented merely because she is one of those rare and priceless friends who understand the glorious necessity of taking risks in this world. She ordered a horse, and bade me ride, until I was black and blue and lame and stiff and aching in every joint. It is my first and last advice to anyone intending a trip to the Canadian Rockies: learn how to ride in time.[111]

‹FIGURE 3.17
Elliott Barnes demonstrating his camera to unidentified Stoney man, photographer unknown, 1907.
[Mary Schäffer] hand-tinted lantern slide
[WMCR V439/PS1-35]

There are many contradictory details in the two stories that cannot—and perhaps need not—be reconciled: in Humphrey's version, Schäffer and Adams were already acquainted, as Adams's diary and correspondence from 1904 attest; and while Schäffer had attributed the impetus of the trip to her accompaniment of a Bostonian to the Saskatchewan River, and claimed that the extra three travellers had asked to join them, Humphrey sets it out as an ambitious, new ride for women mountain trail travellers conceived of by the long-experienced Schäffer, who recruited participants. Adams's correspondence corroborates Humphrey's claim that Schäffer called Adams after their arrival in the Rockies.[112]

Adams's account of events was written in a series of letters to her sister Catherine Elkin immediately before and after the trip. On 17 July, Adams wrote from Laggan, now known as the hamlet of Lake Louise, and at that time a CPR stop.

All our plans as to what next have been entirely changed by hearing from Mrs. Schäffer this morning. She has just come out of the Yoho and is at Field and telephoned to find if we had arrived, and invited us to go on a three weeks pack trip. At first I said no, because I did not think Zephine would care for it, but on the contrary she is wildly enthusiastic, so we are going. I think it will be great. We are going north towards the sources of the Saskatchewan and Athabasca.[113]

The group departed on 24 July, after Sharp had sufficient time to rest and recover from the climbing expedition with Tuzo.[114] On 11 August, one day after arriving back in Laggan at the end of the sixteen-day trip, Adams wrote,

We came in yesterday from our packing trip sooner than we expected, for various reasons—the principal one being that we came to a river and we couldn't get across—to wit, the Saskatchewan. It was a mighty roaring flood and they would not let us attempt it....

I came back with mixed feelings because Zephine, in spite of the enthusiasm with which she started, did not find camping to her taste, and I guess this will learn me a lesson never to take people camping again on such a long trip who don't know anything about it. And yet I could not help enjoying myself, although I knew she was having such a bad time and getting so tired every day, and my apology for a conscience told me as well as it could that it was all my fault for bringing her. I did think it was rash but she liked the horseback rides we took beforehand so much, and did so very well that I thought she would get into training in a few days and then have the time of her life, but she didn't. The dirt of camp was too much for her poetic soul, and of course being tired everything seemed worse....

We were a party of five, and two guides, and we had 5 pack horses.... We hit it off very well except on a few occasions when Mrs. Schäffer and I, the only ones who really like camping as such, could not help taking sides against the others. As soon as we found that we could not cross the Saskatchewan and therefore would have to give up that part of the trip, those three wanted to make a break for home. Zephine had not told me then how tired she was, so I backed up Mrs. S. and we stayed and played about on the Kootenay Plains for 4 days. I daresay we should have done it anyway as it was Mrs. S's party, and she is a lady who quite often gets her own way too.[115]

Adams eventually offers a clue to the reason for the differing accounts, and confirms Schäffer's narrative approach to her writing. In Banff on 24 August, back from the divisive journey and in town to buy a buckskin coat and gloves for better warmth and protection on her second trip with Schäffer to the Kootenay Plains that same summer, she wrote to Catherine Elkin, "I kept a brief diary of facts. Mrs. S. kept one of facts and fiction, very amusing. She may publish part of it. Z. was the only one who did not sit down and write industriously! Miss Tuzo is going to send on an account of it to Rod and Gun but Mrs. S. says Miss T cannot write any better than an infant."[116]

Schäffer's harsh words, as recorded by Adams, may have been uttered in anger or frustration with Tuzo. They differ sharply in tone from those of a letter that Schäffer wrote to Tuzo two months earlier. Schäffer thanked Tuzo,

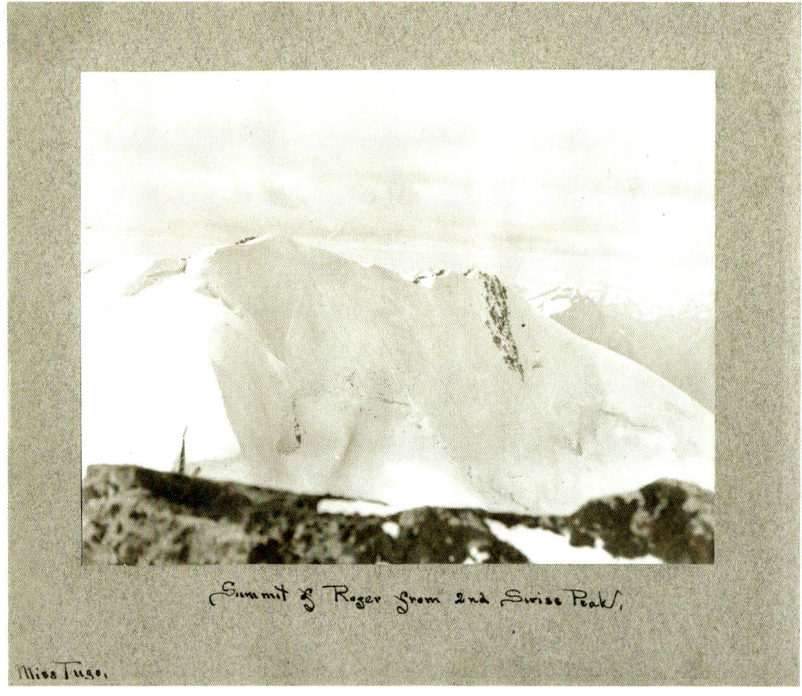

FIGURE 3.18
"Summit of Roger from 2nd Swiss Peak," Henrietta L. Tuzo photograph, 1906.
[WMCR V527/PD-1]

whom she addressed as "Dear New Old Friend," for how "the words of you two dear friends helped the ache. I shall just love you forever for it & you must not mind dear Miss Tuzo if I am very enthusiastic about your dear Mother."[117] Henrietta Tuzo not only published a piece in *Rod and Gun*, she also published in the Banff newspaper, *Crag and Canyon*. Neither article names her companions nor speaks of interpersonal events. Her diary is circumspect as well, but does record pithy observations that echo the others' stories about the trials of camp dirt as well as her particular view of Schäffer's behaviour that suggests a strong and opinionated personality, but not her own or any of the others. In the end, Tuzo gave Schäffer a print of a mountain summit photograph she had made. Schäffer pasted this in her album.

Tuzo first records meeting Schäffer in Banff on 7 June 1906. On 11 June, she wrote that "Mrs. S. is a most pleasant companion, she makes me paint with her & we go about a good deal together." On 2 July, along with Stewardson Brown and William Warren, Tuzo and Schäffer set out on a six-day trip to the Ptarmigan Valley, both women making photographs and, along with Brown, collecting botanical specimens for Brown and Schäffer's alpine manual. On 7 July, Tuzo commented that "Warren was a wonderful guide & the others most pleasant, so we had a jolly time."[118] But matters changed during the later trip to the Saskatchewan River. Tuzo was enthusiastic on their departure 24 July, noting "it was a bit sad saying goodbye to Mother for three weeks. But fancy! being off to the Saskatchewan!" Only three days later, however, the first words of discord appear. On the evening of Thursday, 26 July, "going to bed in good time, Dorothy & I doubled & sent Mrs. S. alone outside." The next morning, "how cross Mrs. S. was when she woke" after an uncomfortable night. That evening, things continued to sour. Following a day of riding, they stopped to camp and began by washing up: "We all had tubs in the river fine. Then Mrs. S. and I wrote while Dorothy started on rice for supper[.] The amounts to be cooked varied from one teaspoon to a cup a head. The result was an enormous [...] full, with stewed apples. Mrs. S.'s complaints were loud & bitter for she didn't properly appreciate it."[119]

The following day, Saturday, "We all had 'tubs' & laundry & a fine supper of ham & onions." Their next stopping point, dubbed "Dustheap camp," was not nearly as picturesque or comfortable as previous sites. On Tuesday, 31 July, Tuzo reported that despite the conditions "our tempers [are] a little improved[;] a great washing day & much cooking." They left that camp on Friday, "every one glad save Mrs. S. who seemed inclined to reproach us w[ith] a [wish] to leave...we are glad to leave that camp. No view & dust & dirt." At the end of the day, "we camped in a lovely meadow w. a deep creek on one side & little one close by so getting water was no hardship—we had lovely views also. Five bath-tubs in a row were in use in the deep creek & a lot of laundry was done. It was a lovely place." That was the weekend that the group decided to stay in camp as "some of the party were rather tired & as Sunday followed we thought it well to rest over." Things came to a head on Tuesday, 7 August, when Tuzo reported "Squalls w. Mrs. S about staying out." Not all ended with hard feelings, however, as on their last day out as they were returning to Laggan, Tuzo noted that Schäffer showed "lots of pluck & stayed on quietly though she was quite white" when her horse stumbled. On Saturday, 11 August, Tuzo reflected on her companions: "I am awfully sorry to leave Dorothy Sharp. She is a dear girl & evidently fond of me wh. is always nice! Miss Humphrey is literary, a poetess I believe. Miss Adams does analysis of igneous rocks at some college. She is to me an enigma." There was no comment on Schäffer other than a promise "to send her some printing paper & an album for Warren."[120]

Do such contradictions in versions of events matter? In some ways, no. These variations of detail are literary devices, which make for well-written and amusing tales. They are also a function of point of view, as well as memory. Adams's letters and Tuzo's diary were written while events were unfolding. Tuzo's articles appeared within months while Humphrey's articles appeared three years after the trip. Schäffer drafted her manuscript almost twenty years after the fact and as part of a larger story. Furthermore, Schäffer's writing was not published, and therefore not subject to comparison or corroboration with Tuzo's and Humphrey's series of articles that had appeared many years earlier. The reason why contradictions do ultimately matter, however, is because Schäffer's written work, published and not, has been recounted as historical fact by both biographers and historians since *Old Indian Trails* was first published in 1911. Taken as fact, they have bolstered the literary persona created by Schäffer as a historically extraordinary woman, someone who has subsequently been admired and even emulated by women following her tracks, or scorned by scholars who have read and reshaped the persona as a historical caricature of colonial contradictions and misbehaviour.[121] Neither of these is an accurate assessment. At best, they are misleading biographical and historical claims. Rather, as Adams testifies and other material evidence corroborates, Schäffer's work is a mixture of fact and invention. It deserves to be assessed and understood this way, as a popular and successful example of the literary practice of memoir rather than a documentary practice of history. The persona created by Schäffer and her work needs to be seen as standing separately from the actual person herself, who emerges spottily in correspondence (if Schäffer left any diaries, they have yet to be found) in all the complexity of any individual whose motives, actions, views, and memory change continuously over a lifetime, and are perceived by others in variable ways as well.

On one point, all accounts about the women on the 1906 trip agree: the party of five separated into two incompatible groups. Humphrey noted that "The adjustment of the party declared itself on that first afternoon. (For of course there must always be some division of five people into classes.) Britannia, Gypsy, and I wanted tea; Doe and Mrs. Selwin scorned it. It would seem a slight matter to stand as a test, but the accuracy of the determination was proved as time went on. Two perfectly hardy Amazons were Doe and Mrs. Selwin, desiring no alleviation of the difficulties of the wilderness; but the frailer children of civilization were Britannia, Gypsy, and I."[122] Given Tuzo's and Sharp's climbing accomplishments that year, and her own determination as a tenderfoot trail rider, Humphrey's description of herself and her like-minded companions is best appreciated as a storytelling device to enhance the tale with heightened contrasts, and one that would have been especially amusing to those who knew, or knew of, the players.

While in 1924 Schäffer described the group as oil and water, in 1909 Humphrey mobilized the contemporary metaphor of wilderness and civilization. Altogether, the four versions of events, as well as Tuzo's comments on the key players, shape a richer portrait of Mary Schäffer. She was clearly a strong-minded woman, who imagined and set out to pursue her goals and ambitions; she was energetic, in her element, intelligent, socially well-connected, serious about her pursuits in the Rockies, and taken seriously by those who knew her, women and men alike. As for the matter of bathtubs, there too there is agreement among Schäffer, Adams, Tuzo, and Humphrey, who wrote, "I have not mentioned the fact, by the way, that washing, particularly on the part of Britannia, Gypsy, and me, was a constant, engrossing occupation. Camp dirt was just too much for our spirits."[123] Adams corroborates this: "I am so glad a little dirt does not make me unhappy. That was almost the worst of poor Zephine's troubles. She could not sit down quietly and be contented when she was dirty, and of course one's hands are never immaculate, and seldom approximately clean for more than five minutes in camp."[124] And Tuzo reported on tubs frequently. Only Humphrey does not admit to an attempt to cut short the journey in favour of a return to "the land of bath-tubs."[125]

As for Schäffer and Adams, a partnership began to emerge on this trip when Adams had her first opportunity to serve as a geology resource for Schäffer: "Mrs. Schäffer is at this moment writing an article to be incorporated in a government report about the country we went over on our last trip, and I am supplying a few correct (I hope) geological phrases to describe it."[126] And so, Adams deployed knowledge that she had cultivated over the previous five years with Ida Ogilvie to assist Schäffer and thereby earn designation as "the geologist" in Schäffer's later recollections.[127] Subsequently, in biographical studies of Mary Schäffer, Molly Adams has been described as a geology teacher at Columbia College, the then male-only undergraduate college at Columbia University in New York City.[128] This description may have been derived from an October 1908 newspaper clipping, "Daring Explorers Make a Remarkable Trip to the Heart of the Canadian Rocky Mountains," preserved in Schäffer's scrapbook of articles about her travels and reviews of *Old Indian Trails*.[129] The unnamed reporter listed the members of the group, including "Miss Adams, who is a geologist connected with Columbian college in New York." There is no record in the Columbia University Archives' official university appointment cards file or administrative correspondence of Adams having been employed there in any capacity, however; nor is Adams listed as an instructor in Columbia's *Directories of Officers and Students 1900–1908*. Nevertheless, three archival remnants suggest that she was indeed "connected," as the reporter claimed—but rather than teaching geology, she appears to have worked in the winter and spring terms of 1907–1908, at least, as an assistant to her friend Professor Ida Ogilvie, who was on faculty at Columbia.

First, when she was admitted to membership in the Geographical Society of Philadelphia on 14 November 1906 as a nominee of Mary Schäffer, Adams's primary residence was recorded in the membership files as 477 Prospect Street, New Haven, Connecticut, where Adams continued to live with her sister and brother-in-law, Catherine and William Elkin (director of Yale Observatory), after her mother's death in 1902. A year later, on 26 November 1907, the address on her membership card was emended to the Brooks Hall residence of Barnard College (built in 1906–1907), adjacent to Columbia College, on Broadway and 116th Street in New York City. The address was changed back to Prospect Street in New Haven on 26 May 1908.[130] These addresses are corroborated in a second historical document: the passport application that Adams filed on 20 May 1908 on which she lists New Haven as her permanent residence and Brooks Hall as her mailing address for the passport. On that application, however, she simply put a stroke through the space designated for one's occupation.[131]

The third piece of evidence is a wistful comment made by Adams in a letter to Ogilvie. Writing from Field, British Columbia, on 26 September 1908, shortly after completion of that summer's journey with Schäffer to Maligne Lake and prior to leaving for Vancouver en route to Japan, Adams remarked, "I suppose college is about beginning soon. I hope you are well braced up from your summer, & I hope you will be able to have a proper assistant so you are not worked to pieces.…I may be back in N.Y. before the winter is over. I shall miss awfully having regular work to do. I feel already as if I were just trying to pass the time until I got at something."[132] Adams implies that she had been Ogilvie's assistant in the past and might have liked to return to the position or some other form of occupation.

The July 1906 trip to the Saskatchewan was just the first of four lengthy journeys north of the CPR line that Schäffer and Adams undertook together over the next two-and-a-half years. On 28 August, less than three weeks after returning from their ill-fated journey with Humphrey, Tuzo, and Sharp, the two set out again, alone except for their two guides, William Warren and Joe Barker, to return to the Kootenay Plains or "Saskatchewan country."[133] Adams wrote that she and Schäffer planned to locate a site on the Kootenay Plains on which to build their own log shack,[134] although nothing came of that plan. On 11 September at the Kootenay Plains, Adams wrote to her sister, "Zephine and that bunch would be dead if they were with us now (and so should we). We travel farther and faster, not stopping for lunch, but having it late when we get in, and then we usually have a walk or small climb in the afternoon."[135] This time they stayed out six weeks—until 12 October, riding about five hundred miles[136]—and were able to cross the North Saskatchewan River, which was "so low now that we crossed yesterday without getting our feet wet by hauling them up on the saddle."[137] There they met and photographed Stoney families who were in camp on their traditional territory, which resulted in a series of portraits of Frances Louise, Leah, and Sampson Beaver made by Schäffer. Adams wrote on 19 October from Field, where they were staying at Mount Stephen House, "We have been spending all day doing photos—and every day. Mrs. S. has some dandies, and some of mine are good as far as they go, and a lot ruined."[138] The lens on Adams's camera had worked loose during jarring rides on her horse, but the damage had gone unnoticed for some time.[139]

For Schäffer, writing in retrospect, Adams was remembered as "the finest pal any woman could ever have had."[140] "We never had a riffle of disagreement in the thousands of miles we meandered with ponies, we had daily pleasures in spite of rain and snow, heat and mosquitoes and heavenly days piled in between."[141] The two women's personalities and ambitions differed, but they seemed to agree on their compatibility as trail riders. Schäffer was extroverted and ambitious, and set specific destinations as goals for her journeys. Adams was introverted and easygoing with others, and most at home in an unstructured, outdoor society where neither sightseeing nor formal social events were required.[142] She travelled in the Rocky Mountains for the pleasure of doing so. Partnering with Schäffer made it possible for her to go farther afield from the railway backbone and experience a greater variety of landscape, geology, botany, and weather. For Schäffer, finding a compatible companion willing to go the distance no matter discomfort or trail troubles made her journeys not only pleasurable but also viable, and made *Old Indian Trails of the Canadian Rockies* not only viable but also successful. Schäffer's recollections years later may have been idealized by time and polished by a storytelling skill.

FIGURE 3.19

"Frances Louise Beaver and Her Family," Mary Schäffer photographs, 1906.

[WMCR V527/PD-1]

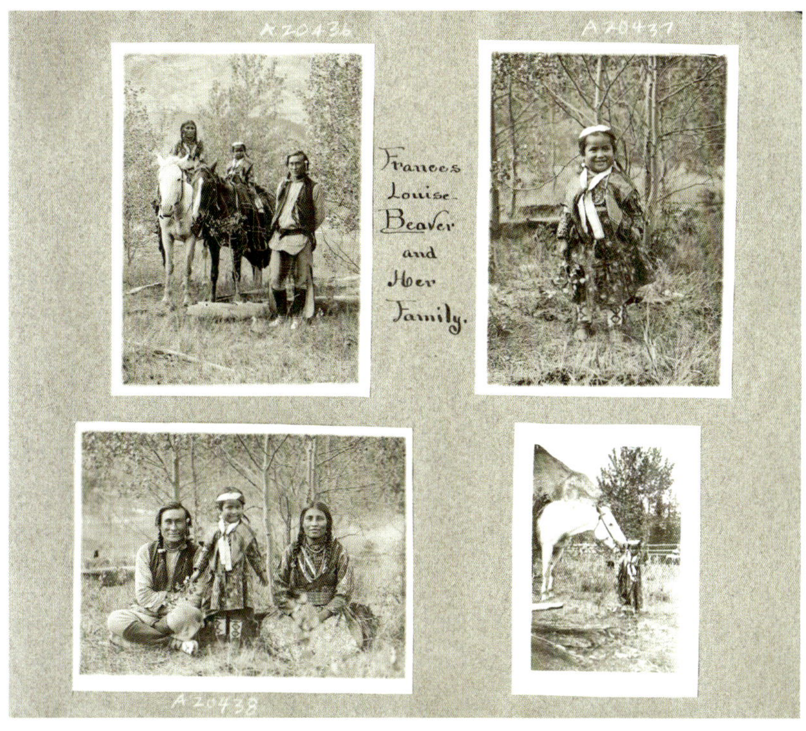

FIGURE 3.20

Frances Louise Beaver and her parents, Sampson and Leah Beaver, Mary Schäffer photographs, 1906.

[WMCR V527/PD-4]

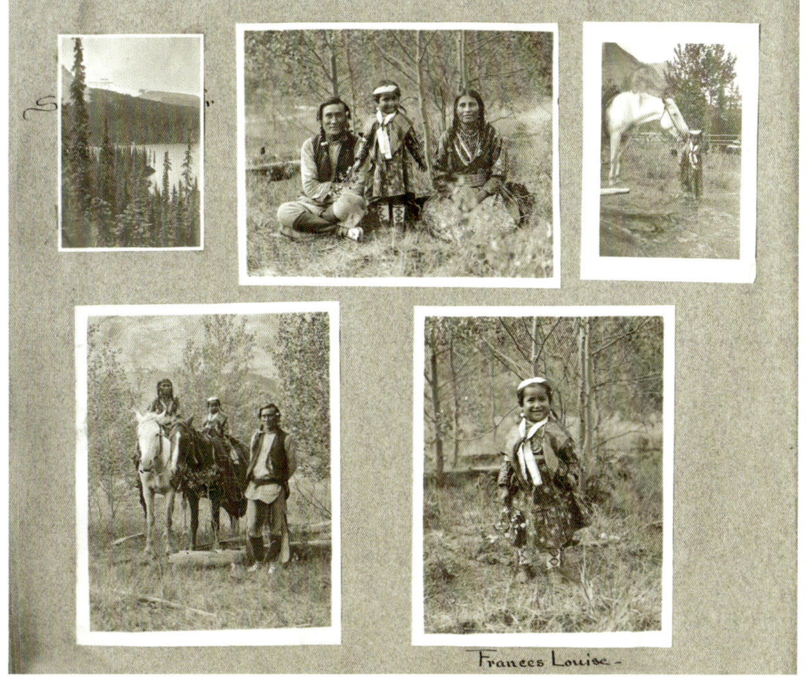

But perhaps not. Despite the number of women camping in the areas near the railway line and more and more who were climbing—one-third of the founding membership of the Alpine Club of Canada in 1906 were women—few were joining the surveyors and prospectors charting the backcountry. It was rugged going, and Schäffer and Adams were fortunate to find another woman able and willing to take it on. Writing from Banff to her sister during her first trip to the Rockies in 1904, when she and her friends first travelled and camped on their own, Adams had declared, "I should love to go from here with pack horses, guide, cook and driver, our selves of course riding too. Off into the mts. by Mt. Assiniboine which is called the Matterhorn of the Rockies, but it is a trip of a week or so and would cost ten dollars a day apiece, so we are not doing it. They have to have a driver for the pack horses as they won't go when led."[143] She did so in 1906 when she joined Schäffer on the two pack horse trips.

1906 proved to be a pivotal summer in the Rockies not only for Adams, but for Schäffer as well. Fieldwork for *Alpine Flora* reached its peak, and Schäffer began, as Zephine Humphrey stated, to expand the scope of her interest and ambition. *Alpine Flora of the Canadian Rocky Mountains* covers the area that Charles and Mary Schäffer had focused on between Banff, Alberta, and Glacier, British Columbia, the Lake Louise area south of the CPR station at Laggan, the Ptarmigan Valley, and part of the Pipestone Valley about thirty miles north of Laggan.[144] Even though Brown was credited as author, it was Schäffer's name and work that were publicized and cited after *Alpine Flora of the Canadian Rocky Mountains* was released in late 1907. In the late 1890s, Schäffer had staked as her scientific and photographic specialty the alpine flowers of the Canadian Rockies, and the quality of her work had been independently confirmed when it was included in the American women photographers' exhibition in Paris in 1900. The *New York Times* described the book as "distinctly a manual of the plants to be found within the limits of the Canadian Pacific Railway between Banff and Glacier. It is delightfully illustrated with over 120 views, thirty-one of which are beautifully colored."[145] The publisher, G.P. Putnam's Sons, gave Schäffer top billing in its display ads in the *New York Times* in December 1907.[146] *Alpine Flora* was also the work that Schäffer in later life named her most valuable, despite her range of journal articles and the popularity of *Old Indian Trails*, which appeared four years later. Even then, she downplayed the skill and quality of her painting and photography, stating, "I often think everything I have written is specially silly, the botany is the only thing of weight

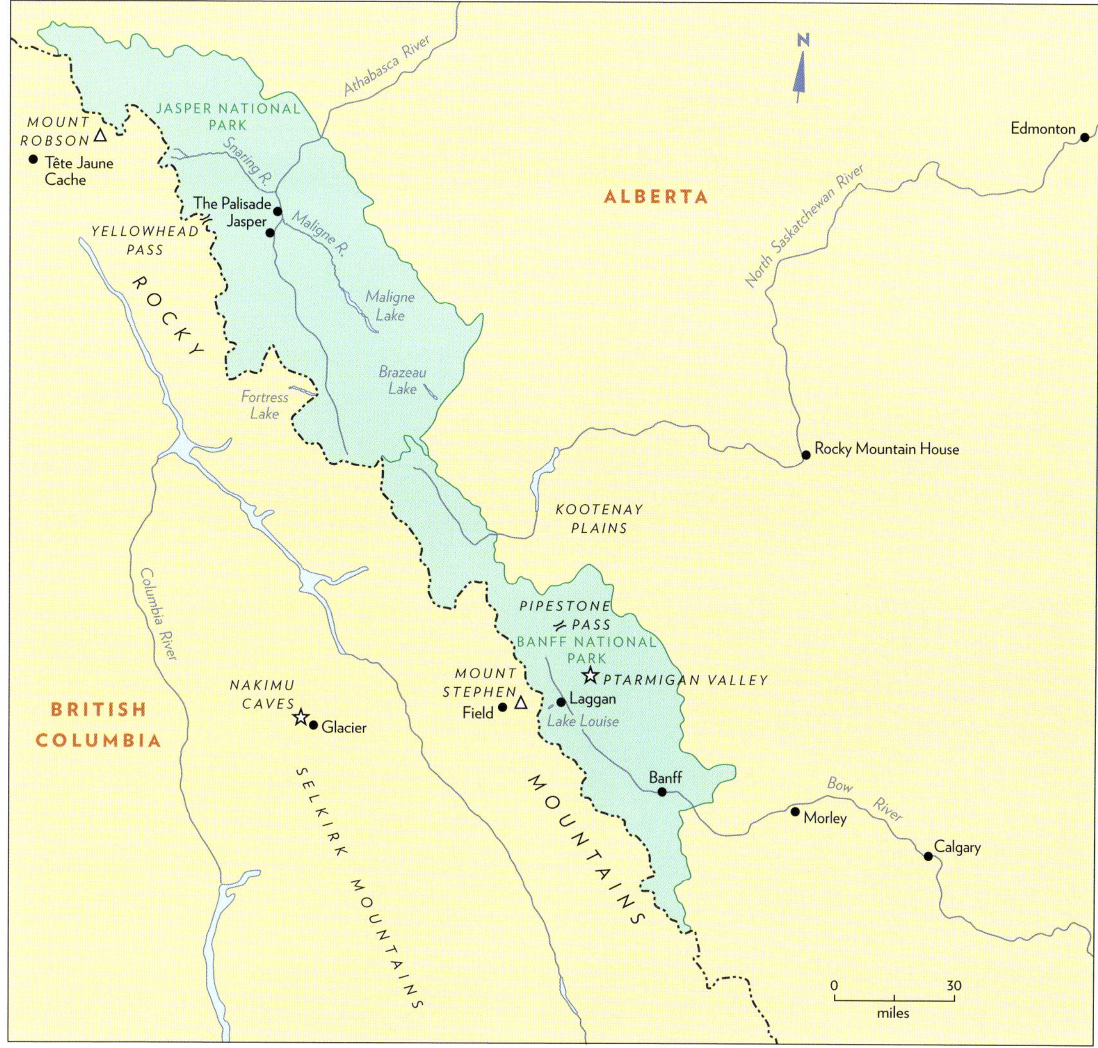

MAP 1
Rocky Mountains of Canada and region travelled by Mary Schäffer between 1889 and 1911.

and what I did about it was the mere mechanical part. Anyone who can sketch (correctly)[,] gather the plants, photograph accurately, and press the specimens, is not so direfully clever."[147]

Despite years of skill and success, in later life Schäffer downplayed her roles in achieving the quality and accomplishments for which both of her books were recognized. Why she did so is not known. It might have been a matter of portraying a persona of appropriately feminine modesty, despite her strength of mind and ambition as reported by Humphreys, Adams, and Tuzo. It might have been a sincere belief in the relative quality and value of her work and the value of science compared to that of travel writing. Or perhaps it was sage perspective toward the end of a varied and eventful life. Whatever the reason for her later views, critics at the time of publication of her works contended otherwise, especially when it came to her second book, *Old Indian Trails*. Even her rival Julia Henshaw was generous with praise for *Old Indian Trails*:

> *The actual difficulties, hardships and dangers of such expeditions are infinitely greater for a woman than the average reader would gather from reading Mrs. Schaeffer's tale. Two plucky women they were who followed these "Old Indian Trails," for they encountered difficulties without fear, and discomforts without a murmur, taking every ounce of delight out of the sunny days, the great guardian mountains, hours spent beneath the blue tent of the sky, and recking [*sic*] little of rain or other trials so far, to them, outweighed by the love of life on the trail....*
>
> *"Old Indian Trails" is an inspiration to go and do likewise, and the beautiful illustrations, reproduced from Mrs. Schaeffer's own photographs, with which the book is lavishly interleaved, will complete what the letterpress has begun—lead other women to go out on the trail in the most wonderful region in Canada, the Rocky Mountains.*[148]

In 1911, an unnamed reviewer for the *New York Times* worked deeply the vein of gender that Schäffer's book presented, recognized the achievement of travelling the trails and charting the lake, and commended the quality of the writing and photography:

> *In reading "Old Indian Trails," by Mary Schäffer, it is difficult to decide just what impresses us most: the excellence of the writing, the picturesqueness of the country described, or the personality of the author herself. All three elements, indeed, work together in making this a most enjoyable outdoor book, but without doubt the average lover of the wilds will dwell longest upon the personality. For always the wildernesses have belonged to the male. Physiological facts and temperamental tendencies have seemingly ordained that it should be so....*
>
> *Now the trails described in this book are hard ones, and the traveler-author is a woman; wherefor [*sic*], any trail-wise man who does not figuratively remove his hat as he reads, is no sportsman and wouldn't "split fair" with a comrade....*
>
> *Mrs. Schäffer, among other things may lay claim to the distinction of having placed a new lake upon the map, which fact in itself should commend her book to all amateur explorers....*

> *Although there was much picturesque scenery along the various trails, there are no verbal flights of sentimental ecstasy to be endured, nor is there any attempt on the part of the author to prove to the reader what a rarely sympathetic soul she has. She is sincere, as all good travelers should be. One sees it all and longs to go there too. A genuine, quiet love of beauty, considerable descriptive ability, and an active sense of humor join to make the book worth reading. The hundred photographs taken by the author are remarkably fine.*[149]

Schäffer was successful in creating a persona that immediately captured early twentieth-century readers' imaginations and continued to do so among the generations that followed. Although the reviewer praises Schäffer alone for the "remarkably fine" photographs, Schäffer acknowledged the contributions of her collaborators and credited the success of her travels to a group effort. She cast her persona as that of an energetic, modest, somewhat witty woman with a strong constitution, whose quest with Adams matched that of men for rigour, and demanded that it be acknowledged and respected as such.

Old Indian Trails of the Canadian Rockies

Mary Schäffer's second book, *Old Indian Trails of the Canadian Rockies*, is of an entirely different genre, and her role in its creation of an entirely different scope from the first. Brown and Schäffer's *Alpine Flora of the Canadian Rocky Mountains* was intended to serve both the annals of botanical knowledge and readers with either professional or amateur interest in the subject matter, as well as the educated, nature-oriented tourist and traveller visiting the Canadian Rockies. It was based upon years of gathering, documenting, and describing natural specimens. In contrast, *Old Indian Trails* is a book about human activity and the writer's personal experience. It was also one that attracted the broader audience that most travel narratives seek—not only tourists but also those reading both to expand their geographic knowledge of the world and to enjoy vicariously the writer's adventures and lessons learned from her experiences in the places to which author and reader journey. Like *Alpine Flora*, *Old Indian Trails* was a product of years of collaborative enterprise, this time with Molly Adams as fellow traveller, diarist, and photographer. As was the processes of writing and illustrating the two books, the journeys recounted in *Old Indian Trails* were also collaborative, involving guides William Warren ("Chief") and Sidney Unwin (called "K" in the book), and others along the way.

Studies of Schäffer's life, writing, and photographs treat *Old Indian Trails* as documentary in nature. It undoubtedly is in many ways—Schäffer, Adams, Warren, and Unwin did follow the routes described and find the geographical landmarks they were seeking. But Schäffer's book is more and other than documentary. *Old Indian Trails* is above all an imaginative and selective memoir of past events that shares both the personal impact and higher meaning experienced by the author. Schäffer recalled that her young nephew, Eric Sharpless,

> *loved my stories and so I gathered them one by one from our diaries leaving out [so] much of the funny part—those who write are forced to leave out the best and there are times when I want to write a new book of an old trail, but there is so much too sacred now on which to touch.*
>
> *"K" fell in France, Mollie lies in Kobe. I could not tell our dear yarns which came out round the camp-fire you know.*[150]

When writing the narrative, however, she cast the stories as truthful: "From now on I shall keep before me the worn, thumbed, much-jeered-at diary; its lead-pencil-smudged pages (in many places nearly obliterated) are dear to the eyes of its owner, and it is at least a record of the heart-beats day by day."[151] In the context of *Old Indian Trails*' storyline, the recordings of their day-to-day activities in diaries, along with the photographs "by the Author and by Mary W. Adams" and Schäffer's map, are deployed as primary evidence of the truth of Schäffer's story. Rather than write a merely descriptive work recounting the facts of where they went and what they saw, Schäffer fleshed out events recorded in Adams's diary, and her own, from which she claims to quote directly from time to time in *Old Indian Trails*,[152] although no such diaries (if she kept any) or letters to family appear to have survived.

Schäffer's voice in *Old Indian Trails* is one of welcome, humour, and friendliness, as if the reader were a companion along the way. It is in many ways a memoirist's voice of "tranquility," such as Helen M. Buss describes in her study of women's memoir, which "re-experiences the event, reprocesses it more fully than it could have been felt and understood in the first instance, and comes to an understanding of the event for the purpose of increasing the 'tranquility' of the memoirist's present self…tranquility…implies the composure, the peace of mind, the more complete understanding that comes from having done the hard work of remembering the past."[153] Schäffer's later reflections on the journeys and her account of them align with this description. In a letter written in 1928, she told her correspondent, Raymond Zillmer, who had been seeking a copy of her book,

> *Just one more about the story which cannot be written in a book. No one may know I went among those hills with a broken heart and only on the high places could I learn that I and mine were very close to-gether. We dare not tell those beautiful thoughts, they like to say "explorer" of me, no, only a hunter of peace. I found it....*
>
> *Its* [sic] *hardly nice to mention the quiet, dear spots, but you liked my wee book and somehow I want you both to know there is a lovely song of thanks in it which could never be ~~read~~ published* [sic].[154]

Here, Schäffer movingly portrays her private experience of the journeys, which underpins the stories told in the book but could not be included among them. And while Schäffer's narrative is of a past of real events that involved more players than the writer alone, Buss reminds us "acts of imagination are involved in constructing a memoir."[155]

As memoir, Schäffer's story is based on her experience; its purpose, however, as expressed in the book's preface, is to explore and express the human experience in a particular time, place, and social context, rather than to document events. It is about gender and social roles, mountain exploration and exploitation, civilization and wilderness in modernity, and emotional health. Buss defines memoir as something that "does not claim to be a 'complete history,' but rather the testimony of the writer who has 'personal knowledge' of the events, the era, or the people that are its subject. As a result, in terms of historical studies, the memoir serves as a historical resource rather than a historical discourse. Thus, memoir continues to occupy a marginal status in historical studies as well as in literary studies. Yet memoir endures as a much used form of discourse in Western culture because of its accessibility."[156]

This tone of accessibility is more literary than documentary and, Buss argues, is established by writing in the first person—that is, in the more intimate and expressive voice of the author who stakes her place in the story.[157] This voice stands in contrast to the third-person voice of the historian, for example, who speaks at a distance and from outside, without first-hand experience of the event under discussion. The first-person voice is that of the diarist as well, and Molly Adams's voice resonates in the published narrative that originates, at least in part, in her diary. Like their travels and photographs, the text of *Old Indian Trails* is a shared and collaborative venture. Unlike a diarist, however, the memoirist already knows how the story ends—in this case, knows of the death of one of the travellers just months later. And yet Schäffer's narrative captivates the reader with a sense of the tension of the unknown, startling, or frightening—and the relief, humour, or joy of the aftermath of an event that Schäffer and her companions experienced. Schäffer's call to those seeking adventure or solace continues to resonate with her readers, especially women, a century later. Michale Lang, for example, opens her 2011 book *An Adventurous Woman Abroad* with a chapter entitled "Mary and Me," and a story:

> *When I hike the trails that Mary Schäffer's hobnail boots trod 100 years ago, I feel a kinship to this famous Victorian woman adventurer of the Canadian Rockies. I consider what I might have in common with her. Perhaps most important, Mary came to the Canadian Rockies as a "hunter of peace." I too come to these mountains seeking peace. I share her love of the mountains, of alpine meadows, clear glacial lakes, wildflowers and wild creatures. Banff has become my home as it was hers. Like her, I am interested in photography and art, although I share her talent for neither. Mary's deep interest in indigenous people and history is the other common ground we walk. Mary was an extraordinary woman for her time, but she is someone I can easily relate to.*[158]

Schäffer's voice is a persuasive one, too, and has spawned a sense of familiarity and even intimacy with her among the many writers who call her "Mary." Not even Molly Adams took that liberty in personal correspondence for the first four years of their acquaintance; she was accorded at first the respectful "Mrs. Schäffer," and then "Mrs. S.," and finally, in 1908, "M." Schäffer's style also inspires a style of writing in the first person that includes personal anecdotes and self-deprecation. The ability to create a narrative to which readers relate so readily, evidenced in reviews at the time of publication as well as a century later, is a mark of the accomplishment of Schäffer's work. But it is also a mark of the success of Schäffer's creation of a persona that was admired as extraordinary and yet resonated with readers and their own senses of identity and ambition.

Where Schäffer's memoir does not venture is into the private and personal realm of her grief or her relationships. Her book is neither documentary nor autobiography. While she admits to seeking and finding peace after grief, she does not share or lay bare the emotional process for her readers. Nor does she include any sense of personal relationships, beyond mutual respect and friendship, among those with whom she travelled. In an overview of American women's travel writing, Susan L. Roberson states, "Not only was the traveling woman at sexual risk, but in the nineteenth century she posed a threat to patriarchy and social order." Perhaps, Roberson contends, that is why women (like Schäffer) travelled with others: "By making it clear that they are not women alone, these authors assure readers that whatever else they may have transgressed, they were not crossing boundaries of sexual comportment or threatening established standards of sexual morality....Even when sexual adventure is part of the journey, the details are left to the reader's imagination as they draw the veil on that part of their story."[159]

In late 1936, writing to a woman who had recently taken a pack horse trip to Maligne Lake following Schäffer and Adams's route, Schäffer wrote of *Old Indian Trails* as her "rather silly book. Of course I love it, because it was so filled with private personalities. Very little of the whole ever showed and we dare not say too many things. But to us, it was a great trip—this seeking for unknown land and lake."[160] Adams, in her usual, more understated way, concurred in 1908: "We are glad we got there, for of course we never should have been satisfied otherwise, but we all agreed that our next trip to the Athabasca would be by train (railroad train, not pack train). It certainly was amusing at times, and like nothing I ever hope to experience again. I mean the society of the trail."[161]

Only in private correspondence did Schäffer so much as allude to interpersonal relationships, the silence about which in the book has led to speculation in later studies.[162]

> *Our evenings at the camp-fire were the best of the day because we could always talk on* ANY *sub. Mollie was the geologist, I am an imitation botanist (sort of copy-cat)[,] Mr. Warren had been a soldier as had Sid in the So. African war and the men with the horses were all educated. I meant by that there was the most perfect harmony and could all parties go out and have the times we did there would be no one left in the hotels. We would be gone 5 mo. and never a dissenting voice. You cannot get that in civilization.*[163]

Schäffer's later recollections contrast with Adams's observations written less than a month after their return from Maligne Lake.

Camplife was as agreeable as ever to me, although plentifully diversified with bugs of all kinds, and the inevitable bad trails or no trail at all, rain, snow and deep rivers, and an occasional lost temper. Which do you suppose feels the most uncomfortable, the one whose temper has gone queer on them, or the others who are left standing on tiptoe trying to say the right thing at the right time? Four people shut off from the world for almost four months and not having a few fights would be an impossibility I suppose, although I really don't see why they should get mad about it. This sounds as if we were scratching and biting all of the time, which is not the case. I forgot, there were six of us at first, and some of the hard feeling departed off with them, the two others, when they left us and drove their reluctant cayuses away from the bunch, on the home trail.[164]

While Schäffer undertook the journeys in part as a means to assuage her grief (and of this there is no doubt; the distressed tone of her letters to George Vaux Jr. in early 1904 is evidence enough), those journeys also served as a bridge from the married life she had so much enjoyed for the intellectual, social, physical, and creative pursuits at its centre to one of widowhood with new companions, ambitions, goals, and accomplishments. As with the journeys and the completion of *Alpine Flora of the Canadian Rocky Mountains*, Schäffer's writing of *Old Indian Trails* may also have had therapeutic value, as she began that manuscript following yet another death of a close companion and wrote it during a winter of health problems, likely the winter of 1909–1910.[165] Molly Adams died of pneumonia in late January 1909 while travelling with Schäffer in Japan, a trip that had immediately followed their return from Maligne Lake the previous summer. She dedicated the book to Adams and directed it most specifically to others suffering pain to encourage them to seek catharsis in the mountains.

Catharsis was not the only motivating force for writing *Old Indian Trails*, however, any more than it had been for completing *Alpine Flora*. Schäffer was ambitious and enjoyed the taste of her work's success both critically and financially. Throughout the years, Schäffer had been telling tales of her journeys both to entertain and to educate her young nephew, but also in public talks to colleagues and friends in Philadelphia and West Chester, Pennsylvania, accompanied by photographs and lantern slides.[166] The interest of others in her journeys, the opportunities that membership in the Geographical Society of Philadelphia offered to make illustrated presentations, the desire and perhaps the encouragement of others to publish, her ambitions to support herself and to demonstrate women's capacity to do so, experiencing and valuing success for herself and on her terms—these all flow and fuse in her work. The warm reception of critics and readers of the book, which was widely reviewed, sold out two printings, and was still being sought twenty years later, secured Schäffer's status among early twentieth-century travel writers.[167] Perhaps more importantly to her, these things also cemented her place in relation to her Canadian mountain peers, those men known as explorers whom she had watched leave for "the wonders of the more northern Rockies…the vast, glorious, unexplored country beyond" while preparing to undertake her own, grander journeys.[168]

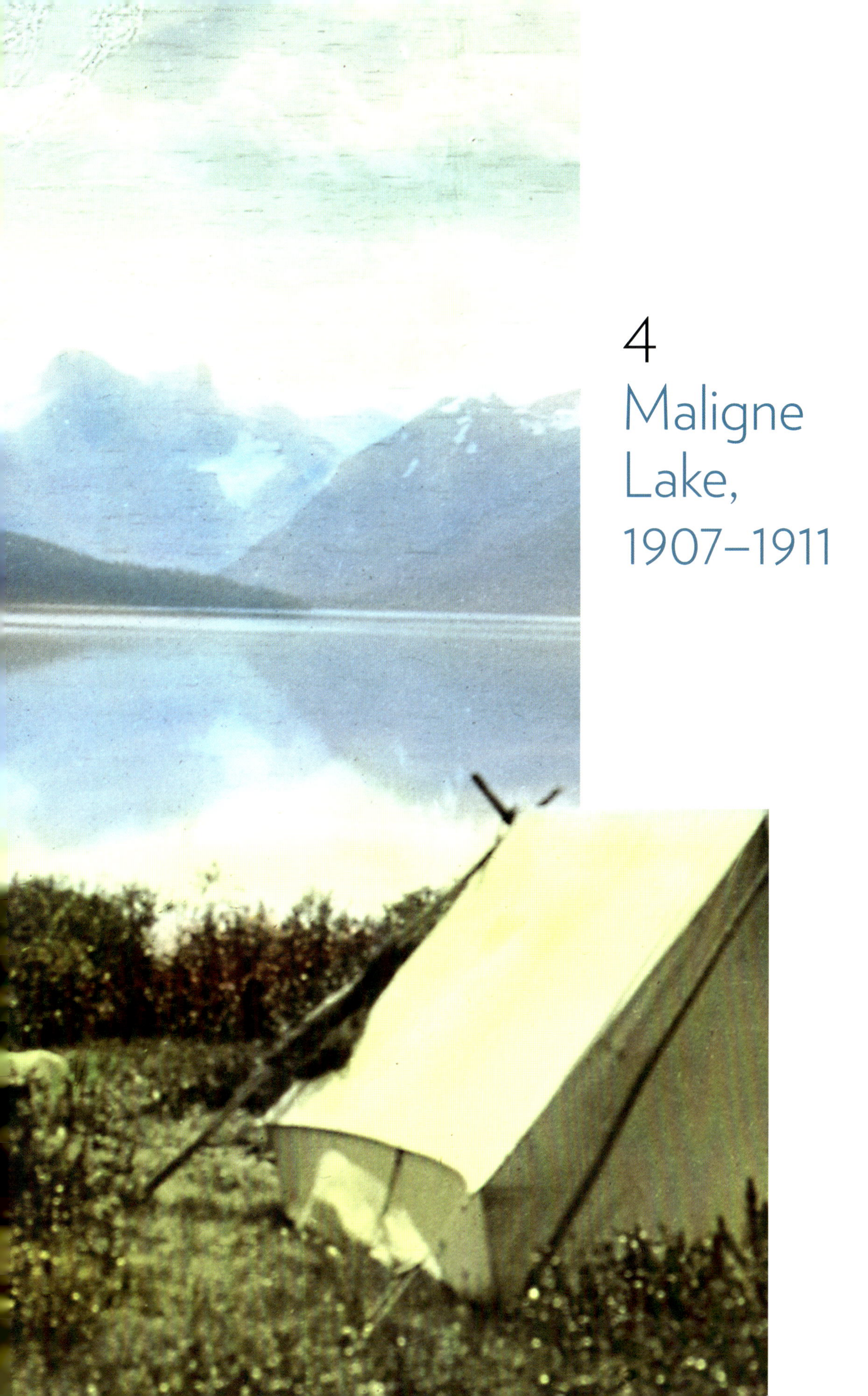

4
Maligne Lake, 1907–1911

ON 8 MAY 1911, Mary Schäffer wrote to George Vaux Jr. in Philadelphia, from the Canadian Pacific Railway's Place Viger Hotel in Montreal.

> *There is still a large bill coming in on "Indian Trails". That will come to thee to pay, as I may be far in the hills when it comes. Does thee call that extravagance? I don't. I'm living now. I'm meeting people, doing things, thinking, working. Mayhaps that thousand dollars will come back to me. If it does thee shall have every red cent of it as principle. I've put in $462. It will foot up [...] over $1000 I think. The C.P.R. is taking it for hotels and trains. The G.T.P. [Grand Trunk Pacific] is doing the same. The latter is also ordering 1000 copies of the map (with the book & my name attached) to be published in a book they are getting out. Putnam's & I think this a good stroke of business.*[1]

By spring 1911, seven and half years had passed since her husband Charles's death, and much had happened in the intervening time. Not the least was Schäffer's emergence as a woman of public renown in Rocky Mountain travel literature and exploration, and one of independent financial means. Moreover, in contrast to the tone of deep grieving evident in her 1904 letter, she was now looking to the future rather than the past, active and optimistic: "meeting people, doing things, thinking, working." In May, she was on her annual trip to the Canadian Rockies. This year, however, she had been contracted by the Geological Survey of Canada to return to Maligne Lake in June to undertake a survey on its behalf. She was about to chart for the Government of Canada the legendary Chaba Imne just as her second book, *Old Indian Trails: Incidents of Camp and Trail Life, Covering Two Years' Exploration through the Rocky Mountains of Canada*, was coming off the press in New York City. In 1909 and 1910, Schäffer had published two articles on the trip to Maligne Lake as well as a booklet about the Rockies for Soo Line Railway in Minneapolis, a subsidiary of the CPR.[2] She had staked her claim to the region, and had attracted the attention of public servants at the Geological Survey of Canada in the process.

In a moment of seemingly serendipitous coincidence, the federal government decided to reduce dramatically the areas in the Rocky and Selkirk Mountains that had been reserved as wilderness parks. One of those areas, the 4,400-square-mile Jasper Forest Reserve, had been established in fall 1907 and encompassed the uncharted area where Schäffer's group found Maligne Lake the following summer. On 19 May 1911, while Schäffer was in Banff prior to departing a second time for Maligne Lake, the Jasper reserve was reduced to a mere 1,000 square miles running just 50 miles long and 10 miles deep on either side of the new Grand Trunk Pacific railway tracks that had been laid through the area. Many of the region's most fragile and compelling ecological and geographical landmarks, including Maligne Lake and its surrounding area, were thereby excluded from the protective boundaries of the forest reserve. The publication of *Old Indian Trails* and Schäffer's return to chart the lake could not have been timelier.

Just as Mary Schäffer crafted a public persona through literary mixing of fact and fiction in accounts of her travels in the Rockies to both inform and entertain readers, so too was she instrumental in crafting an idea of "Maligne Lake." The most enduring impact of Schäffer's travels, magazine articles, and books is that the imagery and texts she published shaped a conceptual evolution of Maligne Lake. For Schäffer, it began as a rumour reported by a non-Indigenous guide who had been told of a legendary lake known by the Stoney. With Schäffer's quest to locate the lake that Indigenous people knew but only one Euro-North American had ever seen, the area entered the imagination as wilderness. With the first published photograph of it, the lake was transformed into landscape, a culturally mediated perception of a wilderness space. Finally, renamed, charted, described, and made physically accessible to travellers, Maligne Lake became a place. Previously known as and named Chaba Imne by the Stoney, the lake, its environs, and its flora, fauna, and inhabitants passed through these phases between 1906 and 1912 in the eyes, imagination, and understanding of members of American and British scientific societies through Schäffer's lantern slide lectures and journal articles. Explorers, climbers, hikers, and other tourists also came to know Maligne Lake as presented by Schäffer's articles in the journal of the Alpine Club of Canada and popular travel magazines, as did readers and reviewers of travel literature through *Old Indian Trails of the Canadian Rockies*.[3] Integral to the documented and imagined Maligne Lake that Schäffer produced are images, specifically photographs and maps, four of which are iconic representatives of the conceptual evolution of Maligne Lake.

This evolutionary process is a concept that toward the end of the twentieth century engaged another woman photographer visiting Alberta—Marlene Creates, who in 1985 observed, "The land is important to me but even more important is the idea that it becomes a 'place' because someone has been there."[4] Later, in her work *Language and Land Use, Alberta 1993*, Creates explored the contradiction and elision of "natural" areas conserved as public spaces for recreation where, she observed, "human activity is considered undesirable"—except for "the roads and parking lots that have been put there for our convenience in arriving. I am fascinated by the different layers of history—'natural' and human—that can occur *in the same place*."[5]

Maligne Lake is a "natural" area of sublime beauty, conserved as a public space for human recreation in Jasper National Park—thanks in part to the intervention of Schäffer herself in 1911.[6] As such, it has been protected from development—except for the roads that lead to it, the parking lot that adjoins it, the groomed walking trails that skirt it, and the boat tours that allow visitors to traverse it as Schäffer did (albeit on a raft built from fallen logs on site when she was first there in 1908). At the same time, Maligne Lake became and remains an area that excludes traditional use by Stoney hunters and their families.

Seeking Chaba Imne

On 20 June 1907, Mary Schäffer and Molly Adams, with guides William Warren and Sidney Unwin, set out from Laggan on their first full summer expedition, a sixteen-week trip into the Rocky Mountain back country. They headed north towards the headwaters of the Saskatchewan and Athabasca Rivers, an ambitious journey of some two hundred miles by trail.[7] The idea was to see parts of the interior mountain country that lay beyond the scope of tourism, such as Fortress Lake and Brazeau Lake, that geologists such as Arthur P. Coleman before them had explored in the early 1890s, as well as to travel through and find new geographical landmarks. Schäffer attributed her determination to find Chaba Imne to a hunter she called "Jim" in her 1911 *Travel* magazine story, "Hunting a Lost Lake." Jim suggested, "'While you are looking for Fortress Lake, why don't you look for a lake up around the Athabaska somewhere, that the Indians told me about. They call it Chaba (Beaver), and say it is very big.'"[8] Elsewhere, she wrote, "The Stoney Indians had spoke with great enthusiasm to 'Jim,' of a large lake (calling it Chaba Imne—Beaver Lake), and he knowing our love of penetrating to new and untried places, had passed the information to us."[9] And in *Old Indian Trails*, she wrote, "Not that the Indians had told us anything of this lake (they are too afraid of the white man trespassing upon their hunting grounds), but they had mentioned its existence to our friend Jim and he had passed the information on for what it was worth."[10] In its report on Schäffer's success in finding and later surveying the renamed Maligne Lake, the *Geographical Journal* of London identified "Jim" as James Simpson, a well-known and regarded hunter and guide.[11] Simpson, better known as "Jimmy," was an English immigrant who arrived in the Rockies in 1897.[12]

It was not just the Stoney who knew the rumoured lake before Simpson alerted Schäffer to its existence. Molly Adams noted in her 1908 diary, "The Crees call the lake Ka-kin-ocha-mash which means Long Lake."[13] Furthermore, she wrote that John Moberly, a Métis trapper and trader who supplied groups travelling through the area and helped those such as Schäffer's group to cross the Saskatchewan River near his homestead, "has been to Maligne Lake four different ways."[14] Henry Macleod, a surveyor with the Canadian Pacific Railway who had travelled through area in 1875, had dubbed it "Sorefoot Lake."[15]

Four images in *Old Indian Trails* figure prominently in the process of the transformation of legend to place for the literary public: the now-iconic portrait photograph of Sampson and Leah Beaver and their daughter Frances Louise on the Kootenay Plains in early autumn 1906 (Fig. 4.4); a landscape photograph, "First Sight of Maligne Lake, from Mount Unwin," attributed to guide Sidney Unwin, who was carrying a camera when he first caught sight of the lake (Fig. 4.2); a sketch map attributed to Sampson Beaver and credited with the success of Schäffer's party in finding the way to Chaba Imne (Fig. 4.9); and the detailed topographical map revised in the second printing of the book in January 1912 (Fig. 4.1). In addition, there is the map of the lake drawn by Schäffer following her return visit to survey it for the Geological Survey of Canada in the summer of 1911, published in the *Geographical Journal* of London and the *Canadian Alpine Journal* in 1912 (Fig. 4.12). This map includes the names of various geographical landmarks bestowed by Schäffer and her companions and approved by the Geographic Board of Canada.

Photographs are often understood as historical documents that picture the fact of a real person, place, or thing at a certain moment. Like memoir, however, photography more often creates perception than portrays fact, "blurring the distinction between the real and the imagined."[16] As with memoir, the imagined or imaginative bears heavily on the meaning that is inferred or derived from a photograph. Elements that contribute to this liminal, indeterminate space and subsequent meanings include the socially positioned gaze that the photographer casts on a scene, as well as the way in which the photograph is presented; the context in which the photo is seen or discussed; and the questions or expectations that a viewer brings to the image. Furthermore, knowledge and meaning are made or changed as photographic images are taken up and used in different times, places, and contexts. Human history, then, is not a stable entity, preserved in fragments of truth captured permanently in a document of the day, such as a photograph, a map, or a text; instead, it changes and even evolves as narratives are reconfigured and layers of memory are accumulated, and lost, over time.

Schäffer's maps, like the texts and photographs in *Old Indian Trails*, were made collaboratively with others who mapped their own knowledge of the mountain ranges. These include not only Schäffer's own maps but also those of Stoney hunter (and later chief) Sampson Beaver, whose sketch map pointed the way to Chaba Imne; mining geologist James McEvoy of the Geological Survey of Canada, who produced a survey map of the Yellowhead Pass between Edmonton and Tête Jaune Cache in 1900;[17] and British chemistry professor and mountaineer J. Norman Collie.[18] Schäffer drew in part on the last, along with her own Maligne Lake survey map, to revise a detailed map of the areas of her journeys for the 1912 reprint of *Old Indian Trails*. This is the map that she reported was purchased in large quantities for distribution by the CPR and the Grand Trunk Pacific Railway. As with photographs, maps and the act of mapping are embedded in human interactions that are distinguished by the particular social circumstances and structures in which the maps are made and used. As such, in addition to (or beyond) serving as records of measurements and geographical placement to guide others, a map functions to create an idea or represent a perception of a space and place. Although commonly perceived as objective or scientific renderings of a physical entity, mapmaking and maps—like other modes of communication, such as writing and books, and photography and photographs—are products of the individual or group in their time and place, with particular communication objectives for specific audiences.[19]

By means of the visual—the photographic and the cartographic, photographs and maps—Maligne Lake evolved conceptually from legend (imagined) to wilderness (a natural environment that included but was not yet dominated by

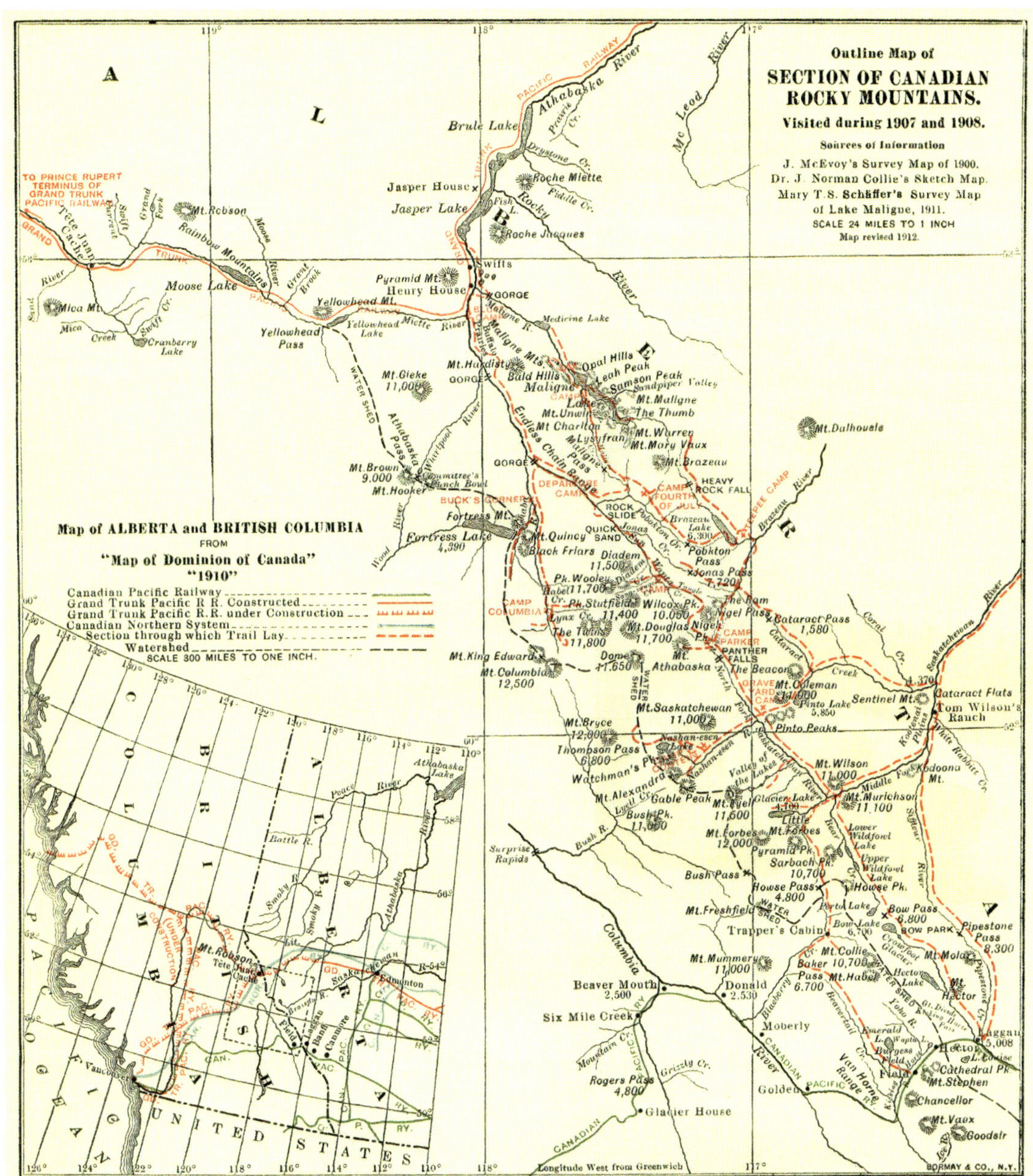

FIGURE 4.1

"Outline Map of Section of Canadian Rocky Mountains. Visited during 1907 and 1908." In *Old Indian Trails* (1911; reprint with revised map 1912), opposite page 360.

humans) to landscape (imaged); it became place when located, named, and shown to others in *Old Indian Trails* and other publications, as well as in lantern slide lectures. The maps, photographs, and texts together form Schäffer's story, which includes Stoney knowledge of Chaba Imne, the physical challenge to locate the elusive lake carved deep into the Rocky Mountain range, and her pragmatic conclusion about its future.

Creates writes, "tourism counts for just one form of human movement in an intersecting mix of experience....Human displacement has been going on since our beginnings, giving rise to the landscape's increasingly complex history as a place of both dwelling and transience."[20] This long view opens space to think about how the very first representations of Maligne Lake, both written and visual, served to create Maligne Lake as a place, one that entered Euro-North American consciousness as something with a layered history of human presence in nature; one that remains active, overlapping, and changing as well, and not one whose history began (or ended) with Schäffer and Adams's visit in 1908, nor one framed in the past as unpeopled wilderness. In his 1983 study of the Vaux family photographic legacy in the Canadian Rockies and Selkirks, Edward Cavell argues that "the era depicted is without today's feelings of environmental guilt. People were considered as an integral aspect of the wilderness, not interlopers....Their photographic skill, artistry and depth of understanding of the mountain environment have created a powerful and incisive document of a living wilderness."[21]

Photography was an integral interest and skill shared by Schäffer and Adams. Working with at least one Pony Premo folding camera owned by Schäffer—a popular camera with accordion bellows that folded into a compact 3.25 x 6 x 6.75 inches in a leather case with a carrying handle—and glass plates until 1906, and with sheet film in 1907 and 1908 (in a variety of negative sizes including 2 x 3, 2.5 x 8, and 4 x 5 inches), they carried supplies with them to the Rockies each summer, and developed and printed their negatives in facilities supplied by their hotels there.[22] (Adams also had a dark room at her home in New Haven.[23] Where Schäffer processed negatives or printed photographs in Philadelphia or West Chester after 1903 is not known.) They shared subject matter too—mountain vistas (that in 1900 Schäffer had claimed impossible to photograph well), alpine wildflowers, their pack-train horses, campsites, guides, other travellers and mountain residents they encountered, and each other. Schäffer also photographed Indigenous people. The photographs they made, and where those were published or projected (or not), are part of the narrative of their lives and journeys as constructed by Schäffer, as well as evidence of their social conditions, interests, activities, and ways of seeing and framing themselves and their journeys in the contexts of their time and place. Credit for the photographs in *Old Indian Trails* is shared equally between Schäffer and Adams.

Finding Chaba Imne

The narrative arc of the entire book is one based on struggle, uncertainty, determination, perseverance, and, ultimately, success in finding the uncharted lake. At the end of the journey in 1907, while resting on the Kootenay Plains and visiting with the Stoney who camped there as well as with photographer Elliott Barnes, who was homesteading there, Sampson Beaver sketched a map that the group used to guide itself to the lake's location the following year. On 8 June 1908, the original four, along with botanist Stewardson Brown and guide Reggie Holmes, set out again for the summer, this time with Chaba Imne as their priority goal.[24] The quest as recounted in *Old Indian Trails* reaches its highest point of tension when, after another two weeks of searching, assisted by Beaver's directions, the group despairs of ever finding the lake.

> *With lunch over, up came the everlasting question: "where is that lake? Do you think we are on the right track?" "K." [Unwin], who had grown more and more solemn for days, suddenly jumped up and shaking himself violently said: "Well, it's two o'clock, but I'm going off to climb something that's high enough to see if that lake's within twenty miles of here, and I'm not coming back till I know!" Anxious as I was to go along, I knew he was in no mood to have a snail in tow, and then it was far more important to locate our quarry than that I should personally be in at the death.*[25]

The rest of the group waited through a long, hot day and well past dark before Unwin returned to the camp and "greeted us with the joyful news, 'I've found the lake!' Ascending the ridge behind our camp, he dropped 2000 feet to another valley, then climbed a fine peak where the aneroid said 8750 feet. Reaching the top, he looked over and there lay the lake below. The quest was over, all doubts were at rest, so there was no turning back, we could go on."[26]

The reader is given a sense of how the crew experienced the discovery of the lake when the mountaintop photo that Unwin made of the first sighting of Maligne Lake appears in the text immediately following the account of the group's arrival at their destination the next morning: "In about two hours, after passing through a little very soft ground we came out on the shores of Chaba Imne (Beaver Lake)....Yes, the long quest was over, the object found, and it seemed very beautiful to our partial eyes."[27] This photo as published is the definitive evidence of Chaba Imne's existence, standing in for the reader who sees what Unwin saw on his solitary hike. It also serves to confirm the veracity

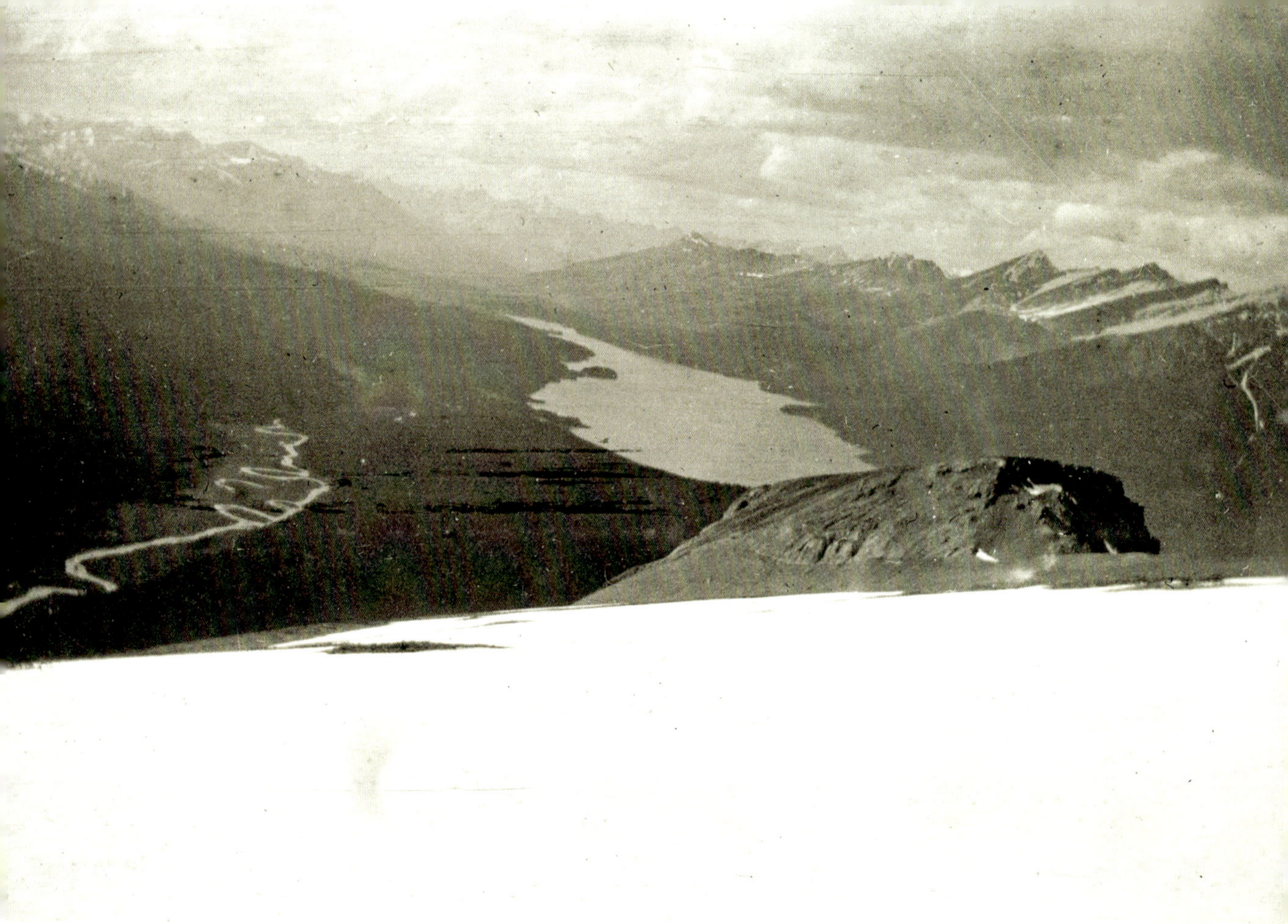

FIGURE 4.2
"First Sight of Maligne Lake, from Mount Unwin," Sidney Unwin photograph, 1908.
In *Old Indian Trails* (1911), 241.
[WMCR V527/PD-1]
(Also Mary Schäffer hand-tinted lantern slide [WMCR V527/PS1-61])

of the maps—both Beaver's sketched map and Schäffer's later topographic and survey maps—demonstrating its shape, including the narrows.

Privately, Adams too reflected on the beauty of the lake. In a letter to her sister and cousin a week after their arrival, she wrote,

> *Well, we sure have been a long time finding this lake, but also it sure is worth finding. We are at its outlet now, first struck it about 6 miles farther up, and rafted from there some 15 miles to the head. The upper half is right in high mts and is pleasing....Are now settled in an ideal camp ground—a strip of meadow and willow bush around the edge of the lake and green woods behind us. The lake composes even better from this point of view than from the last camp, so although we have already taken dozens of pictures in various lights, we shall no doubt take dozens more.*[28]

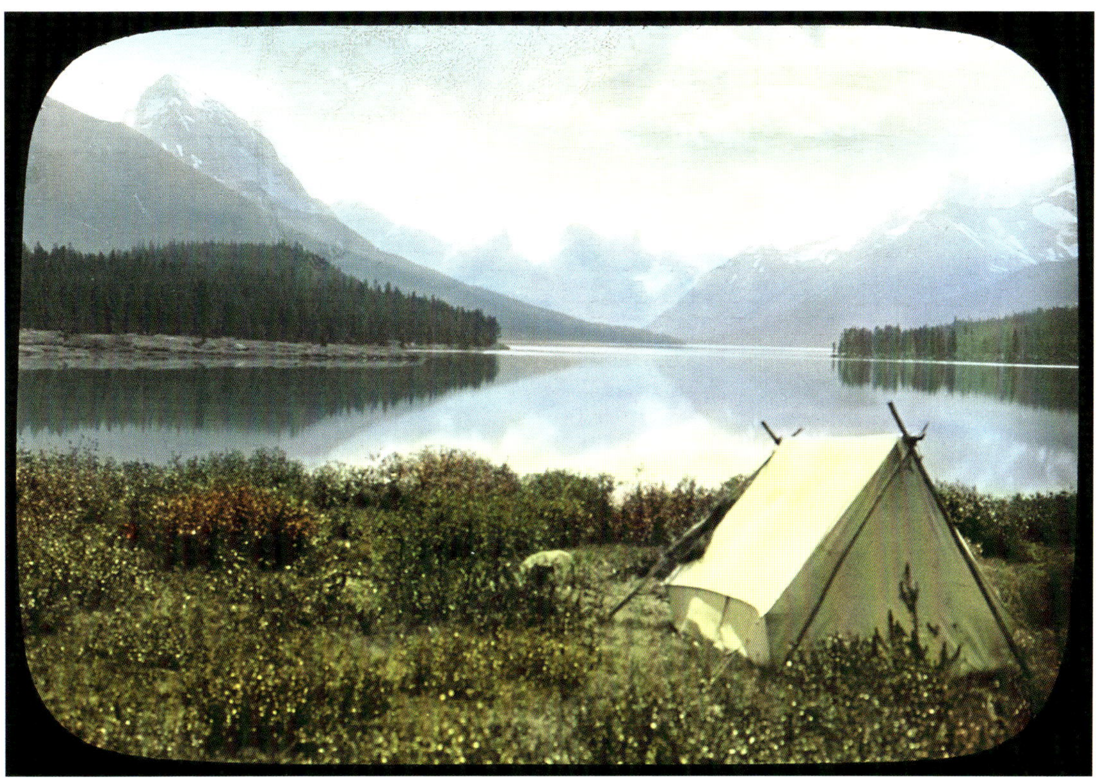

FIGURE 4.3

Camp at Maligne Lake, Mary Schäffer and/or Mary W. Adams photograph, 1908.

[WMCR V527/PD-1]

Mary Schäffer hand-tinted lantern slide

[WMCR V527/PS1-69]

Two decades later, Schäffer recounted in a private letter Unwin's pursuit that led to the first glimpse of the object of their quest as well as the first photograph of what would become known as Maligne Lake: "Sid (K) climbed Mt. Unwin and obtained the first glimpse of the lake for which we had looked so long. Perhaps I tell in the little book of how Sid got desperate and went off one afternoon with a $5. camera and tho he could match any Swiss guide I ever saw, he did not come back to camp till about 11 P.M.…Sid's climb whereby he took the tiny picture of the lake which is found in Trails, could not be surpassed."[29]

Joan Schwartz and James Ryan write that "the rhetoric of transparency and truth that came to surround the photograph enabled it to take up a position between observer and material reality….There, 'photographic seeing' became a surrogate for first-hand observation."[30] Unwin's grainy snapshot of Maligne Lake, seen over the expanse of snow at the mountain's edge (later named Mount Unwin by Schäffer and company), acts in this very way, as the reader seems positioned as viewer between Unwin behind and the scene before them. (Schäffer also tinted a lantern slide copy of the photograph for lecture audiences.) Schwartz and Ryan conclude that "the taking and viewing of photographs was an integral, active and influential part of engagement with material reality, helping to construct imaginative geographies, shape collective memory, define cultural difference and sustain power relations based on gender, race, class and colonialism."[31] *Old Indian Trails* served as a vehicle for all of this, and more. Most significantly, it served as a space for chipping away at those four inextricably entwined social concepts described by Schwartz and Ryan. Two women employed male guides to assist their quest, and the guides respected and became personally invested in the women's ambitions; the Beaver family photo resonates with a visceral connection between Indigenous sitters and a Euro-American photographer, and thus viewers; Schäffer and Adams, members of the class of professional and amateur scientists, travelled, worked, and lived in camp with guides who made their living through physical labour. Finally, *Old Indian Trails* laid a claim to Chaba Imne and the area around it as part not only of imperial possession (as Maligne Lake), but also of women's possession and knowledge: surrounding peaks were named for those involved in the quest rather than in conformity with toponymical conventions and standards of naming after eminent men or as descriptors of physical shape.[32]

The Beaver Family

Those who today travel the well-worn paths of the Rocky Mountains of Canada inevitably encounter Schäffer's 1906 portrait of Frances Louise Beaver and her parents, Sampson and Leah Beaver. The photograph is an icon of Rocky Mountain history in no small part because of its ubiquity on postcard racks throughout the string of mountain parks that ranges from Waterton to Jasper, and its presence in guidebooks and on websites. The photograph was first widely circulated in 1911 in North America and England by means of *Old Indian Trails of the Canadian Rockies*, where it was captioned "Sampson Beaver, His Squaw, and Little Frances Louise."[33] Since 1980, this photograph, distinctive for its time, has been seen and consumed most often outside of its original context in Schäffer's book. It has been circulated and re-circulated not only as a tourist token but also across diverse historical, political, and theoretical fields, generating new knowledge and new meanings among those viewing, reproducing, analyzing, and discussing it.

The portrait was one of four made of the family (Figs. 3.19 and 3.20) in late September 1906, four weeks after Mary Schäffer and Molly Adams, along with William Warren and Joe Barker, had set out on a second excursion following

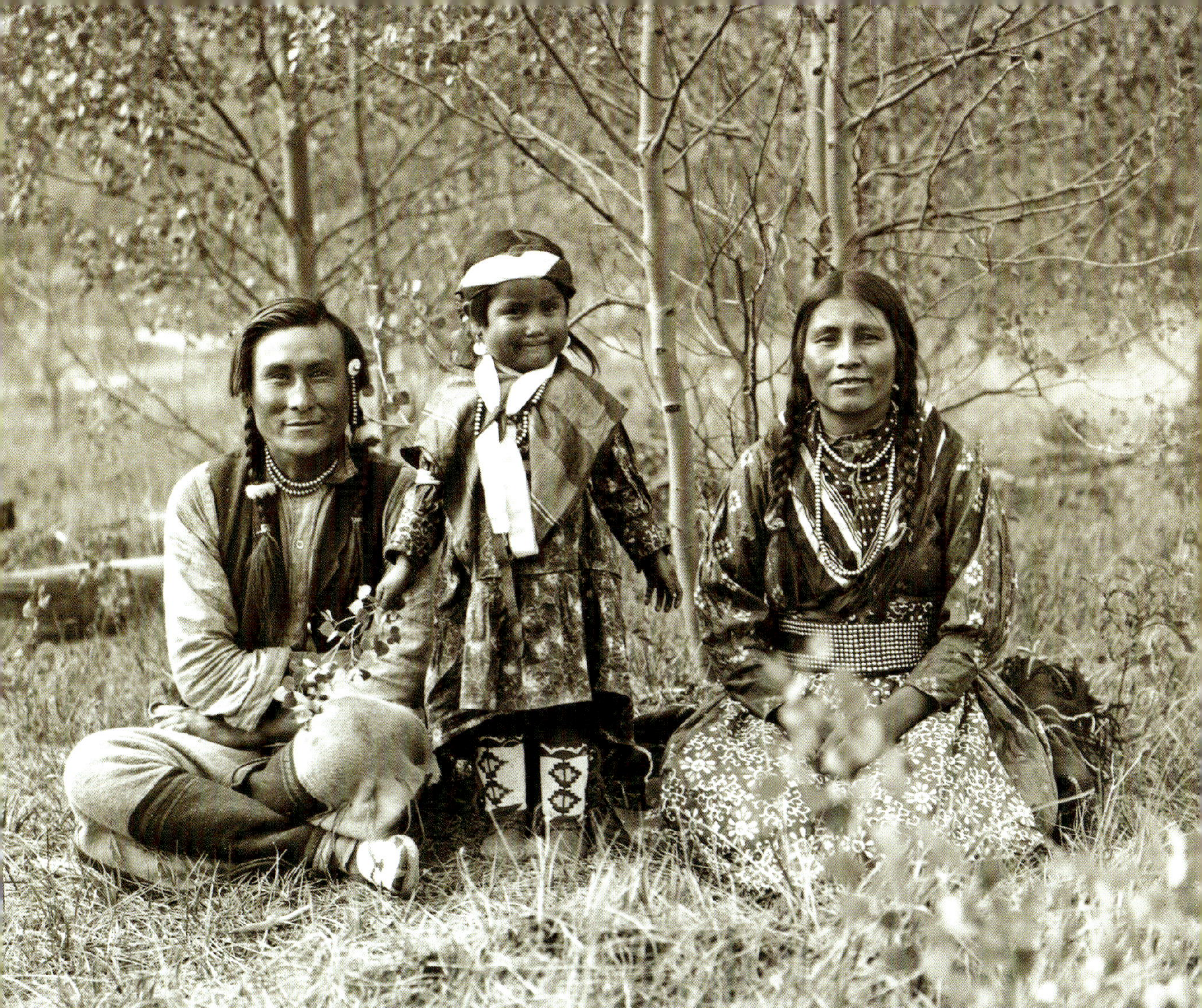

FIGURE 4.4

Sampson, Frances Louise, and Leah Beaver, Mary Schäffer photograph, 1906.

[WMCR V527/PD-1 and V527/PD-4]

Reproduced from original glass negative

[WMCR V527/NG-124]

the earlier ill-fated pack trip with Zephine Humphrey, Henrietta Tuzo, and Dorothy Sharp, departing Laggan on 28 August. In one of Schäffer and Adams's albums of photographs, the four photographs are labelled as a group: "Frances Louise Beaver and Her Family." They met the Beaver family for the first time at a Stoney camp on the Kootenay Plains of the eastern Rockies.[34] A year later, on 27 September 1907, while returning to Field, British Columbia, following their first, unsuccessful season seeking the "lost lake," Schäffer's group again stopped on the Kootenay Plains. There, "we rested and reveled in those golden valleys, visited the Indians, and found life a very pleasant matter in that peaceful sunshine after the snows and storms among the more northern valleys."[35] In a ten-page passage halfway through *Old Indian Trails* and very near the end of the story of the 1907 journey, Schäffer crafts a narrative of a crucial four days in their quest while they paused near the Stoney camp. First, she writes, they were welcomed warmly by the women and children who were there that day while the men were out hunting, and, as Schäffer described the event in a jarring shift to third-person voice, they allowed that "Yahe-Weha might photograph to her heart's content. She had promised pictures the year before, she had kept the promise, and she might have as many photographs now as she wanted."[36]

Schäffer's change of narrative viewpoint for these two sentences—the only ones like this in the 360-page book—is disconcerting to read today. It is a comparatively clumsy rhetorical device that introduces the name that the Stoney bestowed on Schäffer; it seeks to explain why she and Adams were welcome to make numerous photographs, but does so in a way that does not require Schäffer to make immodest or unfeminine claims about herself. The shift in voice, when read in isolation from the rest of the text, also takes on a childlike tone that resonates with a stereotypical representation of Indigenous adults as "simple" people. In the context of the passages before and after these sentences over the ten-page narrative of the visit, Schäffer otherwise seeks to dispel stereotypes. In stories about her and Adams's interactions with Indigenous people, she shows that the individuals they met and portrayed were fundamentally not unlike their visitors and that they mutually enjoyed one another's company.

She did this in two ways. First, when speaking of visiting the women, she refers to herself and Adams as "white squaws" and writes about the pleasure the Stoney women and their female visitors shared in their collaboration as sitters and photographers. There is no hint of Schäffer implying that they and their Stoney counterparts were somehow the same just because of gender, however. Instead, she drew upon both contrasts and common experiences between them, leading into a passage about the afternoon of photograph-making with a description of "three smiling, dirty squaws, who looked as though wash-days were not over numerous, but whose welcome was very cordial."[37] Nor should the description be taken as discriminatory, pejorative, or stereotyping. Washdays on the trails—a source of friction with fellow travellers in 1906 and point of comparison with the Kiplings when emerging from four months on the trails in 1907[38]—were not numerous for Schäffer and Adams either.

Some of Schäffer's words are startling today, when the term "squaw" has long been used as a derogatory and offensive sexual and racial epithet.[39] But as PearlAnn Reichwein and Lisa McDermott remind us, in the early twentieth century the term was understood to be an Indigenous word for "wife" or "woman," and that is the way in which Schäffer uses it, something she would have been unlikely to do in reference to herself and Adams if today's meaning had been the common understanding among her readers at the time.[40] Furthermore, read in context, the descriptor serves as an effective means of suggesting strongly to her readers Indigenous and Euro-North American women's shared experiences, mutual respect, and indeed safety, despite cultural differences. Few of Schäffer's readers encountered or knew Indigenous people, who had largely been confined to reserves at a distance from settler towns and cities. Fear, discomfort, dislike, and discrimination against Indigenous peoples in North America among settler cultures were—and remain—commonplace and status quo, and Schäffer was well aware of this. Molly Adams counted herself among those uncomfortable with Indigenous people, and noted in contrast that Schäffer liked to know and interact with such cultural and (as understood at the time) racial Others.[41] Schäffer knowingly wrote and photographed within and against the grain of popular concepts of the day. Euro-North American culture created sharply contrasting images of white and Indigenous women. In her critical examination, *Capturing Women: The Manipulation of Cultural Imagery in Canada's Prairie West*, Sarah Carter describes this phenomenon concisely: "White women, projected as 'civilizing' agents were central to the creation and reproduction of the new community; also central to the new notions of spatial and social segregation were representations of Aboriginal women as dangerous and sinister."[42] Kipling had traded on this very contrast when he portrayed Schäffer with "the comprehending equal eyes of the civilized white woman which moved in that berry-brown face" as they rode past one another, she in front of a pack train, he in a carriage, along a border of wilderness and civilization.[43]

Schäffer's narrative strategy, viewed from today's vantage point, was to show respect for her acquaintances through her actions. On the Kootenay Plains, she tells a story of delivering on her promise to give the Stoney inhabitants prints of the photographs she made, thus earning the reward of a welcome for her and Adams. Furthermore, Schäffer did not photograph for free, nor expect to do so, travelling as she had for years in a barter and tourist economy, acquiring artifacts and making photographs. "Personal experience has shown me that the Indian has the vanity of his white brethren, but he is not going to pose for nothing. I have no belief in their superstitious dread of photography, at least so far as the Plains Indians are concerned; it is simply a matter of fair trade,"[44] she declared in *Old Indian Trails*.

Schäffer also told a story, which should be understood as an imaginative retelling rather than a literal account, of an exchange she had with two Stoney men during this visit. Sampson Beaver and his friend, Silas Abraham, both members of the Wesley band that lived much of the year on Stoney traditional territory of the Kootenay Plains, joined Schäffer's group in front of a fire after dinner on the last night of their stay. "Silas had been making a few mild jokes (it is so hard to associate jokes with Indians whom most of us have only met in books), and both of them had been laughing heartily at our lame attempt to pronounce some of their words, so that atmosphere seemed propitious" for Schäffer to attempt what she jokingly described as missionary work.[45] The self-deprecating humour upon which the story about gender roles is founded is typical of Schäffer and other women travel writers of the time. She writes that she asked Silas Abraham about the work that Stoney women usually did in camp but for which Schäffer's male guides were responsible, such as setting up, pulling down, and moving camp, packing the horses, and cutting wood, and suggested that Stoney men should do the same. While Schäffer's side of the exchange implied that Abraham was lazy (not an unexpected stereotyped characterization for readers), the tables are turned when Schäffer repositions the reader to see his side, which posited that Schäffer was, in fact, the lazy one for not doing the work that was women's responsibility in his culture. Schäffer's "missionary effort went to the floor with a bang and everyone burst out laughing (at the missionary, of course)....The burst of laughter, however, had shown Silas that his company and wit were appreciated."[46] The narrative also shows the reader that customary good manners welcoming visitors and making them feel comfortable were relevant and effective social currency in the peopled wilderness, and a means to bridge cultures.

While Schäffer made other portraits of the Beaver family in 1906, at least one of which was published prior to publication of *Old Indian Trails* in 1911 and three of which prints were given to Henrietta Tuzo, the seated portrait is the only one included in *Old Indian Trails*.[47] At the time the photograph was made, Sampson Beaver was about thirty years of age, according to Schäffer.[48] Leah Beaver appears to be about the same age as her husband, and Frances Louise appears to be four or five years old. Of the three family members, Leah Beaver is the only one whom Schäffer does not identify by name in the caption or text; nor does she describe an encounter with her at length in her book. She did, however, name adjoining peaks near Maligne Lake for Sampson and Leah

Beaver. These two were among other mountains named to memorialize those who materially aided the expedition's success.

The portrait of the family is one that conveys considerable warmth, both among the three sitters, and between sitters and viewers through the Beavers' animated gazes and smiling expressions. The child's expression and hand gestures suggest barely contained enthusiasm and pleasure. The composition and framing are appealing, stable in the solid triangular shape formed by the sitters. All are well-dressed in the normal mix for the time of fabric and buckskin clothing, accessorized by beaded jewelry, belts, and moccasins. The Beavers are seated on the ground in front of an aspen grove of bare trees in late autumn. The camera is at eye level, and so the viewer too feels seated, creating an informal, inviting circle. It is a portrait that contrasts dramatically with more commonly known studio portraits documenting unsmiling individuals in seemingly traditional clothing. At the same time, it is a portrait that is not unique in an era when some photographers in Canada and the United States were spending considerable periods of time in communities of First Nations, Inuit, and Native American people, and their portraits were marked by the sense of familiarity and ease of established relationships, such as Schäffer among the Stoney on the Kootenay Plains.[49] Above all, what appears to be portrayed is a nuclear family of paternal lineage (especially in the absence of Leah Beaver's name in the photo's title in favour of her descriptor as wife of Sampson Beaver, thus identifying her position in the family). The overall effect is one of a recognizably modern domestic social order, not unlike that experienced by the reader or viewer.

In 1992, when considering Schäffer's portrait of the Beaver family, Lucy Lippard wondered what a reading of the photograph might be if the image were not "cut loose from all knowledge of the people involved."[50] It is an important question, and one that can now be broached. Sampson and Leah Beaver and their children were members of the Wesley Band of the Stoney Indian First Nation at Morley, Alberta, located about thirty-seven miles west of Calgary.[51] The Wesley Band summered on their traditional territory of the Kootenay Plains, and some band families also wintered there. The Canada Census of Manitoba, Saskatchewan, and Alberta for 1906, the year in which this photograph was made, records some details of their family. (In contrast, Alberta Birth, Marriage, and Death records from this period do not include most Indigenous citizens.) When the census taker visited the Stoney Reserve at Morley on 9 July 1906, Sampson and Leah Beaver and their children were there. Both parents were recorded as 35 years old (that is, born in 1870 or 1871) and married, with 6 children: Job, aged 13; William, 11; Patrick, 10; Paul, 9; Frances (the only daughter), 7; and Jacob, 2. The portrait photograph, however, made 6 or 7 weeks later on the Kootenay Plains, about 125 miles north of the reserve, clearly shows that Frances was younger than 7 that year. The 1916 census supports that contention.

In 1916, when the census was taken at Morley, Sampson Beaver is recorded as 45, Leah Beaver as 44, Frances as 15 (thus making her about 5 years of age in 1906), and Jacob as 12. None of the other 4 sons is enumerated as living with his parents or being at Morley when the enumerator visited in 1916. The 1916 census asked for far more detail about individuals, including occupation, religious affiliation, and ability to speak, read, or write English or French. That year, the Beavers were documented as Methodist. Sampson Beaver was identified as a hunter. He and the children were recorded as able to speak English but not French. Their ability to read or write in those languages was not elicited, however, nor was any information on Leah Beaver's abilities in English or French. Their mother tongue was recorded as "Indian." Sampson and Leah Beaver and their children do not appear to be registered in any other federal census, except for Paul, who appears alone in the 1911 census at Morley at age 14.

As yet, no public document recording Sampson or Leah Beaver's non-Indigenous education or that of their children has emerged. The only hint lies in a passing comment published by a Rocky Mountain explorer. In early August 1902, geologist and professor Arthur P. Coleman had employed Beaver as a guide to cross the North Saskatchewan River near the Kootenay Plains at the foot of Sentinel Mountain. While usually fordable earlier in the summer, fifteen Stoney lodges were just then breaking camp on the east side of the river in preparation for crossing the Saskatchewan because of the unusually high flow of water caused by several years of above-average rainfall in Alberta.[52]

> *I got Samson [sic] Beaver, now a married man with a family in a teepee near by, to come as guide to the ford, which he had looked at the day before.*
>
> *Samson can talk no English; he was too sad a truant from the Mission school as a boy ever to learn it; but his sister Becky, a smiling, bright-faced girl, came along as interpreter.*[53]

Beaver's much younger sister, Rebecca ("Becky"), appears in the 1901 and 1911 censuses, but not in those of 1906 or 1916. Rebecca Beaver is listed as 16 years old at the time of the 1901 census (when her older brother would have been 30 years of age), which was taken in April. She was recorded as Methodist, and as a pupil living in residential school at Morley, along with 28 other pupils ranging in age from 5 to 14 and their principal, John Niddrie. The McDougall Orphanage School, established as a day school by Methodist missionaries in about 1875, became a residential school in the mid-1880s and operated in Morley until 1910. Rebecca Beaver's first language (or "mother tongue") was listed as Stoney, and she was recorded as able to read, write, and speak English. Coleman's account corroborates this documentation. No further official documentation from that period or the next 45 years is as yet publicly available.

Decades later, however, both a Becky Beaver and a Frances Beaver are named on voters lists following changes in 1960 to the Canadian Bill of Rights that established Indigenous people's suffrage. In 1962 and 1963 they are listed in Bow Valley, Alberta (where Morley is located). A Frances Beaver (recorded as "Miss Frances") is also on the 1968, 1972, and 1974 voters lists for Rocky Mountain, Alberta (in the Kootenay Plains and Bearspaw Reserve areas), while a Becky Beaver appears on the 1974 Rocky Mountain voters list. Their names do not appear on subsequent lists, and death records from that time are not yet public information, but it is possible that these women—aunt and niece only about fifteen years apart in age—are those whom Schäffer and Coleman knew as children.

Frances Louise had purportedly charmed Schäffer when they first met in late September 1906, and Sampson Beaver garnered distinction in Schäffer's narrative for aiding their quest by sketching from memory a map to guide them to the legendary "lost" lake of Chaba Imne. The portrait may have been shown publicly prior to publication as a hand-coloured lantern slide in Schäffer's lectures on the Rocky Mountains, presented during winters in Pennsylvania, although no surviving lecture manuscripts from that period indicate so definitively. (The portrait of Frances Louise Beaver alone was also made as a hand-coloured lantern slide, and it too may have been included in public presentations.) Beginning in May 1911, the monochromatic print version began to circulate in North America and England when it appeared in her soon-to-be popular book, *Old Indian Trails of the Canadian Rockies*.

It was not long before the photograph circulated beyond the book itself. On 5 August 1911, two months after publication in *Old Indian Trails*, it was reproduced with the same title alongside a review of the book in the *Portland Telegram*.[54] The *Telegram* reviewer pronounced Schäffer's photographs "rarely beautiful" but does not comment on the portrait directly. Instead, the reviewer recounts Schäffer's humorous story of the exchange with Silas Abraham. In other words, the first time it was re-circulated, the photo remained attached to a story about Rocky Mountain Stoney inhabitants from Schäffer's journey. Many newspapers in the United States and Canada—from the *New York Times* to the *Edmonton Bulletin*—published reviews, although the *Portland Telegram* was the only one to print a photo from the book. By all accounts the book sold well, becoming one of the must-reads for travellers and climbers in the Rocky Mountains over the next two decades. Demand was such in the late 1920s that Schäffer managed to get the publisher to bind and distribute 260 extra prints of the book that the publisher had been holding. In the process, she was also upset to learn that G.P. Putnam's Sons had likely destroyed, without her permission, the colour and photo plates that she had produced for *Alpine Flora*, which she in fact owned.[55]

After 1911, the portrait does not appear to have circulated widely again until 1980, when it was included in a newly published but substantially revised version of *Old Indian Trails*. At that time, Schäffer's text, as well as a previously unpublished manuscript in which she recounts a story of her 1911 trip to Maligne Lake and that contains an introduction to her life written by E.J. Hart, was compiled under the title *A Hunter of Peace* and published by the Whyte Museum of the Canadian Rockies in Banff, which holds Schäffer's original glass negative, prints, and hand-tinted lantern slide of the Beaver family portrait. While the text was reprinted word for word, without alteration (although with omission of the preface, index, and other front and back matter), the book was redesigned and presented in a new format, and differed from the original edition in terms of photographs. Some images that had not appeared in the original book were included in the new edition, including hand-coloured slides (colour printing was rare at the turn of the twentieth century and the only colour photograph in *Old Indian Trails* was pasted on the cover), and some images from the original edition did not appear. Many of those images that did appear were inserted at different points in the text from the original edition. The portrait, newly captioned "Sampson Beaver and his family" in *A Hunter of Peace*, was one of the few to retain approximately the same position in the text, near Schäffer's story of the time spent on the Kootenay Plains. The 1980 edition sharpened the focus on the characters involved in the journeys,

FIGURE 4.5

Cover of E.J. Hart's *A Hunter of Peace*, 1st ed., 1980. 8.5 x 11 inches.

[WMCR Archives and Library Collection]

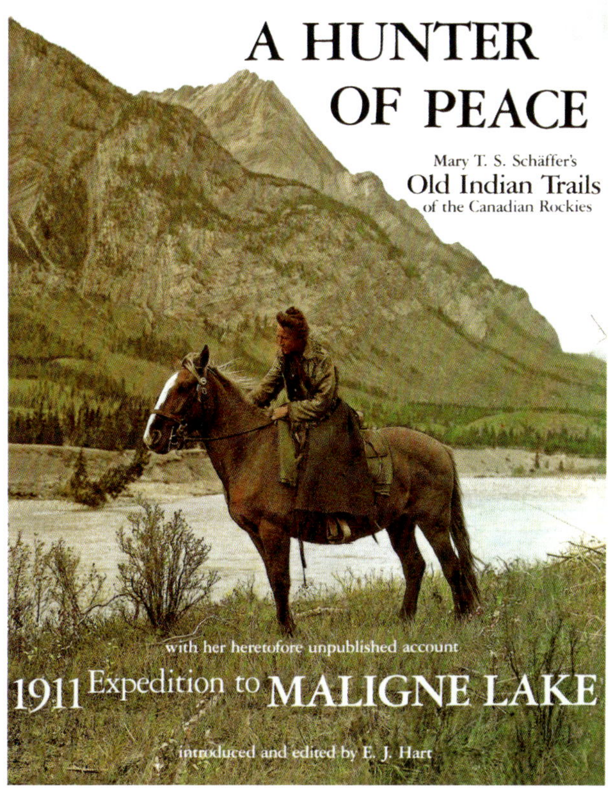

particularly the women themselves, and especially Schäffer, by including more images of the travellers and their pack horses. This stood in contrast to the author's original focus on the physical environment and experiences of the journey in both the text and images.

A Hunter of Peace was followed in the 1980s by a postcard and poster reproduction of the photograph, both of which remain available for purchase at the Whyte Museum and elsewhere in Canadian Rocky Mountain national parks today; in 1988, the portrait also appeared in Ben Gadd's *Handbook of the Canadian Rockies*, the definitive and indispensable handbook of the "geology, plants, animals, history and recreation" of the region. There it is labelled "Stoney band members Sampson Beaver, his wife Leah and daughter Frances Louise at a camp on the Kootenay Plains near today's Two-O'Clock Creek Campground along Highway 11, in August of 1907. Photo by Mary Schäffer."[56] Although its appearance and placement in *Old Indian Trails* imply that the photo was made on the journey in 1907, the photograph was made during the late-summer journey of 1906, when Schäffer and Adams first met the family on the Kootenay Plains.[57] The portrait thus re-emerged in the 1980s for consumption in the same venues in which it was first circulated—that is, in the North American tourist economy and the literary travel writing and reading market. Of course, the sociohistorical context of the 1980s was much different, and this factor is a significant element in the analysis and criticism that subsequently emerged among scholarly writers.

Photographing the Beaver Family

It began in 1990 when Canadian Plains Cree artist and curator Gerald McMaster sent the postcard picture of "Sampson Beaver and his family," as the postcard was labelled, to American art critic and curator Lucy Lippard, who credits the image with inspiring her 1992 groundbreaking book *Partial Recall*.[58] Lippard's imagination was engaged by what she called the image's "crisp presentness," which precluded ethnographical overtones in favour of the individuality of the sitters.[59] She explains it this way: "The Beavers' portrait seems a classic visualization of what anthropologists call 'intersubjective time.' It commemorates a reciprocal moment (rather than a cannibalistic one), where the emphasis is on interaction and communication; a moment in which subject and object are caught in exchange within shared time."[60]

Lippard's analysis takes its starting point from her argument that intellectual inquiry into the "intersections of, and the differences between, the mythic Wests of white culture and of Native cultures"[61] has had to shift or expand beyond what she called the "colonial overview."[62] While meditating on the warm response she felt in gazing at the sitters and positing that empathy could be "a factor in the relationship between race and gender lurking in this subject," Lippard traces the white, middle-class, middle-aged American Quaker widow's biography, based on Hart's introduction to *A Hunter of Peace* and Schäffer's story in *Old Indian Trails* (as reprinted in Hart's edition) of her encounter with Frances Louise and her parents. She cautions readers that her analysis is unusually subjective, as she lacked any information beyond what the back of the postcard provided about the Beavers. "This is the feeling I get from the Beavers' portrait," she wrote. "Am I just kidding myself? Overidentifying with Mary Schaffer?"[63]

In the end, text trumps image, and Lippard concludes that Schäffer's portrait of the Beavers could not be empathetic but only sympathetic because her "journals betray a colonial lens."[64] If Schäffer's 1906 lens was "colonial"—an accurate albeit reductive assessment—Lippard's 1992 lens was, like Schäffer's, transgressive in its day. In retrospect, like Schäffer's, it too appears conventional for its time: an intellectual amalgam of post-structuralism informed by post-colonialism and feminism, framing a Foucauldian view of the world as one of fluid if not destabilized identities and power relations. Furthermore, it turns its focus on the photographer, who, despite an intellectual generation's best efforts to bury the author, survives as the centre of interest and study. As with the *New York Times* critic in 1911, Schäffer herself continues to attract greater interest and attention than her work or its content, whether text or image.

Embedded in *Partial Recall*, the portrait of "Sampson, Frances Louise, and Leah Beaver" (as it is labelled in Lippard's book) was revived, perhaps even appropriated, for circulation in a new discursive field: that of scholarly inquiry and critical analysis. At the same time, it continues, nearly four decades after its revival by Hart in *A Hunter of Peace*, to circulate as a tourist token. Lippard's powerful meditation is the touchstone for every subsequent attempt to engage with this image. Her work brought the portrait to an international audience of visual and literary scholars, and subsequently triggered compelling post-colonial analyses of the photograph. Julia V. Emberley, for example, strongly disagrees with Lippard's reading. Whereas Lippard confined her context for analysis to "then-present" and "now-present" spaces between the sitters, the photographer, and herself, Emberley seeks the "resignification" of the image—that is, a new meaning that emerges from a broader understanding of the context of its production.[65] Her goal is twofold: to demonstrate the complexity of seemingly straightforward photos, such as this family portrait; and to destabilize its received meaning by examining contemporary and historical mechanisms that contribute to the type of meaning that is produced. Emberley argues that the image is transmuted "from a sign of subjugation"—one that was produced, used, and abused "in struggles for power and domination" at the time it was made—"into a renewed site of resistance" a century later that offers a chance for other meanings to emerge for new audiences.[66] As with Lippard, however, the photographer remains central to the analysis of meaning.

Emberley's Schäffer is "a notable female bourgeois traveller of the Canadian northwest."[67] As such, any agency for resistance to the status quo on the part of the photographer, or a destabilization of a received identity of the historical figure or public persona of Mary Schäffer, is neither allowed nor contemplated. Instead, a small sample of Schäffer's photographic practice—a few of the most aesthetically and technically skilled images of Indigenous women and children and family groupings that were published—is assessed in two case studies to illustrate the general concept of how photography was used by "British bourgeois women travellers" in a colonizing society to create Indigenous families in the likeness of white, Christian, nuclear families, thereby visually imposing a settler concept of family on an Indigenous culture.[68] Indeed, the familiar nuclear family presentation of the Beavers creates for Euro-North American and British readers a sense of the Beavers as "civilized" and, by extrapolation, their society and culture in the eastern Rockies and foothills as civilized as well. Like Lippard in 1990, Emberley (in 2005 and 2007) does not have or use information about the family that is available in historical sources—the absence of the sons of the family is notable, for example—and she too relies on her perceptions of the image alone to construct her argument about the perceived identity of the family. Her analysis implies that their "likeness" is one constructed specifically for and by the camera; as such, the image is assessed to be false or fictive, created by staging the Beaver family so that a culturally preferable non-Indigenous idea of family is represented. The historical evidence of census records, however, shows clearly that the group was, in fact, much as it was presented: a family that lived and interacted with a variety of Euro-North American and Indigenous peoples in a contact culture established for roughly two hundred years, not a pre-contact entity, such as some post-colonial assessments imply would otherwise have existed.

At the same time, Emberley draws parallels with the eighteenth-century notion of the noble savage in nature, and notes the resonance of the Beaver family as a "First Family."[69] It is true that the photograph reflects that archetypal reference, especially when the names and lives of the sitters and their history of interaction with the photographer are displaced in favour of reading a universalized, non-historical representation. This assessment, however, does not take into account the fact that the names of the sitters and their relationships to each other were attached to the photograph from the beginning, or the complexity that historically grounded individual agency and site-specific interactions create: the photograph is set where Sampson and Leah Beaver lived and were raising their family, on traditional territory (not yet recognized as reserve land), in a traditional hunting-gathering and trade economy, and a community of lodges that moved through the year. They interacted in economic, political, gender, racial, class, and religious terms, among others, with Euro-North American men, for the most part, as well as with other First Nations and Métis men and women. Schäffer and Adams were the first

Euro-North American women known to have visited the Kootenay Plains, and like many travellers of that time and today, Schäffer sought interaction with local inhabitants, Indigenous and settler alike, wherever she travelled. She clearly enjoyed Frances Louise, as many adults enjoy the company and behaviour of young children. By taking the narrative as written in *Old Indian Trails* as documentary evidence of the author's racist colonial attitudes and behaviour, Emberley overlooks the literary contradictions the author employed both to engage and challenge received ideas about Indigenous people among her Euro-North American and British readers in the early twentieth century. For Schäffer, it was an exceptional opportunity to photograph an Indigenous family with whom she had friendly and possibly even respectful interactions. Furthermore, the photograph not only resonates with conventional meaning—like so much of Schäffer's work, it pushes back against such meaning as well.

The three are posed in a variety of ways in the outdoor environment (Figs. 3.19 and 3.20). The particular image chosen for *Old Indian Trails* is the most visually compelling. (The photo in which Leah Beaver and Frances Louise are seated on horses with Sampson Beaver standing alongside was published elsewhere in a railway promotional pamphlet, where it was captioned "Friends.")[70] The sitters are dressed up and the clothing of each of the three is an important element, demonstrating the mixture of Stoney and European styles, materials, and accessories that was common at the time after many generations of trade with European and other Indigenous groups. This particular image shows to advantage the fine skills of Leah Beaver in clothing her family in garments and accessories she made or acquired. Above all, the sitters are at ease, their facial expressions showing each one clearly enjoying the moment. There is nothing archetypal or inauthentic about the portrayal. As Lippard points out, it is a comparatively rare (although not unique) example of an alternate form of photographic practice among Euro-North American photographers who spent extended periods of time in Indigenous societies.[71] Such portraits pictured Indigenous sitters as they were, rather than as typecast cultural representatives.

The adults are presented as equally important stabilizers in the image, anchoring the sides of the triangle formed by the three figures, with the apex that of the child's head. It is a vibrant image of both stillness (required for the exposure) and energy. While Emberley ascribes a patriarchal hierarchy to the composition because the father is seated to the left and the convention of reading in English is left to right, she reports becoming confused when, instead of retrieving this version of the image from the Whyte Museum archives, she

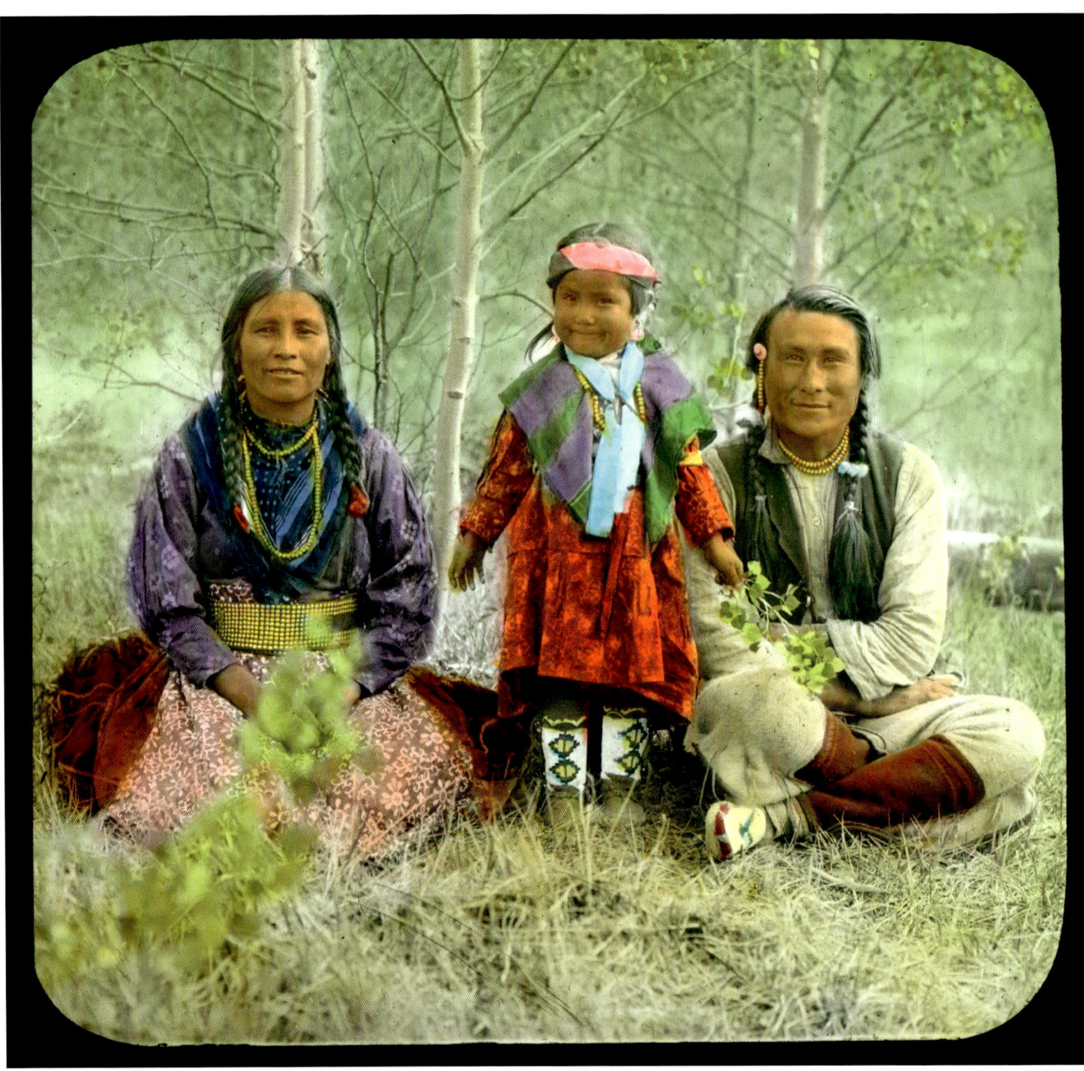

FIGURE 4.6

"Sampson Beaver's Family '06," Mary Schäffer photograph, 1906, and hand-tinted lantern slide (printed in reverse from the negative). [WMCR V527/PS1-5]

received one in which it is reversed, with the mother on the left.[72] There is a simple technical explanation for this reverse "syntax," as Emberley describes it.[73] Schäffer's hand-tinted lantern slide (labelled by Schäffer "Sampson Beaver's Family '06") is a result of the negative being printed backwards as a slide positive, a not uncommon occurrence in the days of analogue film processes—just as reversing 35 mm film slides either accidentally or deliberately when placing them in a slide projector was common throughout the twentieth century. Furthermore, the lantern slide was not tinted to "giv[e] it aesthetic value for inclusion in her book," as Emberley states; the published print in the 1911 book is monochromatic, as it had to be given printing technology of the time, and it is not the reversed image that was published, as Emberley implies.

Why Schäffer did not correct this reversal is unknown. Was it perhaps too expensive or time-consuming to remake the slide? Did it not make an aesthetic difference to Schäffer? Did it not matter because she could simply insert the slide in reverse in the lantern slide projector to little ill effect? Was it a deliberate choice or merely accidental? The answer cannot be established because there is no material evidence to address the question. For Emberley, however, such considerations are irrelevant: "Whatever Schäffer's original intentions may have been, the reversal signifies the instability of a colonial-patriarchal syntax that can be so easily undone. And perhaps, even, a political unconscious at work."[74] Perhaps, but probably not. Over-reading photographs, especially those that are visually and historically provocative, is easily done; but, like reading narrative literally rather than literarily, it leads to unsupported and misleading claims, and strips the image of the nuances and complexities of looking and looking back that are at play. Furthermore, Emberley's findings cannot be replicated when her claim is tested by applying it to another set of images of an Indigenous family. "Mrs. Swift and Her Children" was also reversed when reproduced as a lantern slide. Given the absence from the image of the family patriarch, Lewis Swift, and the cluster of children around Suzette Chalifoux Swift, Emberley's claim for the cause and meaning of the reversal cannot be applied, unless it is stretched to attribute patriarchal superiority to the young boy, an unlikely supposition. Schäffer labelled the album page on which she mounted her prints "Frances Louise Beaver and Her Family," underscoring her abiding interest in the child and the construction of her imagery primarily around the child rather than the father (or, indeed, the mother).

Finally, Emberley insists that the humanist response of Lippard to the ephemeral moment of the photograph must not prevail nor be valorized, for it produces "an historical blindness to the reality of colonization as a radically violent event that obliterated one history by creating another."[75] She is right, if such a humanist response is based on an imagined or romanticized view rather than a historically grounded understanding of the varied and multifaceted histories of Indigenous and European interactions over a three-hundred-year period prior to the Beaver–Schäffer photographic encounter. Where Emberley's argument struggles is with the tendency to the binate either/or, black/white that refuses to acknowledge the elements, groups, or individuals of this society and time who did not hold the majority view and who attempted, sometimes successfully and sometimes not, to represent alternate ways of thinking, as Schäffer did in matters relating to both gender and race.[76] Nonetheless,

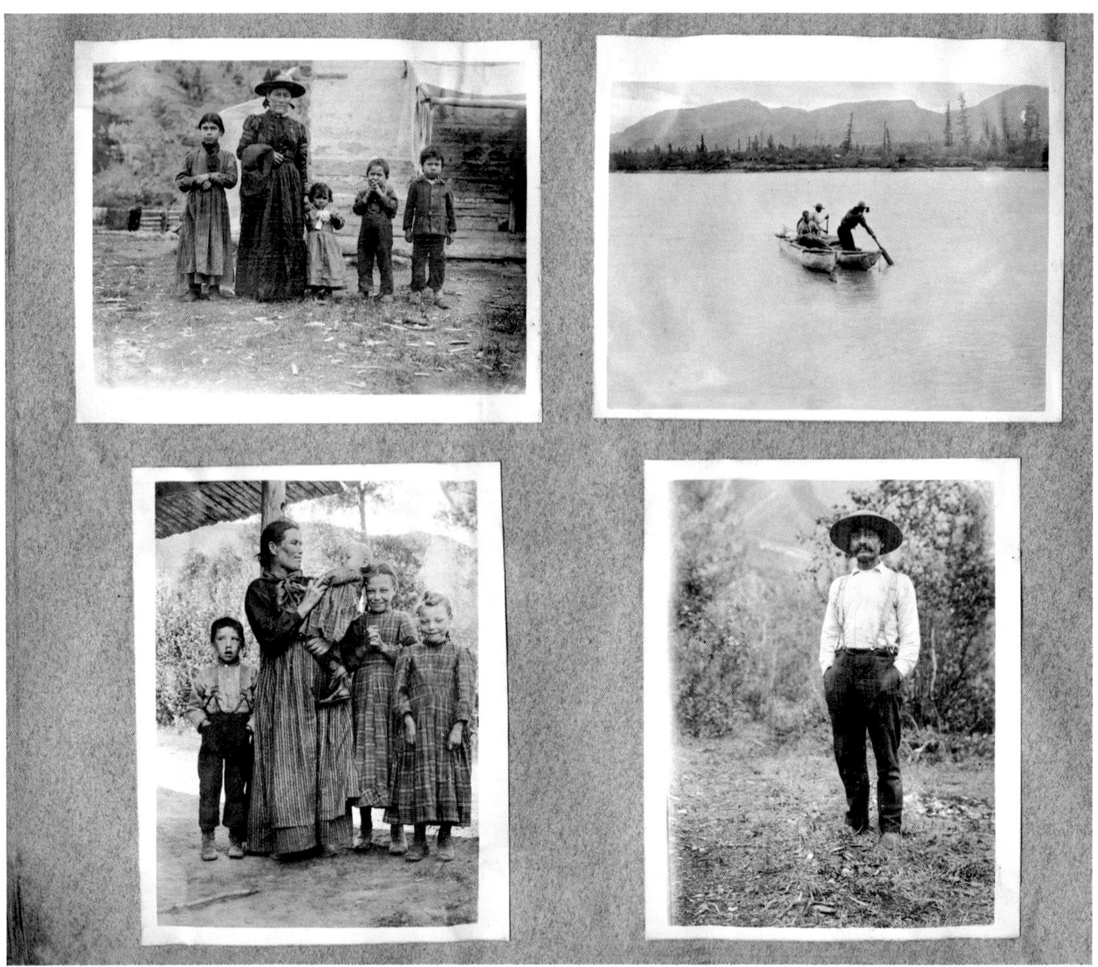

FIGURE 4.7
Album page with Suzette Chalifoux Swift and her children (bottom left); Lewis Swift (bottom right), Mary Schäffer photographs, 1908.
[WMCR V527/PD-1]

Emberley's position is an important counterpoint to Lippard's. It brings into view a crucial and critical accounting of the context of production outside the frame, the sociopolitical foundations on which the Beaver family's circumstances rest. It also resists the aesthetic persuasiveness of the image for viewers a century later. And yet, despite best intentions, photographs, like memoir, create interstitial spaces in which contingent and fluid meanings are created and from which such meanings are taken and shift with time.

The irony of this is that the image of Frances Louise Beaver and her parents recirculates in predominantly non-Indigenous (or predominantly white, Euro-North American) fields. Even the most sharply focused post-colonial glare, despite its desire to claim its location in the field of the colonized, is trapped on the outside—behind the camera, as it were, peering through a neocolonial lens. In his 2001 book *I Hear the Train: Reflection, Inventions, Refraction*, Native

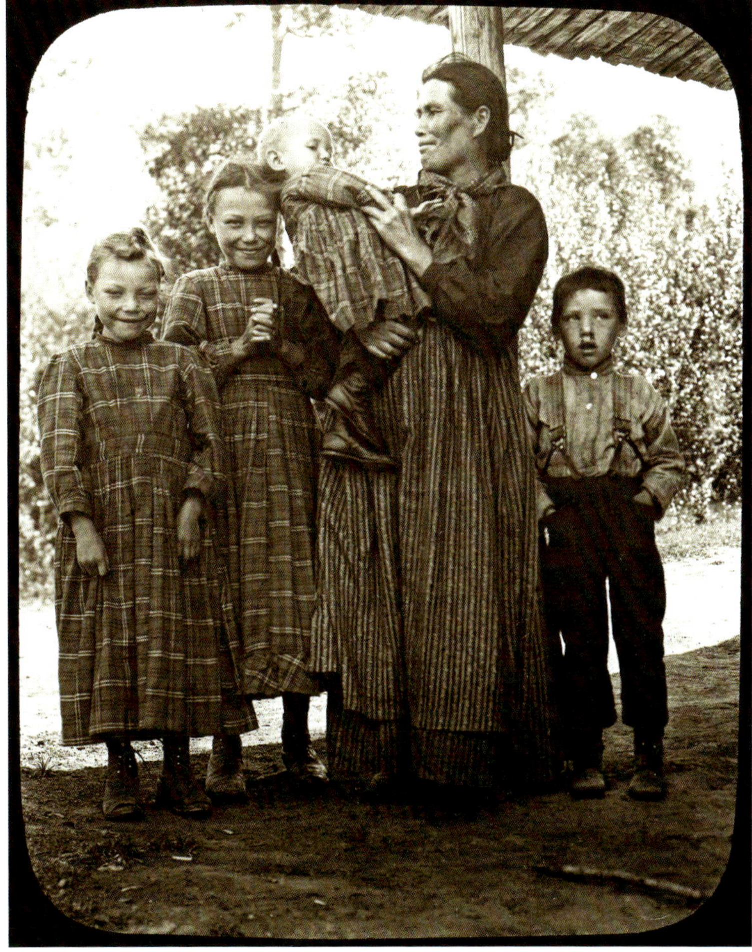

FIGURE 4.8

Suzette Chalifoux Swift and her children, Mary Schäffer photograph, 1908.

[WMCR V527/PD-1-116 and V527/PD-4]

Mary Schäffer monochromatic lantern slide (printed in reverse from the negative)

[WMCR V527/PS1-96]

American studies scholar Louis Owens, of Choctaw, Cherokee, and Irish-American heritage, writes about "[chafing] at the ignorance and erasure of Native American voices within the metropolitan center and within what at times appear to be the loyal opposition to that center called postcolonial theory....It seems that a necessary, if difficult, lesson for all of us may well be that in giving voice to the silent we unavoidably give voice to the forces that conspire to effect that silence."[77] This is precisely what has happened to the sitters, culture, and event occupying the portrait of the Beaver family—a paradox, given its currency as a tourist token evoking voyeurism and as a palimpsest of the historic past that is sought by travellers and readers alike. Even scholars are not immune to this longing. There is no question that the critical discourse that has been constructed around the portrait of Sampson, Frances Louise, and Leah Beaver is a stellar example of Owens's observation.

Owens's lament is one we must heed as we recirculate such photographs, or consume them. Now in the public domain, the photographic portrait circulates as the intellectual, creative, or commercial property of others—not that of the sitters, their descendants, and their community, or the photographer and her descendants.

Recirculation lays down a historical layer each time, made distinct by conditions of the day. In the case of the portrait of the Beavers, matters such as treaty, colonialism, a nascent tourist economy in a new field of capitalist incursion, the Woman Question, masculinity, Indigenous land rights, and education inform the originating context of production and consumption. But its "home," its originating context of display and consumption, was travel literature and memoir—genres that mix fiction and non-fiction, fact and imagination—in which authorial credibility and authority are fortified by the photograph serving as truth, leavening the creative licence that the author applies to her narrative. A century later, scholars draw our attention along a sharply focused angle of view (that of colonialism and the spectre of racism) to something that is represented but not seen—the interaction of those involved in producing the image: the sitters and the photographer, the Beaver family and Mary Schäffer. The "crisp presentness" engages the viewer—academic and tourist alike—while it remains intractable, refusing and frustrating viewers' access to the originating moment. Given the difficulties that contemporary scholars have with this photograph, perhaps the portrait on which Schäffer and the Beavers cooperated does not recall, record, or invent the past (as Susan Sontag famously stated about the work of American photographers),[78] so much as refuse the future—our present.

The tangle of recirculation and consumption sketched here demonstrates that the successive historical contexts in which a photograph circulates are significant and valid: like any work of cultural endeavour, such as music, literature, design, film, or fine art, a photograph is taken up by succeeding generations because something—its quality, content, or purpose, perhaps—speaks to a later time and place in some significant way. Furthermore, the meanings layered by these succeeding engagements cannot be ignored, nor should they be peeled away and discarded in an attempt to recover or reclaim an original and stable meaning. Meaning would have varied even among the first readers of *Old Indian Trails*, female and male, active wilderness visitors and distant armchair explorers alike.

Sketching Chaba Imne

The three maps drawn between 1907 and 1911 serve today as ciphers along the trajectory of the concept of Maligne Lake from rumour and legend (Chabe Imne) to wilderness to landscape to place. Like photographs, maps are generally understood to represent factually both a physical entity and (like memoir) a truth. But as Schwartz and Ryan observe, maps, like memoirs and photographs, are "a complex and culturally-constructed means of representing knowledge" that create a particular sense of a place.[79] For Maligne Lake, it all begins visually with Sampson Beaver's sketched mapping in late summer 1907, which Schäffer describes this way in *Old Indian Trails*:

> *One of the greatest trophies we carried with us when leaving the next day for the North Fork of the Saskatchewan was a tiny grubby bit of paper on which Sampson had with much care traced the lake we had tried so hard to find, which was supposed to lie north of Brazeau Lake. He had been there but once, a child of fourteen, and now a man of thirty, he drew it from memory,—mountains, streams, and passes all included. They had to be labelled for our benefit, for he had probably never seen a geography in his life, and it would be hard to remember for a whole year that a very scribbly spot was a pass, and that something which looked like a squashed spider he called a mountain.*[80]

Rather than leaving it to readers' imaginations to create an idea of Beaver's map in their mind's eye, a pencil sketch labelled "Sampson's map" was reproduced in the midst of this paragraph (Fig. 4.9).[81] Given the ephemeral and transitory nature of such images, it is an unexpected visual pleasure for the reader to encounter it, with the visceral impact it conveys. It is also an intrusion, as the reader's imagination is interrupted and prevented from forming a different impression of how the map may have looked. Such sketched mappings were rarely published at this time, and so the inclusion of this one in *Old Indian Trails* is significant. Beyond the value attributed to it by Schäffer as a turning point in their quest, publishing the sketch serves to secure the truth and credibility of Schäffer's account and the primacy of her claim to have found the real Chaba Imne. For historians today seeking corroborating evidence that Beaver in fact sketched a map, Molly Adams's diary again helps. On 7 July she wrote in camp at Maligne Lake, "So it is discovered at last. Sampson shortened the distance on his map, but it is pretty good all the same."[82]

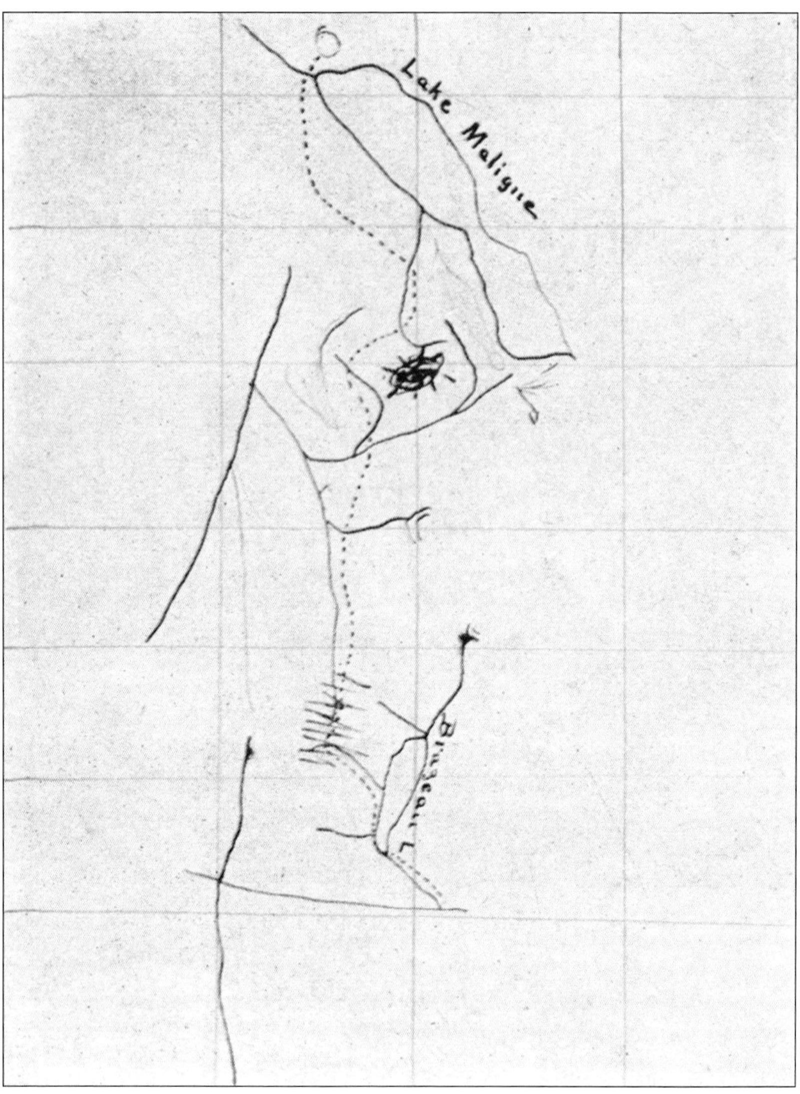

FIGURE 4.9

"Sampson's Map," in *Old Indian Trails* (1911), 183.

Geographer Denis Wood asks, "Where *does* the map's authority come from?" and answers, "It arises directly from the *certainty* guaranteed by the map's object quality, by its being…*a thing in the world*."[83] In the case of the sketched map attributed to Sampson Beaver, the image acts in the context of the book in two important ways: as documentary evidence of Indigenous experience, knowledge, and history in the region, in alignment with an understanding among some of the day that wilderness does not exclude human presence; and as material evidence of Schäffer's first-hand access to and acquisition of that knowledge. In that way, this sketch serves a crucial purpose in authenticating her claim to have found and documented the existence of the legendary but uncharted lake. It also serves to prove that the lake she and her companions found was in fact that of rumour and legend. Its veracity is claimed in its seeming crudeness, which Schäffer attributes to what she suggests is Beaver's likely lack of a geography education, as well as by the fact that it was drawn in some detail from a memory of Beaver's personal experience, despite an intervening decade-and-a-half since he had reportedly last seen the lake.

Beaver's map, by being "a thing in the world," in turn brings into knowledge and thus existence the lake as a "thing," or place, in the non-Indigenous world.[84] The publication of the sketch also serves as tangible evidence of a symbolic claim to the legend and transfer of the landscape and place from Stoney society to Euro-North American culture. Schäffer explains the inscriptions on "the grubby bit of paper," which match the script on other maps she drew, as labels to help the later travellers translate the meaning of the sketched elements. That the found lake is labelled "Maligne," however, suggests that the inscriptions in fact came later, after the lake was found. For it was Chaba Imne, as it was known to the Stoney, that Schäffer and Adams and their guides sought. The lake was not renamed Maligne until after they found it in 1908, and understood that its waters flowed into the already-named Maligne River:

> *Having almost lost two horses at the lake's very quiet looking outlet, and having learned that Maligne River (named these many years, and which empties into the Athabaska River opposite Henry House), headed not from Medicine Lake, as it appears on McEvoy's map, but merely flowing through it, came direct from our "new" lake, all the party decided the river named the lake, and it has since been so recorded.*
>
> *Ten days later, when we stood on the banks of the Maligne River at its junction with the Athabaska, its turbulent condition was reason enough to our minds why some old French half-breed trapper had called it thus—he forgotten, its troublous water never, as long as those waters flow.*[85]

The authenticity of the sketch map that appears in *Old Indian Trails* has not been questioned publicly, to the best of my knowledge. Given Adams's corroborating comments, there is no reason to doubt that Beaver sketched a map to show Schäffer's group the location of the lake and the trail to follow to get there. Whether the sketch published is in fact Beaver's own work is another question. Beyond the probability that the labelling was done after the journey met with success, and in preparation for publication rather than as a guide to finding the lake, there are at least four additional reasons to question the published sketch's authenticity. One is that the "squashed spider" calligraphy of landmarks in the drawing, as it is described by Schäffer, is a feature found also in Schäffer's own printed and hand-drawn (or manuscript) maps of Maligne Lake (Figs. 4.1 and 4.12).[86] It is also seen in the unpublished drawing she made for the Geological Survey of Canada that appends the rationale for the names proposed for various geographical landmarks (Fig. 4.14). A second reason is that another reproduction of Beaver's map, labelled "The Indian's Map," appears in "A Recently Explored Lake," an article that Schäffer published in the *Bulletin of the Geographical Society of Philadelphia* in 1909, two years prior to the publication of *Old Indian Trails* (Fig. 4.10).[87] This map clearly differs from that published in *Old Indian Trails*; it seems roughly traced over the version in the book, and the manner in which it is labelled, as well as the naming of Maligne and Brazeau lakes, also differ. Yet it too is claimed to be (a reproduction of) the original from Beaver's hand. Thirdly, a lantern slide labelled "Sampson's Map '08" appears to be the same as the one published in *Old Indian Trails* (Fig. 4.11). This version, however, lacks the grid, the labelling of the lakes, and the enhanced drawing of some landmarks that Schäffer had claimed were done to help her and her party remember the meaning of the marks on the map when it was put to use a year after Beaver drew it. Finally, it is interesting to note that the shape of the lake in all versions of the sketch is very similar to that seen in the photograph of the lake attributed to Sidney Unwin, and as charted by the survey that Schäffer made on a return trip for that purpose in 1911. Would Beaver have known or remembered the shape of the lake in such detail from his boyhood visit? He may well have gained a bird's-eye perspective of the fourteen-mile long lake in the same way Unwin did by climbing to the top of a mountain offering a panoramic view of the lake. While Unwin estimated the lake to be about eighteen miles long when he returned from his expedition,[88] only a small part of the lake below the narrows was visible from Unwin's vantage point when he made his photograph. Perhaps its full shape was part of Stoney knowledge. The remarkable similarity between the sketch and Unwin's photograph, however, add to my skepticism about the veracity of the published sketches' origins, in light of the variances in the published sketches attributed to Beaver.

Schäffer's published stories of the origins of Beaver's sketched map differ in subtle ways as well. While the unattributed report in the April 1912 journal of the *Royal Geographical Society* states merely that Schäffer's group "met a

FIGURE 4.10

"The Indian's Map," in *Bulletin of the Geographical Society of Philadelphia* 7, no. 3 (July 1909): 124.

2 *A Recently Explored Lake*

ness north of Laggan, armed with the little map, and the unknown lake a prime feature of the expedition.

Our route lay over the now familiar Bow Pass, which owing to our early start, was still heavily clad in the winter's snow, thence down Bear Creek to its junction with the Saskatchewan, and then up the east side of the North Fork of the Saskatchewan to its junction with Nigel Creek. Here we bore to the right, ascended Nigel Creek on its south side, traversed the pass of the same name, and dropped to the head waters of a branch of the Brazeau River.

Camping at an old, well-frequented Indian camp-ground two miles below the lake, our men explored some distance ahead, to see if the way was passable for horses—as Dr. Coleman is the only explorer of that section on record, he having crossed Pobokton Pass in 1892.

The trail was found very readily, with Dr. Coleman's cuttings quite distinct, as well as some very old blazes, which proclaimed it a long-favored Indian highway. The lake was crossed at its mouth where the ford was but three and a half feet deep—surprisingly shallow for a body of water six miles long and a mile wide.

From there a sharp ascent was made to overcome some obstructing cliffs on the lake-shore with as sudden a drop to the lake, where

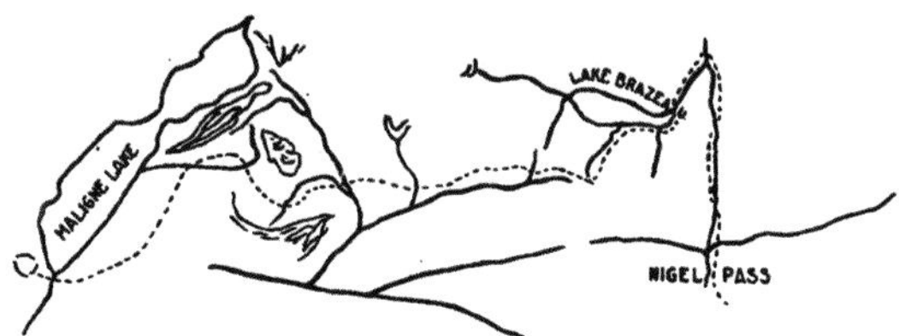

THE INDIAN'S MAP.

we encountered a half mile of bad muskeg. Having successfully surmounted that trail, the way became well defined and led in easy gradations for some time toward the pass.

Horse-feed however was scarce throughout the entire valley, and was only obtained in moderate quantities at 6,300 feet where we camped. The ascent to the summit of Pobokton Pass from that camp proved excessively steep, and furthermore the entire pass was

(124)

Stoney Indian, who gave information as to the best method of reaching the lake,"[89] Schäffer writes in the *Bulletin of the Geographical Society of Philadelphia* of 1909 that Beaver "quickly sketched a crude map of the desired section,"[90] in contrast to tracing the lake "with much care" as written later in *Old Indian Trails*.[91] Furthermore, recounting the sketch's efficacy in 1909 (and in contrast to Adams's diary entry in 1908), Schäffer claimed that "it was at this time we should much have preferred Sampson to his rather indefinite map; and that

FIGURE 4.11

"Sampson's Map '08," Mary Schäffer lantern slide, n.d.

[WMCR V427/PS1-53]

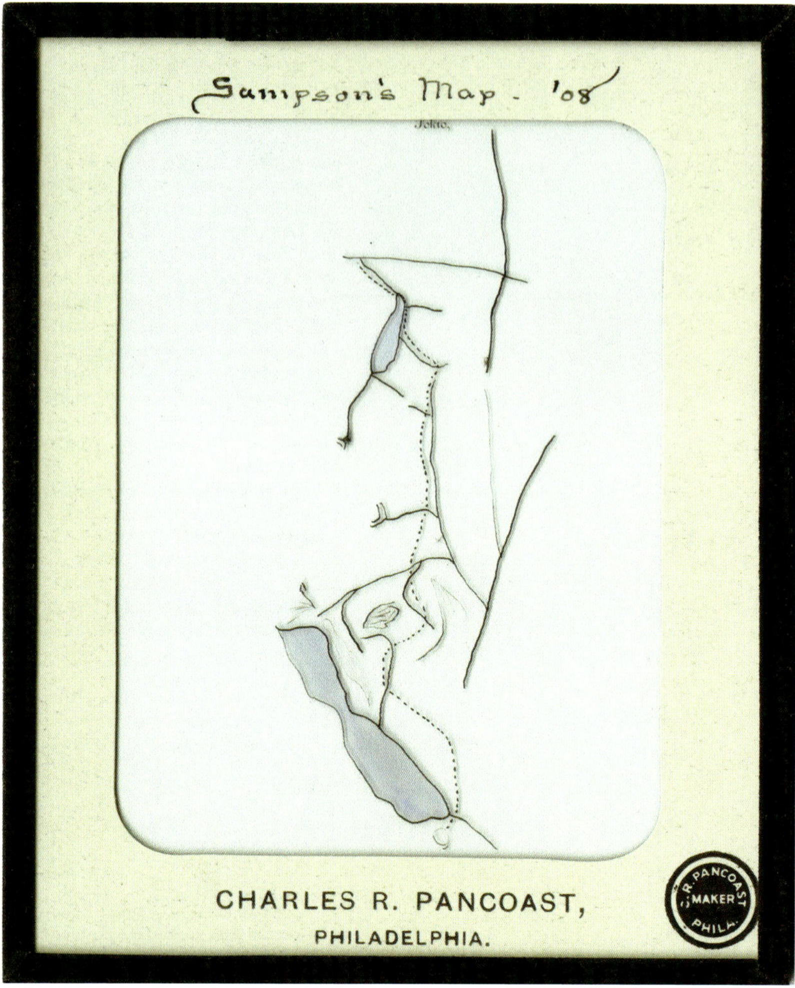

we ever did strike the trail which eventually led us to our destination, was due rather to the dogged persistence and determination of our men, than to any very clear ideas expressed in the little sketch-map."[92] Nevertheless, Schäffer acknowledges that "Sampson had sketched 'narrows' in the upper end of the lake (remember he was only a boy of fifteen when last he was there, and now a man of thirty-five): we found those narrows just where he had drawn them, and above them a towering rocky peak which we named for him."[93] In *Old Indian Trails*, the sketch was said to have been "stowed away in a pocket of the said travel-worn diary"[94]—and when used on the journey of 1908, the map was found to be vague: "The Indians' [*sic*] map told us to leave the valley at the third creek coming in from the right. We had already passed a dozen of them and were now passing another, but no horse-feed was in sight."[95]

Cartographer and scholar Nikolas H. Huffman acknowledges that the discipline and practice of cartography had been traditionally understood by mapmakers and readers to be scientifically based and objective, a rendering of geographical facts unaffected by the experiences and social context of the individuals who constructed a map and thereby visualized an environment for others. He takes the position, however, that there are more complex ways to think about, assess, and undertake cartography that extend the boundaries and practices of the discipline.[96] He argues, for example, that it is critical to recognize that the gender of the mapmaker is a component in the creation of cartographical knowledge.[97] His view is not an isolated one. Huffman aggregates the thinking of a cohort of map scholars who see that "different cultures have different social spaces, and produce very different kinds of maps," and that a map is "'a social construction of reality' that serves to create the social and political spaces…[it represents] by linking the territory depicted on the map with the social and spatial mandates that go with the map."[98] This now-mainstream view emerged among cartographic scholars in the 1980s and 1990s. Geographer Mona Domosh's work is representative. She cautions that meaning should not be derived from who the author is, or from the author's individual experience. Rather, "different people…experience those circumstances differently, depending of course on how they have been positioned in society,"[99] and it is the social, political, economic, or other contexts in which these experiences take place, not the individual or experiences themselves alone, that need to be examined for meaning. The same can be said for photographs and texts.

Will C. van den Hoonaard takes up this strand of thinking in his 2013 study *Map Worlds: A History of Women in Cartography*. He argues that women's participation in cartographic production is a function of the way in which various times and places were socially organized, which in turn "was shaped by the advent of technological advances, social customs, scientific knowledge, and larger political forces."[100] In the case of Schäffer's and Adams's work, the way in which they originally participated and the kind of challenge to the status quo they launched align with Van den Hoonaard's observation that "women are often associated with the 'gathering' of knowledge, such as research, compilation, assistance, and preparation of maps materials."[101] Schäffer's botanical work in the Rocky Mountains of Canada, and the publication of *Alpine Flora* with Stewardson Brown, are cases in point of this kind of activity.

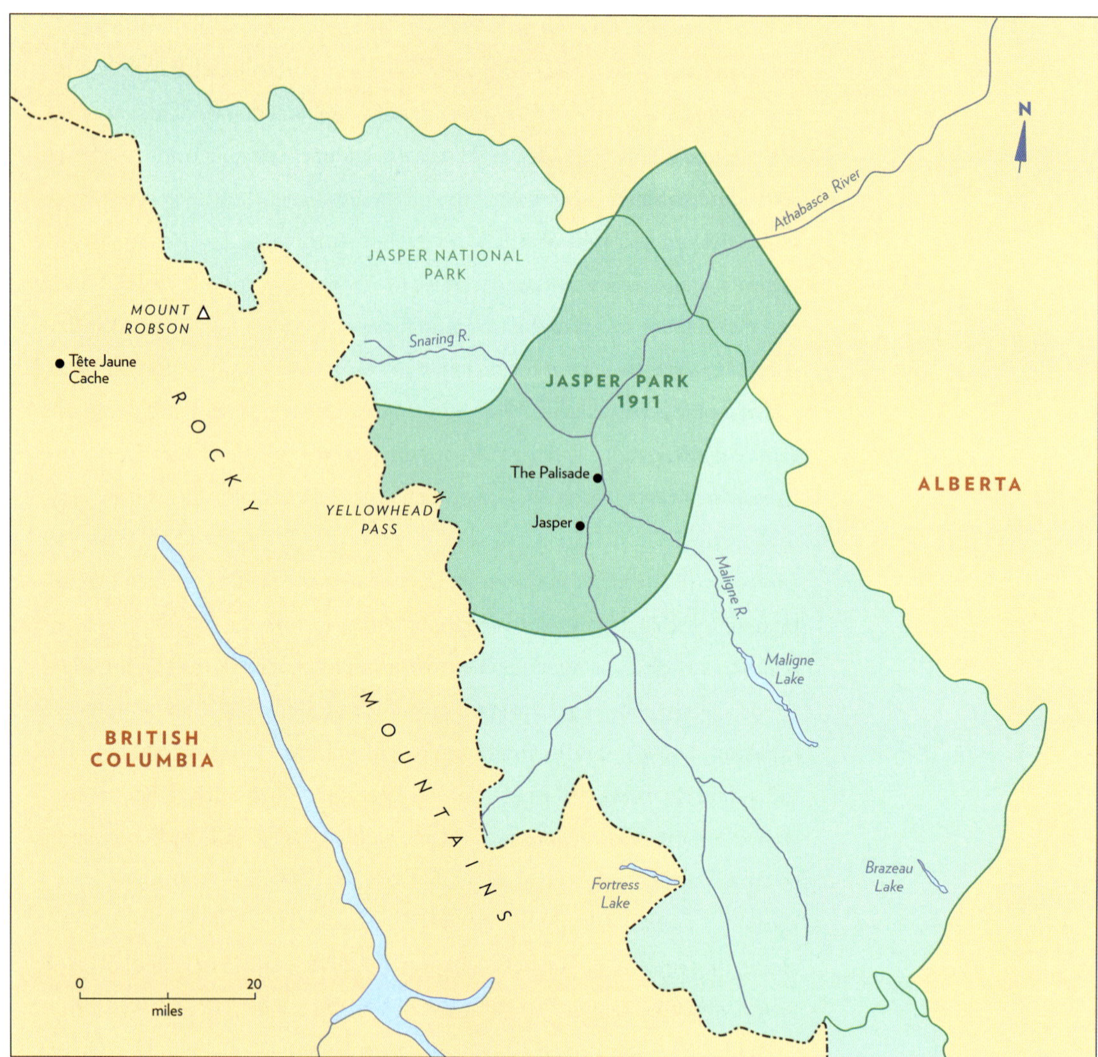

MAP 2
Jasper National Park today with overlay of 1911 boundaries that excluded Maligne Lake from the park, established in 1907, just prior to Mary Schäffer's return to survey the lake.

Schäffer's mapmaking took place in a time when the final object was rendered and received as a scientifically grounded image conveyed in a shared Euro-North American language of cartography. However, the inclusion of Beaver's mapping, read (at the time, and to date) as the authentic original sketch, along with Schäffer's topographical map in *Old Indian Trails*, were editorial decisions that demonstrate an astute understanding of the complexity of factors that informed the reception of a map. These include the circumstances in which it was made and the social perception of the individual who made it. In the same way, the politically astute and strategic choice of the Geological Survey of Canada to commission Schäffer to undertake the official survey of Maligne Lake in 1911, as the boundaries of the area set aside as a national park in 1907 were being reconsidered, demonstrates the same multi-faceted understanding of the significance and impact of social, scientific, economic, and other factors in the construction of meaning in a map. This is also reflected in their subsequent publication of her map and adoption of the place names that she bestowed in the region.

Wood has established the significance of the difference between "mapping" and "mapmaking." This distinction is helpful in understanding how the two maps that are published in Schäffer's book—the sketch map attributed to Beaver and Schäffer's topographic map—serve different functions, but together make crucial contributions to the image and idea of Maligne Lake that Schäffer's work produced at the time of publication, and continues to produce a century later through subsequent study and publication of her work. Nikolas Huffman explains, "For Wood (1993), mappings, such as sketch maps, are ephemeral images that share spatial information between people engaged in interpersonal communications, but whose meaning and utility evaporate upon leaving the communication setting."[102] Beaver's sketch served in exactly the way both Wood and Huffman describe. Recreating the moment of making the sketch, and its impact, in the narrative of *Old Indian Trails* for the benefit of readers is an important and informed narrative strategy. "On the other hand," Huffman continues, "the map is a tangible, graphic record that has a stable presence of its own and is intended to bear its meaning beyond the immediate mapping setting through shared interpretable cartographic codes. Mapmaking differs from mapping because it allows one to consolidate the power of recreating spaces in the form of a map that can be carried away from the scene, manipulated, compared to, and integrated with other images and spaces."[103] Schäffer's topographical map incorporates many details about both natural and human-made features that create new knowledge about the area and confirm established geographical information. At the same time, its standardized format inscribes scientific authority and authorial credibility.

In contrast, Martin Dodge has argued that a map of the kind that Beaver reportedly drew on the spur of the moment, which he calls an impromptu map, "has an intrinsic appeal because of its amateur nature and uniqueness." This type of map also sparks a question from Dodge that, when transposed to the question of Sampson Beaver's map, is especially insightful: "These are made as one-off maps rather than being mass-produced; they are ephemeral and personal objects, made in-the-moment to solve immediate spatial tasks and never meant to be kept. But what happens when you do keep them, and then reproduce them in a professionally designed book? Are they still interesting?"[104]

Applied to the context of *Old Indian Trails*, Dodge's question underscores the comparisons and contrasts that come to mind: the description of the "grubby bit of paper" in contrast to the professionally produced, finely detailed, definitive printed map that Schäffer produced for the book; the suggestion that Beaver's assumed lack of formal education makes the sketch more of a reassurance than a reliable guide, thereby diminishing its substance and significance; and the transient versus enduring natures of the two images, the first being a "mapping," the latter a "map." In his review of a collection of hand-drawn maps, Dodge remarks, the book "has almost nothing to say on the performance of mapping….The book's presentation makes all the maps seem solid, complete artifacts, yet the reason these maps matter is surely that they were living mappings of space. The map images now fixed on the printed page are thoroughly disconnected from the contexts in which they were brought in[to] being: rather than lively mappings, we have a parade of dead maps."[105]

In contrast, in the context of *Old Indian Trails*, we find what Dodge was craving: an engagement of mapping in perpetuity. This is evident in the hand-drawn map's emergence as an integral part of the narrative and a crucial moment leading to the success of the quest, forever tied to the man who is said to have made the map. It is also evident as the two maps—sketched and topographical, ephemeral and printed—play off one another, the existence of the former seemingly essential to both the possibility and truth of the latter. In both cases as well as the third—the survey map—Schäffer recounts in texts and photographs the performances or stories of the various actions and behaviours that took place to constitute each map.

Dodge also succinctly raises the issue of the politics of mapping that is evident in Schäffer's work as well: "The class of professional versus amateur knowledges and rights to the authorship of mapping of the 'here and now,' as against relying on the 'official' maps, are worthwhile points to debate."[106] The tensions between amateur and professional, female and male, aboriginal and white, indigenous and settler, traditional knowledge and formal education, wilderness and civilization are important, although usually only implicit, aspects of Schäffer's story. It is clear in Schäffer's published work that she, like other Euro-North Americans of her time and place, understood wilderness to

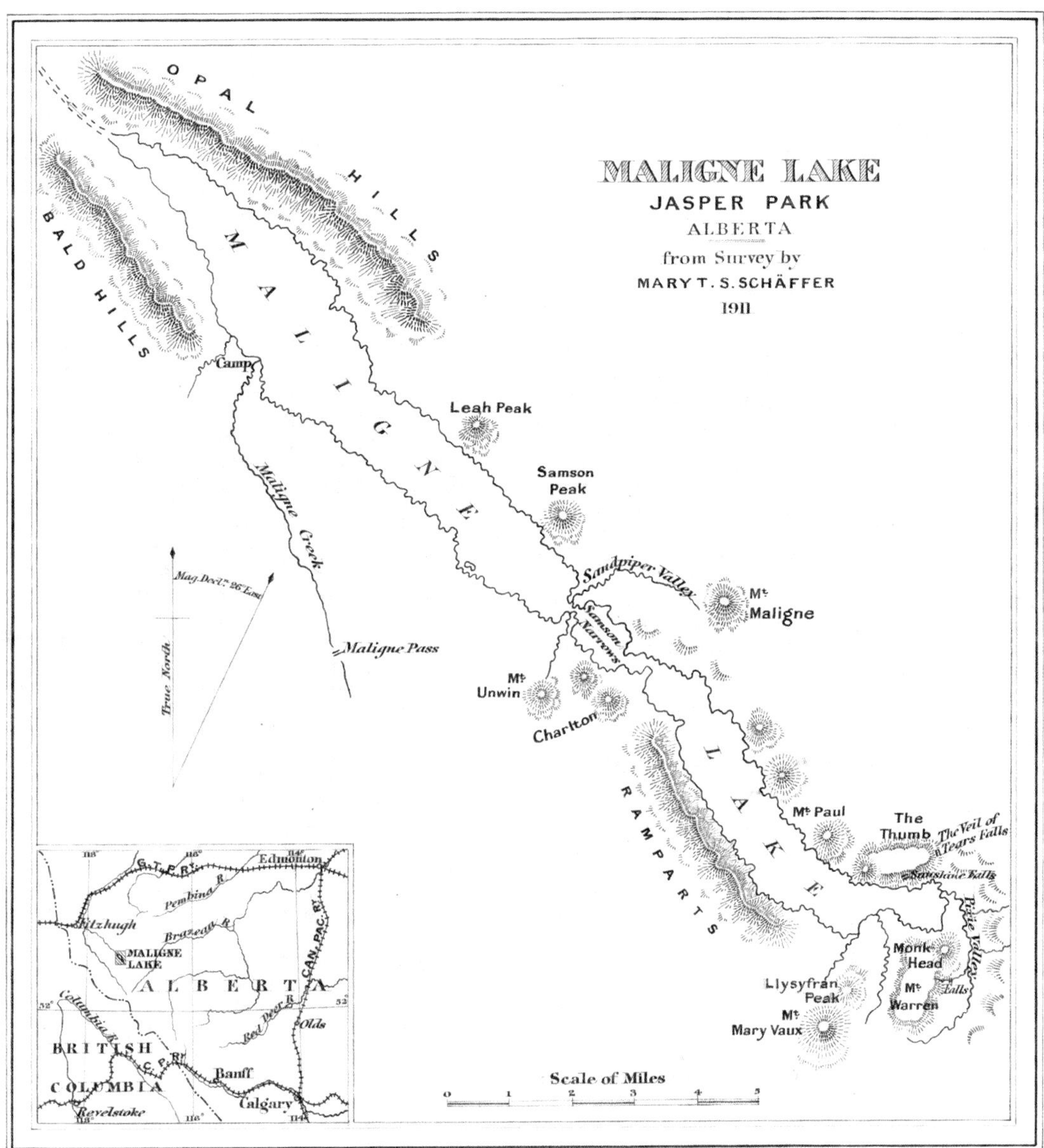

FIGURE 4.12

"Maligne Lake from Survey by Mary T.S. Schäffer, 1911." Reproduced in the *Canadian Alpine Journal* 4 (1912): 95. [WMCR M79/9A Oversize F]

be a place long-traversed by humans. In "Hunting a Lost Lake," published in 1911 in the American magazine *Travel*, Schäffer writes about following

> *the course taken by hunters, traders and Indians for the two centuries that the Yellowhead Pass has been known to the white man as the lowest one north of the border line....For here on the shores of the Athabaska, after traveling at least three hundred miles by trail, we had come upon the first human habitations. Those three hundred miles of most magnificent mountain*

scenery, are scenery alone. From time immemorial the Indian tribes near the boundary have used the country for fall hunting. A network of old, almost obliterated trails are in every direction, but we have never seen the first sign of a permanent camp.[107]

›FIGURE 4.13
Mary Schäffer with Paul Sharpless and Caroline Sharpless, photographer unknown, 1911.
[WMCR V527/NA-78]

Sustained, if transient, human presence in the landscape defines wilderness for Schäffer's generation.

Old Indian Trails also established Schäffer's claim to the legacy of Maligne Lake. This connection was further sealed by the survey of the lake, which Schäffer undertook at the invitation of the Geological Survey of Canada in 1911, just weeks after *Old Indian Trails* was published. She reported her work and findings the following year, including publication of her official map of the lake in both the *Canadian Alpine Journal* and the *Geographical Journal* of London.[108]

Surveying Maligne Lake

When Caroline Sharpless and her ten-year-old son, Paul, arrived in Edmonton on 4 June 1911, she "found Mary at the hotel busy talking to reporters."[109] Most importantly, she met Mary Schäffer, her sister-in-law, with a special package in hand. On the day Sharpless had left home in New York a week earlier, she had gone "to Putnam's where they gave me the two very first copies of 'Indian Trails', just in from their publishing house. They could not give me a copy with the colored picture on the cover so instead of leaving the space blank they put in Sidney Unwin's picture 'baking bannock.' I am delighted to think I am the bearer of the first copy to the author."[110] As a result, Schäffer carried *Old Indian Trails of the Canadian Rockies* with her on her return to the lake by train and on horseback along tote roads and newly cut trails.

In May 1911, Schäffer had returned to Banff for another summer in the Rockies.[111] At the beginning of June, she journeyed by train from Banff to Calgary and then north to the terminus of the Canadian Pacific Railway's Calgary–Edmonton Railway at the Town of Strathcona, on the south side of the North Saskatchewan River. (The CPR's High Level Bridge linking Strathcona to Edmonton would not open until 1913.) Schäffer then travelled over the river by means of the Low Level Bridge in "an ancient stage [a horse-drawn stage-coach]...into the very heart of one of the most modern up-to-date wide-awake cities of the northwest—Edmonton. Rooms such as they were, were obtained, with a muttered, 'You can be thankful you have these. If you were a man, you

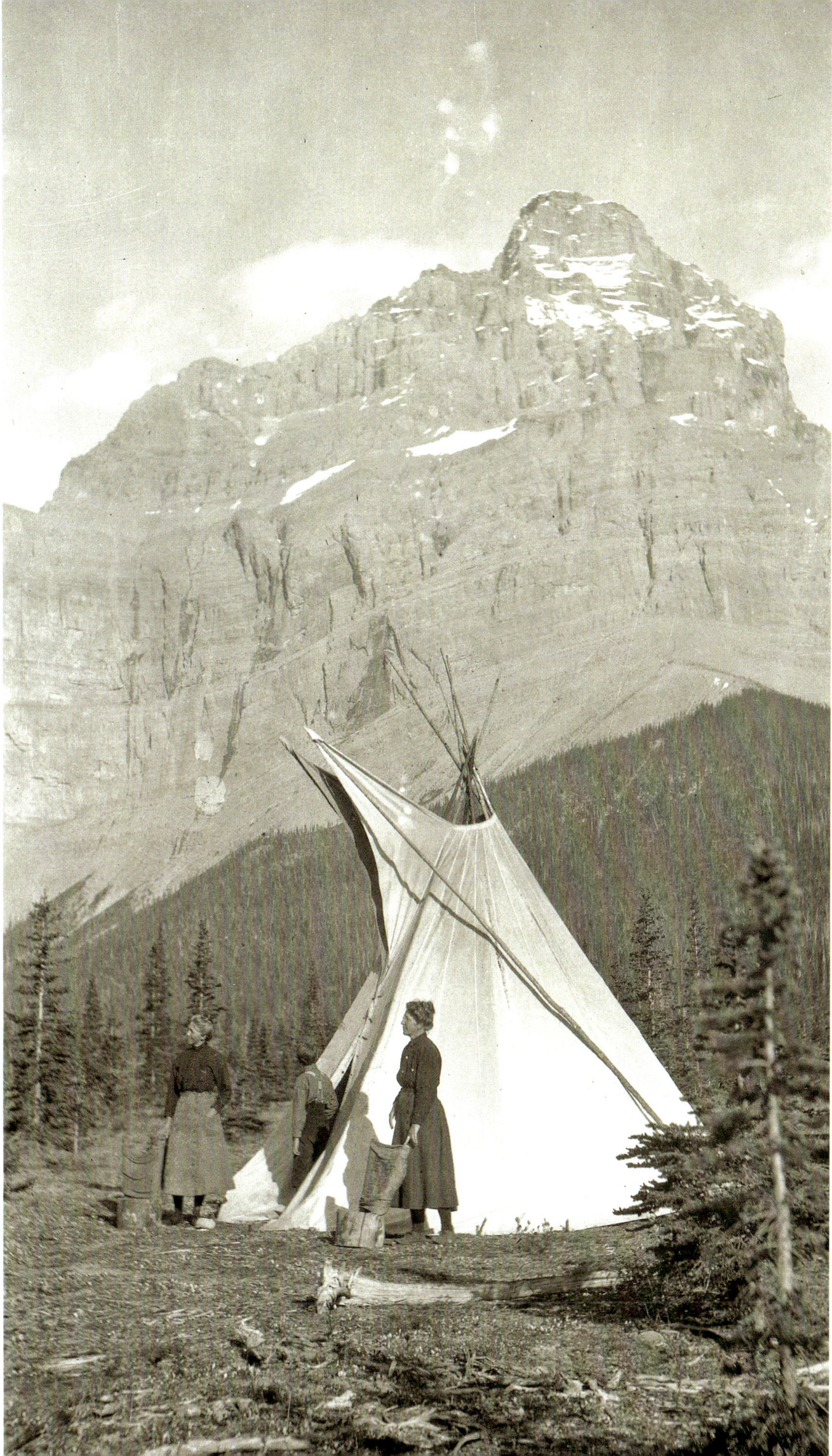

might walk the streets.' (Once more thankful for being a woman.)"[112] She arrived to find that "the city was filled to overflowing with incoming strangers" and counted herself fortunate to find lodging at the King Edward Hotel[113] where "we accepted our fate—the mattress and mud—silently, and wished for the day and the hour when the long trail and its comforts were ours."[114] Schäffer's unpublished narrative is substantiated by Caroline Sharpless's diary description of her first impression of the city and their hotel: "Water here is adulterated mud and they give us only a thimbleful to wash in. The city has a population of 30,000 and is a nice little prairie town, lots of poplar trees around it, some nice houses and is on the Saskatchewan River, a pretty winding river, wooded to its edges."[115]

Here Schäffer, Sharpless, and young Paul paused for almost a week to prepare for travel to Maligne Lake. In 1907 and 1908, Schäffer and Molly Adams had travelled at their own motivation and expense to seek the legendary lake. In 1911, Schäffer was travelling under the auspices of the Geological Survey of Canada. Among her guides and packers was Sidney Unwin ("K" in *Old Indian Trails*). The lead guide this time was Jack Otto; William Warren was not part of the team, nor was Molly Adams, who had died in 1909. Schäffer's sister-in-law and nephew had been recruited from their home in New York City to serve as travelling companions.

In late September 1908, reflecting on their journey, Molly Adams had written, "We are glad we got there, for of course we should never have been satisfied otherwise, but we all agreed that our next trip to the Athabasca would be by train (railroad train, not pack train)."[116] As predicted, in 1911 Schäffer's group travelled on the Grand Trunk Pacific (GTP) Railway, which had begun passenger service through Edmonton in 1910.[117] Passenger service on the new GTP ran from Winnipeg through Edmonton and as far as Hinton, Alberta, in 1911. From there, construction continued to Jasper townsite and through the Yellowhead Pass to terminate finally at Prince Rupert, British Columbia, in 1914. On 7 June, Schäffer, Sharpless, Unwin, and Paul boarded the GTP train for the nearly 180-mile journey to Hinton.[118] They were met by guide Jack Otto and departed from there the next day by a train of pack horses to undertake a twelve-day trip along established tote roads, where they encountered numerous other travellers, and then on newly cut trails to Maligne Lake, arriving on 20 June. The survey, undertaken amid rain, hail, snow, and cold—not unusual mountain weather at that time of year in Schäffer's experience—took a little more than a month. Work was completed on 24 July, and the group left their campsite the next day. On 2 August, a couple of days after encountering along the way Schäffer's sponsor, D.B. Dowling of the Geological Survey of Canada, the pack train arrived at GTP Telegraph Station 65. There they boarded a small train of about a dozen freight and passenger cars travelling along an unstable and crooked track (which was forced to stop three times when one or more cars slid off the rails) to connect with the main GTP passenger train at Edson, Alberta. They departed Edson for Edmonton later the next day, 3 August, and after an eventful trip, which included Caroline Sharpless assisting with a birth on board, arrived in Edmonton.[119] On 11 August, Schäffer returned to Banff to draft the survey map, while Sharpless and her son continued to New York.

The Edmonton press took notice of Schäffer's excursion to Maligne Lake and, on her return, her opposition to the reduction of park areas that had been imposed earlier that summer. She stressed the threat posed to wildlife that was no longer protected from hunters, both Indigenous and settler, outside the new minimal park areas.[120] Schäffer's concern and reasoning for maintaining established park reserves embody the seemingly contradictory motivations for national park conservation: to protect the flora and fauna of a region from the depredations of industrial development, which Schäffer knew to be inexorable in the Rockies, and to provide a place for settler Canadians and other tourists to experience wilderness with the aid of human amenities that the tourism industry could provide, while excluding Indigenous nations from traditional territories and subsistence hunting there. In 1908, the travellers foresaw the future and fate of Maligne Lake. Adams wrote in her diary, "We all agree that Maligne Lake is one of the finest things in the Rockies or Selkirks. The upper half is right in high mountains, the lower more open and gentle looking. It will probably be a great resort some day when the Grand Trunk is done."[121] Schäffer cast the group's pragmatic observation with a melancholy tone in the conclusion to *Old Indian Trails*.

> *The following morning, "all set," we said, "Good-bye; will see you when the first Grand Trunk Pacific train comes through," and passed on, knowing we were coming to the beginning of the end. As we crossed the Athabaska, we realized that next time we came that way our horses would not have to swim for it, all would be made easy with trains and bridges; that the hideous march of progress, so awful to those who love the real wilderness, was sweeping rapidly over the land and would wipe out all trail troubles.*[122]

Schäffer's photographs, articles, maps, and book about her and her companions' quest to locate the "mythical" "lost" lake were published between 1908 and 1912, at a politically sensitive moment in the emergence of the Canadian conservation and national parks movement. Her work both captured and shaped an idea of Maligne Lake as a physical and cultural entity with an ancient past in human knowledge and an immediate future of rapidly escalating human incursion, securing its place in readers' geographical imaginations as a jewel of the Rocky Mountains owned and protected by the government of Canada.

Mistaken Identity

Denis Wood asserts that a map makes a place a thing, and Marlene Creates that "the land is important…but even more important is the idea that it becomes a 'place' because someone has been there."[123] In this context, bestowing names on a landscape's geographical features serves to stake a claim to ownership, if not of the site itself, at least of its first sighting, as in this case. An unsigned, hand-drawn map of Maligne Lake and its surrounding topography that appears to have been made by Schäffer (given its distinctive "squashed spider" calligraphy marking mountains) lists the names bestowed by her group on various landmarks in 1908, along with the reasons for the names chosen (Fig. 4.14). American historian Alan Trachtenberg has argued that "naming lays claim to the view," for political and colonizing purposes. "By the same token," he argues, "a photograph attaches a possessable image to a place name. A named view is one that has been seen, known, and thereby already possessed."[124]

In the case of Maligne Lake and its surroundings, naming staked a claim on two levels—and, at the time, sparked controversy on one. On one level, reinforced by the survey and map produced on the return visit in 1911, which had been commissioned by the Geological Survey of Canada, the naming claimed the land for Canada, disenfranchising the Stoney and Cree of the eastern Rockies. On a second level—the one that proved controversial—it claimed the area as the site of Schäffer and Adams's successful incursion into territory previously unseen and uncharted by their male peers and predecessors. The fact that they were first was not contested; the burr under the saddle of surveyor Arthur O. Wheeler was his disagreement, publicly expressed, with Schäffer's choices of names, and dismay that the Geographic Board of Canada had accepted them.[125] The public disparagement may read today as gentlemanly and mild, if perhaps patronizing; at the time, given Schäffer's references in her private correspondence, it was perceived, at least by her—and rightly so—otherwise. Wheeler wrote,

> *The lake lies at an altitude of 5,525 feet. The key-note of the eastern margin is a high central peak (altitude 10,091 ft.) of grey limestone capped with snow, rising 4,566 feet above the water surface. From all points of view it stands alone, and suggests the name of "Mt. Lone Spur." I had so named it, but find that another name has been given by Mrs. Charles Schaffer that has been adopted by the Geographic Board of Canada. Mrs. Schaffer has spent many summers in the Canadian Rockies, first coming to them with her husband, the late Dr. Charles Schaffer, of Philadelphia, a charming personality, an intense lover of Nature and a good botanist, altogether a man whom it was a delight to meet. So frequently has Mrs. Schaffer visited the Canadian Rockies, that she is altogether Canadian in her love for them, and has done much as an original explorer to bring their attractions to public notice through her writings and lectures. She first visited and brought notice to this beautiful lake, which had previously been known only to the Indian and the hunter. She has, therefore, undoubtedly the right to name its features. I could wish, however, that personal names had not been so prominent, for the surrounding peaks have many striking characteristic features that seem naturally to supply the names.*[126]

Wheeler's report was published in the same issue of the *Canadian Alpine Journal* as Schäffer's article about her 1911 return to Maligne Lake to undertake a survey of the lake on behalf of the Geological Survey of Canada. Her article included the map of Maligne Lake based on the survey that featured the various named landmarks.[127]

Complementing the literary and sales success of *Old Indian Trails* that was to follow was the commercial success of the topographical map Schäffer produced, which was revised following the trip for the second printing of the book (Fig. 4.1). On 27 May 1911, while in Banff preparing for her return trip to survey Maligne Lake, Schäffer asked, in a letter to George Vaux Jr., "Did I tell thee the G.T.R. [Grand Trunk Railway] takes 10000 [*sic*] copies of the map of 'Old Indian Trails' with my name and the book on it?"[128] Later that year, on 21 November, again writing from Banff, where she planned to spend winter for the first time in a rented cabin to test the viability of living there year-round,

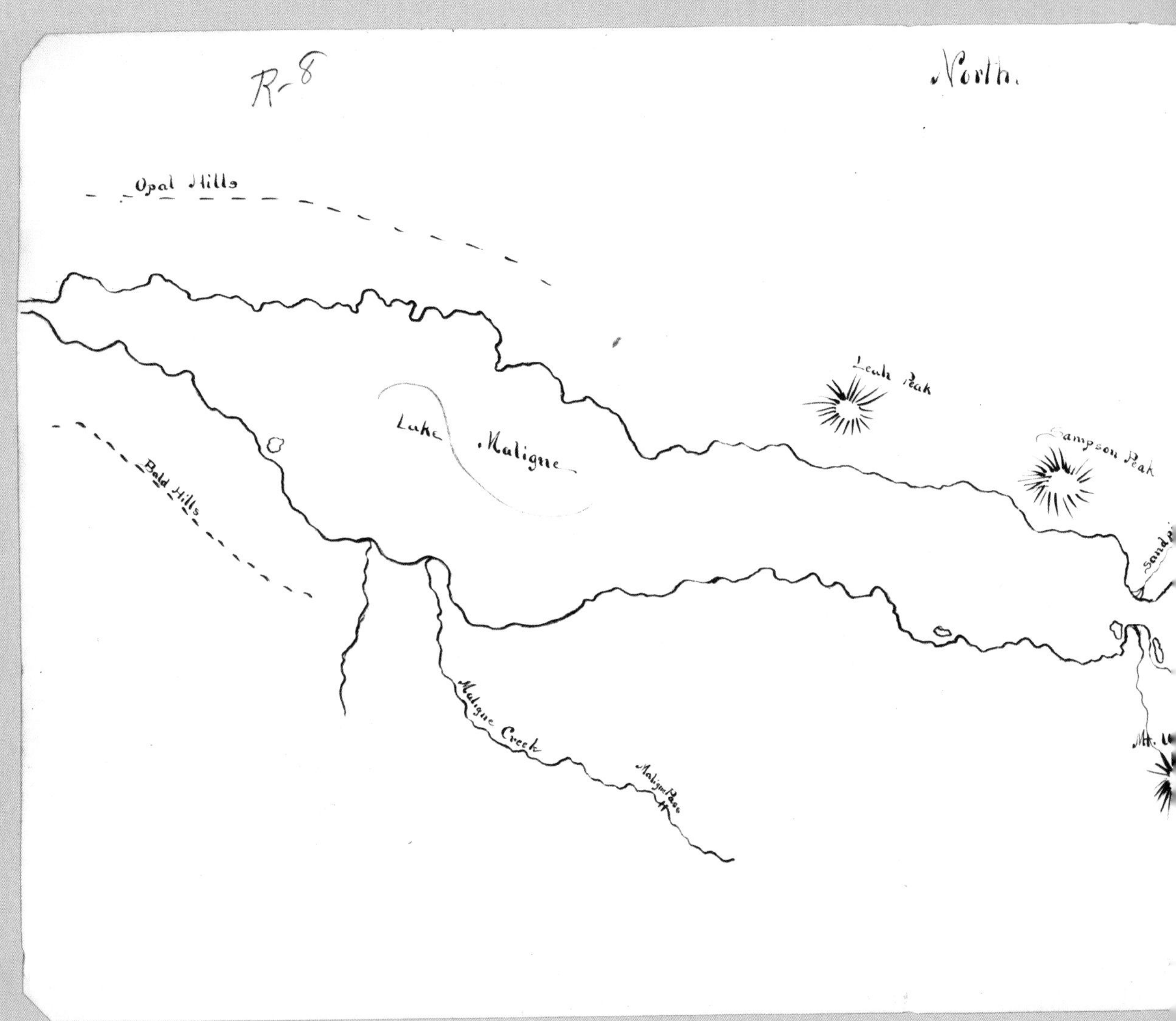

FIGURE 4.14

Annotated hand-drawn map of Maligne Lake, Mary Schäffer, ca. 1911. [WMCR M79/9A Oversize F]

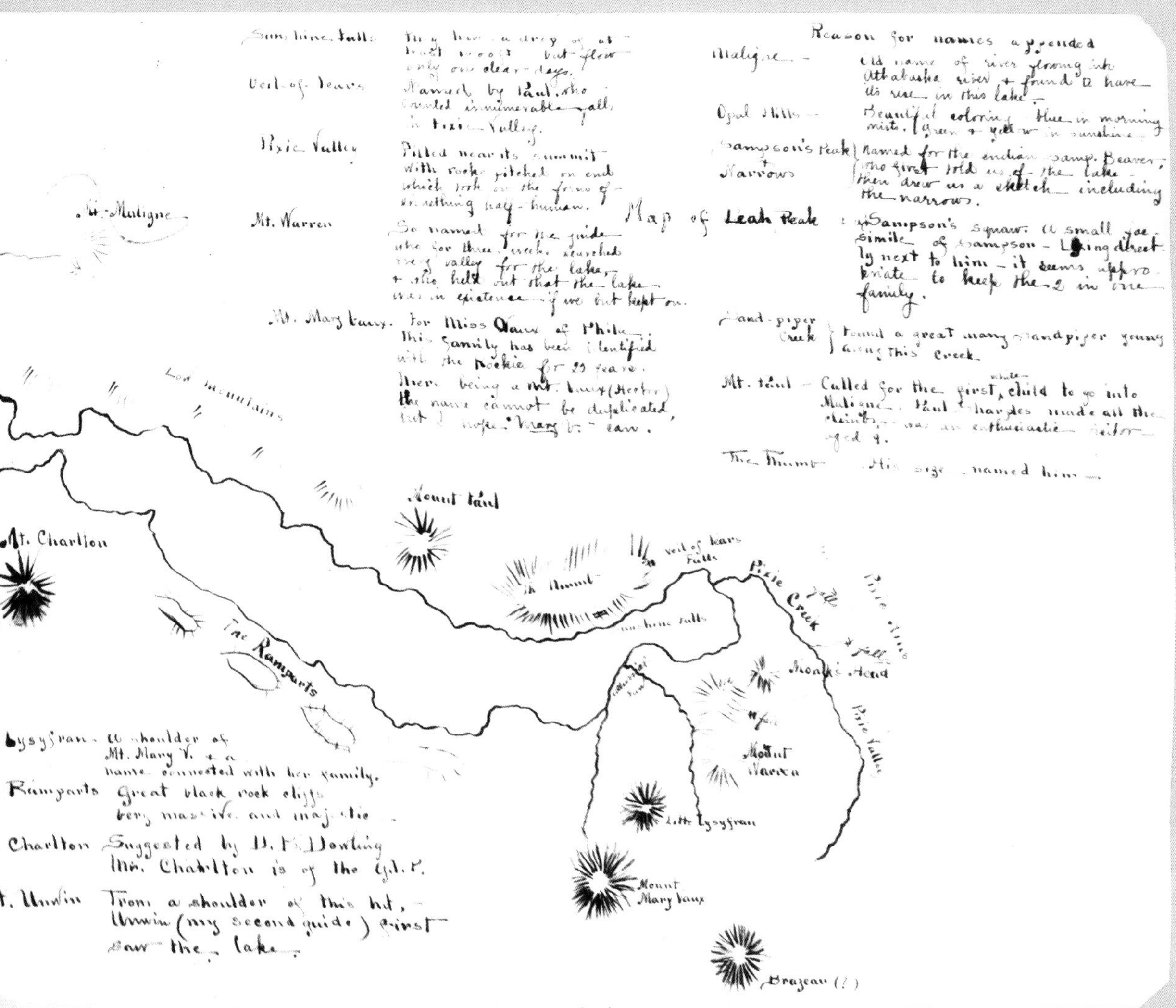
Reason for names appended
Maligne – Old name of river flowing into Athabaska river & found to have its rise in this lake.
Opal Hills – Beautiful coloring blue in morning mist. Green & yellow in sunshine.
Sampson's Peak & Narrows – Named for the indian Samp. Beaver, who first told us of the lake, then drew us a sketch including the narrows.
Map of
Leah Peak – Sampson's squaw. A small fac-simile of Sampson – Lying directly next to him – it seems appropriate to keep the 2 in one family.
Sand-piper Creek – Found a great many sandpiper young along this creek.
Mt. Paul – Called for the first white child to go into Maligne. Paul Sharples made all the climbs, was an enthusiastic sailor aged 9.
The Thumb – His size named him.
Sunshine Falls – They have a drop of at least 1000 ft but flow only on clear days.
Veil-of-Tears – Named by Paul, who counted innumerable falls in Pixie Valley.
Pixie Valley – Pitted near its summit with rocks pitched on end which took on the form of something half-human.
Mt. Warren – So named for the guide who for three weeks searched every valley for the lake, & who held out that the lake was in existence if we but kept on.
Mt. Mary Vaux. For Miss Vaux of Phila. This family has been identified with the Rockies for 20 years. There being a Mt. Vaux (Hector) the name cannot be duplicated, but I hope "Mary V." can.
Mt. Maligne
Mount Paul
Mt. Charlton
Veil of Tears Falls
Pixie Creek
The Ramparts
Monk's Head
Mount Warren
Mount Mary Vaux
Brazeau (?)
Rampart Great black rock cliffs very massive and majestic.
Charlton Suggested by D. B. Dowling. Mr. Charlton is of the G.T.P.
Unwin From a shoulder of this Mt., Unwin (my second guide) first saw the lake.

she again wrote to Vaux: "Thee will be interested to know that the map, which was drafted from the figures which I obtained with log and compass on Maligne Lake, has just been returned home from Ottawa, where it was in the hands of an expert. It is a beauty, and I will have a few blue-prints made from it and send your family one"[129] (Fig. 4.12). Furthermore, "Dr. Scott Keltie writes if I will get out a short paper on the way we did the work and a map and a few pictures, he will try and have it placed in the Royal Geog. Magazine. I am too human not to be very pleased with his suggestion, specially as A.O.W. [Arthur O. Wheeler] has ignored every thing I have done up there."[130] A month later, on 26 December, she wrote that "Wheeler is to be here this week, I hope it will be my good fortune to miss him. He has been so ugly about Lake Maligne, that it is hard to be nice, and I do not want to be anything else."[131] Schäffer's reputation, expertise, and claim on Maligne Lake for having successfully searched out and charted it were made undisputable. To a typed letter to Vaux of 17 April 1912, Schäffer added a handwritten postscript saying, "My report on Lake Maligne has just come out in the Royal Geog. Journal. It will be still harder for Arthur."[132] The "hunter of peace" had become a successful, internationally recognized scientific competitor.

PearlAnn Reichwein and Lisa McDermott argue that "through mapping and place naming, Mary Schäffer's expeditions left their footprints on wilderness as a peopled cultural landscape...She implicitly worked outside the standard boundaries of masculinist professional geography commonly practiced in her era....Schäffer inscribed her story of human experience on the map as a distinctive temporal record of people and places central to her own geographical imagination."[133] Although effacing known or unknown Stoney or Cree names for the landscape did not stir controversy among the players at the time, the action of doing so has had profound impact across Indigenous traditional territories in North America. It has served over time to erase from the historical memory of Euro-Canadian cultures the contents of treaty agreements, such as Treaty Seven of 1877, which was negotiated between First Nations of this region, including Stoney, and the Canadian government. Treaty Seven is an agreement to peace (both among Indigenous nations and with Canada) and to sharing the land. It is not a surrendering of land, an agreement to occupancy restrictions, or a suspension of the right to use of land and its resources, including the right to hunt, particularly in land claimed for national parks.[134] In Canada, Indigenous names are being recovered and reinstated in some places, alongside or in place of later, English or French names. By understanding cartography as a form of social discourse and maps as unstable, mutable, subjective objects, the legacy of naming that Schäffer undertook resonates in instructive ways when reading these two maps today. Cartography historian Karen Piper lays the foundation for such resonance when she claims that colonial cartography "never quite succeeds. It never quite suppresses alternative forms of territoriality, which continue to haunt the map. Similarly, the progress of the map, itself, could be read as a kind of cognitive failure—or a form of mistaken identity."[135]

From Stoney legend to sanctioned map of the Geological Survey of Canada, Maligne Lake came into being in the historical, geographical, and cultural imaginations of Canadian, American, and British scientists, tourists, travel readers, civil servants, and policy makers. The articles and images of Maligne Lake that appeared between 1909 and 1912 helped to prepare the ground for future struggles and compromises over this land and landscape, among conservationists, natural resource and tourism developers, Indigenous inhabitants, and federal policy makers and politicians. Where the photograph representing the first sighting of Maligne Lake serves in *Old Indian Trails* to transform the Chaba Imne of Stoney knowledge and legend into wilderness, landscape, and place, so the imprimatur of the Geographic Board and the Geological Survey of Canada on Schäffer's survey map—backed by the portrait of Sampson, Frances Louise, and Leah Beaver, the mountaintop snapshot of the lake, and the sketch map attributed to Sampson Beaver—closes the circle, establishing the lake and its surrounding mountains as a known, claimed, and appropriated place, one that continues to be both conserved and exploited.

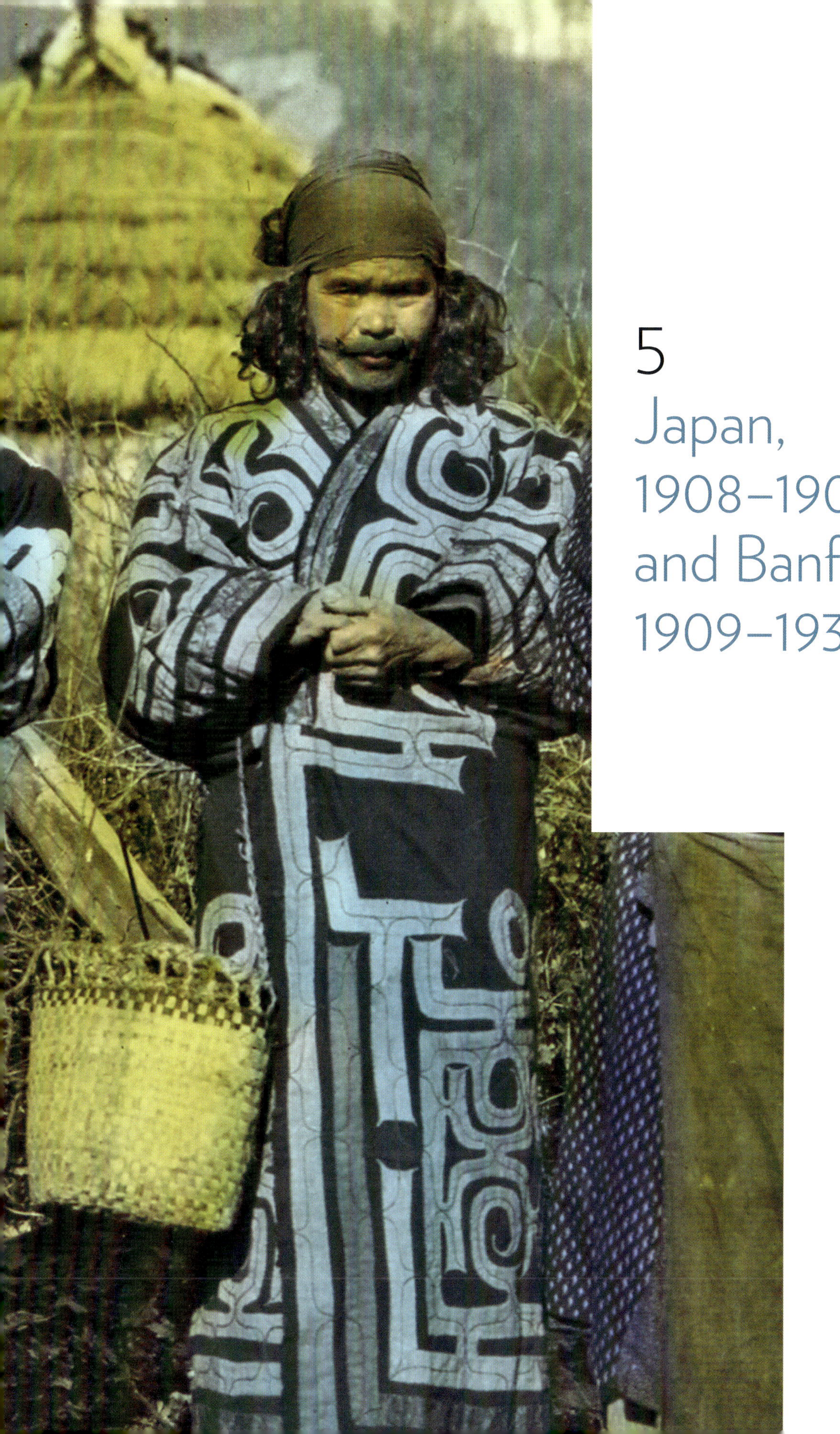

5
Japan, 1908–1909, and Banff, 1909–1939

ON 25 DECEMBER 1908, Mary Schäffer wrote in a letter to her "dear ones at home":

> *As we got out…Mr. M. said with a sigh: 'I'm glad we are back safe.' Was it dangerous? I'm sure I don't know. It was lovely, delightful, and all did go well. That is enough.*[1]

Schäffer could have been describing her response to the four-month excursion in the Rocky Mountains of Canada that she and Molly Adams and their guides had completed earlier that year. But she was not. Rather, she was writing about a visit that day to a village of Atayal Indigenous people in the mountainous interior of Formosa. "Photographs of these strange people were my next desire," Schäffer claimed after she, Adams, and their two women companions had arrived in the area, although their Japanese escort, Mr. Miyoshi, "seemed to feel a little dubious of the reception which might be accorded our cameras."[2]

Schäffer, as usual, was the driving force behind the trip to Japan. For readers of her subsequent article about her encounters with Indigenous people there, she placed her interest in the context of "the general revival of interest in things Japanese."[3] Like Adams, she had a tremendous desire, or possibly need, to travel, and into that context they carried their shared and abiding interests in women, wilderness, and photography. Women travellers and women's travel writing spread around the world in the wake of nineteenth-century imperialism and industrial expansion, including increasing international transportation networks of trains and ships. The commercial and tourist routes and amenities of the Canadian Pacific Railway (CPR), for example, followed by the Grand Trunk Pacific Railway, opened the way to Schäffer's destinations and pursuits. After about 1880 when mass production of dry-plate glass negatives eliminated the need to process a wet-plate negative immediately on exposure in the field, women's (and men's) travel photography expanded as well. American, Canadian, and British women travelled to Europe, the Middle East, Africa, South and East Asia, the western United States, and across Canada from Montreal to Vancouver via the Rocky Mountains. Women, like men, travelled for reasons of adventure, change, curiosity, work in numerous and diverse fields, health, missionary activity, or to accompany spouses posted by their employers—government, church, military, or business—in foreign places. Like today, women who travelled did so with a variety of constraints and freedoms, including financial, family, and health, which vary at different moments in life. Women who wrote about and photographed their travels did so for the same reasons as men: to earn a living in whole or in part (as Schäffer did), to communicate with family and friends (as Adams did), and to privately record, remember, and make sense of what they saw, heard, tasted, smelled, and thought about cultures and environments that were new to them.

Women's ventures into the public activities of travel and travel writing in the Victorian era of the late nineteenth century have been characterized in retrospect as escaping gender oppression and familial restrictions, and in so doing, tearing down the imprisoning walls of domestic space.[4] At the time, however, women's travel writing was not overtly political, calling for social or political change. Instead, women often built narratives around contrasts of culture, gender, race, and class that, when written with self-deprecating humour, skewered social stereotypes and conventions. One convention was never breached, however: personal relationships and events along the way remained private. Schäffer's writing, especially in *Old Indian Trails*, is a classic example of this popular genre.

Interest in Things Japanese, October 1908–January 1909

Publishing *Old Indian Trails of the Canadian Rockies* and enjoying the popularity and critical response that the book evoked lay three years in the future when Schäffer and Adams returned from their successful journey to find the newly christened Maligne Lake. They emerged at Laggan, Alberta, on 20 September and travelled that day by train to settle in at Mount Stephen House in Field, British Columbia, for a couple of weeks. While there, time was spent catching up on correspondence and printing photographs "madly."[5] More travel lay immediately ahead, this time to Japan. Rather than returning to Philadelphia and New Haven, they carried on to Vancouver en route to Tokyo. The CPR's

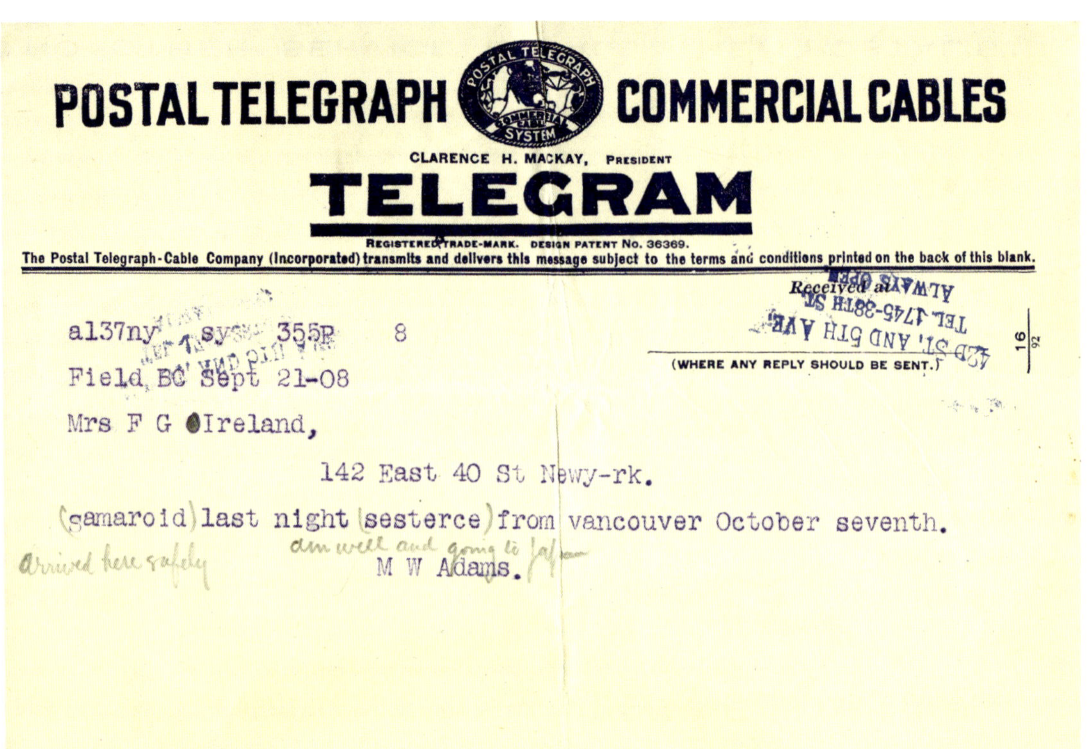

POSTAL TELEGRAPH — COMMERCIAL CABLES

CLARENCE H. MACKAY, PRESIDENT

TELEGRAM

REGISTERED TRADE-MARK. DESIGN PATENT No. 36369.

The Postal Telegraph-Cable Company (Incorporated) transmits and delivers this message subject to the terms and conditions printed on the back of this blank.

Received at (WHERE ANY REPLY SHOULD BE SENT.)

a137ny sy 355P 8

Field BC Sept 21-08

Mrs F G Ireland,

142 East 40 St Newy-rk.

(samaroid) last night (sesterce) from vancouver October seventh.

Arrived here safely — am well and going to Japan

M W Adams.

FIGURE 5.1

Molly Adams to Mrs. F.G. Ireland ["Cousin Alice"], telegram, Field, BC, 22 September 1908.

[Adams Family Collection]

steamship, RMS *Empress of Japan*, had been sailing to Asia from Vancouver since 1891. Schäffer's contacts with the CPR enabled them to secure a stateroom for the price of a regular ticket.[6] Reportedly, it was large enough for three, which meant the luxury of extra space for the two women, and featured a deck—which turned out to be up two flights of stairs from the cabin.[7] While they had passports in hand, obtained the previous spring, and tickets for the 7 October sailing, their return plans were uncertain.[8] Adams wrote, "I have left my camp things in a trunk of M.S.'s in Field. Both my steamer trunks with us and one of M's. We share my steamer trunk. M. now says she is coming back in March, but I tell her she does not know a thing about it yet, and we might just as well lie low and wait, but the idea of going round the world is not popular at present. M. can always get passes on the C.P.R. so she naturally has a leaning this way."[9]

Moreover, Adams expressed mixed emotions about the venture to her friend Ida Ogilvie: "We are going to Japan, sail from Vancouver on S.S. *Empress of Japan* Oct 7. I don't feel so awfully enthusiastic about it as I ought. Going with Mrs. S this way I shall have to do the society act, which bores me stiff. Of course I want to see Japan, but a little sightseeing goes a long way too, almost as far as a little society does."[10] Adams's fears were both confirmed and calmed in the course of their travels. Following a twelve-day excursion to the island of Hokkaido, north of the main island of Japan, she wrote from Tokyo, "Back again after a strenuous journey, and have been doing the sassiety [*sic*] act ever since arriving yesterday noon, which does not amuse me half as much as the queer inns and country places, but M.S. is in her element here."[11] And on 29 December from Formosa, she wrote, "We are still having the time of our life. It is great to be 'the guests of the state,' and it is lovely here."[12]

Although Schäffer and Adams stayed true to their decision in 1906 to travel as a twosome only, they were joined by other women they met in Japan on their two sojourns to isolated areas of the country to see the landscape and Indigenous people in their villages: Michi Kawai to Hokkaido, and Susan Lippincott and Caroline Macdonald to Formosa.[13] They made numerous photographs, which Schäffer later printed and preserved in an album, made into hand-tinted lantern slides presented in public lectures, and published in travel magazines based in London and New York.[14] Neither kept a diary, but both composed long letters that were intended to serve in that capacity and as future reference for articles and lantern slide lecture scripts.[15] Only one letter from Schäffer, lengthy yet incomplete, survives in the archives at Banff, while a host of letters from Adams remain in transcription, preserved in the family's collection.

Adams's letters, written between 6 October 1908 and 3 January 1909, document the destinations, pace, and events of their travels, and her views of the country and their experiences there. Schäffer and Adams landed in Tokyo on or about 21 October after two weeks at sea.[16] Despite the occasional sighting of a rat, Adams found ship life "very sociable—almost as much so as camp life."[17] Over the next three months they travelled, photographed, and wrote about their experiences. Schäffer also purchased artifacts from Indigenous people,[18] and both women shopped—extensively, it would seem. "Each place we go," Adams admitted a month after arrival, "we say we will not buy anything more, but each time we go forth to have an amble around the town we come in loaded down with truck. My trunk will soon burst. My latest specialty is prints, I long for the old expensive ones, but have limited myself to...cheap ones thus far. As we are travelling with hand luggage now our impedimenta is getting fearfully unwieldy."[19]

Adding to the general attraction to Japan for Schäffer were eminent acquaintances living there: Mary Elkinton Nitobe, a Quaker from Philadelphia who worked with Japanese women activists on women's education,[20] and

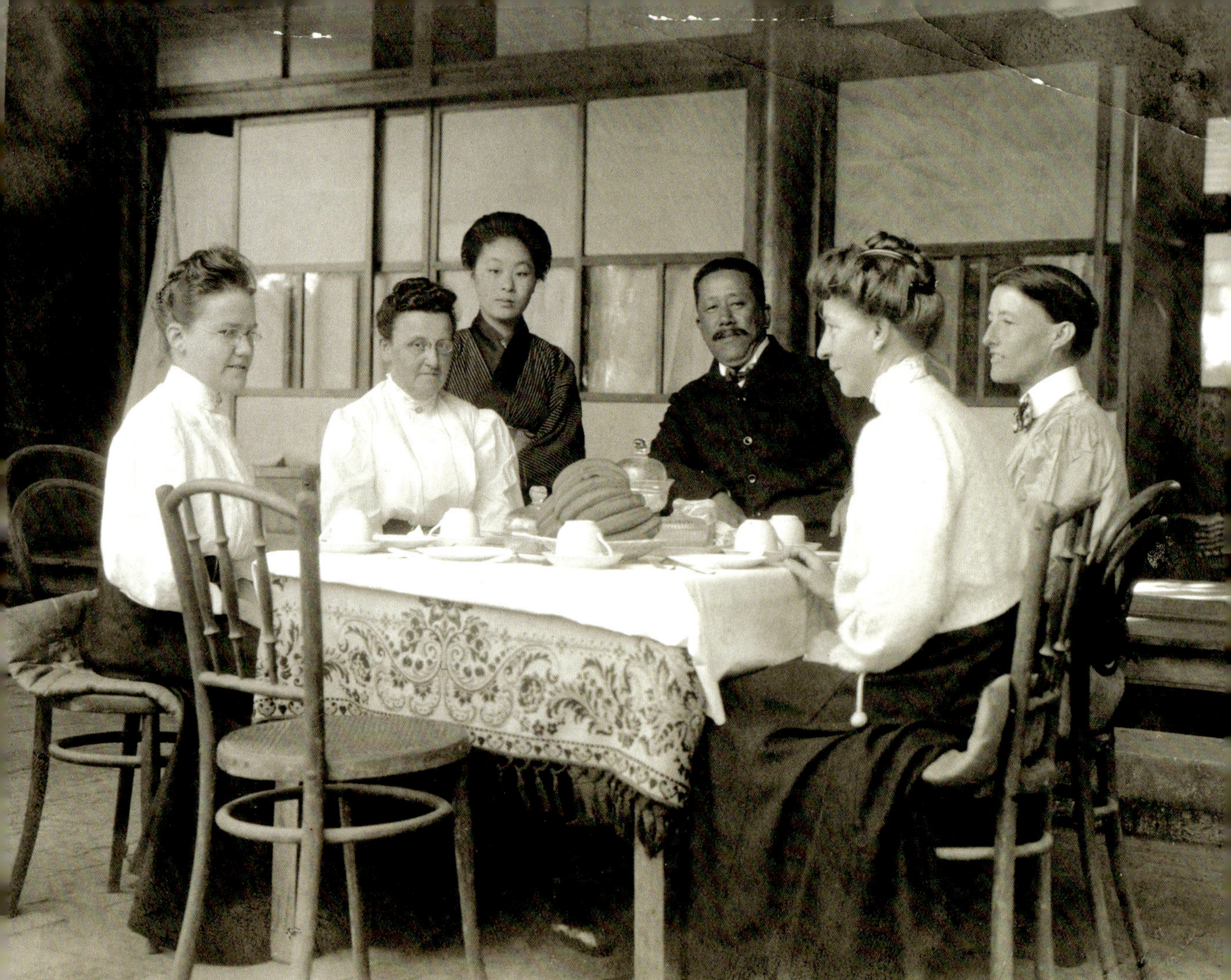

FIGURE 5.2
Clockwise from left: Susan Lippincott, Mary Nitobe, unknown woman, Inazo Nitobe, Molly Adams, and Mary Schäffer, Tokyo, photographer unknown, 1908. [WMCR V527/PD-5]

her husband, the respected Japanese diplomat, agricultural economist, and professor, Inazo Nitobe, who had joined the Quakers while studying at Johns Hopkins University in Baltimore, Maryland, in the mid-1880s.[21] In Tokyo, Adams discovered that she and the Nitobes shared a mutual acquaintance in Miss Umeko Tsuda, who had studied at Bryn Mawr while Adams's cousin, Marian Adams Wright, was also a student there. Tsuda had since returned to Japan and established a new institution for women's advanced education.[22]

The Nitobes enabled entrée to a variety of activities in Japanese government and educational society in Tokyo, which were of interest to and pleasant for Schäffer. Furthermore, Nitobe used his government connections to arrange access and assistance for travel to sites in Formosa beyond established European and North American travellers' destinations. In a letter to cousin Käthchen Cook from Taipeh (now Taipei) on New Year's Eve, 1908, Adams reported, "We have been in Formosa now almost two weeks and have been having the time of our life. There are four of us, and we are 'state guests' because we are friends of Dr. Nitobe, who is a great man down here—as well as in Japan—The governor [of Formosa] has placed the official interpreter [Mr. Miyoshi] at our disposal and he has been 'personally conducting' us."[23] Although honoured as "state guests," the women appear to have paid for their own accommodations and other expenses while on Formosa, as they did throughout their journey to Japan.[24]

Schäffer and Adams stayed in Tokyo at the Imperial Hotel for nearly two weeks after their arrival, even though "M. is most anxious to go to see the Ainu, the Indigenous race of Japan. Perhaps you know all about them, I didn't. No one knows just what race they belong to. It is a long journey, two days to get there."[25] Their departure was delayed first because the American fleet was in port and offered social opportunities through the Nitobes and their friends. The society-averse but wry Adams recounted, "Miss Lippincott, who is staying with Mrs. Nitobe had some invitations to the reception on the flag ship Connecticut….So next day…[we] went and had a limp handshake from Admiral Sperry and a few sickly smiles from the Am. ambassador, Mr. O'Brian, and a few others."[26] There were other events that Schäffer did not want to miss, such as a visit to a prestigious school, in contrast to Adams's dim view of such things: "The Empress may be there and there will certainly be a lot of Imperial princesses and of course we have to seize the opportunity to see all of this."[27] Adams later conceded, however, "The show at the Peeresses' School was really worth going to, aside from the fact that the Empress was there."[28]

On 1 November, Adams reported, "Still we sit here at Tokyo" because of health problems for Schäffer, who "had various indigestions," and was advised by a doctor that "she had better look out or she would get jaundice, so now she is starving herself and going for a two mile vigorous constitutional before breakfast etc."[29] (Schäffer's troubles did not end there. In late December, Adams wrote, "M.S. has to have a lot of dentistry done in Yokohama before she goes back to the wilds of Canada."[30]) In the end, Schäffer and Adams spent most of their time in Tokyo, but took a ten-day trip to Hokkaido and a two-week trip to Formosa. In between, they visited Nikko, Yokohama, Miyanochita, Kyoto, and Kobe.

On 2 November, Schäffer and Adams, accompanied by Michi Kawai, finally departed Tokyo for Hokkaido where the Ainu people lived, travelling by train and boat and stopping at inns along the way, including in Sendai on 3 November and Sapporo on 6 November.[31] From Sapporo they made their way inland to

MAP 3

Cities and villages in Japan visited by Mary Schäffer and Molly Adams in fall 1908.

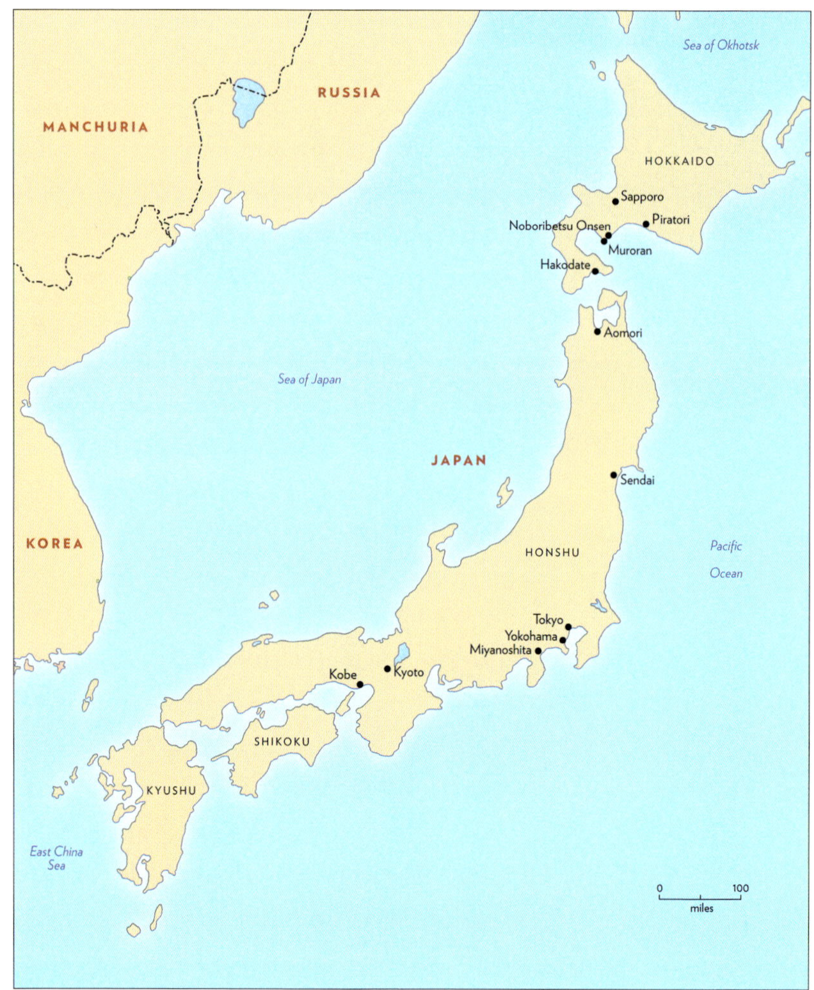

the Ainu village of Piratori by train and cart, then returned in similar mode via Noboribetsu Onsen to Muroran. Travel conditions on this excursion, and others they undertook on Japan's main island and across open water to Formosa about 1,100 miles to the southwest, appear to have been at least as challenging as (and far less comfortable than) the lengthy pack-train horse rides along trails in the Rockies. Molly Adams recounted their journey by boat returning from Muroran on Hokkaido to Aomori on the main island as "strenuous."[32] She elaborated,

> *In good weather a two hour trip, but yesterday we took 4 hrs., and there was a big sea running for a boat of that size ["a trifle larger than a tugboat"] although we were not outside in the ocean. I stayed out on deck all the time,*

MAP 4

Formosa (as Taiwan was known while governed by Japan 1895–1945), located 1,100 miles southwest of Japan, and visited by Mary Schäffer and Molly Adams in late December 1908.

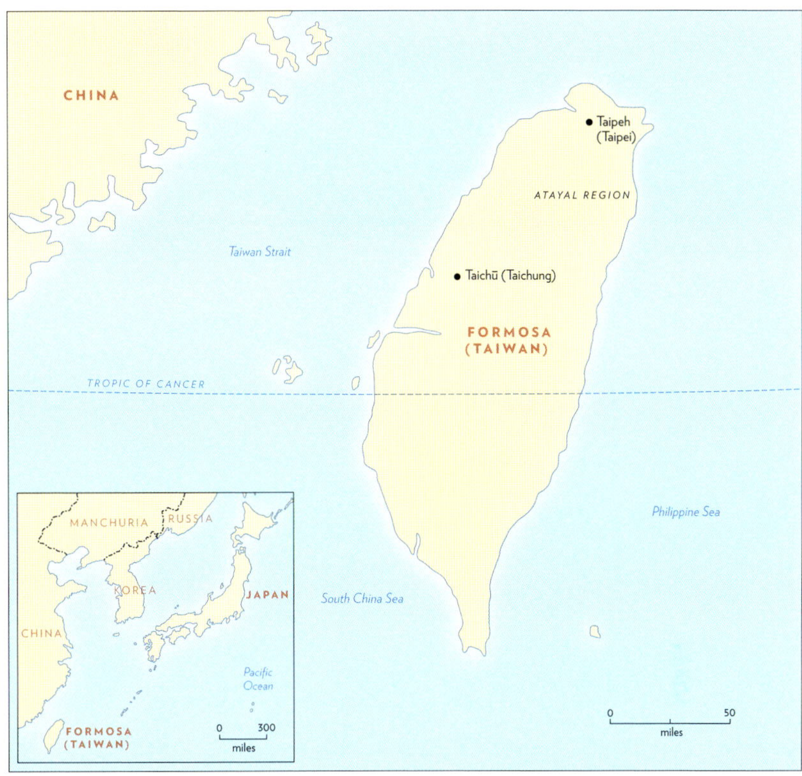

shivering and quaking with cold, but preferring that to probably feeling seasick if I went in the little box of a cabin. The other two [Schäffer and Kawai] did not stick it out long, crawled inside and lay on the floor, very miserable. When I found we were not going straight to the bottom of the sea with every plunge she made, I rather enjoyed it; was behind the little cabin way aft, so only a few small remains of waves dashed over me. It was blowing hard and snowing occasionally.[33]

Seasickness was a common refrain as Schäffer and Adams travelled often by boats of various sizes and purposes. Schäffer's account of the crossing to Formosa a few weeks later is especially vivid:

We had two lovely days at sea coming here. It doesn't seem to me to be as terribly rough, or as very stormy but the boat kept up a constant screw-like motion till everyone one on the ship was sick as a dog. The first day, M and I lay in our berths, and I don't believe said ten words, she ate nothing, and I had

> *a slice of toast. The two others, Miss Lippincott and Miss McDonald were pretty sick all day, I believe, but I couldn't have gone in if they had been reported dying.*[34]

Nevertheless, Mary Schäffer presented herself to readers in the United States and England as being as sanguine as Molly Adams in her attitude towards such travails:

> *The ordinary tourist in Japan sees little of the country north of Sendai, and knows but little of the real Japanese conditions of travel as in the central and southern portions of the island, where the "foreigner" wanders most, European hotels and customs have been largely introduced.*
>
> *The railroads throughout the entire empire are narrow-gauge. I usually find that if travelling facilities are not as we are accustomed to in our own country, we are uncomfortable, so we were uncomfortable.*[35]

They usually stayed in Japanese inns "because the foreign ones in the smaller places are so stuffy" and both wrote humorous accounts of a rat in their room throughout the night on Christmas Eve that knocked over tea cups and ran through their hair as they slept on traditional Japanese floor mats.[36] They ate "foreign" fare when it was offered, "such as beefsteak and bread toasted," but more often local cuisine that was unfamiliar in form, taste, smell, preparation, and presentation: "Gold rice was in one box, garnished with mushrooms, seaweed, strips of egg and a few other things; sweet things made of bean curd and rice flour in another."[37] From time to time in her letters, Adams described various meals, her response to certain foods, as well as her increasing dexterity and confidence with chopsticks. In the one letter home that survives, Schäffer too expressed enjoyment of the inns and food. At an inn on Formosa, for example, she commented on dinner and their accommodation: "My it was good—raw fish, cold fried fish, queer pickles, rice, & finally fried chicken....Our three rooms are separated by 4 screens...it is a most sociable arrangement."[38]

In her articles about the trip to Japan, Schäffer distinguished her topic and her travel by first acknowledging polite interest in seeing the usual sites of beauty but then creating a sense of greater adventure by writing of an expressed desire to venture farther afield, to see not just modern, imperial Japan but also the country's colonized Indigenous people: "Hence it came about, that when I landed in Japan and was asked by a resident what most I wished to see: 'Fuji, temples of course, and some of the lakes and mountains,' I made answer: 'also if it is possible, and if you please, I should much like to see the Ainus.'"[39]

Molly Adams's letters confirms Schäffer's nod to conventional tourist travel. For example, "All globe trotters have to come to Miyanoshita so here we are, and hoping the weather will allow us to take a trip tomorrow to a lake where there is a celebrated view of Fuji."[40] Adams also noted how comparatively little traditional sightseeing they in fact undertook.

> *My letters don't seem to get written as soon as I should think they would! Especially considering how little I do in the sightseeing line. We have been so much of our time in Tokyo that we have hardly seen a thing here which the conscientious tourist ought to, and don't suppose we shall. As for me, I am of course, very much limited by not being able to climb many stairs, and the principal sights of Japan being temples, and those almost invariably perched on a hill-top with long flights of steps leading up to them—I can avoid them with a clear conscience. They are very beautiful sometimes, however, and I would like to see more than is possible.*[41]

Adams's mobility was compromised by an unspecified chronic heart problem that she had referred to in passing in letters over the years. In late July while camped at Maligne Lake, Adams wrote to her sister Catherine, "I don't think Dr. Putnam would recognize me or my game heart in my present condition, appearance and costume. So you will probably get the code telegram which means 'have been very well, am going to Japan'" (Fig. 5.1).[42]

After returning from Maligne Lake, Adams mentioned her health in a number of letters. For example, from Mount Stephen House, Field, British Columbia, on 21 September, she wrote to Cousin Alice, "I am not feeling quite so rumbunctiously [*sic*] vigorous as when I last wrote, but still about a million times better than when I left N.Y. I think it was the hot weather we had at the Yellowhead that took me down a little. My eye still has red streaks in it. I shall be able to tell better whether it is going to do anything queer now that I am out of the camp fire smoke."[43]

And on 28 September also from Field, she wrote to her sister, "I don't think my eye is perfectly good as new yet, it does not seem to like me to read or use it as much as I want to, but perhaps it just needs more exercise of the muscles as I naturally used it very little in that way in camp. If it should go queer again

I would rather have Dr. Thomson fix it up than anyone else."[44] Overall, she concluded, "I think, for an invalid I did pretty well this summer, riding did not seem to make me tired at all unless we were as much as six or seven hours in the saddle, but of course I could only take short walks, and no climbs."[45]

By 12 November she wrote, "I have been going up stairs a lot lately and I am sure my game heart is better."[46] Nevertheless, she suffered a series of ailments while in Japan, reporting on 5 December, for example, "In this interval I have been much occupied with germ No. 3, which thought he would go for my tonsils—at least I suppose it is tonsils when you are all swelled up each side and it is hard to swallow, but it might be follicular pharyngitis for all I know about it. Anyway, the worst is over."[47]

Photographing in Ainu and Atayal Villages

Thirty years before Schäffer and Adams travelled in Japan, the famed British traveller Isabella Bird did so, claiming her place as the first European woman to see the Indigenous "Ainos of Yezo" on the island of Hokkaido. Bird visited in 1878, she claimed, to improve her health, but was "attracted less by the reputed excellence of its climate, than by the certainty that it possessed in an especial degree those sources of novel and sustained interest."[48] Schäffer, too, placed her trip in the context of general interest in Japan in her time and place. Japan was a very different kind of destination than the Canadian Rockies or Europe or Africa; not only was its culture and history distinctive, it was an imperial foreign nation that had made treaties with, but not been colonized by, Europe or North America. For Schäffer, simplicity and familiarity of travel with the CPR likely also played a role in choosing the destination, as well as social connections in Tokyo.

Schäffer's interest in touring Japan was focused especially on Indigenous people, who had been confined to distant regions, specifically the Ainu on the island of Hokkaido in northernmost Japan and the Atayal on the island of Formosa, a colony of Japan since being ceded by China (where it was known as Taiwan) in 1895. Accompanied by an interpreter—first "Kawai San, our guide, philosopher, and friend,"[49] to Hokkaido, and later Mr. Miyoshi on Formosa—Schäffer and Adams travelled by train, boat, wagons ("basha"), and rickshaws or pushcarts ("kuruamas").[50] Michi Kawai appears to have been an excellent match for Schäffer and Adams. Schäffer described how she had been advised by a local "informant" in Sapporo that travel to the Ainu village of Piratori "was out of the question, owing to the difficulties of our getting there. Miss Kawai, however, failed to recognize such things as 'difficulties,' and having laid our plan of action, we laid in a stock of necessary provisions, and started the next day for our goal—Piratori, one of the most typical Ainu villages left."[51] Adams concurred, "She is the nicest thing, a Bryn Mawr graduate, by the way, she is really a perfect dear, and most capable and efficient in bossing things generally."[52]

When writing the illustrated article about the Ainu following her return from Japan, Schäffer relied on missionary John Batchelor's illustrated book of 1901, *The Ainu and Their Folk-lore*, to set a historical background and explain some of the customs she and Adams observed and photographed.[53] Evoking received ideas of her time, she concisely draws a contrast between ancient and contemporary Ainu, and states their fate as a matter of fact: "These gentle, harmless people were at one time a race of savage cannibals. To-day they number about sixteen thousand souls, timid and harmless, and dying off fast. A few more years and the Ainu will be but a memory—so disappears the aborigine." [54]

She reports that responsibility for the demise of Indigenous people is ascribed both to Ainu of the past and the present-day Japanese government: "At one time inhabiting the entire island of Japan…they have been gradually driven farther and farther north by the energetic invaders, until, crossing Tsugaru Straits, they have taken their last refuge in the inhospitable hills of the Hokkaido. Their rapid decrease is said to be due originally to strife among the various clans; also from having been forced into vegetarianism when they are a race of hunters. The Government has stopped the killing of deer, and their fishing stations have been taken from them."[55]

Other forces described as contributing to the declining Ainu population are practices that Schäffer calls superstitions (following Batchelor's description); fatalism; the impact of "strong drink"; and the fact that the island "is far too rich in natural resources to be longer neglected as a wilderness, and the Japanese are constantly pouring in and pushing him [the Ainu] rapidly back into the as yet almost inaccessible hills."[56] It is striking that such descriptions match Schäffer's commentary on the Stoney in *Old Indian Trails* where "washdays were not over numerous, but whose welcome was very cordial."[57] Of the Ainu she writes, "Water was evidently not their strong point; it seldom is in the lower planes of life, but in natural politeness they certainly excelled. Very willingly they allowed us to use the camera, and proved immensely proud of

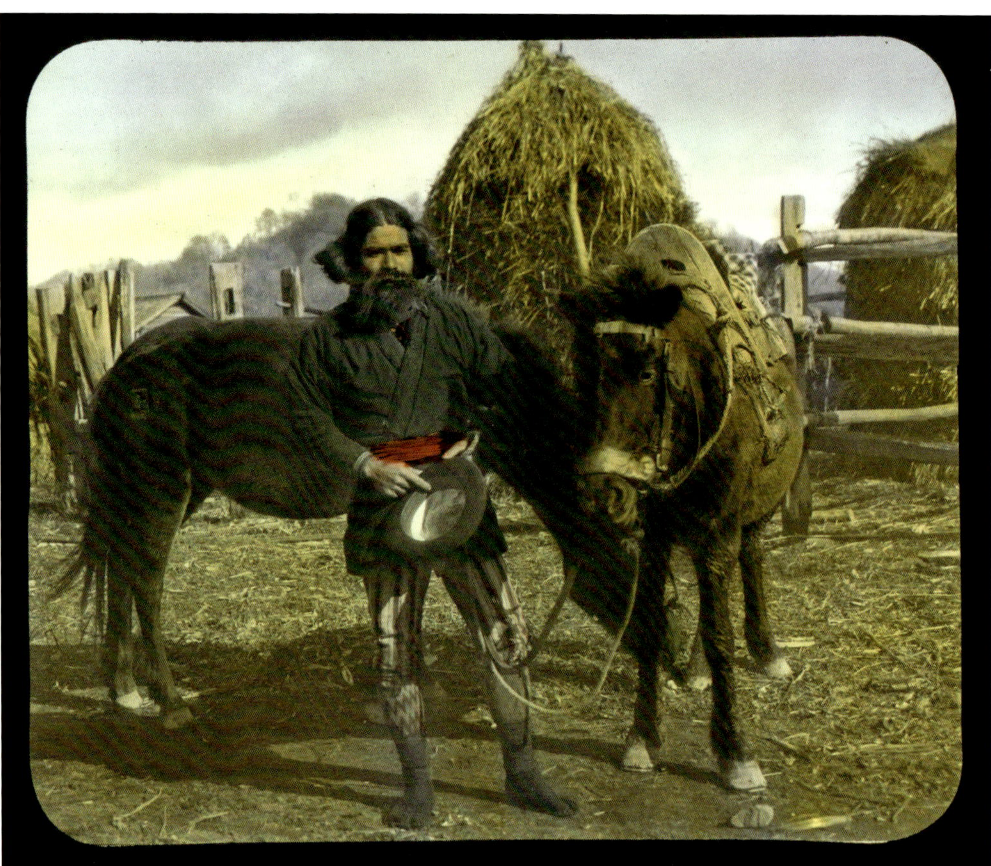

FIGURE 5.3

"A Peasant and His Horses: Some of the horses belonging to the Ainus are remarkably fine animals, superior in appearance to those on the main island of Japan," as captioned in *Travel* 16 (April 1911): 260; "An Ainu Peasant," as captioned in *Travel and Exploration* 3 (January to June 1910): 378. Mary Schäffer and/or Mary W. Adams photograph.

Mary Schäffer hand-tinted lantern slide [WMCR V527/PS1-869]

their tattooing, especially the hands, which they placed conspicuously in front when asked to pose."[58] In contrast, needlework was described as "exceedingly crude."[59] And yet she concludes that "altogether they were the most civilized savages I had ever seen"[60]—in part, she claims, because of contact and subsequent intermarriage with the colonizing Japanese.

Physical appearances were a focus as well. The men's long beards and women's facial, arm, and hand tattoos elicited attention in both the text and photographs, and are described with a flourish for readers: "The most marked physical characteristic of the Ainu is the enormous growth of hair on the men, while the women are hideously tattooed on face and arms....The first sight of these Ainu women gave me the impression of having come across a lot of men masquerading as women, so masculine is the appearance of this tattoo of the lips."[61]

Adams expressed similar views, but in a more constrained tone, when she wrote,

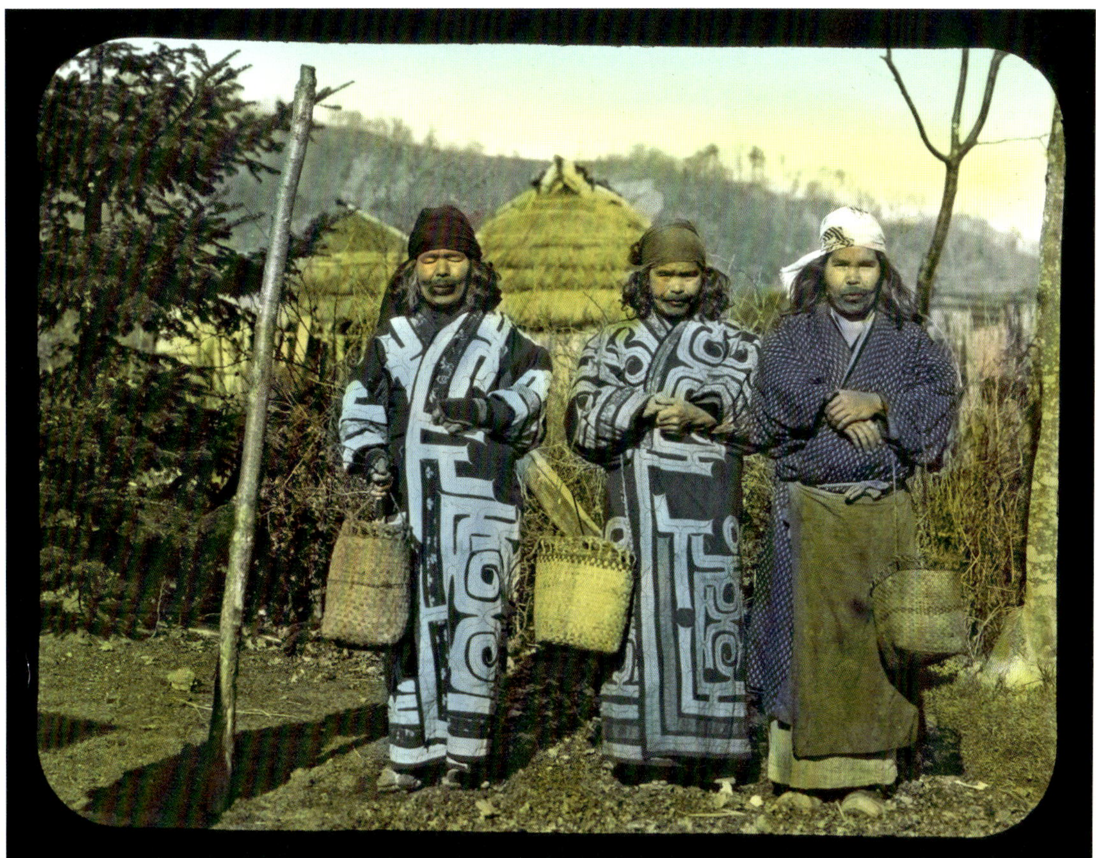

FIGURE 5.4

"Some Ainu Women: The tattooed lips sometimes make it difficult to tell whether these are men or women," as captioned in *Travel* 16 (April 1911): 261. "Ainu Women," as captioned in *Travel and Exploration* 3 (January to June 1910): 378. Mary Schäffer and/or Mary W. Adams photograph.

Mary Schäffer hand-tinted lantern slide [WMCR V527/PS1-839]

> *We did go off into the country to the Ainu village. It was just my kind of a trip, and I enjoyed it like the queer places in Mexico, etc. And it was easy going this time because of course Kawai San did all the arranging of everything....*
>
> *Most of the Ainu men were out working in the fields, but our faithful one-eyed driver rounded up some women and children and we corralled a few men as they were passing by. The women have a strange custom of tattooing a mustache effect around their mouths, very weird looking. M. bought a lot of things from them to give to the Acad. Nat. Sci. in Phila. They seem very gentle in their ways and language, and the men quite handsome, with long flowing beards and hair.*[62]

In contrast to her published photography and writing about the Rockies, Schäffer focused more on Indigenous people and their habitations in Japan than on the landscape or flora. Her descriptions of their travel are, as always, lively and humorous, and the black-and-white published photographs are of excellent technical and aesthetic quality, well-composed and full of fine detail, such as tattoos and clothing, to occupy viewers. The distance between the photographer and her posed subjects is similarly close to those of the Stoney images, and the viewer may have experienced a sense of that physical proximity, especially if the images were viewed as projected coloured lantern slides. In contrast to the portraits of Frances Louise Beaver and her parents on the Kootenay Plains, however, there is no sense of the sitters looking back directly at the viewer in a collaborative way (Fig. 3.19). Instead, there is an aura of archaic anthropological spectacle rather than contemporary interpersonal presence. These photographs contain none of the sense of the singular personalities of the sitters evident in the Beaver photograph, or the sense of the intimacy of the exchange between sitters and photographer (and by proxy, the viewer of the Kootenay Plains photographs), nor could they. Schäffer and Adams were very much transitory travellers in Japan, their visits very brief. Their "glimpse of the head-hunters of Formosa," for example, entailed just a few hours on Christmas Day, 1908.

Adams described the visit in a single paragraph:

> *It was actually clear and sunshiny that morning, Xmas day. The day before had been very dull and dark though not raining, temperature just pleasant in summer clothes riding in my chair, but pretty hot for those who walked all the way. So our cameras were shooting in all directions. We stopped at the savage villages and took pictures which I hope will come out well. All the men were off hunting deer, to our great disappointment, but there were plenty of women and children. We saw just one man—he was squatting by the side of the trail with a basket of green bananas to sell. We did not think he looked very friendly—perhaps it was just as well they were most of them away, or they might not have let us photograph the women and children. These tame savages are well armed with rifles etc. which the Japanese don't dare take away from them for fear of creating hard feeling.*[63]

As for anthropological novelty, Schäffer portrays herself and Adams as being as much of a curiosity to the Ainu on Hokkaido (and, elsewhere, the Atayal on Formosa and Stoney, Cree, and Métis in the Canadian Rockies) as Indigenous people were to them, and claimed in her published account to be discomfited by being the object of a candid gaze. In Japan, she wrote, "Our greatest trial was the frank curiosity of the populace who, accustomed only to an occasional passing missionary, peered into the low windows of the train till we were forced to draw down the blinds, or followed us in generous squads."[64]

In her letter home, however, Schäffer contradicts her later public narrative, writing that after breakfast on Christmas morning, before departing for the day's travel to see the Atayal villages, "we had dressed before an admiring audience of coolies. I have to put in my usual remark here, no white women had ever penetrated this savage district so far before, so we didn't mind them."[65] Nevertheless, both she and Adams write in their letters of this reversal of the gaze, which was discomfiting, it seems, as an intrusion into their privacy when they were weary from travel, and much accustomed to being the ones looking out—especially through camera viewfinders, and precisely when they chose to do so.

As on their Rocky Mountain travels, Schäffer and Adams photographed together in Japan. "M.S. and I spent the whole A.M. in tramping the streets taking photos," Adams wrote on 31 December from Taichū (now Taichung) on Formosa.[66] Schäffer described in greater detail that same outing: "This morning Mollie & I ambled forth with our cameras to take pictures in the city. I think we took about 16. Had no trouble. We have grown accustomed to the crowds who are always gentle & polite. I also bought a few head-hunter curios for the Acad."[67] As with most of the Rockies photographs, the specific photographs each woman made here cannot be discerned. The quality of Schäffer's and Adams's images as well as that of the tinted lantern slides readily rivals that of the H.C. White Co., a studio based in North Bennington, Vermont, that specialized in the large-scale manufacture and distribution of stereoscopic view photography from around the world. Schäffer included three of White's images among the thirteen reproduced in the American version of the Ainu article.[68] How she obtained those photographs is unknown, although Schäffer noted in an aside in her letter home, "The Count [Sakuma Samata, Governor of Formosa] just gave me a fine lot of Savage photos."[69] This may be the source of a number of images in the archives that Schäffer and Adams clearly did not make and that Schäffer never published, such as that of two Indigenous men seated with a decapitated head on display in front of them.[70] Schäffer and Adams did not encounter—or pose—any such scene in the few hours they spent among the Atayal.

Schäffer did not publish any writing or photographs related to the excursion to see the Formosan Atayal, other than some passing comparisons in her article on the Ainu. She did, however, draft a manuscript titled "A Glimpse of the

Head-hunters of Formosa."[71] The manuscript takes the same approach as the Ainu article, beginning with the historical context of the colonial encounter of Japan and Taiwan after 1875, although she does not attribute her description to any particular source. Furthermore, the description of their interaction with Atayal women and children, as with Ainu women and children, echoes the description in *Old Indian Trails* of the day she and Adams spent photographing Stoney women and children on the Kootenay Plains while the men were away hunting.[72] The manuscript also creates a far more colourful description of events that had been recounted in Schäffer's letter, clearly making for a more entertaining and exciting story, and one that plays overtly to stereotypes of colonized Indigenous peoples. The actual events of the day and the images of the Atayal women and man are comparatively less interesting than those experienced with the Ainu, and Schäffer embellished her narrative, perhaps in an attempt to write a more entertaining and educational tale.

It is not surprising that she did not publish "A Glimpse of the Head-hunters of Formosa," but it is an excellent example of Schäffer's deliberate use of creative narrative rather than documentary description to portray people, places, and events when writing for the travel reading market. For example, in her letter Schäffer writes,

> *The day was a perfect one. As we came over a knoll, we met a savage mother & her baby. Giving them a bit of silver I got her picture. Again we met a man selling bananas & he was willing, & I got the pipe out of his mouth. Entering the Chief's village, several women & children were there, so I didn't do so badly. Mr. M said the men might have refused any pictures, so perhaps it's as well they weren't at home.*
>
> *They treat these people as tho they were gun-powder. They are the Attails* [sic]*, one of the most cruel tribes on the island. Back at our police station, they set out tea, bananas & boiled duck eggs; then we said good-bye to our escorts, & taking a boat manned by coolies, shot the rapids of Tamsui River.*[73]

In comparison, the draft manuscript reads,

> *The morning was perfect, we swung along at a brisk pace, meeting and passing the coolies with their aromatic loads of camphor-oil, and keeping one eye out for any strange native.*

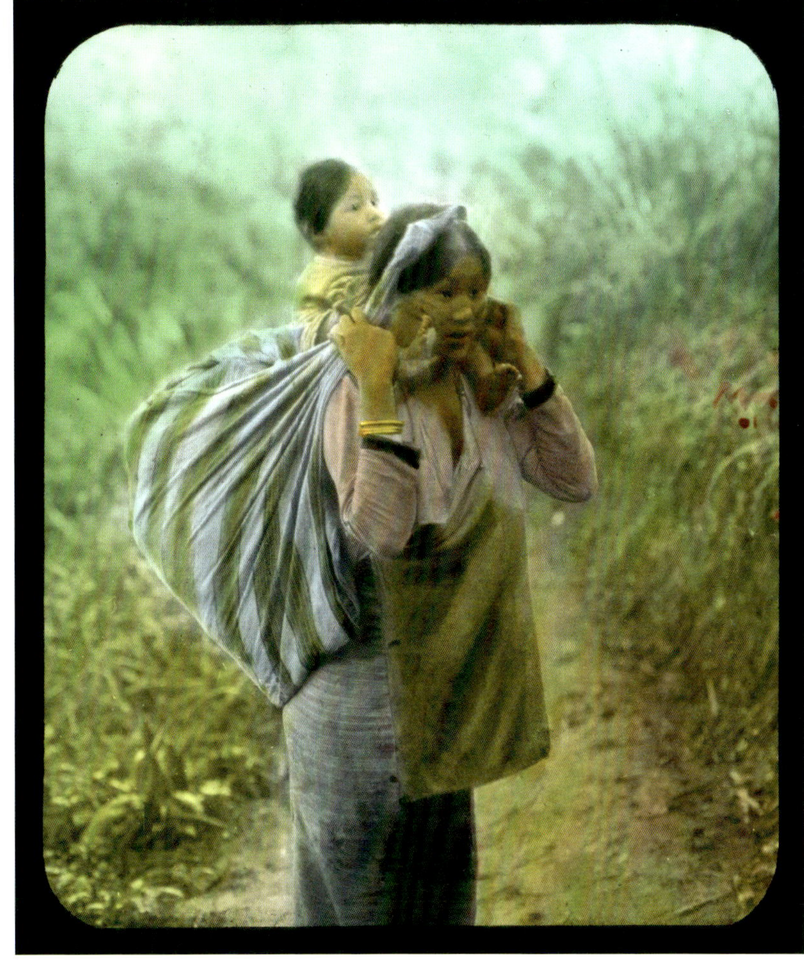

›FIGURE 5.5

"Formosa Savage on the trail" [Atayal woman and baby], Mary Schäffer and/or Mary W. Adams photograph, 1908.

[WMCR V527/PD-5]

Mary Schäffer hand-tinted lantern slide

[WMCR V527/PS1-1045]

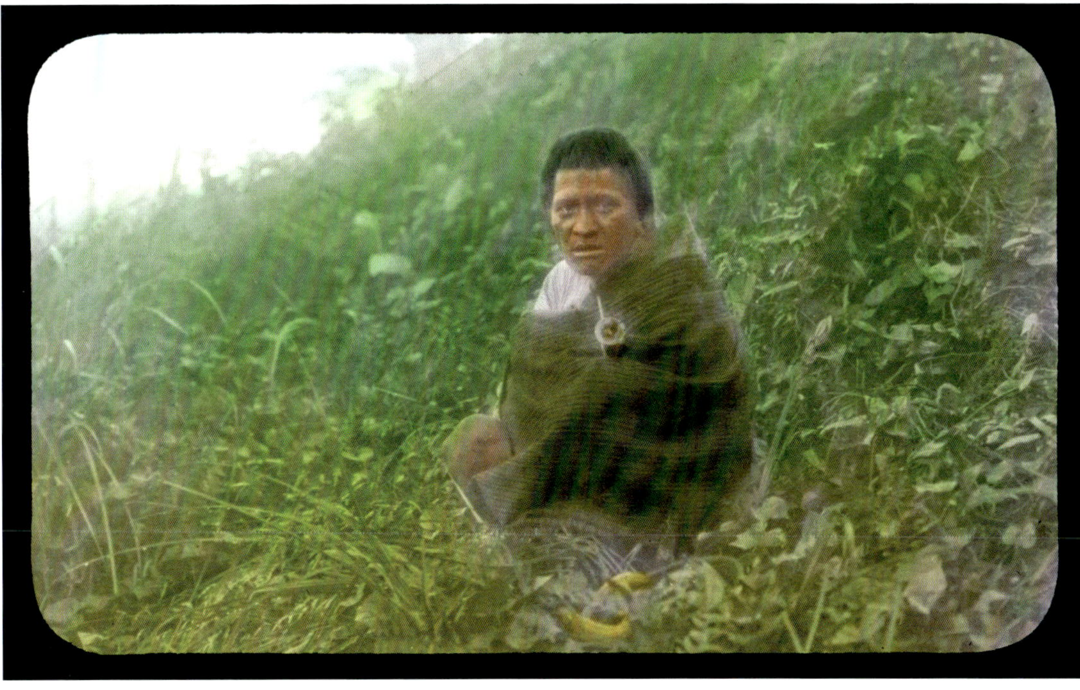

˅FIGURE 5.6

["The banana man"] [Atayal man], Mary Schäffer and/or Mary W. Adams photograph, 1908.

[WMCR V527/PD-5]

Mary Schäffer hand-tinted lantern slide

[WMCR V527/PS1-1015]

I was a little in advance of the others with the guard, when swinging round a sharp bend in the trail, I suddenly came upon a beautiful sight—a savage mother. On her back she carried a huge burden, and poised about it, a tiny child. She showed no fear of the camera, and accepted the small silver coin with a pretty smile.

A little lower down the hill, a man sat crouched on the high bank, with a native pipe in his mouth; huddled up in a little heap he sat there waiting for a prospective buyer of three green unhealthy-looking bananas. We bought the bananas, ditto the pipe, showed our silver, and got a picture. He was quiet but alert and watchful during the camera episode, the beady eyes constantly shifting from one to the other of us; and I felt a considerable satisfaction that the guard was at my elbow. His expression left slight doubts in my mind that the reverence for the law and order had not reached much beneath the skin.

We then arrived at the village we had first passed on our upward journey, took a number of pictures of the women, children and their huts, and obtained from them ear ornaments, necklaces, baskets and portions of dress. They were a genial, laughing crowed, apparently very glad to see us, and examined us as minutely as we did them. It did not take long to discover that they were quite enough in touch with the world to know silver from copper, and accepted only silver.

Obtaining all we could in photographs, we waved a gay good-bye, took up our march on the winding, flower-bedecked trail, and descended to a boat-landing on the Tamsui where a Chinese sampan, manned by coolies, awaited us.[74]

In 2011, the manuscript was printed and illustrated with a selection of colour images in a book about Schäffer's lantern slides. That is, more than a century later, and despite that fact that Schäffer left the manuscript unpublished (and never published the Formosa photographs), the narrative was reproduced as a literal, documentary account of events that included images that Schäffer and Adams did not make themselves and that overlooked the literary style and effect of the writing.[75] Readers of this version must take care to resist accepting it as a purely factual account and should instead consider Schäffer's text to be a work-in-progress of creative non-fiction that attempted to invoke imagination and cater to an early twentieth-century North American audience's expectations regarding stories of adventure among unfamiliar and formerly unseen Indigenous people.

Echoing her lament for the Ainu, as with the Stoney, Schäffer's manuscript on the Atayal concludes, "We…then took a last, long look at the savage hills we were leaving, those hills peopled by a race so little known or understood,—a race which must live out the tragedy of defeat and extermination as Indigenous tribes the world over have done before them."[76] It is clear in her work, both in the published texts and photographs, as well as in private, unpublished writing and photographs, that Schäffer shared the common understanding of Indigenous Japanese and Taiwanese people as having a "savage" or violent past, and of the inevitable passing of global Indigenous cultures that had been displaced and colonized by expanding imperial cultures and their industrializing agendas, whether European, North American, or Asian. This is hardly surprising, given the lack of access at the time to alternative readings of the history of imperial interactions of both China and Japan with the Indigenous peoples of their territories. After more than four hundred years of contact between Europeans and Indigenous people in North and South America and Asia, and the subsequent devastation of Indigenous populations from famine, disease, and displacement, colonizing cultures had accepted as truth the prevailing explanation that Indigenous people's inherent biological traits were the reason for their irreversible global demise.[77] The title and subtitle of Schäffer's article when published in *Travel*—undoubtedly written by an editor rather than Schäffer—is especially provocative and telling: "With the Hairy Ainus: A gentle and harmless people of northern Japan who were at one time a race of savage cannibals—hirsute adornment, real and imitation."[78]

Adams's and Schäffer's letters make it clear that they were subject to views of the Atayal held by the contemporary Japanese governing class, their own preconceived expectations about the relative or comparative modernity of imperial and colonial Japan, and the dissonance of their experiences, which were of both modern comforts and "gentle" rather than "savage" people. Schäffer writes, for example, that in Taipeh, "not the least of our surprises was finding that the Taihoku Railroad Hotel was built and run on elaborate foreign lines, when we had set out to visit a 'savage' country."[79] In her letter home, Schäffer expressed her surprise when they encountered a group of local Japanese and Chinese women watching "a moving-picture show" in the lobby of a hotel on Formosa.[80] At the same time and in contrast, she wrote that the "sad part" about a visit to a Chinese school where Schäffer was invited to speak ("on the American Indian, some stories of our living among them, then of our going to see the Ainus & winding up here to see the Formosan savage") "was to see the little girls with their bound feet. It makes a great bump where the ankle ought to be. They suffer terribly. A man will not marry a large footed woman. So that settles the future of almost all the girls."[81] A sketch of a foot and ankle accompanied this description.

Adams expressed similar conflicting impressions. Letter writing served as a vehicle for expressing first thoughts, and over the course of the trip, evolving views. The last letter in the transcribed collection of Adams's correspondence is dated 3 January 1909, and was written onboard a steamer returning from Formosa to the main island of Japan. After two-and-a-half months in Japan, Adams reflected on its state of affairs as a colonizing country.

> *You say that people you know have fallen in love with the country of Japan but not always with the people. I like the people whom I have met personally very much indeed, and I certainly admire them as a nation. The higher classes, government officials, university people, etc. are just as modern and up to date as we are; but then there is the great mass of the uneducated who are still in the middle ages I suppose, and I should think it would take a long time to pull them up out of it. All the reforms have to come from above, here. Instead of the lower classes demanding them, they have them forced down their throats by the government.*[82]

Schäffer, Adams, Lippincott, and Macdonald began their return trip to Tokyo on 2 January 1909. Adams wrote from their steamship en route to Miyajima, "We have been having a most interesting two weeks visit in Formosa and are now on the way back to Japan. All the rest of the party are in bed seasick, I am sitting out on a somewhat moist deck and it is raining, but very warm and pleasant."[83]

The plan was to stop at Miyajima, Kobe, and Kyoto on their way back to Tokyo, where they expected to arrive on 10 or 11 January.[84] It is unclear whether they made it as far as Tokyo before Molly Adams fell gravely ill, although it seems unlikely. Adams did not indicate any sense that her health was deteriorating or in danger in her letters from Japan. From mid-November, she had been looking to the future and trying to decide on plans for returning home. On 21 November she wrote,

> *I must confess that I am fired with a desire to go home by way of around the world—either by steam around India, or Siberia would suit me equally well.*

However, I am booked for the Empress of Japan to Vancouver Feb. 1st. That is not paid for, so could be given up if any other favorable opportunity should occur. I have met a lady [Susan Lippincott] who is going by Siberia about April 1st and she wants more people to join her party, but that is a long time to stay here. I don't know what may turn up yet. M.S. goes to Vancouver Feb. 1st, anyway.[85]

By early December, Adams had made a decision. Although Schäffer was booked on the *Empress of Japan*, which was then scheduled to depart on 24 January, a week earlier than previously advertised,[86] Adams believed "it would be so much more amusing to go back around the world than the same way I came out,"[87] and on 12 December she advised her sister and cousin,

I have written to the C.P.R. *man giving up the passage engaged on the Empress of Japan for Jan. 24th! Perhaps someone will turn up who is going via the ports (which means India and the Suez Canal) about that time. I heard rumors of somebody's mother and sister who were going; otherwise I shall join the Terrys April 1st via Siberia. I think it is too silly to go back* C.P.R.*, and I certainly don't want to, although I may have to economize all summer to make up for not doing it....Whichever way I go I should probably sail for N.Y. from Naples or Genoa.*[88]

No letters or other documents have come to light as yet to explain what happened during the three weeks between the time when Adams wrote the last extant letter on the ship steaming back to Japan and her death on 23 January. An obituary notice in the *New Haven Evening Register* on 25 January simply announced: "DIED. ADAMS.—In Japan, January 23 1909. Mary Wright daughter of the late Dr. Daniel L. Adams. Interment in Japan."[89] The Burial Register of foreigners maintained in Japan documents the interment of "Mary A. [*sic*] Adams, 41, American" on 23 January 1909, in Kasugano Cemetery in Kobe, one of two cemeteries for foreigners in Japan at the time.[90] That the date of death and burial are recorded as the same suggests that at best Adams and Schäffer had travelled no further than Kobe; it is also possible that Adams died en route. Any letters or telegrams Schäffer may have sent at the time of Adams's death have not come to light.

Schäffer alludes to the death metaphorically in her dedication of *Old Indian Trails* to Molly Adams: "To MARY who with me followed the 'Old Indian Trails,'

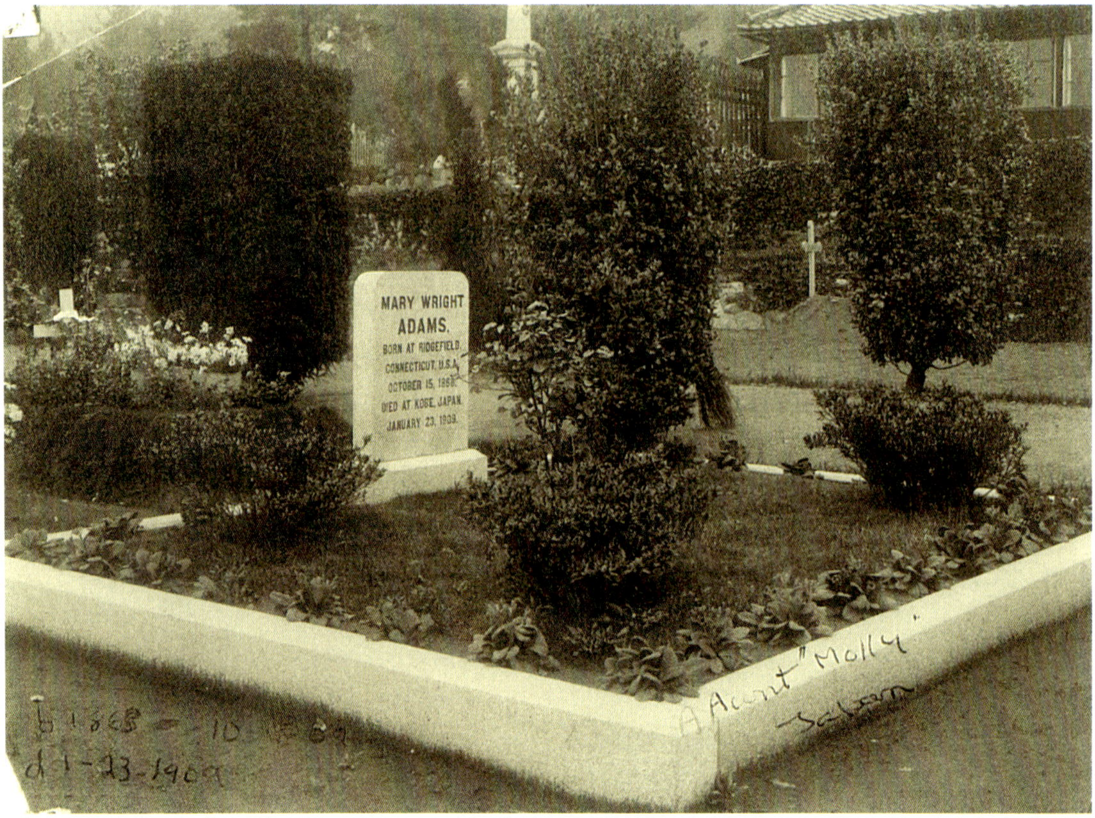

^FIGURE 5.7

Mary W. Adams original gravesite, Kasugano Cemetery, Kobe, Japan, photographer unknown, n.d. [before 1960].

[Adams Family Collection]

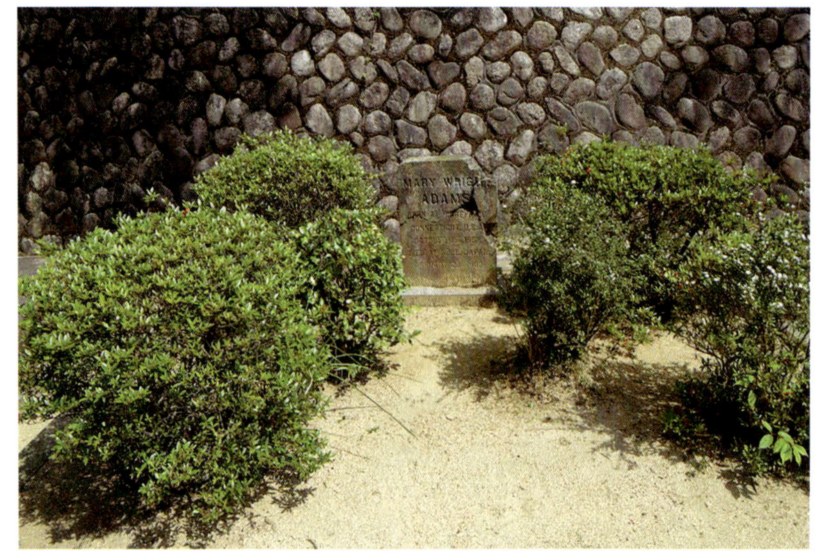

>FIGURE 5.8

Mary W. Adams gravesite, Municipal Foreign Cemetery, Kobe, Japan, 2016.

Photo: Anna Ciriani-Dean.

[Adams Family Collection]

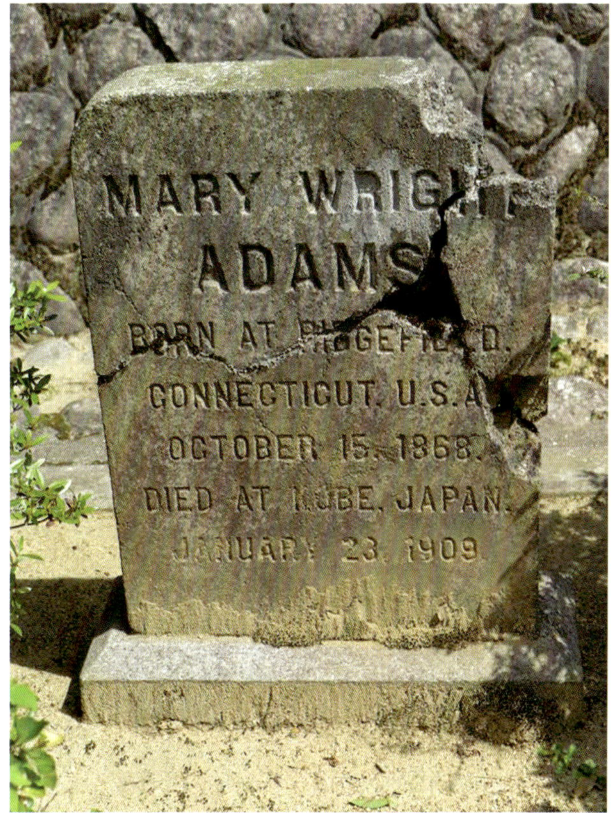

FIGURE 5.9

Mary W. Adams gravestone (showing earthquake damage), Municipal Foreign Cemetery, Kobe, Japan, 2016.

Photo: Anna Ciriani-Dean. [Adams Family Collection]

but who has now gone on the long trail alone."[91] It is only in the mid-1930s, twenty-five years after the event, that a private comment by Schäffer about Adams's death is to be found:

> *The winter after we had re-located the lake my dear friend Mollie Adams and I were in Japan, Hokkaid [sic], Formosa and a snip of China. She caught cold coming back to Japan and I left her sleeping in Kobi [sic] on the beautiful heights overlooking the Pacific, pneumonia from exposure on deck.*
>
> *For something to do, I wrote the little book which cannot fail to show we had unearthed that beauty spot. I dedicated it to Mollie the finest pal any woman could ever have had.*[92]

Would Adams have said the same of Schäffer? There is no question that they were unusually compatible companions on long and rigorous journeys. Schäffer's sociability, confidence, and intellectual curiosity appear to have been complemented by Adams's easygoing, accommodating, mild temperament and literally quiet presence. At dinner on Christmas Eve, 1908, for example, the day before the group was to visit the Atayal region, Schäffer wrote, "We all made speeches (not Molly) & laughed."[93] Keen observers of the world around them, they worked collaboratively as photographers, and wrote long and entertaining diaries and letters for friends and family about their journeys. They shared a willingness to endure discomfort in travel and a desire to see landscapes and people that were believed to be on the brink of disappearance. For all of this, however, they had their differences. Adams was the more peripatetic of the two, travelling more extensively and to more varied destinations as an adult than Schäffer did. In 1908, for example, Adams aspired to travel around the globe to get home from Japan, rather than retrace passage back to Vancouver. Schäffer, however, not only kept an eye on thrift in her passage, whether by rail or ship, but retraced the same route every year between Philadelphia and Banff from 1889 until she finally settled there in 1912 (and even occasionally afterwards when she returned to visit to Philadelphia, West Chester, and New York).

While Adams may well have agreed that they made fine travel companions in mountain wilderness, she was by no means certain that Schäffer was the ideal partner for the trip to Japan. While waiting to depart from Field, British Columbia, Adams wrote to her friend Helène, with whom she had travelled in the past: "We have arrived, & all is well. And we sail for Japan Oct. 7 per S.S. *Empress of Japan* from Vancouver. I wish it was you who were going with me. You & I are more alike in the things we like to do in civilization, not to mention such things as the affections of the heart etc. I seem to have expressed that wrong somehow. It sounds as if I meant the 'game heart', but I didn't. Just the heart as such."[94]

"Things we like to do in civilization" and "affections of the heart": here is where Schäffer and Adams's compatibility appears to have diverged, at least in Adams's view. The meaning of Adams's words, no doubt understood by her correspondent, is vague to strangers reading her letter today. Certainly, Adams made clear in other letters that she had no interest or comfort in participating in the activities and spectacle of urban society, in contrast to Schäffer who was as much in her element in Philadelphia and Tokyo as she was travelling with a pack train along trails in the Rockies. "Affections of the heart"—not the "game heart," that is, the physical heart with which Adams had trouble—may allude to the types of things or people that they loved, or to the kind of love that they experienced or valued and shared, whether romantic, familial, or platonic.

As Adams noted when they first met in 1904, Schäffer was a woman who captured the attention of men, and who enjoyed their companionship.[95] Schäffer wrote frequently of the high opinion in which she held her husbands—the deep grief she suffered with Charles Schäffer's unexpected death, and the admiration she had for William Warren. Adams, in comparison, travelled almost exclusively with women and maintained an extensive correspondence with many of them. It appears from her letters that she may have been especially close to her married sister Catherine (Katy) Elkin, with whom she lived following their mother's death. She also made new women friends readily during her travels with promises to travel together in the future, such as with climber Gertrude Benham in the Rockies in 1904 and Susan Lippincott in Japan. Her surviving letters do not reveal any amorous relationships, or even hints thereof, with either women or men. Her private life was built around her family and friends, and her greatest interest was travel, especially outside of cities, and in being outdoors engaged in casual, unstructured activities, whether in the Adirondacks or the Rocky Mountains, or on the deck of a steamship. It appears that her health was of significant concern to her family and friends, as she reassured them regularly of her well-being during her travels. In short, she lived the life of the turn-of-the-twentieth-century American spinster, the financially independent (but not wealthy), single woman, and many of her friends did so as well. Some of them, such as Käthchen Cook and Ida Ogilvie, formed personal partnerships with a woman companion.[96] Adams did not.

A third significant area of difference between Schäffer and Adams, both of whom lived in an age of overt racism and the crescendo of imperialism, was in their attitude towards Indigenous people in North America and Asia. Both women used common descriptors of their day, such as "squaw" and "savage," in both private writing and in Schäffer's published works. Schäffer's published work vacillates between using such default descriptors, which register today as racist, and displaying the humanity of Indigenous people and respect for them based on personal interactions that belied racial and racist stereotypes. She deliberately sought out Indigenous communities as part of her travel experience and photography interests. From time to time in her letters, Adams commented on Schäffer's interest in and ease with Indigenous people, in contrast to her own discomfort with and dislike, which she stated in blunt terms. The language can be shocking or disappointing today, but remains valuable as material evidence of the complexity, contradictions, and variability of values and viewpoints of the time. For example, Adams was not keen to join Schäffer on a future trip along the Athabasca and Mackenzie Rivers because "I don't like Indians, except to look at from a little distance, they are too grubby, & when you are anywhere within miles of them they are always with you, squatting close at your tent door for hours at a stretch with their eyes glued to you."[97] This view is not simply racism. It does, of course, speak to discomfort with the inversion of the colonial gaze, as Indigenous people in both Canada and Japan examined the colonial women traversing their territory, without benefit of a camera lens to buffer the contact. But that is not all. Adams's sensitivity, which Schäffer did not share, should also be attributed in part to her temperament and to class affinity. Adams was intensely introverted and most comfortable in small groups of people that she knew, especially women. Furthermore, both Schäffer and Adams, despite the latter's distaste for "society" and its obligatory behaviour, travelled and mingled with ease and even friendship among the Japanese and Chinese professional echelons at schools and social events in Japan and Formosa, and with their interpreters Michi Kawai and Mr. Miyoshi, both native Japanese; this suggests that the views Adams expressed had at least as much to do with classism as racism. Commentary on the looks and behaviour of Chinese men and women serving on the *Empress of Japan* and on transportation networks in and around Japan, known at the time as coolies, betray curiosity about the new for both Schäffer and Adams—but also, for Adams, tremendous discomfort with physical proximity to those of lower social status and different social behaviours.

Despite these differences, and Adams's decision to part ways with Schäffer on their return to Tokyo so as to carry on around the world, Schäffer and Adams's trip to Japan was as harmonious as those in the Rockies. Following Adams's death, Schäffer returned from Japan with a collection of photographs that she and Adams had both made and acquired. Coupled with photographs from their 1906, 1907, and 1908 trail rides through the Rockies on a quest for Maligne Lake, and Adams's diary of the last trip, she was equipped to write at length about their journeys. Collaboration, curiosity, and challenging conventions of gender and race, in both texts and photographs, are the markers that distinguish Schäffer's work.

Writing the Rockies, 1909–1939

The four years following Schäffer's return from Japan were her busiest and most intensely productive years as a publishing writer and photographer. Between 1909 and 1912, Schäffer not only produced *Old Indian Trails of the Canadian Rockies*, she wrote and published an illustrated article that appeared in two different magazines on the trip to Hokkaido to see and photograph the Indigenous Ainu. The text is identical in both magazines, except that the concluding line, "We had seen the Ainu," that appeared in *Travel and Exploration*, an illustrated monthly magazine published in London, does not appear in the New York–based *Travel* magazine article of a year later. This may have been simply because of a spacing issue with the layout; an additional page would have been required to accommodate the sentence. Another difference is that the later article, published in the United States, is more extensively illustrated. Schäffer also wrote the unpublished manuscript on her travel to Formosa,[98] and published four articles on Rocky Mountain travel and one commissioned tourist pamphlet on the Canadian Rockies.[99] She returned to the Jasper area to measure Maligne Lake and then draft its first survey map, devoted time to the labour-intensive process of tinting slides from both the Rockies and Japan,[100] and presented lantern slide lectures in both Philadelphia and West Chester, Pennsylvania.[101] Schäffer also decided to build a home in Banff. In spring of 1911, a lease was obtained for property on which to build, and William Warren took on the work of contracting materials and labour. For the first time, she stayed on in Banff through autumn and into the new year of 1912, ostensibly to test the rigours of winter in the mountains. In late November, she described a bit of recent weather to George Vaux Jr.: "Our cold snap seems to be about over. I found 40 below a most interesting experience. For four days we dared not open a window for fresh air, but as it oozed thro [*sic*] every crack, we didn't miss it."[102] The house was finished by the end of the year,[103] and after returning to Philadelphia for a few months in January 1912, she moved into Tarry-a-while, which she completed with furniture and keepsakes shipped from Philadelphia (Figs. 3.1 and 5.10).

During this time, she also attempted to undertake another wilderness excursion, this time into northern Canada along the Athabasca and Mackenzie Rivers. The plan was to travel with the Hudson's Bay Company, whose brochure with passenger tariffs for 1911 is preserved among her papers.[104] Schäffer set her sights on such a journey shortly after returning from Maligne Lake in 1908. While at Field, British Columbia, prior to departing for Vancouver and Japan,

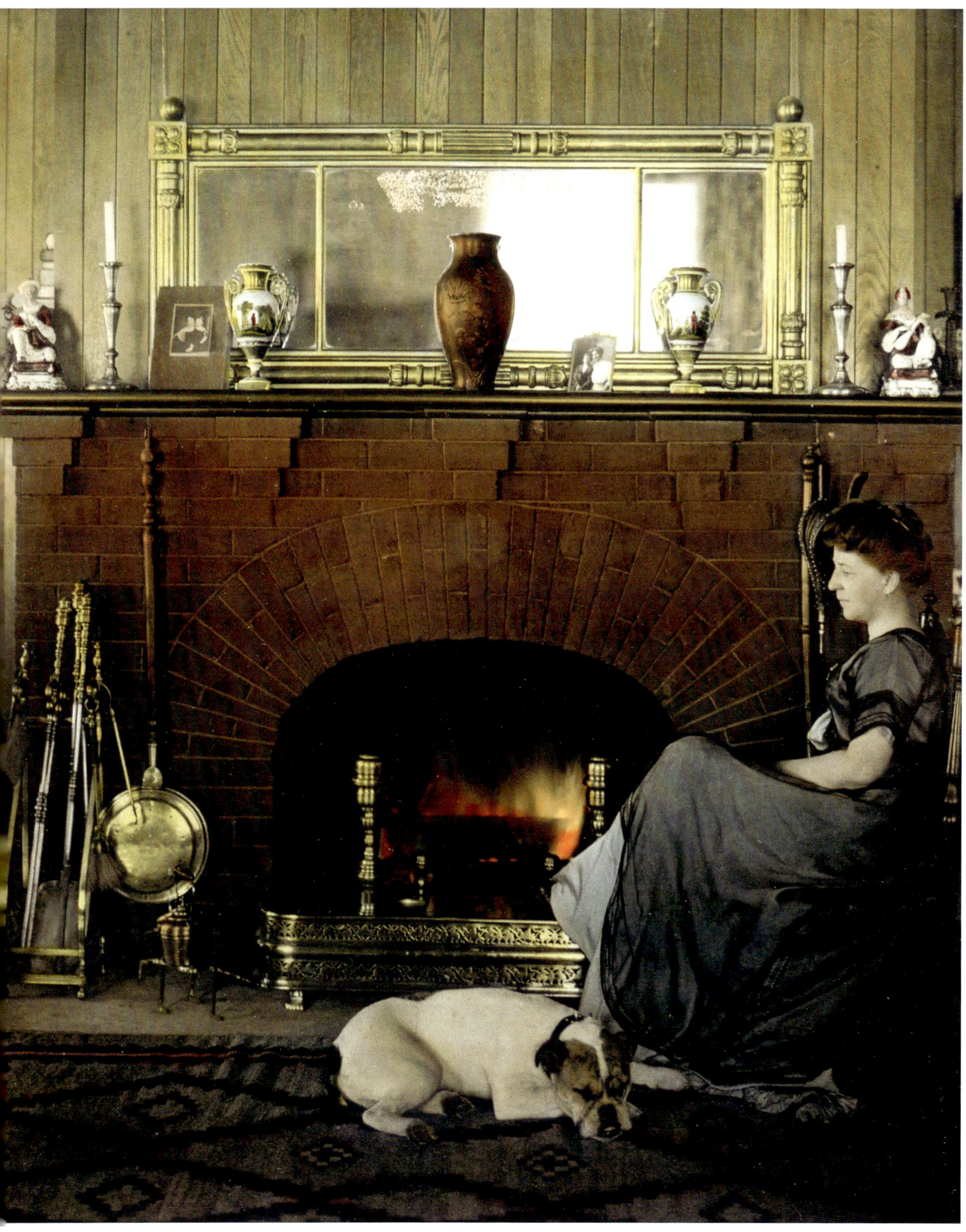

<FIGURE 5.10

Mary Schäffer in her new home, Tarry-a-while, Banff, 1912. Attributed to George Noble. Verso in ink on framed print: "To Mary J. Vaux. A little corner of "Tarry-a-while"/I wonder if thee will recognize any of the trimmings./Wishing you a Happy Christmas./Mary Schäffer." [WMCR V527/PC and NA66-527]

Schäffer and Adams encountered Agnes Laut, an expatriot Canadian writer. Writing to Ida Ogilvie, Adams explained that Laut "has been on a great trip this summer, from Edmonton to Lake Winnipeg, by canoe 1500 miles on the Saskatchewan. Perhaps you have read some of the things she has written about the North West, Indians etc. She was stopping at every Indian encampment, Hudson Bay fort etc picking up facts, historical anthropological etc, & incidentally some beautiful Indian work on buckskin.... M.S. is fired with ambition to go on a similar trip, but it does not really appeal to me."[105]

In December 1911, Schäffer wrote to Vaux that she was "going up to Edmonton to-morrow to see the Hudson Bay people about a trip up to the Mackenzie next summer. I have got in with the right people, and only want to be sure of a companion, tho. they tell me it is easy to go alone."[106] Schäffer's ambition was ultimately thwarted, however. First, a prospective unnamed woman travel companion from England cancelled in March because of financial difficulties.[107] Then, in April, planning to travel with her fourteen-year-old nephew, Eric, but facing escalating costs related to completing her house in Banff, she announced to George Vaux Jr., "The northern trip is off for another year.... I hope to be in the position to have him take the trip next year with me when I am not building houses."[108]

Lack of a woman companion and ill health have been stated as the reasons why Schäffer did not embark on any further wilderness excursions after 1908.[109] Although she continued to experience dental problems and occasionally referred to unspecified bouts of illness as "nerves" or "neuralgia" in her foot or legs in correspondence during the 1920s and 1930s, there is no evidence that poor health was a significant impediment to further travel, or that she lacked companionship. Her sister-in-law Caroline Sharpless, for example, accompanied her on the Maligne Lake survey expedition in 1911. In September 1915, she and a young Banff friend, Stella Painter, travelled first to California then to Edmonton and Jasper by train. There they met up with their husbands, who had gone by trail on horseback from Laggan to Jasper, "a spot where so few years ago all was a wilderness. We all rode to Maligne, where we spent a couple of days, then the men turned south for a short hunting trip and we returned to the r.r."[110]

Between 1914 and 1918, Schäffer's activities and focus changed, as did those of most in Canada, to the First World War. Writing and photography were her means of engagement. In 1916, Schäffer wrote two letters that were published in the *New York Times*, as well as at least one that appeared in the local West

Chester, Pennsylvania, newspaper in 1917.[111] Among immediate family and close friends in Canada who volunteered for service were her American nephew Eric Alfred Sharpless, then living in Calgary with his parents, and her guide and friend Sidney Unwin, a British citizen. Both died in the war—Sharpless during the Battle of the Somme in 1916 and Unwin after being wounded at Vimy Ridge in 1917.[112] She presented lantern slide lectures for war-related fundraising events, including one on Japan and Formosa at the Lux Theatre in Banff in 1918 for the Halifax Relief Fund.[113] She also produced and sent at least one set of slides with a script to England to entertain injured soldiers.[114]

In 1919 and 1927, Schäffer again published Rocky Mountain articles, some of which were illustrated with her photographs or those of others.[115] She maintained copious correspondence with family, friends, and acquaintances, and an active role in Banff social life and community service. During that time, many of her contemporaries and friends died, including George Vaux Jr., Julia Henshaw, and Inazo Nitobe, and she noted their passing, with personal comments, in letters. She also wrote more fiction and creative non-fiction that remained unpublished.[116] Mary Schäffer continued to travel regularly, but as a tourist, and most often with William Warren, whom she married in 1915.[117] They generally travelled to Vancouver en route to American and Caribbean destinations by ship. In contrast to Warren's preference for milder coastal climates, Schäffer remained more inclined to the comfort of cooler and dryer mountain air.[118] On 23 January 1939, Mary Schäffer died in Banff, the same date on which Molly Adams had died thirty years earlier.

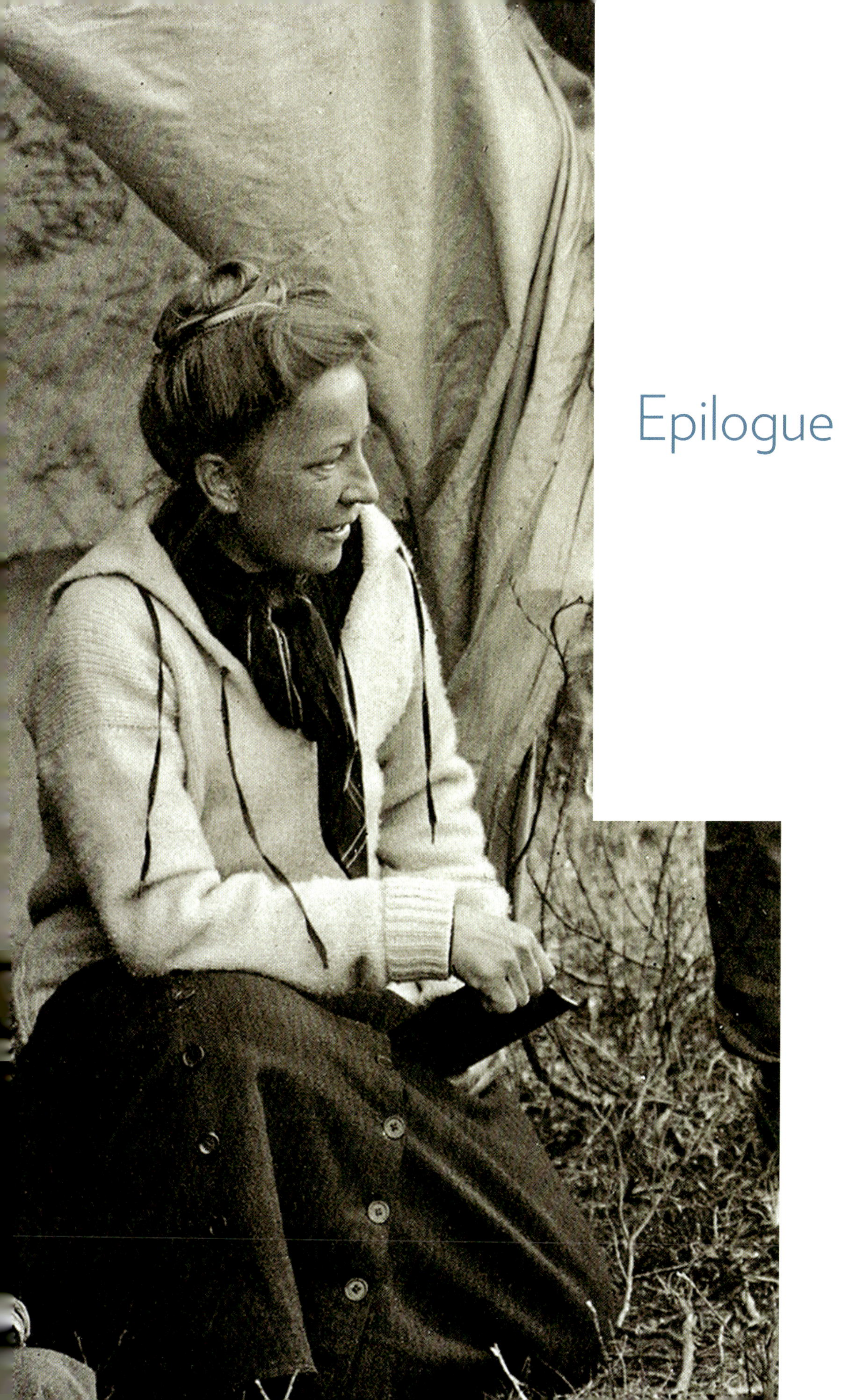

Epilogue

THE ROCKY MOUNTAIN landscape and flora photographs Schäffer produced and exhibited in Philadelphia and Paris in the late 1890s and 1900 laid the foundation for her intellectual and creative achievements between 1904 and 1912. The work on Japan, while less widely circulated and eventually overshadowed by the mountain photographs and publications, demonstrates consistency and focus in her photography and writing interests. It also indicates the ways in which she distinguished her work in the world of travel writing and photography, seeking destinations where Indigenous and imperial cultures remained in deadly contact and white women had not before appeared.

Mary Schäffer came to study, know, and share her experiences and understanding of the natural world, and especially peopled wilderness just beyond the ever-expanding boundaries of industrializing colonialism, first through photography and then through writing. When the two were combined, her work hit its stride and was especially well-received. Historical and archival materials, public and private, show how Schäffer travelled, worked, and socialized among other educated and accomplished women with a range of personalities, interests, vocations, and backgrounds in the Canadian Rockies and Japan. In her own scientific and creative non-fiction writing and photography, she established a credible voice that took advantage of gender stereotypes of her day to craft lively, humorous, and incisive critiques of the expectations for women's behaviour that such stereotypes evoked, challenging and transgressing circumscribed norms.

Private letters and diaries, which have critically informed and enriched this study, are significant sources for writing women's histories. These documents present not only women's own voices describing their activities, experiences, and views for their own purposes, but also bring to light unexpected or unknown histories of women crossing paths, collaborating, and influencing those activities and views. By simply seeking out the names and activities of women, much is learned about an array of issues, ideas, times, and places. Most of the women with whom Schäffer travelled had public and even historically prominent profiles that have subsequently dropped from sight—from Mary M. Vaux to Molly Adams, Zephine Humphrey, Henrietta Tuzo, Suzette Chalifoux Swift, and Michi Kawai. These women in turn crossed paths with others, such as Ida Ogilvie, Gertrude Benham, and Umeko Tsuda. There were still others, including writers Mary Ward, Julia Henshaw, and Agnes Laut, and author, politician, and activist Nellie McClung, who visited Schäffer at her home in Banff.[1] Materials related to Schäffer's photography, writing, and life will doubtless continue to come to light, as has happened from time to time since the late 1970s, and will have an impact on future studies of her photographs, texts, and life. The ways in which such materials are presented and analyzed must be considered with care and respect, especially when referring to those materials created by Schäffer and others for private consumption and left in private hands upon death. How to write about women and their visual and literary practices, as well as their life stories, remains a contested and challenging endeavour. However well-intended, any approach—whether paternalistic, condescending, or disparaging on the one hand or hagiographic, hero(ine)izing, or empathetic on the other—that fails to seek, consider, and question historic evidence clouds the view. "Mary" never existed, except in the imaginations or longing of writers, and perhaps some readers, inspired by the stories told about her. "Schäffer" existed—as a public figure, a name attached to texts and photographs, such as "She Who Colored Slides," and a persona created by the photographer-author and by reviewers of her work. But she, too, is not someone who can be intimately known or knowable, nor can she, her work, or her time and place be better understood when descriptions and analyses fail to be informed by historical material evidence.

Schäffer's work can and will continue to yield paths for inquiry in a range of fields that pursue and ponder lingering or emerging questions about women and social structures, the environment and human histories, global colonization and Indigenous nations and societies, and the creation of knowledge and construction of meaning in visual and written work, both fiction and non-fiction, imaginary and documentary. Schäffer's work in botany, painting, photography, cartography, writing, and travel is a quintessential model of skilled amateur Euro-North American pursuit of knowledge in the natural sciences by women and men alike at the turn of the twentieth century. Writing and photography were the main tools of those practitioners. At the time, the concept of the natural sciences included Indigenous peoples in imperial societies' colonized territories. There is still much to learn, and work such as Schäffer's and that of her collaborators, which attests to broad social, intellectual, and creative currents as well as to confounding individual interactions that contest, confuse, or contradict stereotypical or received cultural norms, are significant artifacts for such studies. Schäffer's and Adams's photography in the Canadian Rockies and Japan made visible, and thereby knowable and comprehensible, the remote, the rumoured, the believed, and the confounded among viewers in North America and Britain. Schäffer's work was invariably and intensively collaborative, from her earliest work in botanical studies alongside Charles Schäffer in the 1890s to her travel and wilderness photography with Molly Adams between 1906 and 1908. Both collaborations were something special, based on shared interests and aspirations in photography, botany, writing, and travel into areas just beyond the horizons of conventional tourism and just before industrial development opened access to general tourist markets.

Mary Schäffer, the photographer and writer, was a woman of education, independent income, and professional and public success. Schäffer brought to her endeavours imagination, discipline, collaboration, and perseverance. She earned the respect, interest, and friendship of male scientists and surveyors, and cultivated the intellectual, creative, and social companionship of women scientists and travellers. She and her work were not anomalies, nor were they extraordinary, even though they were successful, and of high quality and achievement; both were, in fact, very much of a time when women of Schäffer's background and socioeconomic status travelled, botanized, wrote, photographed, and presented their work to public audiences.

Schäffer first practiced photography at the crest of its ascendance in Philadelphia, and witnessed first-hand its rupture with the passing of the American photographic vanguard to pictorialism and New York. Her work in botanical studies and lantern slides took advantage of her skills as a watercolour painter. Here too she was active at a late moment of popularity just prior to obsolescence, as technological invention in colour photography augured the end of the aging, labour-intensive, but popular hand-tinted lantern slide era.[2] The kinds of knowledge and meaning, facts and truths produced by Schäffer's published and public images and texts, both when first circulated and again in more recent decades, has been the focus of this study. Such knowledge and meaning remain provisional and fluid, subject to researchers' and readers' interests, their depth and breadth of historical, literary, and photographic knowledge, and their social places, times, and points of view. Photographic or literary meaning is not constructed, and cannot be construed, by authorial intent alone. Nevertheless, comprehension of the contexts of Schäffer's side of the lens is essential to understanding in a multifaceted and nuanced way the images made and shown to a variety of audiences in their time of origin: American, Canadian, and British, women and men, scientists and tourists, and those Indigenous sitters on the Kootenay Plains whose generosity of time and good humour Schäffer repaid with prints in addition to payment at the time of photographing. The fact that readers and viewers remain interested in, and at times highly critical of, Schäffer's works (and Schäffer herself) a century or more later is testament to the quality, reach, and significance of her images and narratives in her day and our own.

Appendix 1
Mary T.S. Schäffer and Families

Mary Townsend Sharples Schäffer Warren (4 October 1861–23 January 1939)

Mary Townsend Sharples Schäffer was the daughter of Elizabeth Cope Sharples (1830–1903) and Alfred Sharpless (1822–1903), distant cousins and descendants of British Quakers Jane and John Sharples who arrived in Pennsylvania in 1682. The comprehensive genealogy compiled for an 1882 bicentennial reunion of the Sharpless family notes that the spelling of the family name, which according to genealogist Gilbert Cope appears to originally have been Sharples, varied through the generations and numerous branches. Even in the one volume, the spelling varied with individuals across the different records in which they appeared (that is, when recorded as offspring under a father's listing, or as a husband or wife under the man's listing). While her brothers retained the paternal spelling of Sharpless, Schäffer spelled it as Sharples, the maternal lineage.

Schäffer's mother grew up in the Pennsylvania township of East Bradford. Her father was born and raised in West Chester, Pennsylvania, before he moved to Philadelphia in 1839 to begin working at age seventeen. They married in 1857 and lived in Philadelphia until 1870 when Alfred Sharpless retired from his position as superintendent of the Schuylkill Navigation Company and they purchased and began operating her father's farm in East Bradford. In 1883, the couple retired from farming and moved their family to West Chester.

They had four sons and one daughter: Henry Lewis (1858–1861), Joseph Townsend (1859–1869), Mary Townsend (1861–1939), Frederick Fraley (1866–1951), and Herman Hoopes (1871–1949). Only the three youngest survived to adulthood.

Frederick Fraley Sharpless graduated from the University of Michigan at Ann Arbor with a bachelor's degree in chemistry and undertook a career as a mining engineer in Philadelphia and New York. He married Caroline Hawxhurst (1866–1939) who, with their young son Paul (1901–1941), joined Schäffer on her return trip to survey Maligne Lake in 1911. Paul

Sharpless married Elizabeth Stamford (1904–1992) in 1930. Their only child, Eric (b. ca. 1934) was named for Paul's cousin who died in the First World War.

Herman Hoopes Sharpless studied briefly at the University of Michigan. He married Australian Jeannette Smith (1875–1966) in 1896. Along with their only child, Eric (1898–1916), they moved from West Chester to Calgary in 1912, the same year that Mary Schäffer moved permanently to Banff, where he worked for the Canadian Pacific Railway. In 1916, eighteen-year-old Eric, who had enlisted in the Canadian army in the autumn of 1914, died in the Battle of the Somme.

Mary Townsend Sharples was educated at Quaker Friends Select schools in Philadelphia and East Bradford, and lived with her parents until her marriage at age twenty-seven on 24 July 1889 to twice-widowed Philadelphia physician Charles Schäffer (1838–1903). Mary Schäffer visited the Canadian Rockies for the first time that same year.

Schäffer stated in a letter to Lillian Gest, which she signed "Mary Townsend Sharples Schaffer Warren—Nothing like the whole thing," that she was named after the first wife of her uncle, Joe Townsend.

On 28 April 1908, Mary Schäffer described her physical self in detail as required on her passport application: "Age: 46 years; Stature: 5 feet 5 inches; Forehead: high; Eyes: light brown; Nose: straight—prominent; Mouth: medium; Chin: rounded; Hair: light brown; Complex: fair; Face: oval." She put a stroke through the space left for occupation and listed her permanent residence as Philadelphia. This information was recorded on her passport.

Sources

United States Federal Censuses: 1860, 1870, 1880, 1900, 1910, 1920, 1930, and 1940. National Archives of the United States.

Gilbert Cope, *Genealogy of the Sharpless Family, Descended from John and Jane Sharples, Settlers Near Chester, Pennsylvania, 1682* (Philadelphia: Bi-Centennial Committee, 1887), 51, 424, 446, 773.

US Passport Applications, roll 0059, certificates 50879–1827, 27 April 1908–5 May 1908. Washington, DC: National Archives and Records Administration.

Copy of Mary Schäffer 1908 Passport: WMCR M107/II.B.12.

Mary Schäffer Warren to Lillian Gest, letter, Banff, 23 May [ca. 1938]. WMCR M67/8.

Charles Schäffer (1838–1903)

Charles Schäffer was born in Philadelphia, the only child of Charles Schäffer, a druggist, and Priscilla Morgan Schäffer, both of Quaker heritage. He obtained a medical degree in 1859 from the University of Pennsylvania and practiced as a physician in Philadelphia. He was also a respected amateur botanist and botanical photographer. In 1861, Schäffer was elected as a member of the Academy of Natural Sciences of Philadelphia and in 1888 as a member of the Photographic Society of Philadelphia. He was also a founding member of the Geographical Society of Philadelphia in 1891.

Schäffer married Martha T. Potts (1835–1878) in 1862. In 1882, he married physician Ellen E. Zook (1841–1884), and in 1889 married Mary Townsend Sharples. All marriages remained childless.

Sources

United States Federal Censuses: 1860, 1870, 1880, and 1900. National Archives of the United States.

William Biddle Atkinson, ed. *The Physicians and Surgeons of the United States* (Philadelphia: Charles Robson, 1878), 199.

"Charles Schäffer," *Prominent and Progressive Pennsylvanians of the Nineteenth Century*, vol. 2, edited by Leland M. Williamson, Richard A. Foley, Henry H. Colclazer, Louis N. Megargee, Jay H. Mowbray, and Will. R. Antisdel (Philadelphia: The Record Publishing Company, 1898), 439–41.

William Warren (1880–1943)

William Warren was born in Harlow, Essex, England and attended St. Mary's College there. Following service in the South African War, he arrived in Banff in 1902 where he gained employment as a guide with outfitter Tom Wilson. Warren guided Mary Schäffer's first journey as a widow in the Rockies in 1904 and most of her journeys through 1908. They married at St. Martin's Anglican Church in [North] Vancouver, BC, on 24 June 1915. On the marriage certificate, both declared Church of England as their religious denomination. Warren's "rank or profession" was listed as hotel proprietor. Warren's age is recorded as thirty-five and Schäffer's as thirty-eight. Following Schäffer's death in 1939, Warren moved to Vancouver, BC, where he resided until his death.

Warren was survived by his brothers John R., a lawyer in Penticton, BC; Frederick in Boston, MA; and Thomas R. in Hamilton, ON; and by his sister Rose Warren in London, England, who inherited his estate.

Sources

British Columbia Division of Vital Statistics, Civil Marriage Registration 034192, 1915. 1915-09-080192. Microfilm B11379.

"Married in Vancouver—Three Cheers." *Crag and Canyon* (Banff, AB), 3 July 1915, 2.

"Funeral Service for William Warren, Held at Vancouver, Fri," *Crag and Canyon* (Banff, AB), 23 July 1943, 1.

William Warren Probate 1943, Calgary Probate Records, Provincial Archives of Alberta.

Appendix 2
Mary W. (Molly) Adams and Family

Mary Wright (Molly) Adams (15 October 1868–23 January 1909)

Mary Wright (Molly) Adams was born on 15 October 1868 in Ridgefield, Fairfield County, Connecticut, the third of five children born to Cornelia Ann Cook (1830–1902) and Daniel Lucius "Doc" Adams (1814–1899) who had married in 1861. She died in Kobe, Japan, on 23 January 1909 and was buried there.

On her passport application of 20 May 1908, Adams described her physical self in detail, as required: "Age, 40 years; Stature, 5 feet 3 inches; Forehead, low; Eyes, hazel; Nose, small; Mouth, medium; Chin, pointed; Hair, brown; Complexion, fair; Face, thin." Where space was left to name family members as applicants as well, she wrote, "I have never been married." Adams drew a stroke through the space left for occupation and noted her permanent residence as New Haven.

She signed her correspondence in various ways, usually either "Molly" or "M.W.A."

Sources

US Passport Applications, roll 0061, certificates 52785–53684, 14 May 1908–21 May 1908. Washington, DC: National Archives and Records Administration.

UK, Foreign and Overseas Registers of British Subjects, 1627–1965. General Register Office: Foreign Registers and Returns. RG33/125. The National Archives of the United Kingdom, Kew, Surrey, England.

"DIED. ADAMS," *New Haven Evening Register*, 25 January 1909, 2.

Parents

Molly Adams's mother, Cornelia Cook Adams, was born in New York City, one of nine children born to Catherine Ireland Cook (born in England) and her husband Edward Cook of

New York. Cornelia Cook's brother William and his wife, Susan Coffin Boyd Cook, had three children: Catherine ("Käthchen") Ireland (b. 1869 in Berlin, Germany), Robert Boyd (b. 1872 in Lausanne, Switzerland), and William ("Willie") Boyd (b. 1884). Käthchen I. Cook was a first cousin of Molly Adams, and a frequent travel companion. William joined them for a short time while travelling in the southwestern United States in the winter of 1904–1905. "Cousin Alice" appears to have been Mrs. F.G. Ireland, whose husband may have been a nephew of Catherine Ireland Cook and a cousin to Molly Adams's mother.

Molly Adams's father, Daniel Lucius Adams, left a public record that continues to grow today. He attended Yale University and Harvard Medical School, as had his father before him, obtaining his medical degree in 1838. Adams first practiced medicine in his hometown of Mont Vernon, Massachusetts, with his father and then in Boston, before moving to New York City in 1839 where he practiced medicine until 1865. Adams also pursued a recreational interest in baseball, which he had begun playing in his youth, and it is this vocation that has kept his name in the public record and imagination. In 1845, "Doc" Adams joined the Knickerbocker Base Ball Club of New York about a month after they were founded on 23 September. He is credited with establishing and being the first to play the position of shortstop, and with codifying the rules of the field size. In 1865, at age fifty-one, he retired from medicine and baseball for what he stated were health reasons and moved with his wife to Ridgefield, Connecticut, where their four surviving children were born. While in Ridgefield, he served as a member of the state legislative assembly in 1870, and as a bank president for two periods between 1871 and 1886. In 1888, at age seventy-three, Daniel and Cornelia Adams moved with their four children to New Haven, Connecticut, where their two sons attended the Sheffield Scientific School at Yale University.

Today, "Doc" Adams's descendants are pursuing recognition for their great-grandfather's legacy as one of the "Fathers of Baseball" in the United States.

Sources

Nathan Adams Downey, "Mailbox: On Baseball When the Game was Very New," *New York Times*, 13 April 1980, S2.

John Thorn, "The Father of Baseball? You Probably Never Heard of Him," *Elysian Fields Quarterly* 11, no. 1 (1992): 85–91.

Erik Ofgang, "Efforts Ramp Up to Get CT Legend Into Hall of Fame," *Connecticut Magazine*, 6 March 2015, www.connecticutmag.com/Blog/History/March-2015/Efforts-Ramp-Up-to-Get-CT-Baseball-Legend-Into-Hall-of-Fame/.

Corey Kilgannon, "Family Rallies in Late Innings for a Pioneering Shortstop," *New York Times*, 23 September 2015, A21.

"Late Rally for Doc Adams, a Jeter Before There Were Mitts," *New York Times*, 23 September 2015, www.nytimes.com/2015/09/23/nyregion/late-rally-for-doc-adams-a-jeter-before-there-were-mitts.html?_r=0.

Andrew Dalton, "Who's Your Daddy? Baseball May Have New Founder," *The Big Story* 7 April 2016, http://bigstory.ap.org/article/c938542ca6304a9fb85cb72e349d7db9/whos-your-daddy-modern-baseball-may-have-new-founder.

Andrew Dalton, "An 'Uncle,' a Displaced Father, a Legend of the Sport: Who Is Doc Adams?" *Globe and Mail* (Toronto), 25 April 2016, S5.

Siblings

Cornelia and Daniel Adams's first child—a son, Charles—died less than a month after his birth in New York in 1864. Daughters Catherine ("Katy") (1866–1958) and Mary (Molly) Wright (1868–1909) may have been named for their mother's family: Catherine for Cornelia's mother Catherine Ireland Cook, and Mary for Cornelia's married sister Mary Cook Wright (m. James A. Wright 7 May 1850). Neither appears to have pursued post-secondary education or paid employment as adults. Sons Francis Mulliken (birth name of Daniel Lucius Adams's mother Nancy Mulliken) (1871–1949) and Roger Cook (1874–1962) graduated Yale with bachelor of philosophy degrees, in 1892 and 1893, respectively, and began working immediately upon graduation.

Catherine Adams married William Lewis Elkin (1855–1933), an astronomer and director of Yale University Observatory. She was not employed and no children were born. Molly Adams, who remained single, lived with the Elkins following her mother's death.

Roger Adams obtained employment in Buffalo, New York, as an electrician and moved there by 1895. In 1899, he married Jeannette Putnam Keating (1878–1961) of Buffalo, with whom he raised a daughter, Anne, and two sons, Roger and Daniel. Molly Adams occasionally commented in letters about visits with her brother and his family in Buffalo. Daniel's daughters, Nancy and Marjorie, inherited their great aunt Molly Adams's papers.

Francis Adams, in contrast to his siblings, was peripatetic. Francis first served as an assistant in the Yale chemistry department in 1893 and 1894, during which time he was a graduate student, and then as a tutor at Yale University between 1895 and 1897. (In New Haven city directories for each of those three years, he is documented as living at home with parents.) The 1900 US Federal Census shows him aged twenty-eight, boarding in Brooklyn and working as a tutor. In 1903, he married Edythe Peck, who died while Molly Adams was travelling in the Rockies in the summer of 1907. In 1910, he is listed as widowed, living with an aunt by marriage, Juliet E. Peck, in Norfolk, Massachusetts, and working as a secretary in a religious institution. In 1929, his name and that of Helen R. Adams, who is listed as his wife, appears on the passenger list for the ship *Lapland* that arrived in New York from Antwerp, Belgium, on 29 September 1929. By 1930, at age fifty-eight, he and Helen R. Adams, aged fifty-three and listed as Francis's wife, were living in Pasadena, Los Angeles, California. The 1940 US Federal Census lists him as Rev. Francis M. Adams, living with his wife Helen R. in Ridgefield, Fairfield County, Connecticut. The *Connecticut Death Index* lists his death as 25 July 1949 while in Maine although resident in Ridgefield. It also states his marital status as "Never Married (Single)." Helen Rockwell Adams's death is recorded in the

Connecticut Death Index on 17 June 1957, at Newtown, Fairfield, Connecticut, while resident in Bridgeport. Her marital status is listed as "Widowed" and her spouse's name as "Fran." Francis and Helen Rockwell Adams had one daughter, Ann C. Horner, and three grandchildren.

Sources

United States Federal Censuses: 1860, 1870, 1880, 1900, 1910, 1920, 1930, and 1940. National Archives of the United States.

Yale University Class of 1835, "Daniel Lucius Adams," *Biographical and Historical Record of the Class of 1835 in Yale College for the Fifty Years from the Admission of the Class to College* (New Haven, CT, 1881), 18–19.

New Haven City Directory (1894).

Yale Class Book '94 (New Haven, CT, 1894), 75.

Passenger Lists of Vessels Arriving at New York, NY, 1897–1957. Microfilm Publication T715. Records of the Immigration and Naturalization Service, National Archives at Washington, DC.

Catalogue of the Officers and Graduates of Yale University 1701–1901 (New Haven, CT: Yale University, 1901), 35, 232, 233, 294, 301.

Molly Adams to "Jean," Elizabethtown, NY, 30 August 1903, Adams Family Collection.

Molly Adams to "Cousin Alice," Field, BC, 14 October 1907, Adams Family Collection.

Molly Adams, Field, BC, to Mrs. F.G. Ireland, New York City, telegram, 22 September 1908, Adams Family Collection.

"William Boyd Cook," *Harvard College Class of 1904 Second Report, June, 1910* (Cambridge, MA: Crimson Printing Co., 1910).

Connecticut Department of Health, *Connecticut Death Index, 1949–2001* (Hartford, CT: Connecticut Department of Health).

"Rev. Francis Adams," *Lewiston Daily News* (ME), 26 July 1949, 2.

Notes

1 She Who Colored Slides

1. Mary T.S. Schäffer, *Old Indian Trails: Incidents of Camp and Trail Life, Covering Two Years' Exploration through the Rocky Mountains of Canada* (New York: G.P. Putnam's Sons; Toronto: William Briggs, 1911; reprint with revised map, 1912), 13. Schäffer revised the map based on her survey of Maligne Lake in 1911. G.P. Putnam's Sons published the 1912 edition in New York and London under their Knickerbocker Press imprint.
2. Stewardson Brown and Mrs. Charles Schäffer, *Alpine Flora of the Canadian Rocky Mountains* (New York and London: G.P. Putnam's Sons/Knickerbocker Press, 1907).
3. Schäffer published one article about the 1911 trip to survey Maligne Lake: Mary T.S. Schaffer, "The Finding of Lake Maligne," *Canadian Alpine Journal* 4 (1912): 92–97. The Royal Geographical Society in London also published an article about the survey trip based on information supplied by Schäffer: "Mrs. Schäffer's Discovery and Survey of Lake Maligne, Canadian Rockies," *Geographical Journal* 39, no. 4 (April 1912): 379–81; and a reader's response with additional information: "Mrs. Schäffer's Survey of Maligne Lake," *Geographical Journal* 40, no. 3 (September 1912): 334–35.
4. "The Canadian Rockies: A Book of Unknown Trails by Mary T.S. Schaffer," *Springfield Republican* (Massachusetts), 23 July 1911.
5. "Old Indian Trails of the Canadian Rockies," *Portland Telegram* (Oregon), 5 August 1911.
6. For more information about Mary Ward's and Marion Cran's publications based on Mary Schäffer's travels, as well as excerpts, see Colleen Skidmore, ed., *This Wild Spirit: Women in the Rocky Mountains of Canada* (Edmonton: University of Alberta Press, 2006).
7. A.P. Coleman, *The Canadian Rockies: New and Old Trails with 3 Maps and 41 Illustrations* (Toronto: Henry Frowde, 1911).
8. Carolyn G. Heilbrun, *Writing a Woman's Life* (New York: W.W. Norton, 1988), 59.

9. Ibid., 17; Carroll Smith-Rosenberg, *Disorderly Conduct: Visions of Gender in Victorian America* (New York: Oxford University Press, 1985), 24; Schäffer, *Old Indian Trails* (1911), 5.
10. Smith-Rosenberg, *Disorderly Conduct*, 29.
11. Helen M. Buss makes this observation in Helen M. Buss and Marlene Kadar, eds., *Working in Women's Archives: Researching Women's Private Literature and Archival Documents* (Waterloo, ON: Wilfrid Laurier University Press, 2001), 4.
12. Afterwards, Molly Adams's family invited me to deposit these materials in the archives of my choice for the use of future researchers. The Adams Family Collection is now in the Archives and Library of the Whyte Museum of the Canadian Rockies.
13. Schäffer, *Old Indian Trails* (1911), 4–5.
14. Carolyn G. Heilbrun, *Reinventing Womanhood* (New York: W.W. Norton, 1979), 34.
15. Schäffer, *Old Indian Trails* (1911), 5.
16. Heilbrun, *Reinventing Womanhood*, 34.
17. Mary T.S. Schäffer passport application, 28 April 1908, US Passport Applications, roll 0059, certificates 50879–51827, 27 April–5 May 1908, National Archives and Records Administration, Washington, DC.
18. Mary [Schäffer] Warren to Humphrey Toms, Banff, 28 March 1935, WMCR M429. Schäffer wrote, "my husband and I (known to his intimates as Will)."
19. "Married in Vancouver—Three Cheers," *Crag and Canyon* (Banff, AB), 3 July 1915, 2.
20. In 1920, women's suffrage was generally limited to "non-alien" women, that is, those born in Canada and holding Canadian citizenship. Only in 1948 did all Asian Canadians win the right to vote. Suffrage was not universal in Canada until 1960 when Indigenous women and men living on reserve in Canada were no longer barred.
21. "Mrs. Wm. Warren Banff Oldtimer and Explorer of Rockies Passes," *Crag and Canyon* (Banff, AB), 27 January 1939, 1–2. Her husband William Warren's ashes were buried alongside her grave following his death in 1943.
22. Smith-Rosenberg, *Disorderly Conduct*, 265.
23. Joan Wallach Scott, *Feminism and History* (New York: Oxford University Press, 1996), 4.
24. "Illustrated Lecture," *Daily Local News* (West Chester, PA), 2 March 1911, clipping file "Schaeffer, M.," Chester County Archives, West Chester, PA.
25. Colleen Skidmore, "Taking a Deep Interest: Métis and Aboriginal Women," in *This Wild Spirit*, 11; Lisa MacFarlane, "Mary Schäffer's 'Comprehending Equal Eyes,'" in *Trading Gazes: Euro-American Women Photographers and Native North Americans, 1880–1940*, by Susan Bernardin, Melody Gaulich, Lisa MacFarlane, and Nicole Tonkovich (New Brunswick, NJ: Rutgers University Press, 2003), 148. For more on Suzette Chalifoux Swift, see Janet Munro, "Hosts of Mountain Oasis," *Canadian National Railways Magazine* (1929), 24–26, reprinted in *This Wild Spirit*, 20–28; and Elsie Park Gowan, "Jasper's First Lady," *Heritage* 5, no. 4 (July/August 1977): 19–20.
26. Schäffer, *Old Indian Trails* (1911), 325.
27. Mary W. (Molly) Adams, 1908 transcribed diary, Swift Camp, 31 August, WMCR M79/11.

28. Eric Sharpless (b. ca. 1934) is the son of Paul Sharpless, who as a young boy accompanied Schäffer on a trip to survey Maligne Lake in 1911, and the grandson of Schäffer's brother and sister-in-law Frederick and Caroline Sharpless. He was named for Eric Sharpless, the son of Schäffer's second brother Herman and sister-in-law Jeannette, who died in the Battle of the Somme on 15 September 1916 as a lieutenant in the Canadian army. See Hugh A. Dempsey, "Mary Warren's Letters from the Home Front 1916–1917," *Alberta History* 63, no. 1 (Winter 2015): 2–15. See Appendix 1 for an explanation of the various spellings of Schäffer's birth family surname.
29. Margaret Atwood, *Negotiating with the Dead* (Cambridge: Cambridge University Press, 2002), 45.
30. Ibid.
31. Smith-Rosenberg, *Disorderly Conduct*, 30.
32. Atwood, *Negotiating with the Dead*, 132.
33. Ibid., 21.
34. Heilbrun, *Writing a Woman's Life*, 49.
35. E.J. Hart, "Yahe-Weha—Mountain Woman: The Life and Travels of Mary Schäffer Warren, 1861–1939," in *A Hunter of Peace: Mary T.S. Schäffer's Old Indian Trails of the Canadian Rockies*, intro. and ed. E.J. Hart (Banff, AB: Whyte Museum of the Canadian Rockies, 1980), 14; E.J. Hart, "Yahe-Weha—Mountain Woman: The Life and Travels of Mary Schäffer Warren, 1861–1939," in *A Hunter of Peace: Mary T.S. Schäffer's Old Indian Trails of the Canadian Rockies*, 2nd ed., intro. E.J. Hart, foreword Jennifer Rutkair (Banff, AB: Whyte Museum of the Canadian Rockies, 2014), 26.
36. "Homegrown Mountain Movie Maker," *Mountain* 3 (Fall 2000): 28.
37. Among others, Lisa MacFarlane characterizes Schäffer as "white and wealthy, a 'lady,'" in "Mary Schäffer's 'Comprehending Equal Eyes,'" 112. Julia V. Emberley classifies Schäffer as a "bourgeois" woman traveller in two publications: J.V. Emberley, "Colonial Phantasms: Aboriginality and the Family in the Photographic Archives," in *ReCalling Early Canada: Reading the Political in Literary and Cultural Production*, ed. Jennifer Blair, Daniel Coleman, Kate Higginson, and Lorraine York (Edmonton: University of Alberta Press, 2005), 301–34, and Julia V. Emberley, *Defamiliarizing the Aboriginal: Cultural Practices and Decolonization in Canada* (Toronto: University of Toronto Press, 2007), 167–76. Not all who describe Schäffer by class are undertaking critical analyses. See Stephen R. Bown and Nicky L. Brink, "Mountain Woman," *The Beaver* 87, no. 3 (June–July 2007): 42–46; and "Romance in Heart of Rockies: Prospectors Bring Story of Riches on G.T.P. Route and Romantic Tale of Society Dames," *Vancouver Daily World*, 3 October 1908, 1.
38. Lucy Lippard, Introduction to *Partial Recall: Photographs of Native North Americans*, ed. Lucy Lippard (New York: The New Press, 1992), 13, 34–45. An excerpt from Lippard's introduction, subtitled "Doubletake: The Diary of a Relationship with an Image," that focuses on Schäffer's portrait of the Beaver family (Fig. 1.9) is reprinted in *This Wild Spirit*, 61–75.

39. See MacFarlane, "Mary Schäffer's 'Comprehending Equal Eyes,'" 108–50; Emberley, "Colonial Phantasms," 301–34; and Michelle Gilbert and James Gillett, "Into the Mountains and Across the Country: Emergent Forms of Equine Adventure Leisure in Canada," *Loisir et Société/Society and Leisure* 37, no. 2 (2014): 313–25.
40. I.S. MacLaren, "Cultured Wilderness in Jasper National Park," *Journal of Canadian Studies/Revue d'études canadiennes* 34, no. 3 (1999): 17.
41. Mary Schaffer Warren to Miss [Minnie] Nickell, Banff, 21 September [ca. 1935], WMCR M8.
42. Mary [Schäffer] Warren to "My Dear Unseen Friend," Banff, 12 November [ca. 1935], WMCR M8.
43. Rudyard Kipling, "Letters to the Family," *Collier's* 41, no. 5 (25 April 1908), 13–14, reprinted in Rudyard Kipling, *Letters of Travel (1892–1913)* (London: Macmillan & Co., 1920), 188–89.
44. A.O. Wheeler, *The Selkirk Range*, vol. 1 (Ottawa: Government Printing Bureau, 1905).
45. Such correspondents include Raymond Zillmer in 1928 (WMCR M8), Minnie Nickell in ca. 1935–1937 (WMCR M8), Lillian Gest in ca. 1938 (WMCR M67/8), and Humphrey Toms from 1933 to 1939 (WMCR M429).
46. Dan McCowan, *Hill-Top Tales* (Toronto: Macmillan, 1948), vii, 94.
47. M.B. Williams, *Jasper National Park: A Descriptive Guide* (Hamilton, Saskatoon, and Vancouver: Larson Publishing Company, 1949), 57–61. Williams spent two decades working in publicity for the National Parks Branch when it was first established.
48. Elsie Park Gowan, "A Quaker in Buckskin," *Alberta Historical Review* 5 (Summer 1957): 1–6, 24–28. Gowan (1905–1999) emigrated with her family from Scotland to Edmonton in 1912. She earned a bachelor's degree in history from the University of Alberta and became a well-known theatre and radio playwright whose work was seen across Canada and heard in Canada, the United States, the United Kingdom, Australia, South America, and the Caribbean. See Anton Wagner, "Elsie Park Gowan: Distinctively Canadian," *Theatre History in Canada* 8, no. 1 (Spring 1987): 68–82, and Moira Day, ed., *The Hungry Spirit: Selected Plays and Prose by Elsie Park Gowan* (Edmonton, AB: NeWest Press, 1992).
49. Gowan, "A Quaker in Buckskin," 1.
50. Ibid., 2–3.
51. Catharine Robb Whyte moved to Banff at age twenty-four in 1930 with her new husband, Peter Whyte, whom she had met at art school in Boston. Like Schäffer, Whyte grew up in the northeastern United States in a family of means and social standing, trained as an artist, and chose to make a life in the mountains at Banff. The museum, opened in 1968, embodies the Whytes' vision and legacy. For a history of the Whyte family of Banff, Peter and Catharine Whyte's life there, and their legacy in the Whyte Museum of the Canadian Rockies, see Chic Scott, *Mountain Romantics: The Whytes of Banff* (Banff, AB: Whyte Museum of the Canadian Rockies and Assiniboine Publishing, 2014).

52. Hart, "Yahe-Weha" (1980), 14; Hart, "Yahe-Weha" (2014), 26.
53. Hart, "Yahe-Weha" (1980), 12, 14; Hart, "Yahe-Weha" (2014), 24, 26.
54. See United States Bureau of the Census, Historical Time Series, Families and Living Arrangements, Marital Status Table MS-2, "Estimated Median Age at First Marriage, by Sex: 1890 to the Present," 30 October 2014, www.census.gov/hhes/families/data/marital.html.
55. Austin Institute, "Ask a Data Scientist—Age Differences Between Couples," Austin Institute for the Study of Family and Culture, 9 November 2014, www.austin-institute.org/research/ask-a-data-scientist-age-differences-between-couples/.
56. Civil Marriage Registration 034192, 1915, 1915-09-080192, microfilm B11379, British Columbia Division of Vital Statistics; "Married in Vancouver—Three Cheers," *Crag and Canyon* (Banff, AB), 3 July 1915, 2. See Appendix 1 for details of William Warren's life. Thank you to PearlAnn Reichwein, who located the marriage certificate.
57. Schäffer, *Old Indian Trails* (1911), 176.
58. Hart, frontispiece, *A Hunter of Peace* (1980, 2014); Mary [Schäffer] Warren to Mr. [Raymond] Zillmer, Banff, 12 April [1928], WMCR M8.
59. Janice Sanford Beck, *No Ordinary Woman: The Story of Mary Schäffer Warren* (Calgary, AB: Rocky Mountain Books, 2001). This book was reprinted with additional material in 2006.
60. Ibid., inside front jacket.
61. Ibid., 129, 145.
62. Ibid., 14, 15.
63. Ibid., 74.
64. Ibid., 84.
65. Mary Schäffer to George Vaux Jr., Banff, 3 December 1911, 26 December [1911], 21 March [1912], 15 April 1912, WMCR Vaux 1 Series. Schäffer planned to take a Hudson's Bay Company 1,854-mile boat trip between Athabasca Landing and Fort MacPherson. Through the company she was able to find another woman to travel with her. When the unnamed woman cancelled, Schäffer decided to have her fourteen-year-old nephew Eric join her, but then cancelled the trip when the cost of building her new house in Banff made the trip unviable. She expressed the hope that she would make the trip the following year, but did not do so. See Chapter 5 in this volume.
66. Hart, *A Hunter of Peace* (1980), 96; Hart, *A Hunter of Peace* (2014), 113.
67. Beck, *No Ordinary Woman*, 74.
68. Schäffer, *Old Indian Trails* (1911), 248.
69. Mary W. (Molly) Adams, 1908 transcribed diary, Chaba Camp, 10 July, WMCR M79/11.
70. Schäffer, *Old Indian Trails* (1911), 5.
71. MacFarlane, "Mary Schäffer's 'Comprehending Equal Eyes,'" 149.
72. Susan Bernardin, Melody Gaulich, Lisa MacFarlane, and Nicole Tonkovich, "Empire of the Lens: Women, Indians, and Cameras," in *Trading Gazes: Euro-American Women*

Photographers and Native North Americans, 1880–1940 (New Brunswick, NJ: Rutgers University Press, 2003), 27.

73. MacFarlane, "Mary Schäffer's 'Comprehending Equal Eyes,'" 149.
74. Lippard, Introduction, 34–45.
75. Ibid., 35.
76. Lippard, Introduction, 36.
77. MacFarlane, "Mary Schäffer's 'Comprehending Equal Eyes,'" 110.
78. Ibid.
79. Ibid., 112.
80. Ibid., 113.
81. Ibid., 114.
82. MacFarlane, "Mary Schäffer's 'Comprehending Equal Eyes,'" 149.
83. I.S. MacLaren, Introduction to *Culturing Wilderness in Jasper National Park: Studies in Two Centuries of Human History in the Upper Athabasca Watershed*, ed. I.S. MacLaren (Edmonton: University of Alberta Press, 2007), xxx.
84. MacLaren, "Cultured Wilderness," 17.
85. Ibid., 13.
86. Schäffer, *Old Indian Trails* (1911), 3.
87. Ibid., 359.
88. Ben Gadd, *Handbook of the Canadian Rockies: Geology, Plants, Animals, History and Recreation from Waterton/Glacier to the Yukon*, 2nd ed. (Jasper, AB: Corax Press, 1995), 703.
89. William Cronon, "The Trouble with Wilderness; or, Getting Back to the Wrong Nature," in *Uncommon Ground: Rethinking the Human Place in Nature*, ed. William Cronon (New York: W.W. Norton, 1995), 69–90.
90. Ibid., 80, 81.
91. The 2014 edition of *A Hunter of Peace* restores the index and preface; as well, photographs have been edited and revised, with many associated with the original chapters in which they were first published, and others of relevance and interest added.
92. Mary T.S. Schäffer, *Old Indian Trails of the Canadian Rockies*, abr. ed., foreword by Janice Sanford Beck (Vancouver: Rocky Mountain Books, 2007). This incomplete version is part of a series of republications of the texts of early twentieth-century Rocky Mountain books. Suffering a similar fate is the work of one of Schäffer's contemporary alpinists, Arthur P. Coleman, whose book *The Canadian Rockies: New and Old Trails* was also published in 1911 with thirty-three photographs and a map, now absent in the 2006 "reprinted" version.
93. Janice Sanford Beck, foreword to *Old Indian Trails of the Canadian Rockies*, by Mary T.S. Schäffer, abr. ed. (Surrey, BC: Rocky Mountain Books, 2007), xi.
94. Mary T.S. Schäffer, *Old Indian Trails of the Canadian Rockies*, abr. 2nd ed., foreword by Janice Sanford Beck (Vancouver: Rocky Mountain Books, 2011).

95. For reports on the 1899 trip, see "Canadian Pacific Excursion," *Journal of the Photographic Society of Philadelphia* 5, no. 4 (April 1899): 36; "Proceedings of the Society," *Journal of the Photographic Society of Philadelphia* 5, no. 6 (October, November, December 1899): 60; "Annual Report of the Board of Directors," *Journal of the Photographic Society of Philadelphia* 6, no. 3 (April 1900): 27.
96. Beaumont Newhall, *The History of Photography* (New York: Museum of Modern Art, 1964); Naomi Rosenblum, *A History of Women Photographers* (New York: Abbeville Press, 1994); Martin W. Sandler, *Against the Odds: Women Pioneers in the First Hundred Years of Photography* (New York: Rizzoli International Publications, 2002).
97. Bronwyn A.E. Griffith, ed., *Ambassadors of Progress: American Women Photographers in Paris 1900–1901* (Giverny, France: Musée d'Art Américain Giverny, 2001).
98. Ibid., 9.
99. Ibid., 22.
100. C. Jane Gover, *The Positive Image: Women Photographers in Turn of the Century America* (Albany: State University of New York Press, 1988), xiii.
101. Ibid., xiv.
102. Ibid., xviii–xix. A decade later, Judith Fryer Davidov took up the phenomenon of women's networks as a way of "recovering photographic history and thinking about the cultural work that images do, and in opposition to the hierarchical *line* of male photographers descending from Stieglitz." Judith Fryer Davidov, *Women's Camera Work: Self/Body/Other in American Visual Culture* (Durham, NC: Duke University Press, 1998), 8.
103. Gover, *The Positive Image*, 134.
104. Ibid.
105. Ibid., 135.
106. Joan M. Schwartz, "Photographic Reflections: Nature, Landscape and Environment," *Environmental History* 12 (October 2007): 991.
107. Ibid., 992.
108. Trinh T. Minh-ha, *Woman, Native, Other: Writing Postcoloniality and Feminism* (Bloomington: Indiana University Press, 1989), 121.
109. Jill Lepore, "Just the Facts, Ma'am," *The New Yorker* 84, no. 6 (24 March 2008), 81.
110. Ibid., 82.
111. Ibid.
112. Ibid., 83.
113. Ibid.
114. Stephen J. Gould, "A Web of Tales," *Natural History* 97 (October 1988): 23.
115. Ibid., 22.
116. Ibid.
117. Ibid., 23.
118. Stage plays include Elsie Park Gowan, "The Jasper Story," unpublished play, 1955, 87–123, University of Alberta Archives, Edmonton; and Sharon Stearns, *Hunter of Peace* (Victoria, BC: Scirocco Drama, 1993).

119. Todd Babiak, *The Book of Stanley* (Toronto: McClelland & Stewart, 2007).
120. Ibid., 107.
121. Heilbrun, *Writing a Woman's Life*, 77.
122. See also Cyndi Smith, *Off the Beaten Track: Women Adventurers and Mountaineers in Western Canada* (Calgary, AB: Coyote Books, 1989) and Jill Foran, *Mary Schäffer: An Adventurous Woman's Exploits in the Canadian Rockies* (Canmore, AB: Altitude Publishing, 2003).
123. Heilbrun, *Writing a Woman's Life*, 95.
124. Ibid., 93.
125. Ibid., 108.
126. Scott, *Mountain Romantics*, 83–87. Barbara and Ruth Carpenter visited Schäffer in Banff in 1930. While there they met their future husbands, David Jr. (Jackie) White and Allan Mather. The couples married in a joint ceremony in 1931 and settled in Banff.
127. See Doreen Walker, ed., *Dear Nan: Letters of Emily Carr, Nan Cheney and Humphrey Toms* (Vancouver: University of British Columbia Press, 1990).
128. Vaux is pronounced "vox." Mary Morris Vaux travelled with her brothers George Jr. and William, as well as her father George Sr. Her mother, Sarah, had died in 1879. Her uncle William S. Vaux was a mineralogist active in both the Academy of Natural Sciences and the Photographic Society of Philadelphia.
129. Heilbrun, *Writing a Woman's Life*, 109.
130. "Lure of the Rockies," *Brooklyn Eagle*, 7 June 1911, clipping, WMCR M79/9B.
131. Mary [Schäffer] Warren to Mr. [Raymond] Zillmer, Banff, 12 April [1928], WMCR M8.
132. Heilbrun, *Writing a Woman's Life*, 110. Heilbrun wrote a popular series of mystery novels under the pseudonym Amanda Cross.
133. Ibid., 111.
134. Atwood, *Negotiating with the Dead*, 132.
135. Heilbrun, *Writing a Woman's Life*, 25.
136. Laura Wexler, *Tender Violence: Domestic Visions in an Age of U.S. Imperialism* (Chapel Hill: University of North Carolina Press, 2000), 36–37.

2 Philadelphia, Paris, and the Rocky Mountains of Canada, 1889–1903

1. Frances Benjamin Johnston, Master of generic letter sent to invitees, Washington, DC, n.d. [ca. 11 June 1900], reel 20, Papers of Frances Benjamin Johnston, 1855–1954 (Microfilm Reel Edition), Manuscript Division, Library of Congress.
2. "Proceedings of the Society," *Journal of the Photographic Society of Philadelphia* 4, no. 5 (May and June 1899): 41.
3. Gilbert Cope, *Genealogy of the Sharpless Family, Descended from John and Jane Sharples, Settlers Near Chester, Pennsylvania, 1682* (Philadelphia: Bi-Centennial Committee, 1887), 773.
4. Charles Schäffer was born at 485 Arch Street, later numbered 1125, in 1838. An only child, he moved with his parents in 1844 to 1309 Arch Street (west of 13th Street). See

"Charles Schäffer," in *Prominent and Progressive Pennsylvanians of the Nineteenth Century*, vol. 2, ed. Leland M. Williamson, Richard A. Foley, Henry H. Colclazer, Louis N. Megargee, Jay H. Mowbray, and Will. R. Antisdel (Philadelphia: The Record Publishing Company, 1898), 439–41. He purchased the residence from his mother, Priscilla M. Schäffer in June 1867 (Philadelphia City Archives, Property Deed entered August 1, 1867, Lot no. 76, Plan Book no. 1N, p. 21, 1309 Arch Street, 10 Ward, Division no. 1). His third wife and widow, Mary T.S. Schäffer, disposed of the property within six months of his death, transferring the deed to the Academy of Natural Sciences on 10 May 1904 (Philadelphia City Archives, Property Deed entered June 13, 1904, Lot no. 76, Plan Book no. 1N, p. 21, 1309 Arch Street, 10 Ward, Division no. 1) in return for a lifetime pension. In a letter written by Mary Schäffer's attorney, George Vaux Jr., to United States Internal Revenue in 1924, it is noted that the gift of the house to the Academy of Natural Sciences was "subject to the payment to her annually of the sum of $1800; this payment to cease upon her death." WMCR Vaux Collection Addition 2007.

5. Williamson et al., "Charles Schäffer," 439.
6. Nathanial Burt, *The Perennial Philadelphians: The Anatomy of an American Aristocracy* (Boston: Little, Brown & Co., 1963), 529.
7. In addition to Johnston's master draft of her letter, the responses she received from Henry Troth, Alfred Stieglitz, and others she consulted, as well as those from most of the thirty-one women whose work she took to Paris, are preserved among the Papers of Frances Benjamin Johnston, Manuscript Division, Library of Congress.
8. Mary T.S. Schäffer to Frances Benjamin Johnston, Philadelphia, 12 June 1900, reel 20, Papers of Frances Benjamin Johnston, 1855–1954 (Microfilm Reel Edition), Manuscript Division, Library of Congress.
9. Joseph T. Keiley, "The Philadelphia Salon: Its Origins and Influence," *Camera Notes* 2, no. 3 (January 1899): 128–29.
10. Two key primary sources for information on the membership and activities of the Photographic Society of Philadelphia are John C. Browne's *History of the Photographic Society of Philadelphia* (Philadelphia: The Photographic Society of Philadelphia, 1884) and the *Journal of the Photographic Society of Philadelphia*, published between 1893 and 1913. Browne's list of members between 1862 and 1884 includes no women. There is then a gap in the documentation until 1893, when the first *Journal* was published. While new members' names were noted in proceedings of meetings published in the *Journal*, the first time a full membership list appeared was in 1903. The Schäffers were included in that list, but there is no mention of Mary Schäffer as a new member in the previous ten years. In the proceedings of the 9 December 1903 meeting, Charles Schäffer's death is noted, along with the fact that he was elected to membership on 3 October 1888. As there is no documentation of when Mary Schäffer became a member of the Photographic Society, it is likely that she joined some time between her marriage and move to Philadelphia in 1889 and the first publication of the *Journal* in 1893. Mary Schäffer resigned her membership in 1906. "List of Members, March 1st, 1903,"

Journal of the Photographic Society of Philadelphia 9, no. 1 (January–February 1903): 9; "Proceedings of the Society," *Journal of the Photographic Society of Philadelphia* 9, no. 4 (October, November, December 1903): 36; "Proceedings of the Society," *Journal of the Photographic Society of Philadelphia* 12, no. 1 (January–February 1906): 2.

11. On 4 May 1893, Charles Schäffer presented a lantern slide lecture on the Selkirk Mountains, the California Sierra mountains, and the Yosemite Valley. Minutes of the Board of Directors, Geographical Club of Philadelphia, March 30, 1891–December 10, 1895, Manuscripts collection no. 93, 1997-787ms, American Philosophical Society Library, Philadelphia.
12. Mrs. Charles Schäffer, "The Valleys of the Saskatchewan with Horse and Camera," *Bulletin of the Geographical Society of Philadelphia* 5, no. 2 (April 1907): 108–14; Mary T.S. Schäffer, "Among the Sources of the Saskatchewan and Athabasca Rivers," *Bulletin of the Geographical Society of Philadelphia* 6 (April 1908): 48–62; Mary T.S. Schäffer, "A Recently Explored Lake in the Rocky Range of Canada," *Bulletin of the Geographical Society of Philadelphia* 7, no. 3 (July 1909): 123–34.
13. Mary Panzer, *Philadelphia Naturalistic Photography 1865–1906* (exhibition catalogue) (New Haven, CT: Yale University Art Gallery, 1982), 14.
14. Browne, *History of the Photographic Society*, 21.
15. "Proceedings of the Society," *Journal of the Photographic Society of Philadelphia* 5, no. 5 (May and June 1899): 41. A report on the proceedings of the Society in vol. 5, no. 3 (March 1899): 17–18 also cites Mrs. Charles Schaffer [*sic*] as well as Miss Mary Vaux among other members showing slides at the 22 February meeting that year. That same spring, Schäffer served on a committee that proposed a members' excursion to the Rocky Mountains of Canada. This presentation may have been made to promote interest in the trip. "Proceedings of the Society," 25 and "Canadian Pacific Excursion," *Journal of the Photographic Society of Philadelphia* 5, no. 4 (April 1899): 36.
16. The Unlabelled Minutes Book of the Board of Directors of the Geographical Club of Philadelphia for November 11, 1908–April 12, 1916 notes that on 8 February 1911, "Mrs. Mary T.S. Schäffer will speak on the Canadian Rockies at the March meeting." Manuscripts Collection no. 93, 1997-787ms, American Philosophical Society Library, Philadelphia.
17. In his *History of the Photographic Society of Philadelphia*, John C. Browne notes, "the large number of amateur photographers lately coming into the society has been brought about by the introduction of Gelantine [*sic*] Dry Plates as a commercial article" (33). The gelatin dry plate was a new kind of glass negative technology that eliminated the need to coat the plate with chemicals prior to exposure and develop it immediately afterwards.
18. *Photographic Times* 19 (February 1889): 177, quoted in Panzer, *Philadelphia Naturalistic Photography*, 6.
19. Panzer, *Philadelphia Naturalistic Photography*, 7.

20. Keiley, "The Philadelphia Salon," 113–32; "Some Salon Statistics," *Camera Notes* 2, no. 3 (January 1899): 132. *Camera Notes* was published between 1897 and 1903 by the Camera Club of New York, and edited by Alfred Stieglitz, the club's founder and driving force, who had served by invitation on the 1898 jury. Of the five jurors, one was a woman, Alice Barber Stephens of Philadelphia, a painter and engraver well known for her magazine illustrations.
21. United States Department of Commerce and Labor, Bureau of the Census, *Statistics of Women at Work: Based on Unpublished Information Derived from the Schedules of the Twelfth Census: 1900* (Washington, DC: Government Printing Office, 1907).
22. United States Department of Commerce and Labor, Bureau of the Census, *Occupations at the Twelfth Census, Prepared under the Supervision of William C. Hunt* (Washington, DC: Government Printing Office, 1904), lii, cxxvii, cxxxvi, cxxxviii.
23. United States Department of Commerce and Labor, Bureau of the Census, *Occupations*, cxxvii.
24. United States Department of Commerce and Labor, Bureau of the Census, *Statistics of Women at Work*, 10.
25. Ibid.
26. Ibid.
27. United States Department of Commerce and Labor, Bureau of the Census, *Occupations*, 678, 676.
28. Ibid., 678–79.
29. United States Department of Commerce and Labor, Bureau of the Census, *Statistics of Women at Work*, 13.
30. Jabez Hughes, "Photography as an Industrial Occupation for Women," *Anthony's Photographic Bulletin* 4 (1873): 162–66, reprinted in *Camera Fiends & Kodak Girls: 50 Selections by and about Women in Photography, 1840–1930*, ed. Peter E. Palmquist (New York: Midmarch Arts Press, 1989), 29–36. Hughes, "Photography" (1989), 30.
31. Hughes, "Photography" (1989), 36.
32. Ibid., 32.
33. Hughes estimated that "about one-third of the photographic assistants are women, but there is no reason why there should not be at least one-half." Ibid., 35. In Canada, women were employed as assistants in significant numbers at the Notman Studio in Montreal, although no women were employed as photographers there. See Colleen Skidmore, "Women Workers in Notman's Studio: 'Young Ladies of the Printing Room,'" *History of Photography* 20, no. 2 (1996): 122–28.
34. Hughes, "Photography" (1989), 32.
35. Ibid., 31.
36. Frances Benjamin Johnston, "What a Woman Can Do with a Camera," *Ladies' Home Journal* (September 1897), 6.
37. Between 1883 and 1885, Frances Benjamin Johnston studied at the Académie Julian in Paris, a private studio school established in 1868, which, unlike the École des

Beaux-Arts, admitted women students. It was especially popular with North American students as an alternative to the highly structured, competitive, and male-only École des Beaux-Arts. The human figure in drawing, painting, and sculpture was the basis and focus of study. Returning home to Washington, she joined the Art Students League, established by artists in New York in 1875 and based on the nineteenth-century French atelier model of instruction, such as that of the Académie Julian. Johnston studied photography with Thomas William Smillie of the Smithsonian Institution Division of Photography, and opened her own studio in 1890. See Naomi Rosenblum, *A History of Women Photographers* (New York: Abbeville Press, 1994), 307–08.

38. Ibid.
39. The Vaux family's Quaker ancestors are counted among the pre–Civil War founding families of Philadelphia. See E. Digby Baltzell, *Philadelphia Gentlemen: The Making of a National Upper Class* (Glencoe, IL: The Free Press, 1958).
40. N.B. Fagin, *William Bartram: Interpreter of the American Landscape* (Baltimore, MD: Johns Hopkins Press, 1933), 37, quoted in Larry R. Clarke, "The Quaker Background of William Bartram's View of Nature," *Journal of the History of Ideas* 46, no. 3 (July–September 1985): 438.
41. Robert W. Rydell, "Gateway to the 'American Century': The American Representation at the Paris Universal Exposition of 1900," in *Paris 1900: The "American School" at the Universal Exposition*, ed. Diane P. Fischer (New Brunswick, NJ: Rutgers University Press, 1999), 138, 214n43. Rydell notes that "Bok's argument was reported in 'American Women at Paris in 1900,' *The Nineteen Hundred* 7, no. 1 (July 1898): 3–4.
42. "The Paris Exposition," *New York Times*, (9 June 1899), 1.
43. Bronwyn A.E. Griffith, "'Dainty and Artistic or Strong and Forceful—Just as You Wish': American Women Photographers at the Universal Exposition of 1900," in *Ambassadors of Progress: American Women Photographers in Paris 1900–1901*, ed. Bronwyn A.E. Griffith (Giverny, France: Musée d'Art Américain Giverny, 2001), 17.
44. See Alfred Stieglitz's explanation for the boycott in "Why American Pictorial Work Is Absent from the Paris Exhibition," *Amateur Photographer* 35 (20 July 1900): 44. Concluding his letter to the editor of the London-based journal, Stieglitz states with some frustration that "if European exhibitions care to have American work upon their walls, give us sufficient notice, and let us have entry blanks at least ten to twelve weeks before the closing of dates." This serves as some evidence of the severity of the constraint that Johnston suffered with just six weeks to prepare.
45. Michel Poivert, "A Taste of the Avant-Garde: The Reception of American Women Photographers in Paris (1900–1901)," in *Ambassadors of Progress: American Women Photographers in Paris 1900–1901*, ed. Bronwyn A.E. Griffith (Giverny, France: Musée d'Art Américain Giverny, 2001), 38.
46. Ellen M. Henrotin to Frances Benjamin Johnston, Chicago, 12 April 1900, reel 5, Papers of Frances Benjamin Johnston, 1855–1954 (Microfilm Reel Edition), Manuscript Division, Library of Congress.

47. Amy S. Doherty, "Frances Benjamin Johnston, 1864–1952," *History of Photography* 4, no. 2 (April 1980): 97; Verna Posever Curtis, "Frances Benjamin Johnston in 1900: Staking the Sisterhood's Claim in American Photography," in *Ambassadors of Progress: American Women Photographers in Paris 1900–1901*, ed. Bronwyn A.E. Griffith (Giverny, France: Musée d'Art Américain Giverny, 2001), 26.
48. Ellen M. Henrotin to Frances Benjamin Johnston, Chicago, 25 May 1900 and 24 April 1900, reel 5, Papers of Frances Benjamin Johnston, 1855–1954 (Microfilm Reel Edition), Manuscript Division, Library of Congress.
49. See Doherty, "Frances Benjamin Johnston, 1864–1952."
50. Judith Fryer Davidov, *Women's Camera Work: Self/Body/Other in American Visual Culture* (Durham, NC: Duke University Press, 1998), 90.
51. Alfred Stieglitz to Frances Benjamin Johnston, Lake George, NY, 8 June 1900, reel 5, Papers of Frances Benjamin Johnston, 1855–1954 (Microfilm Reel Edition), Manuscript Division, Library of Congress.
52. Alfred Stieglitz to F. Holland Day, 31 March 1899, Alfred Stieglitz Collection, Yale University, quoted in Panzer, *Philadelphia Naturalistic Photography*, 16.
53. Henry Troth to Frances Benjamin Johnston, Philadelphia, 7 June 1900, reel 5, Papers of Frances Benjamin Johnston, 1855–1954 (Microfilm Reel Edition), Manuscript Division, Library of Congress.
54. Henry Troth to Frances Benjamin Johnston, list accompanying letter, Philadelphia, 7 June 1900, reel 20, Papers of Frances Benjamin Johnston, 1855–1954 (Microfilm Reel Edition), Manuscript Division, Library of Congress. Troth's list is filed separately from his letter in the Johnston papers.
55. Frances Benjamin Johnston, master of generic letter sent to invitees, Washington, DC, n.d. [ca. 11 June 1900], reel 20, Papers of Frances Benjamin Johnston, 1855–1954 (Microfilm Reel Edition), Manuscript Division, Library of Congress.
56. Mary T.S. Schäffer to Frances Benjamin Johnston, Philadelphia, n.d. [ca. 25 June 1900], reel 20, Papers of Frances Benjamin Johnston, 1855–1954 (Microfilm Reel Edition), Manuscript Division, Library of Congress.
57. Apologizing for earlier ill humour, Schäffer wrote to Lillian Gest in ca. 1938, "I have had plenty of 'ailments' my whole life but that neuritis in my right foot with the knowledge that I HAD to go to the dentist stumped me terribly." Mary Townsend Sharples Schäffer Warren to Miss [Lillian] Gest, Banff, 23 May [ca. 1938], WMCR M67/8.
58. Williamson et al., "Charles Schäffer," 439.
59. Mary T.S. Schäffer to Frances Benjamin Johnston, Philadelphia, n.d. [ca. 25 June 1900], reel 20, Papers of Frances Benjamin Johnston, 1855–1954 (Microfilm Reel Edition), Manuscript Division, Library of Congress.
60. Frances Benjamin Johnston, master of generic letter sent to invitees, Washington, DC, n.d. [ca. 11 June 1900], reel 20, Papers of Frances Benjamin Johnston, 1855–1954 (Microfilm Reel Edition), Manuscript Division, Library of Congress. The paper that Johnston prepared for reading in Paris is not among her papers.

61. Mary T.S. Schäffer to Frances Benjamin Johnston, Philadelphia, 24 June 1900, reel 9, Papers of Frances Benjamin Johnston, 1855–1954 (Microfilm Reel Edition), Manuscript Division, Library of Congress.
62. Johnston's own work was not included in the list of exhibitors made by her mother, Mrs. Frances Antoinette Benjamin Johnston, and so it is unknown what may have been included in the exhibition. Nevertheless, her work was strongly represented in two other venues at the Paris Exposition, with 150 platinum prints of her Hampton Institute photographs of African Americans featured in the American Negro Exhibit in the Palace of Congress and Social Economy, and 350 photographs of high school student activities, representing progressive instruction in Washington public schools as part of the American contribution to an international display on education. Curtis, "Frances Benjamin Johnston," 27.
63. Mary T.S. Schäffer to Frances Benjamin Johnston, Philadelphia, n.d. [ca. 25 June 1900], reel 20, Papers of Frances Benjamin Johnston, 1855–1954 (Microfilm Reel Edition), Manuscript Division, Library of Congress.
64. Davidov, *Women's Camera Work*, 53–54.
65. Mary T.S. Schäffer to Frances Benjamin Johnston, Philadelphia, n.d. [ca. 25 June 1900], reel 20, Papers of Frances Benjamin Johnston, 1855–1954 (Microfilm Reel Edition), Manuscript Division, Library of Congress.
66. Mark V. Barrow Jr., "The Specimen Dealer: Entrepreneurial Natural History in America's Gilded Age," *Journal of the History of Biology* 33, no. 3 (Winter 2000): 493–94.
67. *Act of Incorporation and By-Laws of the Academy of Natural Sciences of Philadelphia* (Philadelphia, June 1903), 5.
68. "Schäffer, Chas. M.D.," membership card file, Academy of Natural Sciences Library and Archives, Philadelphia; *Proceedings of the Academy of Natural Sciences of Philadelphia* 55 (1903): 760.
69. "Schäffer, Mrs. Mary T.S.," membership card file, Academy of Natural Sciences Library and Archives, Philadelphia.
70. Mary T.S. Schäffer to Dr. Nolan, Philadelphia, 2 April 1896, Coll. 567, Academy of Natural Sciences Library and Archives, Philadelphia. Dr. Benjamin Sharp was the husband of photographer Virginia Guild Sharp.
71. "List of Indian implements rec'd from Mrs. Chas Schaffer," 3 March 1904, Coll. 241, Academy of Natural Sciences Library and Archives, Philadelphia.
72. Ann Bermingham, *Learning to Draw: Studies in the Cultural History of a Polite and Useful Art* (New Haven, CT: Yale University Press, 2000), 224.
73. Mary Schäffer to George Vaux Jr., Banff, 20 September 1911, WMCR Vaux 1 Series.
74. Agreement between Mary T.S. Schäffer & Stewardson Brown, Philadelphia, 12 April 1906, WMCR Vaux 1 Series.
75. Stewardson Brown and Mrs. Charles Schäffer, *Alpine Flora of the Canadian Rocky Mountains* (New York and London: G.P. Putnam's Sons/Knickerbocker Press, 1907).

76. Roger L. Williams, *"A Region of Astonishing Beauty": The Botanical Exploration of the Rocky Mountains* (Lanham, MD: Roberts Rinehart Publishers, 2003), ix.
77. Sharon E. Kingsland, *The Evolution of American Ecology, 1890–2000* (Baltimore, MD: Johns Hopkins University Press, 2005), 19.
78. Kingsland raises the question of North American botanists' relationships with Indigenous people and their knowledge of native plants. Brown and Schäffer do not make any reference to Indigenous knowledge. See Kingsland, *The Evolution of American Ecology*, 46.
79. John M. Coulter, *Manual of the Botany of the Rocky Mountain Region* (New York: American Book Company, 1885); John M. Coulter, *New Manual of Botany of the Central Rocky Mountains (Vascular Plants)* (New York: American Book Company, 1909), 3.
80. Stewardson Brown, "Botanizing in the Canadian Rockies," *Proceedings of the Academy of Natural Sciences of Philadelphia* 58, no. 3 (October–December 1906): 429–30.
81. See Kingsland, *The Evolution of American Ecology*, 19, 69–70 for a discussion of the impetus towards a reformed, systematized, and contextualized botany.
82. For more about aspects of the history of botanical painting and drawing, see William Wheeler, *Botanical Illustration* (Paris: L'Aventurine, 2003) and Martyn Rix, *The Golden Age of Botanical Art* (Chicago: University of Chicago Press, 2012). For a brief overview of the emerging role of photography in botanical illustration in the nineteenth century, see Brendan Cull, "The Art and Science of Early Canadian Photography: *Sites et végétaux du Canada* at the 1867 Exposition Universelle in Paris" (master's thesis, Queen's University, 2015).
83. Mary T.S. Schaffer, "Haunts of the Wild Flowers of the Canadian Rockies (Within reach of the Canadian Pacific Railroad)," *Canadian Alpine Journal* 3 (1911): 131–32.
84. Julia W. Henshaw, *Mountain Wild Flowers of Canada: A Simple and Popular Guide to the Names and Descriptions of the Flowers That Bloom Above the Clouds* (Toronto: William Briggs, 1906); Julia W. Henshaw, *Mountain Wild Flowers of America: A Simple and Popular Guide to the Names and Descriptions of the Flowers That Bloom Above the Clouds* (Boston: Ginn & Company, The Athenæum Press, 1906). A decade later, Henshaw published *Wild Flowers of the North American Mountains* (New York: Robert M. McBride & Company, 1915), a slightly revised edition of the earlier publications. Julia Wilmotte Henderson (1869–1937) was born in Durham, England, and emigrated to Canada in 1887 following marriage to Charles Henshaw, originally of Montreal. She wrote for the *Vancouver Province* for a few years under the name of Julian Durham but spent most of her career as an independent writer of articles and books.
85. Henshaw, *Mountain Wild Flowers of Canada*, ix.
86. Ibid., xii.
87. Mary W. [Schäffer Warren] to Humphrey Toms, Banff, 26 November [ca. 1937], WMCR M429/1.
88. Henshaw, *Mountain Wild Flowers of Canada*, xii.
89. Ibid., xiii.

90. Brown and Schäffer, *Alpine Flora*, viii.

91. Paul W. Riegert, "Fletcher, James," in *Dictionary of Canadian Biography Online 1901–1910*, vol. 13 (University of Toronto/Université Laval, 2003–), www.biographi.ca/en/bio/fletcher_james_13E.html; R.M. Anderson, "John Macoun, 1832–1920," *Journal of Mammalogy* 2, no. 1 (February 1921): 32–35; W.A. Waiser, "Macoun, John," in *Dictionary of Canadian Biography Online 1911–1920*, vol. 14 (University of Toronto/Université Laval, 2003–), www.biographi.ca/en/bio/macoun_john_14E.html.

92. Henshaw, *Mountain Wild Flowers of Canada*, xiii.

93. Julia W. Henshaw, "The Mountain Wildflowers of Western Canada," *Canadian Alpine Journal* 1, no. 1 (1907): 130–37. "Editorial Note," *Canadian Alpine Journal* 1, no. 1 (1907): 137. The editor also notes that this article was originally published in the *Montreal Standard* and republished "with amplifications, for the information of our members."

94. Colour photography was not yet a viable process, and so hand-tinting glass slides was the alternative that Schäffer employed. In 1904, the Lumière brothers in France introduced a colour-positive glass slide process called the autochrome. Autochrome photographs were first made in western Canada in 1914 in Edmonton. See Colleen Skidmore, "Imaging the West: Hugo Viewegar and the Autochrome in Canada," *History of Photography* 27 (Winter 2003): 342–48, and "'Touring An Other's Reality': Aboriginals, Immigrants, and Autochromes," *Ethnologies* 26, no. 1 (2004): 145–64.

95. Oliver Wendell Holmes, "The Stereoscope and the Stereograph," *Atlantic Monthly* 3, no. 20 (June 1859): 744, excerpted in Alan Trachtenberg, ed., *Classic Essays on Photography* (New Haven, CT: Leete's Island Books, 1980), 77.

96. Brown and Schäffer, *Alpine Flora*, 156.

97. Mary T.S. Schäffer to Frances Benjamin Johnston, Philadelphia, n.d. [ca. 25 June 1900], reel 20, Papers of Frances Benjamin Johnston, 1855–1954 (Microfilm Reel Edition), Manuscript Division, Library of Congress.

98. Panzer, *Philadelphia Naturalistic Photography*, 15.

99. Mary T.S. Schäffer to Frances Benjamin Johnston, Philadelphia, 24 June 1900, reel 9, Papers of Frances Benjamin Johnston, 1855–1954 (Microfilm Reel Edition), Manuscript Division, Library of Congress.

100. Ibid.

101. This photograph was mistitled "Mount Sir Ronald" in the collection of the National Museum of American History. An examination of Schäffer's inscription on the back of the 8 x 10 inch mount confirms the correct name for this landmark mountain near Roger's Pass, BC. It was named for Sir Donald Smith, who famously drove in the ceremonial last spike of the Canadian Pacific Railway in 1885.

102. Catharine Weed Barnes, "Photography from a Woman's Standpoint," *Anthony's Photographic Bulletin* 21, no. 2 (25 January 1890): 33–42, reprinted in *Camera Fiends & Kodak Girls: 50 Selections by and about Women in Photography, 1840–1930*, ed. Peter E. Palmquist New York: Midmarch Arts Press, 1989), 63–67. See p. 63.

103. Katherine Milliken, "Quakers in Nature: The Vaux Family's Photographs of Mountains and Glaciers" (master's thesis, University of Alberta, 2005).
104. See Edward Cavell, *Legacy in Ice: The Vaux Family and the Canadian Alps* (Banff, AB: Whyte Foundation, 1983), 14–15.
105. Milliken, "Quakers in Nature," 17.
106. William S. Vaux Jr., "Climbing in the Selkirk Mountains," *Minneapolis Journal* (24 December 1898), WMCR M107, quoted in Milliken, "Quakers in Nature," 34.
107. Cavell, *Legacy in Ice*, 10. The mineral known as vauxite was found by Americans in Bolivia in 1921. It was named after George Vaux Jr., who helped to sponsor the expedition undertaken through the Academy of Natural Sciences in Philadelphia during which the new specimen was found. Vaux was a member of the Academy.
108. The Vaux family photographs and papers are held in the Archives and Library of the Whyte Museum of the Canadian Rockies.
109. "Annual Members' Exhibition: A Review by Mr. Herbert A. North, Read at the Stated Meeting, December 14, 1898," *Journal of the Photographic Society of Philadelphia* 5, no. 1 (January 1899): 7.
110. "Members' Annual Exhibition: A Criticism by C. Yarnall Abbott, Read at the Stated Meeting January 9, 1901," *Journal of the Photographic Society of Philadelphia* 7, no. 1 (December 1900–January 1901): 12.
111. Cavell, *Legacy in Ice*, 18.
112. See W.I. Sreznewsky, "The Collection of Photographs Taken by American Women Amateur Photographers," trans. Harold M. Leich, *Fotograficheskoe obozrienie* (1901), 1–5, reprinted in *Ambassadors of Progress: American Women Photographers in Paris 1900–1901*, ed. Bronwyn A.E. Griffith (Giverny, France: Musée d'Art Américain Giverny, 2001), 190–91; "Progress in Photography. Collection of Specimens for the Paris Exposition. All the Work of American Women—A Proposed Exhibit in This City," *Evening Star* (Washington, DC), 6 July 1900, 1, 11. Also see Poivert, "A Taste of the Avant-Garde."
113. Mary T.S. Schäffer to Frances Benjamin Johnston, Philadelphia, 24 June 1900, reel 9, Papers of Frances Benjamin Johnston, 1855–1954 (Microfilm Reel Edition), Manuscript Division, Library of Congress.
114. Arthur O. Wheeler, "The Congress of Alpinism at Monaco," *Canadian Alpine Journal* 11 (1920): 65–68.
115. Mary Schäffer to George Vaux Jr., Banff, 21 May 1912, WMCR Vaux 1 Series.

3 The Rocky Mountains of Canada, 1904–1906

1. Mary Schäffer to George Vaux Jr., [Schäffer's location unknown], 16 May [1904], WMCR Vaux Collection Addition 2007. Schäffer is referring to Mary Morris Vaux (1860–1940), George Vaux Jr.'s sister. In 1907, George Vaux Jr. married Mary Walsh James. Middle initials are essential to distinguish the two women after 1907.

2. Mary [Schäffer] Warren to "My dear unseen friend," Banff, 12 November [ca. 1935], WMCR M8.
3. Mary Schäffer, "Lake Louise of Early Days," n.d., unpublished manuscript, WMCR M79/7. Many secondary sources state that Schäffer first travelled to the Rockies in 1888, apparently derived from the obituary for Schäffer published in the Banff *Crag and Canyon* on 27 January 1939. In 1888, however, Schäffer had travelled across the United States and then north by ship to Juneau, Alaska. See letter from Chas. Schäffer to Mr. Stone, 19 June 1900, Coll. 450, Academy of Natural Sciences Library and Archives, Philadelphia. From 1886, the CPR offered artists, photographers, and writers free passes to travel to the Rockies to paint and photograph the scenery. The goal was to entice tourists to travel on the railway to see the magnificent scenery depicted. Schäffer's response suggests the success of the venture. See E.J. Hart, *The Selling of Canada: The CPR and the Beginnings of Canadian Tourism* (Banff, AB: Altitude Publishing, 1983).
4. Stewardson Brown and Mrs. Charles Schäffer, *Alpine Flora of the Canadian Rocky Mountains* (New York and London: G.P. Putnam's Sons/Knickerbocker Press, 1907). *Alpine Flora* was not Schäffer's first published work. In 1904, between January and August, three articles by Schäffer appeared in the outdoor sport magazine *Rod and Gun in Canada*. See Mary S.S. Schaffer, "Sir James Hector," *Rod and Gun in Canada* 5, no. 8 (January 1904), 416–18; Mary S.S. Schaffer, "The Burial of Cher-on-kee," *Rod and Gun in Canada* 5, no.11 (April 1904), 530–32; and Mary M. Schaffer, "Breaking the Way," *Rod and Gun in Canada* 6, no. 3 (August 1904), 111–12. The latter is an account of Gertrude Benham's climbs of Mounts LeFroy and Victoria earlier that summer. In 1905, fifteen of Schäffer's photographs, ranging from alpine flora to fish and wildlife, as well as eminent Rocky Mountains visitors, were published in A.O. Wheeler, *The Selkirk Range*, vol. 1 (Ottawa: Government Printing Bureau, 1905). These photographs demonstrate the photographic range and skill Schäffer had already achieved in her work. The botany manual marked a significant focusing of subject matter, however. Schäffer's articles from 1907 onwards were about the flora, fauna, and geography of the region, and were based on her own experiences and first-hand knowledge.
5. Mary [Schäffer] Warren to Miss [Minnie] Nickell, Banff, 13 December [ca. 1937], WMCR M8.
6. E.J. Hart, "Yahe-Weha—Mountain Woman: The Life and Travels of Mary Schäffer Warren, 1861–1939," in *A Hunter of Peace: Mary T.S. Schäffer's Old Indian Trails of the Canadian Rockies*, intro. and ed. E.J. Hart (Banff, AB: Whyte Museum of the Canadian Rockies, 1980), 1–14; E.J. Hart, "Yahe-Weha—Mountain Woman: The Life and Travels of Mary Schäffer Warren, 1861–1939," in *A Hunter of Peace: Mary T.S. Schäffer's Old Indian Trails of the Canadian Rockies*, 2nd ed., intro. E.J. Hart, foreword Jennifer Rutkair (Banff, AB: Whyte Museum of the Canadian Rockies, 2014), 11–26.
7. Mary T.S. Schäffer, *Old Indian Trails: Incidents of Camp and Trail Life, Covering Two Years' Exploration through the Rocky Mountains of Canada* (New York: G.P. Putnam's Sons; Toronto: William Briggs, 1911; reprint with revised map, 1912), v–vi.

8. Julie Rak, *Boom! Manufacturing Memoir for the Popular Market* (Waterloo, ON: Wilfrid Laurier University Press, 2013), 8.
9. Mary [Schäffer] Warren to Humphrey Toms, Banff, 25 May [1935], WMCR M429/1.
10. "Last Will and Testament of Elizabeth Sharpless," WMCR Vaux Collection Addition 2007.
11. Mary [Schäffer] Warren to Humphrey Toms, Banff, 25 May [1935], WMCR M429/1.
12. Paul Whitfield, "Follow-Through Day of 1903 Was Much Like Any Other," *Investor's Business Daily*, 27 June 2014, http://education.investors.com/investors-corner/706592-how-to-identify-the-start-of-an-uptrend.htm.
13. Mary Schäffer [Warren] to Mr. George Vaux Jr., "Business" letter, Banff, 14 May 1916, WMCR Vaux Collection Addition 2007. Based on a consumer price index comparative calculation of purchasing power, the $1 million in 1898 would be the equivalent of about $29.5 million in 2015. See Samuel H. Williamson, "Seven Ways to Compute the Relative Value of a U.S. Dollar Amount, 1774 to Present," *MeasuringWorth*, 2015, www.measuringworth.com/uscompare/. Thank you to André Plourde for his generous advice on comparative methodology and resources.
14. Mary Schäffer [Warren] to George Vaux Jr., "Personal" letter, Banff, 14 May 1916, WMCR Vaux Collection Addition 2007.
15. Charles Schäffer married Martha T. Potts (1835–1878) in 1862 and Ellen E. Zook (1841–1884) in 1882. Zook was a practicing physician who retired upon marriage. She earned a medical degree from the Women's Medical College of Philadelphia in 1872. Leland M. Williamson, Richard A. Foley, Henry H. Colclazer, Louis N. Megargee, Jay H. Mowbray, and Will. R. Antisdel, eds., "Charles Schäffer," in *Prominent and Progressive Pennsylvanians of the Nineteenth Century*, vol. 2 (Philadelphia: The Record Publishing Company, 1898), 439–41.
16. "Last Will & Testament of Charles Schäffer/Died November 23, 1903/Will moved Decr 2, 1903," WMCR Vaux Collection Addition 2007.
17. Ibid. In 2015, the value of Schäffer's inherited assets, based on a consumer price index comparative calculation of purchasing power, would have been about $2.6 million, including an equivalence of about $294,000 cash, $1.1 million in investments, and the house valued at about $1.2 million. See Williamson, "Seven Ways."
18. Charles Schäffer was born in 1838 to Charles and Priscilla Morgan Schäffer (née Potts) at 485 Arch Street; at age 6 in 1844, the family moved to 1309 Arch Street. On 1 June 1867, Charles Schäffer acquired the house from his mother who continued to live there with her son, his wife Martha T. Potts and her mother Serena Potts, and two servants. This location on Arch Street is now encompassed by the grounds of the Pennsylvania Convention Centre. See Williamson et al., "Charles Schäffer," 439; Philadelphia City Archives, Deeds: Folder: Book 1N, p. 21, Lots 61–90; and the 1870 United States Federal Census, Philadelphia Ward 10, District 29. Decades later, Mary Schäffer passed along a different family memory: "My first husband's people lived at 13th and Arch before 1800. I think my aunt said they were 'out of the city' when the house was built." Mary

Townsend Sharples Schaffer Warren to Miss Gest, Banff, 23 May [ca. 1938], WMCR M67/8.

19. Charles and Mary Schäffer had donated specimens and artifacts from travels in the past. In 1900, for instance, they donated a lynx skin, "one that Mrs. Schäffer bought at Juneau, Alaska in 1888." Chas. Schäffer to Mr. Stone, 19 June 1900, Coll. 450, Academy of Natural Sciences Library and Archives, Philadelphia.
20. "Report of the Botanical Section," *Proceedings of the Academy of Natural Sciences of Philadelphia* 56, no. 3 (September–December 1904): 851; "Additions to the Museum, Plants," *Proceedings of the Academy of Natural Sciences of Philadelphia* 56, no. 3 (September–December 1904): 864.
21. "Report of Librarian," *Proceedings of the Academy of Natural Sciences of Philadelphia* 56, no. 3 (September–December 1904): 844.
22. The handwritten "List of Indian implements etc rec'd from Mrs. Chas Schaffer" dated 3 March 1904 included: "1 pair snowshoes, 1 carved dish, 1 chilcat blanket, 1 bag gambling sticks (?), 1 flask shaped Mexican basket, 17 indian baskets (various sizes), 1 birch bark basket with lid, 7 mats, 1 pair leggings, 1 pair grass stockings, 1 pair sandals, 1 sack (made of grass), 1 skin bag, wooden fork & spoon, 2 pieces carved wood, 6 carved pieces (charms? etc), 1 beaded pocket book, 9 horn spoons, 1 whetstone, 1 beaded pouch, 1 beaded buffalo-horn 'axe', 1 stone hammer, 1 pipe, 1 string of beads, 1 buffalo horn, 3 small objects (paper knife etc), 1 skin knife sheath (?), 1 silver band." (Coll. 241, Academy of Natural Sciences Library and Archives, Philadelphia.)
23. "Additions to the Museum," *Proceedings of the Academy of Natural Sciences of Philadelphia*, 56, no. 3 (September–December 1904): 856–64. On 2 November 1906, Schäffer deposited with the Academy a set of 8 x 10 inch black-and-white geological photographs she had made in the Rocky Mountains. See Coll. 485, Academy of Natural Sciences Library and Archives, Philadelphia. In 1930, the Academy of Natural Sciences withdrew from archeology to focus on natural sciences and sold parts of its collection, including the Schäffer objects. Some were dispersed to the University of Pennsylvania, while most went to the George G. Heye Foundation's Museum of the American Indian in New York City, which was transferred in 1989 to the Smithsonian Institution as the foundation for the National Museum of the American Indian.
24. George Vaux Jr. to United States Internal Revenue, Philadelphia, 1924, WMCR Vaux Collection Addition 2007. The 1924 annual $1,800 payment from the Academy would be worth about $25,000 in 2015 based on a consumer price index comparative calculation of purchasing power (see Williamson, "Seven Ways"). Approximately $63,000 was paid out over the thirty-five years until Schäffer's death in January 1939. The Academy of Natural Sciences of Philadelphia sold the house in 1920. Philadelphia City Archives, Deeds: Folder: Book 1N, p. 21, Lots 61–90.
25. "Continues the Work," *Crag and Canyon* (Banff, AB), 4 June 1904, 5. Miss James is believed to be Mary Walsh James of Concord, Massachusetts, who was a niece of author Henry James and psychologist and philosopher William James. Mary James married

Schäffer's friend and attorney, George Vaux Jr., in 1907. They first met in Lake Louise in 1904. Henry Vaux Jr., personal correspondence (email) 25 October 2015.

26. "Mrs. Schaffer and Miss James...," *Crag and Canyon* (Banff, AB), 22 April 1905, 4. For a partial account of 1905 activities, see Sister [Mary Schäffer], "The Flora of Canada: Mrs. Charles Schaffer, Formerly Miss Mary T. Sharpless, Writes of Her Work upon a Book Devoted to Scientific Research," *Daily Local News* (West Chester, PA), 15 November 1905, clipping file "Schaeffer, M," Chester County Archives, West Chester, PA, and clipping, WMCR M79/9B.
27. "Mrs. Schaffer and Miss Farr...," *Crag and Canyon* (Banff, AB), 10 June 1905, 7. Edith M. Farr (1864–1956) published *Contributions to a Catalogue of the Flora of the Canadian Rocky Mountains and Selkirk Range* (Philadelphia: University of Pennsylvania) in 1907.
28. Mary Schäffer to George Vaux Jr., Banff, 20 September 1911, WMCR Vaux 1 Series.
29. Stephen R. Bown and Nicky L. Brink describe Schäffer as "a pampered and charming socialite" in "Mountain Woman," *The Beaver* 87, no. 3 (June–July 2007), 42–46; E.J. Hart calls her "wealthy" in "Yahe-Weha" (1980), 5, and "Yahe-Weha" (2014), 16; in his introduction to *Culturing Wilderness in Jasper National Park*, I.S. MacLaren writes, she is "well-heeled and -schooled, she sounds like a snob" (xxx). Lisa MacFarlane's Schäffer is "white and wealthy, a 'lady' with a degree of mobility and opportunity denied to people of color" in "Schäffer's 'Comprehending Equal Eyes,'' in *Trading Gazes: Euro-American Women Photographers and Native North Americans, 1880–1940*, by Susan Bernardin, Melody Graulich, Lisa MacFarlane, and Nicole Tonkovich (New Brunswick, NJ: Rutgers University Press, 2003), 112.
30. "Romance in the Heart of Rockies: Prospectors Bring Story of Riches on G.T.P. Route and Romantic Tale of Society Dames," *Vancouver Daily World*, 3 October 1908, 1, clipping, WMCR M79/9B.
31. Eric C. Sharpless to E.J. Hart, Wayne, PA, 30 March 1985, WMCR Schäffer Biography File.
32. "Son of West Chester Wins High Honors," *Daily Local News* (West Chester, PA), July 1921, clipping file "Sharpless, F.," Chester County Archives, West Chester, PA.
33. Mary Schäffer [Warren] to George Vaux Jr., Banff, 14 April 1917, WMCR Vaux 1 Series.
34. "Income Tax, United States Internal Revenue" [1914], WMCR Vaux Collection Addition 2007. Based on a consumer price index comparative calculation of purchasing power, Schäffer's US income would be the equivalent of $216,000 in 2015. See Williamson, "Seven Ways."
35. Based on a consumer price index comparative calculation of purchasing power, Schäffer's Canadian income would be the equivalent of $57,302.56 in 2015. See Bank of Canada Inflation Calculator, www.bankofcanada.ca/rates/related/inflation-calculator/.
36. Mary Schäffer to George Vaux Jr., Banff, 27 May 1911, WMCR Vaux Collection Addition 2007.
37. See Mary Schäffer–George Vaux Jr. correspondence in WMCR Vaux 1 Series and Vaux Collection Addition 2007.

38. Mary Schäffer to George Vaux Jr., letter and Putnam's Sons' bill, Banff, received by Vaux 9 May 1911, WMCR Vaux Collection Addition 2007. The $1,500 investment would be about $38,600 in 2015 based on a consumer price index comparative calculation of purchasing power. See Williamson, "Seven Ways."
39. "Cost of Bungalow to Date April 18," handwritten account, WMCR Vaux Collection Addition 2007. Based on a consumer price index comparative calculation of purchasing power and using the earliest date available for calculation (1914), Schäffer's original price would be the equivalent of about $49,000 in 2015 and her later cost about $111,000. See Bank of Canada Inflation Calculator, www.bankofcanada.ca/rates/related/inflation-calculator/.
40. "Mary S. Warren Will and Probate," acc. 99.834, Calgary Probate Records Q–Z, box 311, file 11210, Provincial Archives of Alberta. Schäffer's estate was the equivalent of approximately $65,542 in 2015. See Bank of Canada Inflation Calculator, www.bankofcanada.ca/rates/related/inflation-calculator/. The probate record also shows that Schäffer's brother Herman Sharpless, whom she had supported in part and whose trust she had managed (see Mary Schäffer to George Vaux Jr., Banff, 23 May 1917, WMCR Vaux Collection Addition 2007), undertook a search of her will and probate six months after her death.
41. "William Warren Probate," acc. 99.834, Calgary Probate Records Q–Z, box 376, file 14269, Provincial Archives of Alberta. Based on a consumer price index comparative calculation of purchasing power, Warren's estate was the equivalent of about $2.3 million in 2015. See Bank of Canada Inflation Calculator, www.bankofcanada.ca/rates/related/inflation-calculator/. Warren bequeathed the residue of his estate, after gifts to friends totalling $65,200 ($901,460 in 2015), to his sister Rose Warren in London, England.
42. Lease documentation, Lot 23, Block 27 [Tarry-a-while], Banff, AB, WMCR M317.
43. United States Department of Commerce and Labor, Bureau of the Census, *Statistics of Women at Work: Based on Unpublished Information Derived from the Schedules of the Twelfth Census: 1900* (Washington, DC: Government Printing Office, 1907).
44. Mary M. Schaffer, "Breaking the Way," *Rod and Gun in Canada* 6, no. 3 (August 1904): 111–12. On 27 June 1904, Mary Schäffer wrote to George Vaux Jr. from Lake Louise, commenting that "Miss Benham ascended LeFroy to-day with the Kauffmanns [*sic*]. Bad day—snowed up there the entire day." WMCR Vaux Collection Addition, 2007.
45. Raymond John Howgego, "Benham, Gertrude Emily (1867–1938)," *Oxford Dictionary of National Biography*, online ed., October 2008.
46. Photographs from the Vauxes' 1904 excursion reside in the Whyte Museum of the Canadian Rockies. WMCR V653/NA-1235 to 1335.
47. Mary W. (Molly) Adams, transcribed diary, [Camp near Lake Louise], 3 August 1904 and 12 August 1904, Adams Family Collection. During the late 1930s and early 1940s, Molly Adams's sister, Catherine Adams Elkin, transcribed and integrated into the typescript her diaries and letters from July 1891 to January 1909. The original

letters and diaries and the transcriptions have been preserved by the family and were generously loaned for research. In 2017, the Adams family donated their collection to the Archives and Library of the Whyte Museum of the Canadian Rockies.

48. Elizabeth A. Wood, "Memorial to Ida Helen Ogilvie (1874–1963)," *Geological Society of America Bulletin* 75, no. 2 (February 1964): 35–39. See I.H. Ogilvie, "Geological Notes on the Vicinity of Banff, Alberta," *Journal of Geology* 12, no. 5 (July–August 1904): 408–14; and I.H. Ogilvie, "The Effect of Superglacial Débris on the Advance and Retreat of Some Canadian Glaciers," *Journal of Geology* 12, no. 8 (November–December 1904): 722–43. In Banff, on 26 July 1904, Adams noted in her diary, "Ida went to the museum to read and then wrote a geological article. In P.M. went down to falls and took photographs to illustrate article." On 22 October 1904, from Berkeley, California, Adams wrote to her sister, "Ida has been reading in the University library for two days to see if any one else has already written articles saying the same things she did in hers. Her Banff article is published already. They sent her the proof to correct but it never reached her so they printed it without her seeing it." Adams Family Collection.

49. Adams mentions Käthchen Ireland Cook from her earliest extant correspondence in 1891 letters to her mother and sister while travelling in Europe. Cook was born in Berlin (then the capital of Prussia) in 1869 and named Catherine. It appears that she used the German version of her name. Adams also appears to have been at least conversant in German as she regularly used German words and expressions in her correspondence. (She also had at least a rudimentary ability in Italian, studied Spanish in early 1905 while in New Mexico in preparation for travelling on to Mexico, and acquired some rudimentary understanding of Japanese in late 1908.) Adams first mentions Ogilvie in a letter to her sister, Catherine, of July 1901 from the Adirondacks, calling her "the geologist" and "Miss Ogilvie." Ogilvie was pursuing fieldwork, accompanied by Cook, and thereafter the two are always mentioned as a pair by Adams. For example, from Mary W. (Molly) Adams's diary New York, 5 July [1904]: "Met I.H.O. and K.I.C. at Abercrombie's and bought camp duffle." During the 1904 journey, Adams wrote often of what the pair was doing together while she did something else. See Mary W. (Molly) Adams, transcribed diary, Penticton to Sicamous, 8 October [1904], Adams Family Collection. Obituaries and other biographical entries on Ogilvie are silent on her personal life.

50. Adams visited the Adirondacks regularly in the 1890s and early 1900s, as well as Dorset, Vermont (where her friend Zephine Humphrey lived), Chocorua, New Hampshire, and Pompton, New Jersey. In a letter to her sister of 5 July 1901 from the town of Paradox in the Adirondacks Adams writes, "We don't allow the geologist to go off alone on her wild tears, for fear of sprained ankle or such and it has fallen to my lot to go with her for several days now." Käthchen Cook was there as well. Adams Family Collection.

51. Mary W. (Molly) Adams, transcribed diary, train on prairies, [22 July 1904], 7 P.M., and Banff, 23 July 1904, Adams Family Collection.

52. Mary W. (Molly) Adams, transcribed diary, Camp near Lake Louise, 3 August [1904], Adams Family Collection.
53. Molly Adams to Catherine Elkin, Banff, 25 July 1904, Adams Family Collection.
54. Molly Adams to Catherine Elkin, Glacier, BC, 28 September 1904, Adams Family Collection.
55. Mary W. (Molly) Adams, transcribed diary, Camp Lake Louise, 14 August 1904 and Yoho, 28 August 1904, Adams Family Collection.
56. Ibid., Glacier, BC, 22 September 1904.
57. Ibid., Glacier, BC, 2 October 1904.
58. Letters and diaries of Mary W. (Molly) Adams, 1893–1909, transcribed, Adams Family Collection.
59. Molly Adams to Catherine Elkin, North Bend, BC, 9 October [1904], Adams Family Collection.
60. Molly Adams to "Jean," Dolores, NM, 23 February 1905, Adams Family Collection.
61. Molly Adams to Catherine Elkin, North Bend, BC, 9 October [1904], Adams Family Collection.
62. Molly Adams to Catherine Elkin, Dolores, NM, 13 March [1905], Adams Family Collection.
63. Molly Adams to Catherine Elkin, Portland, OR, 14 October 1904, and thereafter in letters during travels continuing until April 1905 through the southwest United States and Mexico.
64. Letters and diaries of Mary W. (Molly) Adams, 1893–1909, transcribed, Adams Family Collection.
65. On 11 August 1901, from Crane Pond in the Adirondacks, Adams wrote to her sister, "One more commission for you. Anne Clinton wants to borrow some of my Adirondack photos for illustrating some story and I have written her that I would ask you to send them to her.... You will find the film album in the darkroom on the shelf, I think, or else in the book case outside the door..." Adams Family Collection.
66. Just days before leaving New Mexico for Mexico, Adams wrote to her sister, "I am sending you a registered package of films. Will you please have them developed at Mr. Malone's place, and keep them for me. I'll let you look at them and print them if it amuses you. They are from California on. Two of them by the way should have been developed by March 1st." The Rockies photos are placed last in the album, even though the Rockies were the first stop. Molly Adams to Catherine Elkin, Dolores, NM, 13 March [1905], Adams Family Collection. This 1904 album is in the Adams Family Collection.
67. M.W.A. and M.T.S.S., Photograph album, "From Laggan to the Wilcox Pass 1906," WMCR V527/PD-4.
68. Zephine Humphrey, with photographs by Mary W. Adams, "Five Women on the Trail," *Outing Magazine* 54 (April–September 1909), 195–205, 341–51, 426–33.

69. There are no letters or diaries about activities while home in the West Chester, New Haven, and New York areas, and therefore no documentation of time that Schäffer and Adams may have spent together during winters.
70. M.S.W, "Tepee Life in Northern Hills" (unpublished manuscript, [1924]), 23, WMCR M79/6, published posthumously in Janice Sanford Beck, *No Ordinary Woman: The Story of Mary Schäffer Warren* (Calgary, AB: Rocky Mountain Books, 2001), 170–91.
71. Molly Adams to Catherine Elkin, Berkeley, CA, 23 October 1904, Adams Family Collection.
72. Mary W. [Schäffer Warren] to Humphrey Toms, Banff, 26 November [ca. 1937], WMCR M429/1.
73. Women, like men (although this was rarely acknowledged), relied on the expertise of climbing guides to achieve their successes. In 1899, the CPR began to employ Swiss guides at its mountain hotels to attract more tourists, and these guides were responsible for leading clients on both new and established climbs. Popular histories, such as R.W. Sanford's *High Ideals: Canadian Pacific's Swiss Guides, 1899–1999* (Canmore, AB: Alpine Club of Canada, 1999) and Chic Scott's *Pushing the Limits: The Story of Canadian Mountaineering* (Calgary, AB: Rocky Mountain Books, 2000) as well as biographies of some mountaineering guides have been written, but studies of the roles and impact of guides and guiding, and matters of class, race, ethnicity, and gender in guiding at the turn of the twentieth century and later in the Rocky Mountains are only now emerging. For an introduction to women mountaineers in the Canadian Rockies, see *This Wild Spirit: Women in the Rocky Mountains of Canada*, ed. Colleen Skidmore (Edmonton: University of Alberta Press, 2006), 349–410. A foundational study of twentieth-century mountaineering that maps the social complexities of mountain culture is PearlAnn Reichwein, *Climber's Paradise: Making Canada's Mountain Parks, 1906–1974* (Edmonton: University of Alberta Press, 2014).
74. "First Ladies to Visit Cave," *The Revelstoke Herald and Railway Men's Journal* (10 August 1905), 1, clipping, WMCR M79/9B. See also Schäffer's retrospective commentary in Mary [Schäffer] Warren to Mr. [Raymond] Zillmer, Banff, 12 April [1928], WMCR M8.
75. Schäffer, *Old Indian Trails* (1911), 13.
76. Molly Adams to Catherine Elkin, Berkeley, CA, 23 October 1904, Adams Family Collection.
77. Phoebe Kropp, "Wilderness Wives and Dishwashing Husbands: Comfort and the Domestic Art of Camping in America, 1880–1910," *Journal of Social History* 43, no. 1 (2009): 8.
78. Ibid., 25.
79. [Mary Schäffer], "Lake Louise of Early Days" (unpublished manuscript, n.d.), WMCR M79/7. After the CPR opened hotels along its line at Glacier, Field, and Banff between 1886 and 1888, outfitters and guides became essential to tourists and the tourist economy in Banff. While some popular histories tell tales of some of the characters of the time, need remains for a critical in-depth history of outfitters, trail guides, camping,

and tourists in the Rockies and Selkirks that includes the roles of Indigenous women and men and Euro-North American women, as well as the mainly Canadian and British men who established outfitting and guiding after 1886.

80. Molly Adams to Catherine Elkin, Banff, 25 July 1904, Adams Family Collection.

81. Kropp, "Wilderness Wives," 21.

82. Rudyard Kipling, "Letters to the Family," *Collier's* 41, no. 5 (25 April 1908): 13–14, reprinted in Rudyard Kipling, *Letters of Travel (1892–1913)* (London: Macmillan & Co., 1920), 188–89.

83. Mary Schäffer kept a clipping of the relevant part of the letter, labelled "Kipling in Collier—Spring 1908" in a scrapbook along with copies of reviews of *Old Indian Trails*. WMCR M79/9B.

84. Schäffer, *Old Indian Trails* (1911), 199–200.

85. M.W.A. and M.T.S.S., Photograph album, "From Laggan to the Wilcox Pass 1906," WMCR V527/PD-4.

86. Molly Adams to Catherine Elkin, Banff, 24 August 1906, Adams Family Collection.

87. Molly Adams to Cousin Alice, Field, BC, 26 August 1906, Adams Family Collection.

88. Mary W. (Molly) Adams, 1908 transcribed diary, Mrs. N's Camp, 28 June, WMCR M79/11. "Mr. B." was botanist Stewardson Brown.

89. Molly Adams to Catherine Elkin, Banff Springs Hotel, 25 July 1904; Mary W. (Molly) Adams, transcribed diary, Camp above Lake Louise, 30 July 1904; Molly Adams to "Dear Children," Mount Stephen House, Field, BC, 9 September 1904, Adams Family Collection.

90. Molly Adams to "Helène," Mount Stephen House, Field, BC, 24 September 1908, Adams Family Collection.

91. M.S.W. "Tepee Life in Northern Hills" (unpublished manuscript, [1924]), WMCR M79/6. "Tepee Life" is a lengthy and disjointed compilation of memories and experiences written in reaction to a series of articles in the *Saturday Evening Post* by a "dude wrangler." Schäffer may have recognized its weaknesses when she wrote in the manuscript, "This sounds a very rambling sort of article to offer to the Public."

92. Zephine Humphrey, with photographs by Mary W. Adams, "Five Women on the Trail," *Outing Magazine* 54 (April–September 1909), 195–205, 341–51, 426–33. Humphrey's account may have benefitted from a diary that Adams kept especially for Humphrey on the second pack trip to the area that Adams and Schäffer took late that same summer: "There is no use going into detail as I have kept a most virtuous diary which you may read later if it does not bore you with details. Zephine implored me to write one for her to read so I have put in things which will seem queer to you, but she knowing more of the people will be interested in." Molly Adams to Catherine Elkin, Kootenay Plains, AB, 11 September 1906. The diary does not survive among the Humphrey, Adams, or Schäffer papers.

93. Molly Adams to Catherine Elkin, Lake Louise, BC, 11 August 1906, Adams Family Collection. On 17 August 1906 from Mount Stephen House at Field, BC, Adams wrote

that "we [Mary Schäffer and Adams] have been doing nothing but develop and print since I got here" five days earlier. And on "Sunday, 19th. Still in the photo business. I rigged up an enlarging apparatus with Mrs. Schäffer's 4 x 5 camera and many blankets and some of my pictures are going to be dandy." Molly Adams to Catherine Elkin, Field, BC, 17 August and 19 August 1906, Adams Family Collection.

94. Henrietta L. Tuzo, "A Glimpse of the Saskatchewan," draft manuscripts, [1906], John Tuzo Wilson Personal Papers, accn. B86-0066, box 59, file "Alpine materials," University of Toronto Archives.
95. H.L. Tuzo, "A Glimpse of the Saskatchewan," *Crag and Canyon* (Banff, AB), 8 September 1906, 1–2, and H.L. Tuzo, "A Glimpse of the Saskatchewan Concludes," *Crag and Canyon* (Banff, AB), 22 September 1906, 1–3; Miss Tuzo, "Lady Explorers on the Trail. Through the Pipestone Pass to the Saskatchewan River," *Rod and Gun and Motor Sports in Canada* 8 (December 1906), 564–68. Tuzo preserved some of the photographs in an album, Wilson Family Collection.
96. Molly Adams to Catherine Elkin, Field, BC, 19 August 1906, Adams Family Collection.
97. Henrietta L. Tuzo to John Wilson, 4 October 1906, John Tuzo Wilson Personal Papers, accn. B86-0066, box 8, file 8, University of Toronto Archives.
98. Mary T.S. Schäffer to Dr. Nolan, Philadelphia, 2 April 1896, Coll. 567, Academy of Natural Sciences Library and Archives, Philadelphia. See Chapter 2 in this volume.
99. The Sharp family moved from Philadelphia to the Boston area in 1905 where they subsequently maintained homes in Brookline and Nantucket. See Sharp Family Papers, 1872–1989, MS270, Nantucket Historical Association Research Library; and the year 1900 in the "The History of the Building" timeline for *317 North 35th Street*, 23 May 2015, http://poweltonvillage.org/interactivemap/files/317n35th.htm; United States Federal Census, 1900.
100. Henrietta L. Tuzo, September 1904–1917 diary, 24 July [1906], Wilson Family Collection.
101. Dorothy Sharp, Alpine Club of Canada application card, WMCR M2W/AC385-10.
102. Henrietta L. Tuzo, September 1904–1917 diary, 23 July 1906, Wilson Family Collection.
103. Mary W. (Molly) Adams letters and diaries, 1891, 1901, and 1904, transcribed, Adams Family Collection.
104. M.S.W., "Tepee Life in Northern Hills" (unpublished manuscript, 1924), WMCR M79/6.
105. Ibid.
106. Ibid.
107. Schäffer was a Quaker, while Adams was raised in a Congregationalist home (Marjorie Adams, personal correspondence [email] 26 August 2014). Adams did not practice her religion in adulthood. In a letter written while on board the SS *Rotterdam* in Europe in July 1891, Adams wrote to her sister, "Sunday 1030 A.M. I feel as cross as two sticks this morning because I have just been obliged to go to church!…I feel like a fool and a hypocrite." In 1899, Adams wrote to her sister, "I went to church this A.M.!! I can't remember when I last was, and I cannot say that I enjoy it." Molly Adams to Catherine

Elkin, Dorset, VT, Sunday, October [n.d.], 1899. And on 29 September 1908, again writing from Field, BC, she reported that she had been offered a position to teach and serve as registrar at the American Women's College in Turkey, but the president had asked an acquaintance "about my Christian character before she offered it to me. I told Miss Weeks she ought to have said that what character I had was heathen." Molly Adams to Catherine Elkin, Field, BC, 29 September 1908, Adams Family Collection.

108. Molly Adams wrote, "Our head guide, Mr. Warren, was just as nice as they make them....Our other guide, Mr. Dan Campbell, was n.g. [no good]. He was the head of the livery and guide business at Field two years ago, but I don't wonder he lost his position. His brother has it now, and another brother is here. It was supposed to be pretty fine to get anything named Campbell to go out with you, but better acquaintance with Danny changed our opinion." Molly Adams to Catherine Elkin, Lake Louise, BC, 11 August 1906, Adams Family Collection.
109. Humphrey, "Five Women on the Trail," 429. Henrietta Tuzo notes in her diary that William Warren and Robert Campbell, who owned the guiding company that employed Warren, assisted with preparations. Henrietta Tuzo diary, September 1904–1917, 24 July [1906], Adams Family Collection.
110. Humphrey, "Five Women on the Trail," 195.
111. Ibid., 199.
112. Molly Adams to Catherine Elkin, Laggan, AB, 17 July 1906, Adams Family Collection.
113. Ibid.
114. Henrietta L. Tuzo, September 1904–1917 diary, 23 July [1906], Wilson Family Collection.
115. Molly Adams to Catherine Elkin, Lake Louise, AB, 11 August 1906, Adams Family Collection.
116. Molly Adams to Catherine Elkin, Banff, 24 August 1906, Adams Family Collection.
117. Mary T.S. Schäffer to Henrietta L. Tuzo, Glacier House, BC, 20 June [1906], Wilson Family Collection.
118. Henrietta L. Tuzo, September 1904–1917 diary, 7 July [1906], Wilson Family Collection.
119. Henrietta L. Tuzo, September 1904–1917 diary, 27 July [1906], Wilson Family Collection.
120. Ibid., 11 August [1906], Wilson Family Collection.
121. See Chapters 1 and 4 in this volume for sources and a fuller discussion.
122. Humphrey, "Five Women on the Trail," 343–44.
123. Ibid., 348.
124. Molly Adams to Catherine Elkin, Field, BC, 19 August 1906, Adams Family Collection.
125. M.S.W., "Tepee Life in Northern Hills" (unpublished manuscript, [1924]), WMCR M79/6.
126. Molly Adams to Cousin Alice, Field, BC, 26 August 1904, Adams Family Collection.
127. Mary [Schäffer] Warren to Mr. [Raymond] Zillmer, Banff, 28 February 1928, WMCR M8.

128. E.J. Hart described Adams as "originally from Boston, a teacher of geology at Columbia College in New York," in "Yahe-Weha" (1980), 8, "Yahe-Weha" (2014), 19. Later, Janice Sanford Beck called her "a geology teacher from New York," in *No Ordinary Woman: The Story of Mary Schäffer Warren* (Calgary, AB: Rocky Mountain Books, 2001), 33.
129. "Daring Explorers Make a Remarkable Trip to the Heart of the Canadian Rocky Mountains," unnamed newspaper clipping, ca. October 1908, WMCR M79/9B.
130. Adams was elected to the Geographical Society of Philadelphia on 14 November 1906. The list of active members published in the *Bulletin of the Geographical Society of Philadelphia* 7, no. 2 (April 1909) included Mrs. Charles Schaffer of 200 Penn Street, West Chester, PA (p. 117); Miss Mary W. Adams, 477 Prospect Street, New Haven, Conn. (p. 121), and Miss Mary M. Vaux, 1715 Arch Street, Philadelphia, PA (p. 119). That year, twenty-five of the forty-four members were female. That same volume included publication of Schäffer's article "A Recently Explored Lake," which recounted the journey to Maligne Lake. Adams's membership card is archived in Card file box 1, 97-787ms(30) in the collection of the Geographical Society of Philadelphia at the American Philosophical Society Library, Philadelphia, PA. The final, undated inscription on the card is "Deceased."
131. Mary W. Adams, US passport application, 20 May 1908, US Passport Applications, roll 0061, certificates 52785–53684, 14 May 1908–21 May 1908, National Archives and Records Administration, Washington, DC. William L. Elkin, her brother-in-law, witnessed her application and listed his professional address at the Yale Observatory in New Haven.
132. Molly Adams to Ida Ogilvie, Field, BC, 26 September [1908], Adams Family Collection.
133. Mrs. Charles Schäffer, "The Valleys of the Saskatchewan with Horse and Camera," *Bulletin of the Geographical Society of Philadelphia* 5, no. 2 (April 1907): 108–14.
134. Molly Adams to "Helène," Mount Stephen House, Field, BC, 19 August 1906, Adams Family Collection.
135. Molly Adams to Catherine Elkin, Kootenay Plains, AB, 11 September 1906, Adams Family Collection.
136. Molly Adams to Catherine Elkin, Mount Stephen House, Field, BC, 13 October 1906, Adams Family Collection.
137. Molly Adams to Catherine Elkin, Kootenay Plains, AB, 30 September 1906, Adams Family Collection.
138. Molly Adams to Catherine Elkin, Field, BC, 19 October 1906, Adams Family Collection.
139. Molly Adams to Catherine Elkin, Mount Stephen House, Field, BC, 13 October 1906, Adams Family Collection.
140. Mary Schäffer Warren to Miss [Minnie] Nickell, Banff, 21 September [ca. 1935], WMCR M8.
141. M.S.W., "Tepee Life in Northern Hills" (unpublished manuscript, [1924]), WMCR M79/6.

142. In September 1908, for example, contemplating the upcoming trip to Japan that she and Schäffer had planned, Adams wrote, "I wish I liked sight seeing better. I do like it well enough under some favorable conditions sometimes, and it may be more amusing than I think it will to do the sassiety [*sic*] set." Molly Adams to Cousin Alice, Mount Steven House, Field, BC, [n.d.] September 1908, Adams Family Collection.
143. Molly Adams to Catherine Elkin, Banff, 25 July 1904, Adams Family Collection. In 2015, the daily cost of the trip would have been about $275 based on a consumer price index comparative calculation of purchasing power. See Williamson, "Seven Ways." Adams often commented on Ogilvie's and Cook's preference to camp while in California and New Mexico because it was more economical than staying in hotels. Adams herself never commented on any financial concerns. She was financially independent, and occasionally in passing would mention to her sister, Catherine, that she would reimburse her for bills that were covered in her absence from New Haven. The source of her financial means has not come to light but perhaps derived from her mother's estate.
144. Mary T.S. Schäffer, "Haunts of the Wild Flowers of the Canadian Rockies (Within reach of the Canadian Pacific Railroad)," *Canadian Alpine Journal* 3 (1911): 135; Stewardson Brown, "Botanizing in the Canadian Rockies," *Proceedings of the Academy of Natural Sciences of Philadelphia* 58, no. 3 (October–December 1906): 429–30.
145. "Season's Offering of Garden Books: Volumes Dealing with Out-of-Door Life Grow More Highly Specialized Year by Year," *New York Times Saturday Review of Books*, 9 May 1908, 264.
146. "Now Ready," display ad G.P. Putnam's Sons, *New York Times Saturday Review of Books*, 14 December 1907, n.p., and 18 December 1907, 5.
147. Mary [Schäffer] Warren to Humphrey Toms, Banff, 28 March 1935, WMCR M429/1.
148. J.W.H. [Julia Wilmotte Henshaw], "The Bookshelf: Old Indian Trails in [*sic*] the Canadian Rockies," *The Chronicle: A Weekly Newspaper for Women* (Vancouver) 1, no. 8 (20 October 1911), 21, clipping, WMCR M79/8.
149. "Two Women in an Untrod Land: Exploring in the Canadian Rockies, They Add a New Lake to the Map," *New York Times Saturday Review of Books*, 16 July 1911, BR3, clipping WMCR M79/9B.
150. Mary [Schäffer] Warren to Mr. [Raymond] Zillmer, Banff, 2 January 1928, WMCR M8.
151. Schäffer, *Old Indian Trails* (1911), 19.
152. See especially Chapter VI of the "Expedition of 1908" in Schäffer, *Old Indian Trails*, 282–84.
153. Helen M. Buss, *Repossessing the World: Reading Memoirs by Contemporary Women* (Waterloo, ON: Wilfrid Laurier University Press, 2002), 15.
154. Mary [Schäffer] Warren to Mr. [Raymond] Zillmer, Banff, 12 April [ca. 1928], WMCR M8. After typing the letter, Schäffer struck through the typed word "read" with a pen and in ink inserted the word "published." Raymond Zillmer (1887–1960) was a Wisconsin attorney, mountaineer, and conservationist whose travels included the

Canadian Rockies. Mount Zillmer in the Cariboo Mountains near Valemount, BC, is named in his honour.

155. Buss, *Repossessing the World*, 19.
156. Ibid., 2.
157. Ibid., 15.
158. Michale Lang, *An Adventurous Woman Abroad: The Selected Lantern Slides of Mary T.S. Schäffer* (Victoria, BC: Rocky Mountain Books, 2011), 9.
159. Susan L. Roberson, "American Women and Travel Writing," in *The Cambridge Companion to American Travel Writing*, ed. Alfred Bendixen and Judith Hamera (Cambridge: Cambridge University Press, 2009), 223, 224.
160. Mary [Schäffer] Warren to Miss [Minnie] Nickell, Banff, 13 December [ca. 1937], WMCR M8.
161. Molly Adams to Catherine Elkin, Mount Stephen House, Field, BC, 21 September 1908, Adams Family Collection.
162. Wendy Wacko, for example, conjectures, "I always thought that Mary Schaffer and her regular travelling companion Mollie Adams were in love—I'm sure they were lesbians. We know they were very, very close—effectively soulmates—and they both had a crush on their guide Billy Warren. It was the ultimate love triangle." "Homegrown Mountain Movie Maker," *Mountain* 3 (Fall 2000): 28.
163. Mary [Schäffer] Warren to Mr. [Raymond] Zillmer, Banff, 28 February 1928, WMCR M8.
164. Molly Adams to "Elizabeth," SS *Empress of Japan* "in the middle of the Pacific Ocean," 15 October 1908, Adams Family Collection.
165. In 1916, Schäffer wrote, "several years ago, while quite an invalid I amused myself one winter writing 'old [*sic*] Indian Trails of the Canadian Rockies.'" Mary Schäffer Warren to Mr. [William Henderson] Watts, Banff, 22 May 1916, WMCR M553.
166. "Mrs. Schaefer Tells of Rocky Mountains," *Daily Local News* (West Chester, PA), n.d., [ca. 1907], clipping, WMCR M79/9B; "Illustrated Lecture," *Daily Local News* (West Chester, PA), 2 March 1911, clipping file "Schaeffer, M.," Chester County Archives, West Chester, PA; "Mrs. Schaffer's New Book," *Daily Local News* (West Chester, PA), 13 June 1911, clipping file "Schaeffer, M.," Chester County Archives, West Chester, PA. The 8 February 1911 entry in the Unlabelled Minutes Book of the Board of Directors of the Geographical Society of Philadelphia for 11 November 1908–12 April 1916 notes that "Mrs. Mary T.S. Schäffer will speak on the Canadian Rockies at the March meeting." Manuscripts Collection no. 93, 1997-787ms, American Philosophical Society Library, Philadelphia.
167. In 1928, Schäffer discovered that 260 unbound copies remained with the New York publisher, G.P. Putnam's Sons. These were then bound and distributed for sale. Mary [Schäffer] Warren to Mr. [Raymond] Zillmer, Banff, 12 April [1928], WMCR M8.
168. Schäffer, *Old Indian Trails* (1911), 5.

4 Maligne Lake, 1907–1911

1. Mary Schäffer to George Vaux Jr., Banff, 8 May 1911, WMCR Vaux Collection Addition 2007. Putnam's June 1911 bill was for $1,018.98 and noted that Mrs. Schäffer owned the electrotype plates. On 30 November 1911, Schäffer wrote to Vaux that "I found 'Trails' in every shop in Calgary, and we are expecting to get out a second edition in Jan. No money out of it yet." WMCR Vaux Collection Addition 2007.
2. Mary T.S. Schäffer, "A Recently Explored Lake in the Rocky Range of Canada," *Bulletin of the Geographical Society of Philadelphia* 7, no. 3 (July 1909): 123–34; [Mary T.S. Schäffer], "Jasper Park: The Mountain Park on the Line of the Grand Trunk Pacific Railway, [Illustrated with Photographs by Mary Schäffer]," *Canadian Life and Resources* (January 1910), 20–23; Mary T.S. Schäffer, *Untrodden Paths in the Canadian Rockies* (Minneapolis, MN: Soo Line, ca. 1910).
3. See Mary T.S. Schäffer, "A Recently Explored Lake in the Rocky Range of Canada," *Bulletin of the Geographical Society of Philadelphia* 7, no. 3 (July 1909): 123–34; Mary T.S. Schäffer, "Hunting a Lost Lake," *Travel* (May 1911), 321–23, 364; Mary T.S. Schaffer, "The Finding of Lake Maligne," *Canadian Alpine Journal* 4 (1912): 92–97; "Mrs. Schäffer's Discovery and Survey of Lake Maligne, Canadian Rockies," *Geographical Journal* 39, no. 4 (April 1912): 379–81.
4. Jacqueline Fry, untitled essay, trans. Elizabeth Ritchie, in *The Distance Between Two Points Is Measured In Memories, Labrador 1988*, by Marlene Creates (exhibition catalogue) (North Vancouver, BC: Presentation House Gallery, 1990), 57.
5. Marlene Creates, *Marlene Creates: Language and Land Use, Alberta 1993* (exhibition catalogue) (Lethbridge, AB: Southern Alberta Art Gallery, 1993), n.p.
6. See PearlAnn Reichwein and Lisa McDermott, "Opening the Secret Garden: Mary Schäffer, Jasper Park Conservation, and the Survey of Maligne Lake, 1911," in *Culturing Wilderness in Jasper National Park: Studies in Two Centuries of Human History in the Upper Athabasca River Watershed*, ed. I.S. MacLaren (Edmonton: University of Alberta Press, 2007), 155–98. See also Glenda Riley, *Women and Nature: Saving the "Wild"* (Lincoln: University of Nebraska Press, 1999).
7. Mary T.S. Schäffer, "Untrodden Ways," *Canadian Alpine Journal* 1, no. 2 (1907–1908): 288.
8. Schäffer, "Hunting a Lost Lake," 321.
9. Schäffer, "A Recently Explored Lake," 123.
10. Mary T.S. Schäffer, *Old Indian Trails: Incidents of Camp and Trail Life, Covering Two Years' Exploration through the Rocky Mountains of Canada* (New York: G.P. Putnam's Sons; Toronto: William Briggs, 1911; reprint with revised map, 1912), 134.
11. "Mrs. Schäffer's Discovery and Survey of Lake Maligne, Canadian Rockies," *Geographical Journal* 39, no. 4 (April 1912): 380. In a letter written two decades later, Schäffer again attributed the idea of looking for "a mystifying lake called Chabe Imne" to Jimmy Simpson. See Mary Schaffer Warren to Miss [Minnie] Nickell, Banff, 21 September [ca. 1935], WMCR M8.

12. See E.J. Hart, *Jimmy Simpson: Legend of the Rockies* (Canmore, AB: Altitude Publishing, 1991).
13. Mary W. (Molly) Adams, 1908 transcribed diary, Moberly Camp 11, 2 September, WMCR M79/11.
14. Ibid. John Moberly's mother, Suzanne Karakonti, was born in 1824 in the Jasper area. His father had been a Hudson's Bay Company trader who had left the family before John was born in 1861. He and his brother established homesteads in Jasper. Their land was expropriated and they were forced to leave when the Jasper Forest Reserve was established in 1907. See "Moberly Descendants Ignored in Totem Dispute," *The Fitzhugh* (Jasper, AB), 13 May 2010.
15. In a letter to the *Geographical Journal* of London following publication of the story of Schäffer's journey and survey map in April 1912, a former member of the Geological Survey of Canada informed readers of surveyor Henry Macleod's 1875 visit, and said that the lake, which Macleod saw and dubbed "Sorefoot," had been drawn but left unlabelled on a CPR map of 1877 and a Canadian Department of the Interior map of 1902—although the latter map "bears no resemblance to the reality either in size or contours." See "The Monthly Record: Mrs. Schäffer's Survey of Maligne Lake," *Geographical Journal* 40, no. 3 (September 1912): 334–35.
16. Joan M. Schwartz and James R. Ryan, "Introduction: Photography and the Geographical Imagination," in *Picturing Place: Photography and the Geographical Imagination*, ed. Joan M. Schwartz and James R. Ryan (London: I.B. Tauris, 2003), 6.
17. In Schäffer's book collection, now in the Archives and Library of the Whyte Museum of the Canadian Rockies, was James McEvoy's *Report on the Geology and Natural Resources of the Country Traversed by the Yellowhead Pass Route from Edmonton to Tête Jaune Cache Comprising Portions of Alberta and British Columbia* (Ottawa: Geological Survey of Canada, 1900). McEvoy's report was based on one season of exploration in 1898 and filed with the Geological Survey of Canada in May 1899.
18. See Collie's foldout map in Hugh E.M. Stutfield and J. Norman Collie, *Climbs & Exploration in the Canadian Rockies* (London: Longmans, Green and Co., 1903).
19. See Denis Wood, "What Makes a Map?," *Cartographica* 30, no. 2 & 3 (Summer/Autumn 1993): 81–86, and "The Fine Line Between Mapping and Mapmaking," *Cartographica* 30, no. 4 (Winter 1993): 50–60.
20. Marlene Creates, "Questions about the Place, Nova Scotia 1998," in *Marlene Creates: Signs of Our Time*, by Marlene Creates, Lucy R. Lippard, and Robin Metcalfe (exhibition catalogue) (St. John's, NL: The Rooms Corporation of Newfoundland and Labrador and Tom Thomson Memorial Art Gallery, 2006), 50.
21. Edward Cavell, *Legacy in Ice: The Vaux Family and the Canadian Alps* (Banff, AB: Whyte Foundation, 1983), 18.
22. Schäffer's Pony Premo folding camera, manufactured by Rochester Optical Co., is in the Whyte Museum of the Canadian Rockies. WMCR Heritage Collection 104.41.0007.

23. Molly Adams to Catherine Elkin, Crane Pond, NY, 11 August 1901, Adams Family Collection.
24. For the first published account of the successful quest, see Schäffer, "A Recently Explored Lake."
25. Schäffer, *Old Indian Trails* (1911), 238–39.
26. Ibid., 240.
27. Ibid., 241, 242.
28. Molly Adams to Catherine Elkin and Cousin Alice, Maligne Lake, 16 July and 17 July [1908], Adams Family Collection.
29. Mary [Schäffer] Warren to Mr. [Raymond] Zillmer, Banff, 28 February 1928, WMCR M8.
30. Schwartz and Ryan, *Picturing Place*, 8.
31. Ibid., 18.
32. Glenda Riley writes in her study *Women and Nature: Saving the "Wild" West*, "Nor were women afraid of the dangers posed by men. Given prevailing worries about decorum and safety, it seems that women would maintain an acceptable distance from men in the field. This was not the case. Such botanists…hired male assistants, who went into the field with them. In addition, women and men travelling together slept in the same tent, dormitory, or barracks" (54). Photographs of camps in Schäffer and Adams's albums, however, show that two tents were erected and at some distance apart.
33. Schäffer, *Old Indian Trails* (1911), 181.
34. Mrs. Charles Schäffer, "The Valleys of the Saskatchewan with Horse and Camera," *Bulletin of the Geographical Society of Philadelphia* 5, no. 2 (April 1907): 108–14.
35. Schaffer, "Untrodden Ways," 292.
36. Schäffer, *Old Indian Trails* (1911), 178.
37. Ibid., 175.
38. Ibid., 200.
39. Some scholars have chastised Schäffer and characterized her as racist for using this now-derogatory term. See J.V. Emberley, "Colonial Phantasms: Aboriginality and the Family in the Photographic Archives," in *ReCalling Early Canada: Reading the Political in Literary and Cultural Production*, ed. Jennifer Blair, Daniel Coleman, Kate Higginson, and Lorraine York (Edmonton: University of Alberta Press, 2005), 320; and Susan Bernardin, Melody Graulich, Lisa MacFarlane, and Nicole Tonkovich, *Trading Gazes: Euro-American Women Photographers and Native North Americans, 1880–1940* (New Brunswick, NJ: Rutgers University Press, 2003), 25, 133.
40. Reichwein and McDermott, "Opening the Secret Garden," 194.
41. Molly Adams to "Elizabeth," SS *Empress of Japan* "in the middle of Pacific Ocean," 15 October [1908], Adams Family Collection.
42. Sarah Carter, *Capturing Women: The Manipulation of Cultural Imagery in Canada's Prairie West* (Montreal and Kingston: McGill-Queen's University Press, 1997), xiii.

43. Rudyard Kipling, "Letters to the Family," *Collier's* 41, no. 5 (25 April 1908): 13–14, reprinted in Rudyard Kipling, *Letters of Travel (1892–1913)* (London: Macmillan & Co., 1920), 188–89.
44. Schäffer, *Old Indian Trails* (1911), 178.
45. Ibid., 180.
46. Ibid., 182.
47. Mary T.S. Schäffer, *Untrodden Paths in the Canadian Rockies* (Minneapolis, MN: Soo Line, ca. 1910); Photograph album, n.d., among Letters, Diaries, and Photograph Albums of Henrietta L. Tuzo, 1904–1917, Wilson Family Collection; Schäffer, *Old Indian Trails* (1911), 181. The photograph of Leah and Frances Louise Beaver on horseback with Sampson Beaver standing alongside was labelled "Friends" when published in Schäffer, *Untrodden Paths*.
48. Schäffer, *Old Indian Trails* (1911), 183.
49. Geraldine Moodie, who worked in the Arctic in the early 1900s, is counted among such photographers in Canada. See Susan Close, *Framing Identity: Social Practices of Photography in Canada (1880–1920)* (Winnipeg, MB: Arbeiter Ring Publishing, 2007), 50–72.
50. Lucy Lippard, Introduction to *Partial Recall: Photographs of Native North Americans*, ed. Lucy Lippard (New York: The New Press, 1992), 36.
51. For a history of the Stoney Nation, see Chief John Snow, *These Mountains Are Our Sacred Places: The Story of the Stoney People*, 2nd ed. (Calgary, AB: Fifth House Publishers, 2005).
52. A.P. Coleman, "The Brazeau Ice-Field," *Geographical Journal* 21, no. 5 (May 1903): 502–10.
53. A.P. Coleman, *The Canadian Rockies: New and Old Trails with 3 Maps and 41 Illustrations* (Toronto: Henry Frowde, 1912), 221.
54. "Old Indian Trails of the Canadian Rockies," *Portland Telegram* (Oregon), 5 August 1911.
55. Mary [Schäffer] Warren to Mr. [Raymond] Zillmer, Banff, 12 April [1928], WMCR M8.
56. Ben Gadd, *Handbook of the Canadian Rockies: Geology, Plants, Animals, History and Recreation from Waterton/Glacier to the Yukon*, 2nd ed. (Jasper, AB: Corax Press, 1995), 688.
57. The four photos of the Beaver family that are printed and mounted in Schäffer's and Adams's albums are included in the 1906 section of each album. WMCR V527/PD-1 and WMCR V527/PD-4.
58. Lippard, Introduction, 13.
59. Ibid., 18.
60. Ibid., 37.
61. Ibid., 14.
62. Ibid., 13.
63. Ibid., 38.
64. Ibid., 43.

65. Emberley, "Colonial Phantasms," 305.
66. Ibid., 307, 333.
67. Ibid., 305.
68. Julia V. Emberley, *Defamiliarizing the Aboriginal: Cultural Practices and Decolonization in Canada* (Toronto: University of Toronto Press, 2007), 168; Emberley, "Colonial Phantasms," 320.
69. Emberley, "Colonial Phantasms," 326. See also Emberley, *Defamiliarizing the Aboriginal*, 173.
70. Schäffer, *Untrodden Paths*, 2.
71. Lippard, Introduction, 38.
72. Emberley, *Defamiliarizing the Aboriginal*, 169.
73. Ibid., 169.
74. Ibid., 170.
75. Emberley, "Colonial Phantasms," 326. See also Emberley, *Defamiliarizing the Aboriginal*, 176.
76. An example from 1907 of an unsuccessful intervention is that of Dr. P.H. Bryce, the chief medical officer of the Department of Indian Affairs, who reported that rampant tuberculosis in residential schools in the west that was causing a 50 per cent mortality rate could be reduced by improving school building conditions, such as ventilation, as well as student nutrition and exercise. These empirically grounded recommendations were suppressed, superseded by cultural assumptions about Indigenous people and their fate, and public political and economic policies of assimilation. See P.H. Bryce, *Report on the Indian Schools of Manitoba and the North-West Territories* (Ottawa: Government Printing Bureau, 1907), and P.H. Bryce, *The Story of a National Crime: An Appeal to Justice for the Indians of Canada* (Ottawa: James Hope and Sons, 1922).
77. Louis Owens, *I Hear the Train: Reflection, Inventions, Refractions* (Norman: University of Oklahoma Press, 2001), 226.
78. Susan Sontag, *On Photography* (New York: Farrar, Straus and Giroux, 1977), 67.
79. Schwartz and Ryan, *Picturing Place*, 4.
80. Schäffer, *Old Indian Trails* (1911), 182–84.
81. Ibid., 183.
82. Mary W. (Molly) Adams, 1908 transcribed diary, 1st Maligne Camp, 7 July, WMCR M79/11.
83. Wood, "What Makes a Map a Map?," 83.
84. Alan Morantz notes that maps were "a primary means of transferring the knowledge of Aboriginal civilizations to the Western world." See Alan Morantz, *Where Is Here?: Canada's Maps and the Stories They Tell* (Toronto: Penguin Canada, 2002), xiv. Nevertheless, First Nations people in the eastern Rockies frustrated early explorers by not divulging place names. See Glen W. Boles, Roger W. Laurilla, and William L. Putnam, *Canadian Mountain Place Names: The Rockies and Columbia Mountains* (Surrey, BC: Rocky Mountain Books, 2006), 10.

85. Schaffer, "The Finding of Lake Maligne," 93. Belgian Jesuit missionary Father Pierre-Jean De Smet is credited with naming the river in 1846 while travelling through the area. See Merrily K. Aubrey, ed., *Concise Place Names of Alberta* (Calgary, AB: University of Calgary Press, 2006), 201, and Boles, Laurilla, and Putnam, *Canadian Mountain Place Names*.
86. Schäffer, *Old Indian Trails* (1911), 184.
87. Schäffer, "A Recently Explored Lake," 124.
88. Mary W. (Molly) Adams, 1908 transcribed diary, 1st Maligne Camp, 7 July, WMCR M79/11.
89. "Mrs. Schäffer's Discovery and Survey of Lake Maligne, Canadian Rockies," *Geographical Journal* (London) 39, no. 4 (April 1912): 380.
90. Schäffer, "A Recently Explored Lake," 123.
91. Schäffer, *Old Indian Trails* (1911), 183.
92. Schäffer, "A Recently Explored Lake," 125.
93. Ibid., 128.
94. Schäffer, *Old Indian Trails* (1911), 203. Neither Schäffer's nor Adams's 1907 diary appears to have survived; only a transcribed and typed version of Adams's 1908 diary has come to light and is in the collection of the Whyte Museum of the Canadian Rockies, WMCR M79/11.
95. Schäffer, *Old Indian Trails* (1911), 233.
96. Nikolas H. Huffman, "Charting the Other Maps: Cartography and Visual Methods in Feminist Research," in *Thresholds in Feminist Geography: Difference, Methodology, Representation*, ed. John Paul Jones III, Heidi J. Nast, and Susan M. Roberts (Lanham, MD: Rowman & Littlefield Publishers, 1997), 255.
97. Ibid., 257. Huffman states his position on feminism: "Because gender constitutes the social relationships between men and women…I regard feminism as an inclusive perspective that acknowledges both women and men, placing men on par with women as equally embodied and gendered persons" (257).
98. Ibid., 259.
99. Mona Domosh, "With 'Stout Boots and a Stout Heart': Historical Methodology and Feminist Geography," in *Thresholds in Feminist Geography: Difference, Methodology, Representation*, ed. John Paul Jones III, Heidi J. Nast, and Susan M. Roberts (Lanham, MD: Rowman & Littlefield Publishers, 1997), 232.
100. Will C. van den Hoonaard, *Map Worlds: A History of Women in Cartography* (Waterloo, ON: Wilfrid Laurier University Press, 2013), 72.
101. Ibid., 9.
102. Huffman, "Charting the Other Maps," 260–61. Huffman assesses Wood's series of articles in *Cartographica* 1, 2 & 3, and 4 (1993).
103. Huffman, "Charting the Other Maps," 260–61.
104. Martin Dodge, "From Here to There: A Curious Collection from the Hand Drawn Map Association/Kris Harzinski," *Cartographica* 45, no. 4 (2010): 274.

105. Ibid., 275.

106. Ibid., 276.

107. Schäffer, "Hunting a Lost Lake," 323.

108. Schaffer, "The Finding of Lake Maligne"; "Mrs. Schäffer's Discovery and Survey," *Geographical Journal*.

109. Caroline Sharpless, "Trip to Jasper Park, Rocky Mountains, Canada, May 29th–August 16th, 1911," transcribed diary, [Edmonton], 4 June [1911], WMCR M79/12.

110. Ibid., [New York City], 29 May, WMCR M79/12.

111. Mary Schäffer to George Vaux Jr., Banff, 27 May 1911, WMCR Vaux Collection Addition 2007.

112. Mary T.S. Schäffer, "Title not decided" (unpublished manuscript), n.d., WMCR M79/3, published posthumously as "The 1911 Expedition to Maligne Lake," in E.J. Hart, *A Hunter of Peace: Mary T.S. Schäffer's Old Indian Trails of the Canadian Rockies*, intro. and ed. E.J. Hart (Banff, AB: Whyte Museum of the Canadian Rockies, 1980), 132; and in *A Hunter of Peace: Mary T.S. Schäffer's Old Indian Trails of the Canadian Rockies*, 2nd ed., intro. E.J. Hart, foreword Jennifer Rutkair (Banff, AB: Whyte Museum of the Canadian Rockies, 2014), 154.

113. Caroline Sharpless, "Trip to Jasper Park, Rocky Mountains, Canada, May 29th–August 16th, 1911," transcribed diary, [Edmonton], 4 June, WMCR M79/12.

114. Mary T.S. Schäffer, "Title not decided" (unpublished manuscript, second draft), n.d., WMCR M79/3, published posthumously as "The 1911 Expedition to Maligne Lake," in Hart, *A Hunter of Peace* (1980), 133; and in Hart, *A Hunter of Peace* (2014), 154.

115. Caroline Sharpless, "Trip to Jasper Park, Rocky Mountains, Canada, May 29th–August 16th, 1911," transcribed diary, [Edmonton], 5 June, WMCR M79/12. On this date, Sharpless also notes meeting Mrs. Emily Murphy, whom she identified as the author of "Jennie Canook." Murphy, writing under the pseudonym Janey Canuck, published four books in the *Janey Canuck* series, beginning in 1901. In 1916, Murphy became the first female magistrate in the British Empire, and in 1929, as a member of the Famous Five, successfully campaigned for women to be recognized as persons under the British North America Act and thereby eligible for appointment to the Senate of Canada.

116. Molly Adams to Catherine Elkin, Field, BC, 21 September 1908, Adams Family Collection.

117. Geoffrey Lester, *Atlas of Alberta Railways* (University of Alberta Press, 2005), http://railways.library.ualberta.ca.

118. Caroline Sharpless, "Trip to Jasper Park, Rocky Mountains, Canada, May 29th–August 16th, 1911," transcribed diary, [Hinton, AB], 7 June, WMCR M79/12.

119. Ibid., [Edson and Edmonton, AB], 2–5 August, WMCR M79/12.

120. "Philadelphia Woman Names New Mountain," *Evening Journal* (Edmonton, AB), 8 August 1911; "Maligne Lake One of World's Beauty Spots," *Edmonton Daily Bulletin*, 9 August 1911, clipping, WMCR M79/9B.

121. Mary W. (Molly) Adams, 1908 transcribed diary, Camp Unwin, 12 July, WMCR M79/11.

122. Schäffer, *Old Indian Trails* (1911), 359. The number of annual visitors to Rocky Mountain Park (renamed Banff National Park in 1930) grew from 8,516 in 1902 to 32,209 in 1908, and to 73,725 in 1912. These numbers were reported in *Sessional Paper No. 25, Dominion Parks: Report of the Commissioner of Dominion Parks, 1912* (Ottawa: Department of the Interior, 1912). Schäffer annotated a copy in her possession. WMCR M79/15-1.
123. Marlene Creates quoted in Fry, untitled essay, 57.
124. Alan Trachtenberg, *Reading American Photographs: Images as History Mathew Brady to Walker Evans* (Toronto: Collins Publishers, 1989), 125.
125. The Geographic Board of Canada, established in 1897, was responsible for ensuring a consistency in geographic naming systems and practices in Canada. See W. Stewart Wallace, ed., *The Encyclopedia of Canada*, vol. 3 (Toronto: University Associates of Canada, 1948), 17.
126. Arthur O. Wheeler, "The Alpine Club of Canada's Expedition to Jasper Park, Yellowhead Pass and Mount Robson Region, 1911," *Canadian Alpine Journal* 4 (1912): 77.
127. Schaffer, "The Finding of Lake Maligne."
128. Mary Schäffer to George Vaux Jr., Banff, 27 May 1911, WMCR Vaux Collection Addition 2007.
129. Mary Schäffer to George Vaux Jr., Banff, 21 November 1911, WMCR Vaux Collection Addition 2007.
130. Ibid.
131. Mary Schäffer to George Vaux Jr., Banff, 26 December [1911], WMCR Vaux Collection Addition 2007.
132. Mary Schäffer to George Vaux Jr., Banff, 17 April 1912, WMCR Vaux 1 Series. See "Mrs. Schäffer's Discovery and Survey," 379–81.
133. Reichwein and McDermott, "Opening the Secret Garden," 180.
134. See Treaty 7 Elders and Tribal Council with Walter Hildebrant, Dorothy First Rider, and Sarah Carter, *The True Spirit and Original Intent of Treaty 7* (Montreal and Kingston: McGill-Queen's University Press, 1996). Whereas Treaty 7 was traditionally explained in the imperial context of building a nation, First Nations understandings of the purpose and the agreements reached are markedly different. See Snow, *These Mountains Are Our Sacred Places*, 55.
135. Karen Piper, *Cartographic Fictions: Maps, Race, and Identity* (New Brunswick, NJ: Rutgers University Press, 2002), 14.

5 Japan, 1908–1909, and Banff, 1909–1939

1. [Mary Schäffer] to "Dear Ones at Home," Taipeh, Formosa, Japan, 19–31 December 1908, 8, WMCR M79/1.
2. [Mary T.S. Schäffer], "A Glimpse of the Head-hunters of Formosa," unpublished manuscript, n.d. [ca. 1909], WMCR M79/2, published posthumously in Michale Lang, *An Adventurous Woman Abroad: The Selected Lantern Slides of Mary T.S. Schäffer* (Victoria, BC: Rocky Mountain Books, 2011), 251, 258.

3. Mary T.S. Schaffer, "With the Hairy Ainus," *Travel* (New York) 16 (April 1911): 259, and Mrs. M.T.S. Schaffer, "With the Hairy Ainus," *Travel and Exploration* (London) 3 (January to June 1910): 377. The general interest in Japan included special interest in Japanese women. See Alice Martin, "Little Women of Japan," *Harper's Bazaar* 44 (November 1910), 635, an illustrated article that focuses on the question of education and career.
4. See, for example, Monica Anderson, *Women and the Politics of Travel, 1870–1914* (Madison, WI: Fairleigh Dickinson University Press, 2006).
5. Molly Adams to Catherine Elkin, Field, BC, 28 September 1908, Adams Family Collection.
6. Molly Adams to Catherine Elkin, Field, BC, 21 September 1908, Adams Family Collection.
7. Molly Adams to Cousin Alice and Catherine Elkin, SS *Empress of Japan* travelling through "the narrows out of Vancouver harbor," 7 October [1908], Adams Family Collection.
8. Mary W. Adams, US passport application, 20 May 1908, US Passport Applications, roll 0061, certificates 52785–53684, 14 May 1908–21 May 1908, National Archives and Records Administration, Washington, DC; Mary T.S. Schäffer passport application, 28 April 1908, US Passport Applications, roll 0059, certificates 50879–51827, 27 April–5 May 1908, National Archives and Records Administration, Washington, DC.
9. Molly Adams to Cousin Alice and Catherine Elkin, Vancouver, BC, 6 October 1908, Adams Family Collection.
10. Molly Adams to Ida Ogilvie, Field, BC, 26 September [1908], Adams Family Collection.
11. Molly Adams to "Helen," Tokyo, 14 November [1908], Adams Family Collection. They departed Tokyo on 2 November and arrived back on 12 November.
12. Molly Adams to Catherine Elkin, Taiwan Railway Hotel, Taipeh, Formosa, 25–31 December 1908, Adams Family Collection.
13. Susan Ecroyd Lippincott was a friend of Mary Elkinton Nitobe from Philadelphia, and visiting the Nitobes at the time. Caroline A. Macdonald, a graduate of the University of Toronto, was living and working in Tokyo for the YWCA World's Committee to establish an association there, for which she recruited Michi Kawai's assistance. See Michi Kawai, *My Lantern* (Ginza, Tokyo: Kyo Bun Kwan, 1939), 116–17. Earlier studies of Mary Schäffer have identified a Miss "Bippinorth" as the fourth woman in the group. This appears to have been based on a misreading of Schäffer's cursive handwriting. Molly Adams's letters confirm that the name was Lippincott. Schäffer also misspelled Caroline Macdonald's surname, variously spelling it McDonald or MacDonald in her letter home from Formosa, [Mary Schäffer] to "Dear Ones at Home," Taipeh, Formosa, Japan, 19–31 December 1908, 8, WMCR M79/1.
14. The album contains twenty pages of prints totalling about ninety images. See Mary Schäffer, photograph album [Japan], WMCR V527/PD-5. Lantern slides made from Schäffer's and Adams's own photographs as well as some acquired in Japan are found

in two fonds, WMCR V527/PS1 and WMCR V439/PS1. Thirteen images are included in Mary T.S. Schaffer, "With the Hairy Ainus," *Travel* 16 (April 1911), 259–62, 251. Four images are included in Mrs. M.T.S. Schaffer, "With the Hairy Ainus," *Travel and Exploration* 3 (January to June 1910), 378–84.

15. "I am not keeping a diary," Adams wrote, "so feel it my duty to write something very often." Molly Adams to Catherine Elkin and Cousin Alice, Hokkaido, Japan, 9 November [1908], Adams Family Collection. Schäffer wrote, "This letter too, must be my record of our trip to another little faraway corner so please take care of it & return it to me at Glacier." [Mary Schäffer] to "Dear Ones at Home," Taipeh, Formosa, Japan, 19–31 December 1908, 1, WMCR M79/1.
16. Molly Adams to Catherine Elkin and Cousin Alice, Imperial Hotel, Tokyo, 27 October [1908], Adams Family Collection. Adams wrote, "Here we have been almost a week in Japan" and then writes an account of activities during the previous five days.
17. Molly Adams to "Elizabeth," SS *Empress of Japan* "in the middle of the Pacific Ocean," 15 October 1908, Adams Family Collection.
18. Molly Adams to Catherine Elkin and Cousin Alice, Hokkaido, Japan, 9 November [1908], Adams Family Collection.
19. Molly Adams to Catherine Elkin and Cousin Alice, the Fujiya Hotel, Hot Mineral Springs, Miyanoshita, Sagami, Japan, 21 November 1908, Adams Family Collection.
20. Kawai, *My Lantern*, 122.
21. For a concise Quaker-oriented biography, see Samuel M. Snipes, "The Life of Japanese Quaker Inazo Nitobe," *Friends Journal*, 1 August 2011, www.friendsjournal.org/life-japanese-quaker-inazo-nitobe-1862-1933/.
22. Molly Adams to Catherine Elkin and Cousin Alice, Imperial Hotel, Tokyo, 1 November [1908], and 1 December [1908], Adams Family Collection. Umeko Tsuda studied at Bryn Mawr from 1889 to 1892. While there, she raised funds to establish an endowment to support Japanese women who wished to study at Bryn Mawr. In 1900, she established the Women's Institute for English Studies in Tokyo, renamed Tsuda College in 1948. See Sally A. Hastings, "Travelling to Learn, Learning to Lead: Japanese Women as American College Students," in *Modern Girls on the Go: Gender, Mobility, and Labour in Japan*, ed. Alisa Freedman, Laura Miller, and Christina Reiko Yano (Stanford, CA: Stanford University Press, 2013), 193–208; and Barbara Rose, *Tsuda Umeko and Women's Education in Japan* (New Haven, CT: Yale University Press, 1992.) Marian Adams Wright (later Mrs. Thomas Henry O'Connor, married 1894) graduated with the class of 1891. Bryn Mawr College, *Program Bryn Mawr College, 1894* (Philadelphia: Sherman & Co. Printers, 1894), 39.
23. Molly Adams to K.I.C. [Käthchen Ireland Cook], Taipeh, Formosa, 31 December 1908–3 January 1909, Adams Family Collection. Schäffer identified their interpreter on Formosa as the governor general's personal interpreter, "Mr. Miyoshi, a graduate of Harvard College" in her unpublished manuscript "A Glimpse of the Head-hunters

of Formosa," n.d. [ca. 1909], n.p., WMCR M79/2, published posthumously in Lang, *An Adventurous Woman Abroad*, 249.

24. [Mary Schäffer] to "Dear Ones at Home," Taipeh, Formosa, Japan, 19–31 December 1908, 1, WMCR M79/1.
25. Molly Adams to Catherine Elkin and Cousin Alice, Imperial Hotel, Tokyo, 27 October [1908], Adams Family Collection.
26. Molly Adams to Catherine Elkin and Cousin Alice, Imperial Hotel, Tokyo, 27 October [1908], Adams Family Collection.
27. Ibid.
28. Molly Adams to Catherine Elkin and Cousin Alice, Imperial Hotel, Tokyo, 1 November [1908], Adams Family Collection. Umeko Tsuda's first teaching position after returning to Tokyo from Bryn Mawr in 1892 was as an English teacher at the Peeresses' School, as well as an appointment at the Tokyo Normal College for Women. Kawai, *My Lantern*, 114–15. Tsuda established her own school in 1900.
29. Molly Adams to Catherine Elkin and Cousin Alice, Imperial Hotel, Tokyo, 1 November [1908], Adams Family Collection.
30. Molly Adams to Catherine Elkin, the Taiwan Railway Hotel, Taipeh, Formosa, 25–31 December 1908, Adams Family Collection.
31. Molly Adams to Catherine Elkin, Sendai, 3 November [1908], Adams Family Collection; Molly Adams to Catherine Elkin [Katy] and Cousin Alice, Sapporo, Japan, 6 November [1908], Adams Family Collection.
32. Molly Adams to "Helen," Tokyo, 14 November [1908], Adams Family Collection.
33. Molly Adams to Catherine Elkin and Cousin Alice, Aomori, Japan, 12 November [1908], Adams Family Collection.
34. [Mary Schäffer] to "Dear Ones at Home," Taipeh, Formosa, Japan, 19–31 December 1908, 1, WMCR M79/1.
35. Schaffer, "With the Hairy Ainus," 260.
36. Molly Adams to Catherine Elkin, Taiwan Railway Hotel, Taipeh, Formosa, 25–31 December 1908, Adams Family Collection; [Mary Schäffer] to "Dear Ones at Home," Taipeh, Formosa, Japan, 19–31 December 1908, 7, WMCR M79/1; Mary T.S. Schäffer, "A Glimpse of the Head-hunters of Formosa," unpublished manuscript, n.d. [ca. 1909], n.p., WMCR M79/2, published posthumously in Lang, *An Adventurous Woman Abroad*, 258.
37. Molly Adams to Catherine Elkin and Cousin Alice, Sapporo, Japan, 6 November [1908], Adams Family Collection.
38. [Mary Schäffer] to "Dear Ones at Home," Taipeh, Formosa, Japan, 19–31 December 1908, 9, WMCR M79/1.
39. Schaffer, "With the Hairy Ainus," 259.
40. Molly Adams to Catherine Elkin and Cousin Alice, the Fujiya Hotel, Hot Mineral Springs, Miyanoshita, Sagami, Japan, 21 November 1908, Adams Family Collection.

41. Molly Adams to "Jean," Imperial Hotel, Tokyo, and [Kyoto Hotel], Kyoto, 11 December [1908], Adams Family Collection.
42. Molly Adams to Catherine Elkin, 1st Maligne Camp, 20 miles from the lake, 25 July 1908, Adams Family Collection.
43. Molly Adams to Cousin Alice, Mount Stephen House, Field, BC, [21] September 1908, Adams Family Collection.
44. Molly Adams to Catherine Elkin, Field, BC, 28 September 1908, Adams Family Collection.
45. Molly Adams to "Elizabeth," SS *Empress of Japan* "in the middle of the Pacific Ocean," 15 October 1908, Adams Family Collection.
46. Molly Adams to Catherine Elkin and Cousin Alice, Aomori, Japan, 12 November [1908], Adams Family Collection.
47. Molly Adams to Catherine Elkin and Cousin Alice, Tokyo, 1–5 December [1908], Adams Family Collection.
48. Isabella Bird, *Unbeaten Tracks in Japan: An Account of Travels on Horseback in the Interior,* 2 vols. (New York: G.P. Putnam's Sons, 1881), 1:vii. The second volume is devoted to Bird's travel on Hokkaido. She did not go to the eastern areas of the island where Schäffer and Adams travelled. Lorraine Sterry examines two types of women travel writers in Japan: those who travelled independently for their own reasons (such as Bird, but also Schäffer and Adams); and those who travelled as diplomats' spouses in *Victorian Women Travellers in Meiji Japan: Discovering a "New" Land* (Kent, UK: Global Oriental Ltd., 2009).
49. Molly Adams to Catherine Elkin and Cousin Alice, Sapporo, Japan, 6 November [1908], Adams Family Collection. Kawai was a beneficiary of Umeko Tsuda's scholarship fund for Japanese women at Bryn Mawr, from which she graduated in 1904. See Hastings, "Travelling to Learn," 196. On her return to Tokyo, Kawai taught at Tsuda's newly founded school, the Women's Institute for English Studies, in Tokyo. In 1927, she established her own school, Keisen Girls' School. For a brief biography, see Marlene Richie, "Michi Kawai: An Inspiring Woman with a Mission," *Child Research Net*, 21 May 2010, www.childresearch.net/papers/new/2010_02.html. See also Kawai's memoir, *My Lantern*.
50. Molly Adams to "Jean," Imperial Hotel, Tokyo, and [Kyoto Hotel], Kyoto, 11 December [1908], Adams Family Collection.
51. Schaffer, "With the Hairy Ainus," 261.
52. Molly Adams to "Helen," Muroran, Hokkaido, Japan, 10 November [1908], Adams Family Collection.
53. Schaffer, "With the Hairy Ainus," 251. See John Batchelor, *The Ainu and Their Folk-lore* (London: The Religious Tract Society, 1901).
54. Schaffer, "With the Hairy Ainus," 259.
55. Ibid.
56. Schaffer, "With the Hairy Ainus," 251. Hokkaido was also known as Yezo.

57. Mary T.S. Schäffer, *Old Indian Trails: Incidents of Camp and Trail Life, Covering Two Years' Exploration through the Rocky Mountains of Canada* (New York: G.P. Putnam's Sons; Toronto: William Briggs, 1911; reprint with revised map, 1912), 175.
58. Schaffer, "With the Hairy Ainus," 251. See Lars Krutak, "Tattooing among Japan's Ainu People," 2008, http://larskrutak.com/tattooing-among-japans-ainu-people/.
59. Schaffer, "With the Hairy Ainus," 251.
60. Ibid.
61. Ibid., 259.
62. Molly Adams to Catherine Elkin and Cousin Alice, Noboribetsu Onsen, Hokkaido, Japan, 9 November [1908], Adams Family Collection.
63. Molly Adams to Catherine Elkin, the Taiwan Railway Hotel, Taipeh, Formosa, 25–31 December 1908, Adams Family Collection.
64. Schaffer, "With the Hairy Ainus," 260.
65. [Mary Schäffer] to "Dear Ones at Home," Taipeh, Formosa, Japan, 19–31 December 1908, 7, WMCR M79/1.
66. Molly Adams to Catherine Elkin, the Taiwan Railway Hotel, Taipeh, Formosa, 25–31 December 1908, Adams Family Collection.
67. [Mary Schäffer] to "Dear Ones at Home," Taipeh, Formosa, Japan, 19–31 December 1908, 12, WMCR M79/1.
68. Schaffer, "With the Hairy Ainus," 259–62, 251.
69. [Mary Schäffer] to "Dear Ones at Home," Taipeh, Formosa, Japan, 19–31 December 1908, WMCR M79/1. The H.C. White Co. images remain in the Schäffer collections at the Whyte Museum of the Canadian Rockies.
70. "Formosa" (photograph), WMCR V527/PS1-905.
71. Schäffer, "A Glimpse of the Head-hunters of Formosa," unpublished manuscript, n.d. [ca. 1909], WMCR M79/2, published posthumously in Lang, *An Adventurous Woman Abroad*, 236–63.
72. Schäffer, *Old Indian Trails* (1911), 175–78.
73. [Mary Schäffer] to "Dear Ones at Home," Taipeh, Formosa, Japan, 19–31 December 1908, 8, WMCR M79/1.
74. Mary T.S. Schäffer, "A Glimpse of the Head-hunters of Formosa," unpublished manuscript, n.d. [ca. 1909], WMCR M79/2, published posthumously in Lang, *An Adventurous Woman Abroad*, 259–61.
75. Michale Lang, *An Adventurous Woman Abroad: The Selected Lantern Slides of Mary T.S. Schäffer* (Victoria, BC: Rocky Mountain Books, 2011). Janice Sanford Beck also used Schäffer's published article and unpublished letter from Japan as documentary fact in *No Ordinary Woman: The Story of Mary Schäffer Warren* (Calgary, AB: Rocky Mountain Books, 2001), 80–84.
76. Mary T.S. Schäffer, "A Glimpse of the Head-hunters of Formosa," unpublished manuscript, n.d. [ca. 1909], WMCR M79/2, published posthumously in Lang, *An Adventurous Woman Abroad*, 263.

77. James Daschuk, *Clearing the Plains: Disease, Politics of Starvation, and the Loss of Aboriginal Life* (Regina, SK: University of Regina Press, 2013), 176, 185.
78. Schaffer, "With the Hairy Ainus," 259.
79. Mary T.S. Schäffer, "A Glimpse of the Head-hunters of Formosa," unpublished manuscript, n.d. [ca. 1909], WMCR M79/2, published posthumously in Lang, *An Adventurous Woman Abroad*, 250. Taihoku was the Japanese name for Taipeh, the Chinese name. Schäffer and Adams used the names interchangeably.
80. [Mary Schäffer] to "Dear Ones at Home," Taipeh, Formosa, Japan, 19–25 December 1908, 3, WMCR M79/1.
81. Ibid., 4.
82. Molly Adams to "F.B.," "written on the steamer of the Osaka Mercantile S.S. Co.," between Formosa and Japan, 3 January 1909, Adams Family Collection.
83. Ibid.
84. Molly Adams to Catherine Elkin, the Taiwan Railway Hotel, Taipeh, Formosa, 25–31 December 1908, Adams Family Collection.
85. Molly Adams to Catherine Elkin and Cousin Alice, the Fujiya Hotel, Hot Mineral Springs, Miyanoshita, Sagami, Japan, 21 November 1908, Adams Family Collection. Adams wrote of the possibility of travelling with Lippincott in her letter to her sister and Cousin Alice from Tokyo, 1–5 December [1908], Adams Family Collection.
86. Molly Adams to Catherine Elkin and Cousin Alice, Tokyo, 1–5 December [1908], Adams Family Collection.
87. Molly Adams to "Jean," Imperial Hotel, Tokyo, and [Kyoto Hotel], Kyoto, 11 December [1908], Adams Family Collection.
88. Molly Adams to Catherine Elkin and Cousin Alice, Kyoto Hotel, Kyoto, 11–14 December [1908], Adams Family Collection.
89. "DIED. ADAMS," *New Haven Evening Register*, 25 January 1909, 2.
90. UK, Foreign and Overseas Registers of British Subjects, 1627–1965, Foreign Registers and Returns, RG33/125, General Register Office, National Archives of the United Kingdom, Kew, Surrey, England. Foreigners' graves in Karunga Cemetery were moved to the Kobe Municipal Foreign Cemetery in the 1960s. Cemeteries for foreigners were originally established to accommodate the need for Christian burial services for non-Japanese seamen and other travellers who died while in the area. Until the 1850s, such burials took place at sea. In 1854, the United States negotiated an agreement with Japan that provided for a burial ground. See Darren Swanson, "A Place for the Dead—the Foreign Cemeteries of Kobe and Osaka, 1867 to the Present Day," (2010), 2, 14, www.academia.edu/6123999/A_Place_for_the_Dead_The_Foreign_Cemeteries_of_Kobe_and_Osaka.
91. Schäffer, *Old Indian Trails* (1911), n.p.
92. Mary Schaffer Warren to Miss [Minnie] Nickell, Banff, 21 September [ca. 1935], WMCR M8.

93. [Mary Schäffer] to "Dear Ones at Home," Taipeh, Formosa, Japan, 19–25 December 1908, 7, WMCR M79/1.
94. Molly Adams to "Helène," Mount Stephen House, Field, BC, 24 September 1908, Adams Family Collection.
95. Molly Adams to Catherine Elkin, Berkeley, CA, 23 October 1904, Adams Family Collection.
96. For a deeper understanding of the sociohistorical context in which Adams lived as a spinster, see Trisha Franzen, *Spinsters and Lesbians: Independent Womanhood in the United States* (New York: New York University Press, 1996), 11–24, 47–77.
97. Molly Adams to Ida Ogilvie, Mount Stephen House, Field, BC, 26 September [1908], Adams Family Collection.
98. Schäffer, "A Glimpse of the Head-hunters of Formosa," unpublished manuscript, n.d. [ca. 1909], WMCR M79/2, published posthumously in Lang, *An Adventurous Woman Abroad*, 236–63.
99. Mary T.S. Schäffer, "A Recently Explored Lake in the Rocky Range of Canada," *Bulletin of the Geographical Society of Philadelphia* 7, no. 3 (July 1909): 123–34; Mary T.S. Schaffer, "Haunts of the Wild Flowers of the Canadian Rockies (Within reach of the Canadian Pacific Railroad)," *Canadian Alpine Journal* 3 (1911): 130–35; Mary T.S. Schäffer, "Hunting a Lost Lake," *Travel* (May 1911), 321–23, 364; Mary T.S. Schaffer, "The Finding of Lake Maligne," *Canadian Alpine Journal* 4 (1912): 92–97; Mary T.S. Schäffer, *Untrodden Paths in the Canadian Rockies* (Minneapolis, MN: Soo Line, ca. 1910).
100. For a description of the process, see James Boniface Schriever, "Colouring Lantern Slides," in *Complete Self-Instructing Library of Practical Photography*, vol. 5, *Photographic Printing Part II: Copying, Enlarging, Lantern Slides* (Scranton, PA: American School of Art and Photography, 1909), 341–48.
101. "Explorations in the Canadian Rockies," *Bulletin of the Geographical Society of Philadelphia* 9, no. 1 (1911): 101–02; "Illustrated Lecture," *Daily Local News* (West Chester, PA), 2 March 1911, clipping file "Schaeffer, M.," Chester County Archives, West Chester, PA.
102. Mary Schäffer to George Vaux Jr., Banff, 21 November 1911, WMCR Vaux Collection Addition 2007.
103. Mary Schäffer to George Vaux Jr., Banff, 16 December 1911, WMCR Vaux Collection Addition 2007.
104. Hudson's Bay Company, *Athabasca and McKenzie* [*sic*] *Rivers Transport Effective 15th May, 1911* (brochure), Winnipeg, MB: R.H. Hall, Fur Trade Commissioner, n.d., WMCR M79/15.
105. Molly Adams to Ida Ogilvie, Mount Stephen House, Field, BC, 26 September [1908], Adams Family Collection. Agnes Laut (1871–1936) was born in Ontario and moved permanently to New York State in 1901. She published a story of her journey. See Agnes C. Laut, "Fifteen Hundred Miles Down the Saskatchewan, Illustrated from Photographs," *Scribner's Magazine* 45 (January–June 1909): 459–74.

106. Mary Schäffer to George Vaux Jr., Banff, 16 December 1911, WMCR Vaux Collection Addition 2007. Schäffer likely obtained the Hudson's Bay Company brochure during this visit to Edmonton.
107. Mary Schäffer to George Vaux Jr., Banff, 21 March 1912, WMCR Vaux 1 Series.
108. Mary Schäffer to George Vaux Jr., Banff, 15–17 April 1912, WMCR Vaux 1 Series.
109. Beck, *No Ordinary Woman*, 84.
110. Mary [Schäffer] Warren to George Vaux Jr., Banff, 13 October 1915, WMCR Vaux 1 Series. Stella (Estelle) Painter's husband was Walter S. Painter, who had been appointed chief architect for the Canadian Pacific Railway in 1906 and worked on a number of projects in the Banff area, including additions to the Banff Springs Hotel, the Cave and Basin Hot Springs, and various railway stations.
111. Mrs. William Warren, "America from the Front: Opinions on Our Attitude Expressed by a Canadian Soldier," *New York Times*, 30 April 1916, 18; Mary S. Warren, "Americans at the Front: A Mother Who Would Give Another Son to the Allies," *New York Times*, 25 October 1916, 10; and, Mary S. Warren, "A Letter from the Somme Battle Front," [*Daily Local News*, West Chester, PA, ca. late November 1917], WMCR M553. An Anglican minister, William Henderson Watts, read the first letter and contacted Schäffer, sparking the beginning of a two-year-long private correspondence in which she expressed her embarrassment and dismay with public opinion in the United States against sympathizing with or assisting Britain in the war. See Hugh A. Dempsey, "Mary Warren's Letters from the Home Front 1916–1917," *Alberta History* 63, no. 1 (Winter 2015): 2–15.
112. "Sargeant Sidney J. Unwin—Canadian Artillery," *Canadian Alpine Journal* 8 (1917): 130–32.
113. "A lecture under the auspices…," *Crag and Canyon* (Banff, AB), 12 January 1918, 8.
114. Mary S. Warren, "In the Heart of the Canadian Rockies with Horse and Camera, Part I and Part II," lantern slide show typescripts, WMCR M79/10C. An illustrated version of the scripts is published posthumously in Lang, *An Adventurous Woman Abroad*, 70–196.
115. Mary S. Warren, "The Byways of Banff," *Canadian Alpine Journal* 10 (1919): 78–91; M.S.W., "Attractions in the Canadian Rockies," *Crag and Canyon* (Banff, AB), 4 September 1920, 6; Mary Schaeffer Warren, "Ptarmigan Valley Twenty Years Ago," *Trail Riders of the Canadian Rockies Bulletin* 10 (16 July 1926): 1–3; Mary Schaeffer Warren, "A Personal Touch of One of the Great Trail Riders of the North," *Trail Riders of the Canadian Rockies Bulletin* 14 (May 1927): 4; Mary Schaeffer Warren, "A Short Synopsis of the Work of the Palliser Expedition," *Trail Riders of the Canadian Rockies Bulletin* 14 (May 1927): 8.
116. See the Bibliography for a list of Schäffer's unpublished and draft manuscripts.
117. "Married in Vancouver—Three Cheers," *Crag and Canyon* (Banff, AB), 3 July 1915, 2.
118. "Will and Mary" [Warren] to Charles Reid, "At Sea," 29 March [ca. mid-1930s], WMCR M413/2; Mary [Schäffer Warren] to Humphrey Toms, Banff, 24 June 1936, WMCR M429/1.

Epilogue

1. Mary [Schäffer] Warren to Miss [Minnie] Nickell, Banff, 11 April [ca. 1936], WMCR M8.
2. The autochrome glass-slide colour positive, invented by the Lumière brothers in France, became commercially available in 1907. German immigrant photographer Hugo Viewegar of Edmonton made the first such photographs in Alberta in 1912. See Colleen Skidmore, "Imaging the West: Hugo Viewegar and the Autochrome in Canada," *History of Photography* 27 (Winter 2003): 342–48, and Colleen Skidmore, "'Touring an Other's Reality': Aboriginals, Immigrants, and Autochromes," *Ethnologies* 26, no. 1 (2004): 145–64. The Kodachrome negative-positive colour process was introduced in the mid-1930s, followed by the Ektachrome colour slide positive in the 1940s.

Bibliography

This bibliography includes primary and secondary material. Primary material is organized alphabetically by the archive or other collection in which it located to aid current and future readers and researchers seeking the material. Original published or handwritten spellings of Mary Schäffer's and Mary W. (Molly) Adams's names have been retained.

Primary Documents and Historical Archives

Academy of Natural Sciences of Drexel University, Academy Library and Archives (*Philadelphia, PA*)

Charles Schaffer 1882–1890 Correspondence Folder. ANSP Coll. 567.

Charles Schaffer 1891–1898 Correspondence Folder. ANSP Coll. 567.

Geological Photographs from Mrs. Charles Schaeffer. ANSP Coll. 485.

Mrs. Charles Schaffer Correspondence Folder. ANSP Coll. 567.

Act of Incorporation and By-Laws of the Academy of Natural Sciences of Philadelphia, Philadelphia, June 1903.

"Additions to the Museum." *Proceedings of the Academy of Natural Sciences of Philadelphia* 56, no. 3 (September–December 1904): 856–64.

"Additions to the Museum, Plants." *Proceedings of the Academy of Natural Sciences of Philadelphia*, 56, no. 3 (September–December 1904): 863–64.

Atkinson, W. Biddle, ed. *The Physicians and Surgeons of the United States, 1878*. Philadelphia: Charles Robson, 1878.

Brown, Stewardson. "Botanizing in the Canadian Rockies." *Proceedings of the Academy of Natural Sciences of Philadelphia* 58, no. 3 (October–December 1906): 429–30.

Chas. Schäffer to Mr. Stone, Philadelphia, 19 June 1900. ANSP Coll. 450.

Harshberger, John W. *The Botanists of Philadelphia*. Philadelphia, 1899.

"List of Indian implements rec'd from Mrs. Chas Schaffer," 3 March 1904. ANSP Coll. 241.

Mary T.S. Schäffer to Dr. Nolan, Philadelphia, 2 April 1896. ANSP Coll. 567.
Proceedings of the Academy of Natural Sciences of Philadelphia 55 (1903).
"Report of Librarian." *Proceedings of the Academy of Natural Sciences of Philadelphia* 56, no. 3 (September–December 1904): 842–44.
"Report of the Botanical Section." *Proceedings of the Academy of Natural Sciences of Philadelphia* 56, no. 3 (September–December 1904): 851–52.
"Schäffer, Chas. M.D.," Academy of Natural Sciences of Philadelphia membership card. ANSP Membership card file.
"Schäffer, Mrs. Mary T.S.," Academy of Natural Sciences of Philadelphia membership card. ANSP Membership card file.

American Philosophical Society Library *(Philadelphia, PA)*

Minutes of the Board of Directors, Geographical Club of Philadelphia, March 30, 1891–December 10, 1895. Manuscripts Collection no. 93.
Minutes of the Board of Directors, Geographical Club of Philadelphia, No. 1 Jan 7, 1896–Oct 14, 1908. Minutes Book, Board of Directors. 1997-787ms, Manuscripts Collection no. 93.
Scrapbook—Geographical Society of Philadelphia 1891–1903. Manuscripts Collection no. 93.
The Unlabelled Minutes Book of the Board of Directors of the Geographical Society of Philadelphia for 11 November 1908–12 April 1916. 1997-787ms, Manuscripts Collection no. 93.

"Adams, Miss Mary W." Geographical Society of Philadelphia membership card. Card file box 1, 97-787ms(30), Manuscripts Collection no. 93.
"Board of Directors." *Bulletin of the Geographical Society of Philadelphia* 4, no. 1 (January 1904): Inside front cover.
"List of Members of the Geographical Society of Philadelphia." *Bulletin of the Geographical Society of Philadelphia* 7, no. 2 (April 1909): 101–22.
Schäffer, Mary T.S. "Among the Sources of the Saskatchewan and Athabasca Rivers." *Bulletin of the Geographical Society of Philadelphia* 6, no. 2 (April 1908): 48–62.
———. "Explorations in the Canadian Rockies." *Bulletin of the Geographical Society of Philadelphia* 9, no. 1 (1911): 101–02.
———. "A Recently Explored Lake in the Rocky Range of Canada." *Bulletin of the Geographical Society of Philadelphia* 7, no. 3 (July 1909): 123–34.
Schäffer, Mrs. Charles. "The Valleys of the Saskatchewan with Horse and Camera." *Bulletin of the Geographical Society of Philadelphia* 5, no. 2 (April 1907): 108–14.

Barnard Archives and Special Collections, Barnard Library, Barnard College *(New York, NY)*

Committee in Instruction 1900–1910. BC 19.1, vol. 1.

Dean's Office Records, 1894–1952, Series 2, 1901–1907.

Faculty, Staff, Visitors—Biographical Files BC 34. 1144. Ogilvie, Ida (Geology).

Minutes of the Faculty 1900–1912. BC 6.2, vol. 2.

Barnard College, *The Mortarboard 1904–1908* [yearbook].

Chester County Archives *(West Chester, PA)*

"Illustrated Lecture." *Daily Local News* (West Chester, PA), 2 March 1911. Clipping file "Schaeffer, M."

"Mrs. Schaffer's New Book." *Daily Local News* (West Chester, PA), 13 June 1911. Clipping file "Schaeffer, M."

Sister [Mary Schäffer]. "The Flora of Canada: Mrs. Charles Schaffer, Formerly Miss Mary T. Sharpless, Writes of Her Work upon a Book Devoted to Scientific Research." *Daily Local News* (West Chester, PA), 15 November 1905. Clipping file "Schaeffer, M."

"Son of West Chester Wins High Honors." *Daily Local News* (West Chester, PA), July 1921. Clipping file "Sharpless, F."

Columbia University Archives *(New York, NY)*

Directories of Officers and Students, 1900–1908.

Instructors Appointment Cards. Index box 1.

Office of the President. Administrative correspondence. Series I: Central Files, 1895–1971. Box 1.

Glenbow Museum, Library and Archives *(Calgary, AB)*

Chas. Schäffer to Tom Wilson, Philadelphia, 8 February 1900. M1322/f17.

Chas. Schäffer to Tom Wilson, Philadelphia, 7 May 1903. M1322/f17.

M.T.S. Schäffer to Tom Wilson, Field, BC, 1 September [1900]. M1322/f17.

Mary [Schäffer] Warren to Tom Wilson, Banff, AB, 15 August 1922 M1322/f19.

Mary [Schäffer] Warren to Tom Wilson, Banff, AB, 2 August 1926. M1322/f19.

Historical Society of Pennsylvania *(Philadelphia, PA)*

Schäffer, Charles. "Meteorological record books, 1860–1903." Am.819.

Scrapbook presented by Mrs. Charles Schäffer, 12 March 1904: "Serena, Emily and Priscilla Potts's scrap book, 1825." WZZ.543.

Library of Congress *(Washington, DC)*

Papers of Frances Benjamin Johnston, 1855–1954, Manuscript Division.

Frances Benjamin Johnston Collection [Photographs], Prints and Photographs Division.

Ellen M. Henrotin to Frances Benjamin Johnston, Chicago, 12 April 1900, 24 April 1900, 25 May 1900. Reel 5, Papers of Frances Benjamin Johnston, 1855–1954 (Microfilm Reel Edition), Manuscript Division.

Henry Troth to Frances Benjamin Johnston, Philadelphia, 7 June 1900. Reel 5, Papers of Frances Benjamin Johnston, 1855–1954 (Microfilm Reel Edition), Manuscript Division.

Henry Troth to Frances Benjamin Johnston, list accompanying letter, Philadelphia, 7 June 1900. Reel 20, Papers of Frances Benjamin Johnston, 1855–1954 (Microfilm Reel Edition), Manuscript Division.

Alfred Stieglitz to Frances Benjamin Johnston, Lake George, NY, 8 June 1900. Reel 5, Papers of Frances Benjamin Johnston, 1855–1954 (Microfilm Reel Edition), Manuscript Division.

Frances Benjamin Johnston. Master of generic letter sent to invitees, n.d. [ca. 11 June 1900]. Reel 20, Papers of Frances Benjamin Johnston, 1855–1954 (Microfilm Reel Edition), Manuscript Division.

Mary T.S. Schäffer to Frances Benjamin Johnston, Philadelphia, 12 June 1900, n.d. [ca. 25 June 1900]. Reel 20, Papers of Frances Benjamin Johnston, 1855–1954 (Microfilm Reel Edition), Manuscript Division.

Mary T.S. Schäffer to Frances Benjamin Johnston, Philadelphia, 24 June 1900. Reel 9, Papers of Frances Benjamin Johnston, 1855–1954 (Microfilm Reel Edition), Manuscript Division.

Nantucket Historical Association Research Library *(Nantucket, MA)*

Sharp Family Papers 1872–1989, MS270.

The National Archives at Philadelphia *(Philadelphia, PA)*

Adams, Mary W. US Passport Application, 20 May 1908. Roll 0061, certificates 52785–3684, 14 May 1908–21 May 1908. Washington, DC: National Archives and Records Administration.

Passenger Lists of Vessels Arriving at New York, NY, 1897–1957. Microfilm Publication T715. Records of the Immigration and Naturalization Service, National Archives at Washington, DC.

Schäffer, Mary T.S. US Passport Application, 28 April 1908. Roll 0059, certificates 50879–1827, 27 April 1908–05 May 1908. Washington, DC: National Archives and Records Administration.

United States Federal Censuses: 1860, 1870, 1880, 1900, 1910, 1920, 1930, and 1940. Washington, DC: National Archives and Records Administration.

National Museum of American History, Smithsonian Institution *(Washington, DC)*

Mary Schäffer Photograph Collection, Division of Culture & the Arts.

New Haven Free Public Library *(New Haven, CT)*

New Haven Directory. New Haven, CT: Price and Lee, Co., 1894.

The New Haven Register [newspaper].

New York Public Library (Stephen A. Schwarzman Building) *(New York, NY)*

"Annual Members' Exhibition: A Review by Mr. Herbert A. North, Read at the Stated Meeting, December 14, 1898." *Journal of the Photographic Society of Philadelphia* 5, no. 1 (January 1899): 5–8.

"Proceedings of the Society." *Journal of the Photographic Society of Philadelphia* 5, no. 3 (March 1899): 17–18.

"Canadian Pacific Excursion." *Journal of the Photographic Society of Philadelphia* 5, no. 4 (April 1899): 36.

"Proceedings of the Society." *Journal of the Photographic Society of Philadelphia* 5, no. 4 (April 1899): 25–28.

"Proceedings of the Society." *Journal of the Photographic Society of Philadelphia* 5, no. 5 (May and June 1899): 41–43.

"Proceedings of the Society." *Journal of the Photographic Society of Philadelphia* 5, no. 6 (October, November, and December 1899): 60.

"Annual Report of the Board of Directors." *Journal of the Photographic Society of Philadelphia* 6, no. 3 (April 1900): 27.

"Members' Annual Exhibition: A Criticism by C. Yarnall Abbott, Read at the Stated Meeting January 9, 1901." *Journal of the Photographic Society of Philadelphia* 7, no. 1 (December 1900–January 1901): 8–13.

"List of Members, March 1st, 1903." *Journal of the Photographic Society of Philadelphia* 9, no. 1 (January–February 1903): 9.

"Proceedings of the Society." *Journal of the Photographic Society of Philadelphia* 9, no. 4 (October, November, December 1903): 29–36.

"Proceedings of the Society." *Journal of the Photographic Society of Philadelphia* 12, no. 1 (January–February 1906): 2.

Philadelphia City Archives *(Philadelphia, PA)*

Philadelphia City Archives, Property Deed entered June 13, 1904, Lot no. 76, Plan Book no. 1N, p. 21, 1309 Arch Street, 10 Ward, Division no. 1.

Philadelphia City Archives, Property Deed entered August 1, 1867, Lot no. 76, Plan Book no. 1N, p. 21, 1309 Arch Street, 10 Ward, Division no. 1.

Philadelphia Street Directories. Philadelphia: Free Library of Philadelphia, 1978. Microfilm.

Private Collections

Letters, Diaries, and Photograph Album of Mary W. (Molly) Adams, 1893–1909. Adams Family Collection.

"Woman Lost in the Mountains." *Pasadena Star* (California), 14 December 1904. (Transcribed version). Adams Family Collection.

Letters, Diaries, and Photograph Albums of Henrietta L. Tuzo, 1904–1917. Wilson Family Collection.

Provincial Archives of Alberta *(Edmonton, AB)*

"Mary S. Warren Will and Probate." Acc. 99.834, Calgary Probate Records Q–Z, Box 311, File 11210.

"William Warren Probate." Acc. 99.834, Calgary Probate Records Q–Z, Box 376, File 14269.

University of Alberta Libraries Bruce Peel Special Collections *(Edmonton, AB)*

Canadian Women's Press Club, Edmonton Branch. "Club Women's Records, Edmonton: Women's Institutes of Alberta, United Farm Women of Alberta." Canadian Women's Press Club, Edmonton Branch, 1916. Peel's Prairie Provinces Database 4201.

Gowan, Elsie Park. "The Jasper Story." Unpublished play, 1955.

Grand Trunk Pacific Railway Company General Passenger Dept. *The Canadian Rockies Yellowhead Pass Route: Two Hundred Miles of Majestic Mountain Scenery* (Promotional booklet). Winnipeg, 1911.

MacGregor, Daisy. Canadian Women's Press Club, Calgary Branch. *The Alberta Club Woman's Bluebook, 1917*. Calgary: Canadian Woman's [*sic*] Press Club, Calgary Branch, 1917. Peel's Prairie Provinces Database 4320.

Schaffer, Mary T.S. *Untrodden Paths in the Canadian Rockies*. Minneapolis, MN: Soo Line, ca. 1910.

University of Toronto Archives *(Toronto, ON)*

Henrietta L. Tuzo, "A Glimpse of the Saskatchewan," draft manuscripts, [1906]. John Tuzo Wilson Personal Papers, accn. B86-0066, box 59, file "Alpine materials."

Henrietta L. Tuzo to John Wilson, 4 October 1906. John Tuzo Wilson Personal Papers, accn. B86-0066, box 8, file 8.

Whyte Museum of the Canadian Rockies *(Banff, AB)*

Mary Schäffer correspondence

Mary Schäffer to George Vaux Jr., 1904–1927. WMCR Vaux 1 Series.

Mary Schäffer to George Vaux Jr., 1904–1927. WMCR Vaux Collection Addition 2007.

[Mary Schäffer] to "Dear Ones at Home," Taipeh, Formosa, Japan, 19–31 December 1908. WMCR M79/1.

Mary Schäffer Warren to Mr. [William Henderson] Watts, Banff, 22 May 1916. WMCR M553.

Mary [Schäffer] Warren to Mr. [Raymond] Zillmer, Banff, 1928. WMCR M8.

Mary [Schäffer] Warren to Humphrey Toms, Banff, 1935–1937. WMCR M429/1.

Mary [Schäffer] Warren to Miss [Minnie] Nickell, Banff, [ca. 1935–1937]. WMCR M8.

Mary [Schäffer] Warren to "My dear unseen friend," Banff, 12 November [ca. 1935], WMCR M8.

Mary Townsend Sharples Schaffer Warren to Miss [Lillian] Gest, Banff, 23 May [ca. 1938]. WMCR M67/8.

"Will and Mary" [Warren] to Charles Reid, ca. 1935–1937. WMCR M413/2.

Mary Schäffer draft manuscripts

"An American Boy in the Canadian Rockies." [4 drafts]. n.d. WMCR M79/4.

"The Beginning, the Middle, and the End of a Hunting Trip." n.d. WMCR M79/13.

"The Byways of Banff." [Typescript published with revisions in *Canadian Alpine Journal* 1919]. WMCR M79/5.

"A Chapter of Accidents." n.d. WMCR M79/7. [Published posthumously in Beck, Janice Sanford. *No Ordinary Woman: The Story of Mary Schäffer Warren*, 146–50. Calgary, AB: Rocky Mountain Books, 2001.]

"Fairy-land of the North." n.d. WMCR M79/7.

"A Glimpse of the Head-hunters of Formosa." n.d. [ca. 1909]. WMCR M79/2. [Published posthumously in Lang, Michale. *An Adventurous Woman Abroad: The Selected Lantern Slides of Mary T.S. Schäffer*, 236–63. Victoria, BC: Rocky Mountain Books, 2011.]

"The Heart of a Child." n.d. WMCR M79/7.

"Jonas." n.d. WMCR M79/7.

"Lake Louise of Early Days." n.d. WMCR M79/7.

"Locating and Measuring Lake Maligne." n.d. WMCR M79/2.

"The Monarch of the Plains." n.d. WMCR M79/2.

"My Garden." n.d. WMCR M79/2. [Published posthumously in Beck, Janice Sanford. *No Ordinary Woman: The Story of Mary Schäffer Warren*, 152–57. Calgary, AB: Rocky Mountain Books, 2001.]

"A New Year in the Wilds." n.d. WMCR M79/6. [Published posthumously in Beck, Janice Sanford. *No Ordinary Woman: The Story of Mary Schäffer Warren*, 191–201. Calgary, AB: Rocky Mountain Books, 2001.]

"A Ptarmigan Story." n.d. WMCR M79/7. [Published posthumously in Beck, Janice Sanford. *No Ordinary Woman: The Story of Mary Schäffer Warren*, 150–52. Calgary, AB: Rocky Mountain Books, 2001.]

"Story of Famous Ride of Doctor, Red Deer Valley." n.d. WMCR M79/5.

"The Story of Revelstoke." n.d. WMCR M79/5. [Published posthumously in Beck, Janice Sanford. *No Ordinary Woman: The Story of Mary Schäffer Warren*, 157–69. Calgary, AB: Rocky Mountain Books, 2001.]

Untitled manuscript. [A story of "Stella"]. n.d. WMCR M79/2.

"Title not decided." Unpublished manuscript, second draft. n.d. WMCR M79/3. [Published posthumously as "The 1911 Expedition to Maligne Lake," in E.J. Hart, *A Hunter of Peace: Mary T.S. Schäffer's Old Indian Trails of the Canadian Rockies*, introduction and edited by E.J. Hart, 131–53. Banff, AB: Whyte Museum of the Canadian Rockies, 1980, and in E.J. Hart, *A Hunter of Peace: Mary T.S. Schäffer's Old Indian Trails of the Canadian Rockies*, 2nd ed., introduction by E.J. Hart, foreword by Jennifer Rutkair, 151–83. Banff, AB: Whyte Museum of the Canadian Rockies, 2014.]

"Trail Life at Lake Louise." n.d. WMCR M79/5.

Untitled history of Howse, Yellowhead, and Athabasca passes. n.d. WMCR M79/5.

M.S.W. "Tepee Life in Northern Hills." [1924]. WMCR M79/6. [Published posthumously in Beck, Janice Sanford. *No Ordinary Woman: The Story of Mary Schäffer Warren*, 170–91. Calgary, AB: Rocky Mountain Books, 2001.]

Schaffer, Mary T.S. "Flora of the Saskatchewan and Athabasca River Tributaries." WMCR M79/2.

Warren, Mary S. "Palliser's Expedition: Some Intimate Glimpses." n.d. [published in the *Calgary Daily Herald*]. WMCR M79/8.

Lantern slide show typescripts

Warren, Mary S. "In the Heart of the Canadian Rockies with Horse and Camera, Part I." n.d. WMCR M79/10C. [Published posthumously in Lang, Michale. *An Adventurous Woman Abroad: The Selected Lantern Slides of Mary T.S. Schäffer*, 70–136. Victoria, BC: Rocky Mountain Books, 2011.]

Warren, Mary S. "In the Heart of the Canadian Rockies, Part II." n.d. WMCR M79/10C. [Published posthumously in Lang, Michale. *An Adventurous Woman Abroad: The Selected Lantern Slides of Mary T.S. Schäffer*, 137–96. Victoria, BC: Rocky Mountain Books, 2011.]

Miscellaneous materials

Agreement between Mary T.S. Schäffer & Stewardson Brown. Philadelphia, 12 April 1906. WMCR Vaux 1 Series.

"Cost of Bungalow to Date April 18." Handwritten account in WMCR Vaux Collection Addition 2007.

"Daring Explorers Make a Remarkable Trip to the Heart of the Canadian Rocky Mountains." Unnamed newspaper clipping, ca. October 1908. WMCR M79/9B.

Department of the Interior. *Sessional Paper No. 25, Dominion Parks: Report of the Commissioner of Dominion Parks, 1912*. Ottawa: Department of the Interior, 1912. WMCR M79/15-1.

Dorothy Sharp, Alpine Club of Canada application card. WMCR M2W/AC385-10.

Eric C. Sharpless to E.J. Hart, Wayne, PA, 30 March 1985. WMCR Schäffer Biography File.

George Vaux Jr. to United States Internal Revenue, Philadelphia, 1924. WMCR Vaux Collection Addition 2007.

Hudson's Bay Company. *Athabasca and McKenzie* [sic] *Rivers Transport Effective 15th May, 1911* (brochure). Winnipeg, MB: R.H. Hall, Fur Trade Commissioner, n.d. WMCR M79/15.

"Income Tax, United States Internal Revenue" [1914]. WMCR Vaux Collection Addition 2007.

"Last Will & Testament of Charles Schäffer/Died November 23, 1903/Will moved Decr 2, 1903." WMCR Vaux Collection Addition 2007.

"Last Will and Testament of Elizabeth Sharpless." WMCR Vaux Collection Addition 2007.

Lease documentation, Lot 23, Block 27 [Tarry-a-while], Banff, AB. WMCR M317.

Mary W. (Molly) Adams. 1908 transcribed diary. WMCR M79/11.

Moore Family Fonds WMCR V439/PS1.

M.W.A. and M.T.S.S. [Mary W. Adams and Mary Townsend Sharples Schäffer]. Photograph album, "From Laggan to the Wilcox Pass 1906." [ca. 1906–1907]. WMCR V527/PD-4.

Schäffer, Mary, and Mary W. (Molly) Adams. Photograph album. [ca. 1906–1908]. WMCR V527/PD-1.

Schäffer, Mary. Photograph album [Japan, 1908–09]. [ca. 1909]. WMCR V527/PD-5.

Schäffer, Mary. Lantern Slides. WMCR V527/PS1 and WMCR V439/PS1.

Schäffer, Mary. Scrapbook. WMCR M79/9B.

Mary Schäffer to George Vaux Jr., letter and Putnam's Sons' bill, Banff, received by Vaux 9 May 1911. WMCR Vaux Collection Addition 2007.

Sharpless, Caroline. "Trip to Jasper Park, Rocky Mountains, Canada, May 29th–August 16th, 1911." Transcribed diary. WMCR M79/12.

Vaux family photographs from 1904 excursion to the Canadian Rockies. WMCR M107/V653/NA-1235 to 1335.

Vaux, William S., Jr. "Climbing in the Selkirk Mountains." *Minneapolis Journal*, 24 December 1898, n.p. WMCR M107.

Mary Schäffer's Published Works

Books

Brown, Stewardson, and Mrs. Charles Schäffer. *Alpine Flora of the Canadian Rocky Mountains*. New York and London: G.P. Putnam's Sons/Knickerbocker Press, 1907.

Schäffer, Mary T.S. *Old Indian Trails: Incidents of Camp and Trail Life, Covering Two Years' Exploration through the Rocky Mountains of Canada*. New York: G.P. Putnam's Sons; Toronto: William Briggs, 1911. Reprint with revised map, 1912.

Articles and other publications

Schaffer, Mary S.S. [*sic*]. "Sir James Hector." *Rod and Gun in Canada* 5, no. 8 (January 1904): 416–18.

Schaffer, Mary S.S. [*sic*]. "The Burial of Cher-on-kee." *Rod and Gun in Canada* 5, no. 11 (April 1904): 530–32.

Schaffer, Mary M. [*sic*]. "Breaking the Way." *Rod and Gun in Canada* 6, no. 3 (August 1904): 111–12.

Schaffer, Mrs. Charles. "The Infinite Variety of the Canadian Rockies." *Rod and Gun in Canada*, n.d. Clipping, WMCR M79/9B.

Sister [Mary Schäffer]. "The Flora of Canada: Mrs. Charles Schaffer, Formerly Miss Mary T. Sharpless, Writes of Her Work Upon a Book Devoted to Scientific Research." *Daily Local News* (West Chester, PA), 15 November 1905. Clipping file "Schaeffer, M.," Chester County Archives, West Chester, PA, and in WMCR M79/9B.

Schäffer, Mary T.S. "Flora of the Saskatchewan and Athabasca River Tributaries." *Canadian Alpine Journal* 1, no. 2 (1907–1908): 268–70.

Schäffer, Mary T.S. "Untrodden Ways." *Canadian Alpine Journal* 1, no. 2 (1907–1908): 288–94.

Schäffer, Mrs. Charles. "The Valleys of the Saskatchewan with Horse and Camera." *Bulletin of the Geographical Society of Philadelphia* (April 1907): 108–14.

Schäffer, Mary T.S. "Among the Sources of the Saskatchewan and Athabasca Rivers." *Bulletin of the Geographical Society of Philadelphia* 6 (April 1908): 48–62.

Schäffer, Mary T.S. "A Recently Explored Lake in the Rocky Range of Canada." *Bulletin of the Geographical Society of Philadelphia* 7, no. 3 (July 1909): 123–34.

[Schäffer, Mary T.S.] "Jasper Park: The Mountain Park on the Line of the Grand Trunk Pacific Railway." *Canadian Life and Resources* (January 1910): 20–23. [Illustrated with photographs by Mary Schäffer.] WMCR M79/9B.

Schäffer, Mary T.S. *Untrodden Paths in the Canadian Rockies*. Minneapolis, MN: Soo Line, ca. 1910. University of Alberta Libraries Bruce Peel Special Collections.

Schaffer, Mrs. M.T.S. "With the Hairy Ainus." *Travel and Exploration* (London) 3 (January to June 1910): 377–84.

Schaffer, Mary T.S. "Haunts of the Wild Flowers of the Canadian Rockies (Within reach of the Canadian Pacific Railroad)." *Canadian Alpine Journal* 3 (1911): 130–35.

Schaffer, Mary T.S. "With the Hairy Ainus." *Travel* (New York) 16 (April 1911): 259–62.

Schäffer, Mary T.S. "Hunting a Lost Lake." *Travel* (New York) (May 1911): 321–23, 364.

Schaffer, Mary T.S. "The Finding of Lake Maligne." *Canadian Alpine Journal* 4 (1912): 92–97.

Warren, Mrs. William. "America from the Front: Opinions on Our Attitude Expressed by a Canadian Soldier." *New York Times*, 30 April 1916, 18.

Warren, Mary S. "Americans at the Front: A Mother Who Would Give Another Son to the Allies." *New York Times*, 25 October 1916, 10.

Warren, Mary S. "A Letter from the Somme Battle Front." [*Daily Local News*, West Chester, PA, ca. late November 1917]. Clipping, WMCR M79/9B.

"Sargeant Sidney J. Unwin—Canadian Artillery." *Canadian Alpine Journal* 8 (1917): 130–32.

Warren, Mary S. "Palliser's Expedition: Some Intimate Glimpses." *Calgary Daily Herald*, n.d. Clipping, WMCR M79/8.

Warren, Mary S. "The Byways of Banff." *Canadian Alpine Journal* 10 (1919): 78–91.

M.S.W. "Attractions in the Canadian Rockies." *Crag and Canyon* (Banff, AB), 4 September 1920, 6.

Warren, Mary Schaeffer. "Ptarmigan Valley Twenty Years Ago." *Trail Riders of the Canadian Rockies Bulletin* 10 (16 July 1926): 1–3.

Warren, Mary Schaeffer. "A Personal Touch of One of the Great Trail Riders of the North." *Trail Riders of the Canadian Rockies Bulletin* 14 (May 1927): 4.

Warren, Mary Schaeffer. "A Short Synopsis of the Work of the Palliser Expedition." *Trail Riders of the Canadian Rockies Bulletin* 14 (May 1927): 8.

Historical published reviews and commentary on Schäffer's work

A.H. "Mary Warren." *Canadian Alpine Journal* 27 (1939–1940): 108–10.

"Anyone who has not read...." *Crag and Canyon* (Banff, AB), 2 September 1911, 8.

"The Canadian Rockies: A Book of Unknown Trails by Mary T.S. Schaffer." *Springfield Republican* (Massachusetts), 23 July 1911.

[Mrs. Emily Murphy]. "'Old Indian Trails' by Mary. T.S. Schaffer." *Winnipeg Telegram* [attributed in Schäffer's handwriting, n.d., ca. 1911]. Clipping, WMCR M79/9B.

"First Ladies to Visit Cave." *The Revelstoke Herald and Railway Men's Journal* (10 August 1905): 1. Clipping, WMCR M79/9B.

"Foreign Parts." *The Sun* (New York, NY), 24 June 1911, 7.

J.W.H. [Julia Wilmotte Henshaw]. "The Bookshelf: Old Indian Trails in [*sic*] the Canadian Rockies." *The Chronicle: A Weekly Newspaper for Women* (Vancouver) 1, no. 8 (20 October 1911): 21.

Kipling, Rudyard. "Letters to the Family." *Collier's* 41, no. 5 (25 April 1908): 13–14. Reprinted in Rudyard Kipling, *Letters of Travel (1892–1913)*, 188–89. London: Macmillan & Co., 1920. Excerpt clipping, WMCR M79/9B.

Love, Currie. "Pushing Ahead of Trails." *Canada Monthly* 10, no. 10 (August 1911), 273–79.

"Lure of the Rockies." *Brooklyn Daily Eagle* (Brooklyn, NY), 7 June 1911, 24. Clipping, WMCR M79/9B.

"Maligne Lake One of World's Beauty Spots." *Edmonton Daily Bulletin*, 9 August 1911. Clipping, WMCR M79/9B.

"The Monthly Record: Mrs. Schäffer's Survey of Maligne Lake." *Geographical Journal* 40, no. 3 (September 1912): 334–35.

"Mrs. Schaefer Tells of Rocky Mountains." *Daily Local News* (West Chester, PA), n.d. [ca. 1907]. Clipping, WMCR M79/9B.

"Mrs. Schäffer's Discovery and Survey of Lake Maligne, Canadian Rockies." *Geographical Journal* 39, no. 4 (April 1912): 379–81.

"Mrs. Schäffer's Survey of Maligne Lake." *Geographical Journal* 40, no. 3 (September 1912): 334–35.

"Mrs. Schaffer's New Book." *West Chester Local News* (West Chester, PA), 13 June 1911. Clipping, WMCR M79/9B.

"Now Ready." Display ad G.P. Putnam's Sons. *New York Times*, 14 December 1907, n.p., and 18 December 1907, 5.

"Old Indian Trails of the Canadian Rockies." *Portland Telegram* (Oregon), 5 August 1911. Clipping, WMCR M79/9B.

"Philadelphia Book News." *New York Times*, 23 April 1911, 257.

"Philadelphia Woman Names New Mountain," *Evening Journal* (Edmonton, AB), 8 August 1911.

"Putnam's New Books." Display ad. *New York Times*, 18 June 1911, BR385.

"Romance in the Heart of Rockies: Prospectors Bring Story of Riches on G.T.P. Route and Romantic Tale of Society Dames." *Vancouver Daily World*, 3 October 1908, 1. Clipping, WMCR M79/9B.

"Romantic Canada." *The Nation*, 28 September [1911]. Clipping, WMCR M79/9B.

"Schäffer, Mrs. Mary T.S." A.L.A. *Booklist: A Guide to the Best New Books* 8, no. 2 (October 1911): 72.

Thomson, John. "Old Indian Trails." *Public Ledger* (Philadelphia, PA), n.d. Clipping, WMCR M79/9B.

"Two Women in an Untrod Land: Exploring in the Canadian Rockies, They Add a New Lake to the Map." *New York Times Saturday Review of Books*, 16 July 1911, BR3. Clipping, WMCR M79/9B.

Wheeler, Arthur O. "The Congress of Alpinism at Monaco." *Canadian Alpine Journal* 11 (1920): 65–68.

"A Woman in the Rockies." *The Argonaut* (San Francisco, CA), 19 August [1911]. Clipping, WMCR M79/9B.

"Women Who Have Revealed Hidden Paths." *Edmonton Journal*, 5 June 1911.

Historical Published Sources, 1859–1949

"American Women at Paris in 1900." *The Nineteen Hundred* 7, no. 1 (July 1898): 3–4.

Anderson, R.M. "John Macoun, 1832–1920." *Journal of Mammalogy* 2, no. 1 (February 1921): 32–35.

Baedeker, Karl. *The Dominion of Canada with Newfoundland and an Excursion to Alaska: Handbook for Travellers*. Leipsic [*sic*]: Karl Baedeker, 1900.

———. *The Dominion of Canada with Newfoundland and An Excursion to Alaska: Handbook for Travellers*. Leipzig: Karl Baedeker, 1907.

Barnes, Catharine Weed. "Photography as a Profession for Women." *American Amateur Photographer* 3, no. 5 (3 May 1891): 172–76.

———. "Photography from a Woman's Standpoint." *Anthony's Photographic Bulletin* 21, no. 2 (25 January 1890): 39–42. Reprinted in *Camera Fiends & Kodak Girls: 50 Selections by and about Women in Photography, 1840–1930*, edited by Peter E. Palmquist, 63–67. New York: Midmarch Arts Press, 1989.

———. "Why Ladies Should Be Admitted to Membership in Photographic Societies." *American Amateur Photographer* 1, no. 6 (December 1889): 223–24.

———. "Woman's Work: A Woman to Women." *American Amateur Photographer* 2, no. 5 (May 1890): 185–88.

———. "Women as Photographers." *American Amateur Photographer* 3, no. 9 (September 1891): 33–341.

Batchelor, John. *The Ainu and Their Folk-lore*. London: The Religious Tract Society, 1901.

Bentzon, Thomas. "Women at the Paris Exhibition." *The Outlook* 66, no. 5 (29 September 1900): 259–65.

Bird, Isabella. *Unbeaten Tracks in Japan: An Account of Travels on Horseback in the Interior* (2 volumes). New York: G.P. Putnam's Sons, 1881.

British Columbia Division of Vital Statistics. Civil Marriage Registration 034192, 1915. 1915-09-080192. Microfilm B11379.

Browne, John C. *History of the Photographic Society of Philadelphia*. Philadelphia: The Photographic Society of Philadelphia, 1884.

Bryce, P.H. *Report on the Indian Schools of Manitoba and the North-West Territories*. Ottawa: Government Printing Bureau, 1907.

———. *The Story of a National Crime: An Appeal to Justice for the Indians of Canada*. Ottawa: James Hope and Sons, 1922.

Bryn Mawr College. *Program Bryn Mawr College, 1894*. Philadelphia: Sherman & Co. Printers, 1894.

Connecticut Department of Health. *Connecticut Death Index, 1949–2001*. Hartford, CT: Connecticut Department of Health.

Coleman, A.P. "The Brazeau Ice-Field." *Geographical Journal* 21, no. 5 (May 1903): 502–10.

———. *The Canadian Rockies: New and Old Trails with 3 Maps and 41 Illustrations*. Toronto: Henry Frowde, 1912. First published London: T. Fisher Unwin, 1911. (Reprinted without maps or illustrations by Rocky Mountain Books, Surrey, BC, 2006).

Coulter, John M. *Manual of the Botany of the Rocky Mountain Region*. New York: American Book Company, 1885.

———. *New Manual of Botany of the Central Rocky Mountains (Vascular Plants)*. New York: American Book Company, 1909.

Cope, Gilbert. *Genealogy of the Sharpless Family, Descended from John and Jane Sharples, Settlers Near Chester, Pennsylvania, 1682*. Philadelphia: Bi-Centennial Committee, 1887.

Crane, Frank W. "American Women Photographers." *Munsey's Magazine* 11, no. 4 (July 1894): 398–408.

Davie, Helen L. "Women in Photography." *Camera Craft* 5, no. 4 (August 1902): 130–38.

"DIED. ADAMS." *New Haven Evening Register*, 25 January 1909, 2.

"Dr. Daniel Lucius Adams," *New Haven Evening Register*, 5 January 1898, 3.

"Dr. D.L. Adams, Memoirs of the Father of Baseball." *The Sporting News*, 29 February 1896, 3.

"Editorial Note." *Canadian Alpine Journal* 1, no. 1 (1907): 137.

Emerson, Peter Henry. "Photography A Pictorial Art" [*sic*]. *The Amateur Photographer* 3 (19 March 1886): 138–39.

Farr, Edith M. *Contributions to a Catalogue of the Flora of the Canadian Rocky Mountains and Selkirk Range*. Philadelphia: University of Pennsylvania, 1907.

"Funeral Service for William Warren, Held at Vancouver, Fri," *Crag and Canyon* (Banff, AB), 23 July 1943, 1.

Harvard College. "William Boyd Cook." *Harvard College Class of 1904 Second Report, June, 1910*. Cambridge, MA: Crimson Printing Co., 1910.

Henshaw, Julia W. *Mountain Wild Flowers of America: A Simple and Popular Guide to the Names and Descriptions of the Flowers That Bloom Above the Clouds*. Boston: Ginn & Company, The Athenæum Press, 1906.

———. *Mountain Wild Flowers of Canada: A Simple and Popular Guide to the Names and Descriptions of the Flowers That Bloom Above the Clouds*. Toronto: William Briggs, 1906.

———. "The Mountain Wildflowers of Western Canada." *Canadian Alpine Journal* 1, no. 1 (1907): 130–37.

———. *Wild Flowers of the North American Mountains*. New York: Robert M. McBride & Company, 1915.

Hines, Richard, Jr. "Women and Photography." *American Amateur Photographer* 11, no. 3 (March 1899): 118–24.

———. "Women and Photography (continued from page 124)." *American Amateur Photographer* 11, no. 4 (April 1899): 144–52.

Holmes, Oliver Wendell. "The Stereoscope and the Stereograph." *Atlantic Monthly* 3, no. 20 (June 1859): 738–48. Reprinted in *Classic Essays on Photography*, edited by Alan Trachtenberg, 71–82 (New Haven, CT: Leete's Island Books, 1980).

Hughes, Jabez. "Photography as an Industrial Occupation for Women." *Anthony's Photographic Bulletin* 4 (1873): 162–66. Originally published in *The London Photo News*. Reprinted in *Camera Fiends & Kodak Girls: 50 Selections by and about Women in Photography, 1840–1930*, edited by Peter E. Palmquist, 29–36. New York: Midmarch Arts Press, 1989.

Humphrey, Zephine, with photographs by Mary W. Adams. "Five Women on the Trail." *Outing Magazine* 54 (April–September 1909): 195–205, 341–51, 426–33.

Johnston, Frances Benjamin. "What a Woman Can Do with a Camera." *Ladies' Home Journal* (September 1897): 6–7.

Keiley, Joseph T. "The Philadelphia Salon: Its Origins and Influence." *Camera Notes* 2, no. 3 (January 1899): 113–32.

Keller, I.A., and Stewardson Brown. *Handbook of the Flora of Philadelphia and Vicinity*. Philadelphia: Philadelphia Botanical Club, 1905.

Laut, Agnes C. "Fifteen Hundred Miles Down the Saskatchewan, Illustrated from Photographs." *Scribner's Magazine* 45 (January–June 1909): 459–74.

Martin, Alice. “Little Women of Japan.” *Harper’s Bazaar* 44 (November 1910): 635.

McEvoy, James. *Report on the Geology and Natural Resources of the Country Traversed by the Yellowhead Pass Route from Edmonton to Tête Jaune Cache Comprising Portions of Alberta and British Columbia*. Ottawa: Geological Survey of Canada, 1900.

Mitchell, Charles M. “The Third Philadelphia Photographic Salon.” *American Amateur Photographer* 12, no. 12 (December 1900): 560–68.

Morris, Alexander. *The Treaties of Canada with the Indians of Manitoba and the North-West Territories including the Negotiations on which they were based*. Toronto: Belfords, Clarke & Co., 1880. (Facsimile reprint Saskatoon, SK: Fifth House Publishers, 1991.)

“Mr. and Mrs. [*sic*] Vaux, of Philadelphia….” *Crag and Canyon* (Banff, AB), 27 August 1904, 6.

Munro, Janet. “Hosts of Mountain Oasis.” *Canadian National Railways Magazine*, 1929, 24–26. Reprinted in *This Wild Spirit: Women in the Rocky Mountains of Canada*, edited by Colleen Skidmore, 20–28. Edmonton: University of Alberta Press, 2006.

“New Canada Opened Up by New Railroad Line: Latest of Transcontinental Routes Taps Region of Great Wealth, Superb Scenery, and Boundless Possibilities for the Future.” *New York Times*, 4 June 1916, SM13.

National Council of Women of Canada. *Women of Canada: Their Life and Work*. [Ottawa], 1900.

Ogilvie, I.H. “The Effect of Superglacial Débris on the Advance and Retreat of Some Canadian Glaciers.” *Journal of Geology* 12, no. 8 (November–December 1904): 722–43.

———. “Geological Notes on the Vicinity of Banff, Alberta.” *Journal of Geology* 12, no. 5 (July–August 1904): 408–14.

Palmer, Howard. *Mountaineering and Exploration in the Selkirks: A Record of Pioneer Work Among the Canadian Alps, 1908–1912*. New York and London: G.P. Putnam’s Sons/Knickerbocker Press, 1914.

“The Paris Exposition.” *New York Times*, 9 June 1899, 1.

Pector, M.S. *Congrès international de photographie*. Paris: Gauthier-Villars, 1901.

“Progress in Photography. Collection of Specimens for the Paris Exposition. All the Work of American Women—A Proposed Exhibit in This City.” *Evening Star* (Washington, DC), 6 July 1900, 1, 11.

“Rev. Francis Adams.” *Lewiston Daily News* (ME), 26 July 1949, 2.

Schriever, James Boniface. “Colouring Lantern Slides.” In *Complete Self-Instructing Library of Practical Photography*. Vol. 5, *Photographic Printing Part II: Copying, Enlarging, Lantern Slides*, 341–48. Scranton, PA: American School of Art and Photography, 1909.

“Season’s Offering of Garden Books: Volumes Dealing with Out-of-Door Life Grow More Highly Specialized Year by Year.” *New York Times Saturday Review of Books*, 9 May 1908, 264.

A Short but Accurate History of H.C. White Stereoscopes and Stereoviews—in the Company’s Own Words. [publisher unknown], 1908.

“Some Salon Statistics.” *Camera Notes* 2, no. 3 (January 1899): 132.

Sreznewsky, W.I. "The Collection of Photographs Taken by American Women Amateur Photographers." Translated by Harold M. Leich. *Fotograficheskoe obozrienie* (1901), 1–5. Reprinted in *Ambassadors of Progress: American Women Photographers in Paris 1900–1901*, edited by Bronwyn A.E. Griffith, 190–91. Giverny, France: Musée d'Art Américain Giverny, 2001.

Stieglitz, Alfred. "Why American Pictorial Work Is Absent from the Paris Exhibition." *Amateur Photographer* 35 (20 July 1900): 44.

Stutfield, Hugh E.M., and J. Norman Collie. *Climbs & Exploration in the Canadian Rockies*. London: Longmans, Green and Co., 1903.

"The Third Annual Joint Exhibition of Photographs." *Photographic Times* 19, no. 394 (February 1889): 176–77.

"To Again Visit Mountain Lake." *Edmonton Bulletin*, 5 June 1911. Clipping, WMCR M79/9B.

[Tuzo, H.L.] "A Glimpse of the Saskatchewan." *Crag and Canyon* (Banff, AB), 8 September 1906, 1–2.

Tuzo, H.L. "A Glimpse of the Saskatchewan Concluded." *Crag and Canyon* (Banff, AB), 22 September 1906, 1–3.

Tuzo, Miss [H.L.] "Lady Explorers on the Trail. Through the Pipestone Pass to the Saskatchewan River." *Rod and Gun and Motor Sports in Canada* 8 (December 1906): 564–68.

UK, Foreign and Overseas Registers of British Subjects, 1627–1965. Foreign Registers and Returns, RG33/125. General Register Office. National Archives of the United Kingdom, Kew, Surrey, England.

United States Bureau of the Census. Historical Time Series, Families and Living Arrangements, Marital Status Table MS-2, "Estimated Median Age at First Marriage, by Sex: 1890 to the Present." 30 October 2014. www.census.gov/hhes/families/data/marital.html.

United States Department of Commerce and Labor, Bureau of the Census. *Occupations at the Twelfth Census, Prepared under the Supervision of William C. Hunt*. Washington, DC: Government Printing Office, 1904.

———. *Statistics of Women at Work: Based on Unpublished Information Derived from the Schedules of the Twelfth Census: 1900*. Washington, DC: Government Printing Office, 1907.

Vickers, George Edward. *Philadelphia: The Story of an American City*. Philadelphia: Dunlap Printing Co., 1893.

Wade, Elizabeth Flint. "Amateur Photography Through Women's Eyes." *Photo-American* 5, no. 8 (June 1894): 235–39.

Wheeler, A.O. *The Selkirk Range*, vol. 1. Ottawa: Government Printing Bureau, 1905.

Wheeler, Arthur O. "The Alpine Club of Canada's Expedition to Jasper Park, Yellowhead Pass and Mount Robson Region, 1911." *Canadian Alpine Journal* 4 (1912): 1–83.

White, James. *Place Names in the Rocky Mountains Between the 49th Parallel and the Athabaska River*. Pawtucket, RI: Quintin Publications, 2000. Originally published in 1916 in *The Transactions of the Royal Society of Canada*.

Wilcox, Walter D. *The Rockies of Canada*. New York and London: G.P. Putnam's Sons/ Knickbocker Press, 1900. Revised edition 1916.

Williamson, Leland M., Richard A. Foley, Henry H. Colclazer, Louis N. Megargee, Jay H. Mowbray, and Will. R. Antisdel, eds. "Charles Schäffer." In *Prominent and Progressive Pennsylvanians of the Nineteenth Century*, vol. 2, 439–41. Philadelphia: The Record Publishing Company, 1898.

"Women Photographers." *Photo Era: The American Journal of Photography* 12, no. 6 (June 1904): 101.

Yale University. *Catalogue of the Officers and Graduates of Yale University 1701–1901*. New Haven, CT: Yale University, 1901.

Yale University Class of 1835. *Biographical and Historical Record of the Class of 1835 in Yale College for the Fifty Years from the Admission of the Class to College*. New Haven, CT, 1881.

Banff *Crag and Canyon* Social Notes on Mary Schäffer's Activities

"Continues the Work." *Crag and Canyon*, 4 June 1904, 5.

"Mrs. Schaffer and Miss James…" *Crag and Canyon*, 22 April 1905, 4.

"Mrs. Schaffer and Miss Farr…" *Crag and Canyon*, 10 June 1905, 7.

"Mrs. Schaffer, the botanist…" *Crag and Canyon*, 9 September 1905, 2.

"Mrs. C. Schafer, who has recently returned…" *Crag and Canyon*, 25 August 1906, 5.

"Mrs. Dr. Schaffer, the well-known lady botanist…" *Crag and Canyon*, 30 May 1908, 4.

"W. Warren returned this week…" *Crag and Canyon*, 26 September 1908, 3.

"Mrs. Charles Schäffer, of Philadelphia, Mrs. H.H. Sharples…" *Crag and Canyon*, 29 May 1909, 6.

"Mrs. Mary T.S. Schäffer, who has been up in the region north…" *Crag and Canyon*, 23 September 1911, 8.

"Interesting Lecture." *Crag and Canyon*, 15 August 1914, 4.

"Appreciative Lecture." *Crag and Canyon*, 23 January 1915, 1.

"I.O.D.E. [Imperial Order Daughters of the Empire] Entertain—Historical Lecture on Matters of Local Import." *Crag and Canyon*, 30 January 1915, 1.

"Married in Vancouver—Three Cheers." *Crag and Canyon*, 3 July 1915, 2.

"Mrs. Wm Warren is confined…" *Crag and Canyon*, 17 February 1917, 8.

"A lecture under the auspices…." *Crag and Canyon*, 12 January 1918, 8.

"Boys at Front Write Interesting Letters Home." *Crag and Canyon*, 2 March 1918, 1.

"They Did Well." *Crag and Canyon*, 6 July 1918, 5.

"Mrs. Wm Warren, Mrs. Oliver…" *Crag and Canyon*, 3 September 1921, 8.

"Mrs. W. Warren, accompanied by Mrs. Nicholson…." *Crag and Canyon*, 28 July 1923, 8.

"Mrs. Wm Warren returned on Wednesday…." *Crag and Canyon*, 1 March 1924, 8.

"Mrs. Wm Warren has been a patient…." *Crag and Canyon*, 4 December 1925, 8.

"Mrs. William Warren is confined to the house…." *Crag and Canyon*, 19 March 1926, 6.

"Mrs. William Warren was a guest…." *Crag and Canyon*, 23 September 1927, 8.

"Banff and the I.O.D.E." *Crag and Canyon*, 8 October 1927, 1.

"Friends of Mrs. W. Warren will be pleased to learn…" *Crag and Canyon*, 2 May 1930, 1.

"Mrs. Wm. Warren Banff Oldtimer and Explorer of Rockies Passes." *Crag and Canyon*, 27 January 1939, 1–2.

Secondary Sources, 1933–2016

"1900—The History of the Building." *317 North 35th Street* [Philadelphia, PA]. 23 May 2015. http://poweltonvillage.org/interactivemap/files/317n35th.htm.

Abernethy, Lloyd M. "Progressivism, 1905–1919." In *Philadelphia: A 300-Year History*, edited by Russell F. Weigley, 524–65. New York: W.W. Norton, 1982.

Adams, Marjorie. Personal correspondence (email), 26 August 2014.

Allen, John L. "Lands of Myth, Waters of Wonder: The Place of the Imagination in the History of Geographical Exploration." In *Geographies of the Mind: Essays in Historical Geography in Honor of John Kirtland Wright*, edited by David Lowenthal and Martyn J. Bowden, 41–62. New York: Oxford University Press, 1976.

Alotta, Robert I. *Street Names of Philadelphia*. Philadelphia: Temple University Press, 1975.

Anderson, Monica. *Women and the Politics of Travel, 1870–1914*. Madison, WI: Fairleigh Dickinson University Press, 2006.

Atwood, Margaret. *Negotiating with the Dead*. Cambridge: Cambridge University Press, 2002.

Aubrey, Merrily K., ed. *Concise Place Names of Alberta*. Calgary, AB: University of Calgary Press, 2006.

Austin Institute. "Ask a Data Scientist—Age Differences Between Couples." Austin Institute for the Study of Family and Culture, 9 November 2014. www.austin-institute.org/research/ask-a-data-scientist-age-differences-between-couples/.

Babiak, Todd. *The Book of Stanley*. Toronto: McClelland & Stewart, 2007.

Baltzell, E. Digby. *Philadelphia Gentlemen: The Making of a National Upper Class*. Glencoe, IL: The Free Press, 1958.

Banta, Martha. *Imaging American Women: Idea and Ideals in Cultural History*. New York: Columbia University Press, 1987.

Barrow, Mark V., Jr. "The Specimen Dealer: Entrepreneurial Natural History in America's Gilded Age." *Journal of the History of Biology* 33, no. 3 (Winter 2000): 493–534.

Beck, Janice Sanford. Foreword to *Old Indian Trails of the Canadian Rockies* by Mary T.S. Schäffer. Abr. ed. Surrey, BC: Rocky Mountain Books, 2007.

———. *No Ordinary Woman: The Story of Mary Schäffer Warren*. Calgary, AB: Rocky Mountain Books, 2001. (Reprinted with additional material 2006.)

Bederman, Gail. *Manliness and Civilization: A Cultural History of Gender and Race in the United States, 1880–1917*. Chicago: University of Chicago Press, 1995.

Benjamin, Philip S. *The Philadelphia Quakers in the Industrial Age, 1865–1920*. Philadelphia: Temple University Press, 1976.

Bermingham, Ann. *Learning to Draw: Studies in the Cultural History of a Polite and Useful Art*. New Haven, CT: Yale University Press, 2000.

Bernardin, Susan, Melody Gaulich, Lisa MacFarlane, and Nicole Tonkovich. "Empire of the Lens: Women, Indians, and Cameras." In *Trading Gazes: Euro-American Women Photographers and Native North Americans, 1880–1940*, by Susan Bernardin, Melody Gaulich, Lisa MacFarlane, and Nicole Tonkovich, with an afterword by Louis Owens, 1–31. New Brunswick, NJ: Rutgers University Press, 2003.

Black, Jeremy. *Maps and Politics*. London: Reaktion Books, 1997.

Boles, Glen W., Roger W. Laurilla, and William L. Putnam. *Canadian Mountain Place Names: The Rockies and Columbia Mountains*. Surrey, BC: Rocky Mountain Books, 2006.

Bown, Stephen R., and Nicky L. Brink. "Mountain Woman." *The Beaver* 87, no. 3 (June–July 2007): 42–46.

Brey, William, Marie Brey, and John C. Browne. *Philadelphia Photographers, 1840–1900: A Directory with Biographical Sketches: Includes a History of the Photographic Society of Philadelphia*. Cherry Hill, NJ: Willowdale Press, 1992.

Brody, Hugh. *Maps and Dreams: Indians and the British Columbia Frontier*. Vancouver: Douglas & McIntyre, 2004.

Burt, Nathaniel. *The Perennial Philadelphians: The Anatomy of an American Aristocracy*. Boston: Little, Brown & Co., 1963.

Burt, Nathaniel, and Wallace E. Davies. "The Iron Age 1876–1905." In *Philadelphia: A 300-Year History*, edited by Russell F. Weigley, 471–523. New York: W.W. Norton, 1982.

Buss, Helen M. *Repossessing the World: Reading Memoirs by Contemporary Women*. Waterloo, ON: Wilfrid Laurier University Press, 2002.

Buss, Helen M., and Marlene Kadar, eds. *Working in Women's Archives: Researching Women's Private Literature and Archival Documents*. Waterloo, ON: Wilfrid Laurier University Press, 2001.

Campbell, Suzan, ed. *Women of the Stieglitz Circle*. Santa Fe, NM: Owings-Dewey Fine Art, 1998. Exhibition catalogue.

Carter, Sarah. *Capturing Women: The Manipulation of Cultural Imagery in Canada's Prairie West*. Montreal and Kingston: McGill-Queen's University Press, 1997.

Cavell, Edward. *Legacy in Ice: The Vaux Family and the Canadian Alps*. Banff, AB: Whyte Foundation, 1983.

Clarke, Larry R. "The Quaker Background of William Bartram's View of Nature." *Journal of the History of Ideas* 46, no. 3 (July–September 1985): 435–48.

Close, Susan. *Framing Identity: Social Practices of Photography in Canada (1880–1920)*. Winnipeg, MB: Arbeiter Ring Publishing, 2007.

Creates, Marlene. "Language and Land Use, Newfoundland 1994." In *Marlene Creates: Signs of Our Time*, by Marlene Creates, Lucy R. Lippard, and Robin Metcalfe, 42–43.

St. John's, NL: The Rooms Corporation of Newfoundland and Labrador and Tom Thomson Memorial Art Gallery, 2006. Exhibition catalogue.

———. *Marlene Creates: Language and Land Use, Alberta 1993*. Lethbridge, AB: Southern Alberta Art Gallery, 1993. Exhibition catalogue.

———. "Questions about the Place, Nova Scotia 1998." In *Marlene Creates: Signs of Our Time*, by Marlene Creates, Lucy R. Lippard, and Robin Metcalfe, 50–51. St. John's, NL: The Rooms Corporation of Newfoundland and Labrador and Tom Thomson Memorial Art Gallery, 2006. Exhibition catalogue.

Cronon, William. "The Trouble with Wilderness; or, Getting Back to the Wrong Nature." In *Uncommon Ground: Rethinking the Human Place in Nature*, edited by William Cronon, 69–90. New York: W.W. Norton, 1995.

Cull, Brendan. "The Art and Science of Early Canadian Photography: *Sites et végétaux du Canada* at the 1867 Exposition Universelle in Paris." Master's thesis, Queen's University, 2015.

Curtis, Verna Posever. "Frances Benjamin Johnston in 1900: Staking the Sisterhood's Claim in American Photography." In *Ambassadors of Progress: American Women Photographers in Paris 1900–1901*, edited by Bronwyn A.E. Griffith, 24–37. Giverny, France: Musée d'Art Américain Giverny, 2001.

Dalton, Andrew. "An 'Uncle,' a Displaced Father, a Legend of the Sport: Who Is Doc Adams?" *Globe and Mail* (Toronto), 25 April 2016, S5.

———. "Who's Your Daddy? Baseball May Have New Founder," AP *Big Story*, 7 April 2016. http://bigstory.ap.org/article/c938542ca6304a9fb85cb72e349d7db9/whos-your-daddy-modern-baseball-may-have-new-founder.

Daschuk, James. *Clearing the Plains: Disease, Politics of Starvation, and the Loss of Aboriginal Life*. Regina, SK: University of Regina Press, 2013.

Davidov, Judith Fryer. *Women's Camera Work: Self/Body/Other in American Visual Culture*. Durham, NC: Duke University Press, 1998.

Day, Moira, ed. *The Hungry Spirit: Selected Plays and Prose by Elsie Park Gowan*. Edmonton, AB: NeWest Press, 1992.

Dempsey, Hugh A. "Mary Warren's Letters from the Home Front 1916–1917." *Alberta History* 63, no. 1 (Winter 2015): 2–15.

Dever, Maryanne. "Reading Other People's Mail." *Archives and Manuscripts* 24, no. 1 (May 1996): 116–29.

Dodge, Martin. "From Here to There: A Curious Collection from the Hand Drawn Map Association/Kris Harzinski." *Cartographica* 45, no. 4 (2010): 274–76.

Doherty, Amy S. "Frances Benjamin Johnston, 1864–1952." *History of Photography* 4, no. 2 (April 1980): 97–111.

Domosh, Mona. "With 'Stout Boots and a Stout Heart': Historical Methodology and Feminist Geography." In *Thresholds in Feminist Geography: Difference, Methodology, Representation*, edited by John Paul Jones III, Heidi J. Nast, and Susan M. Roberts, 225–38. Lanham, MD: Rowman & Littlefield Publishers, 1997.

Domosh, Mona, and Joni Seager. *Putting Women in Place: Feminist Geographers Make Sense of the World*. New York: Guilford Press, 2001.

Downey, Nathan Adams. "Mailbox: On Baseball When the Game was Very New." *New York Times*, 13 April 1980, S2.

Emberley, J.V. "Colonial Phantasms: Aboriginality and the Family in the Photographic Archives." In *ReCalling Early Canada: Reading the Political in Literary and Cultural Production*, edited by Jennifer Blair, Daniel Coleman, Kate Higginson, and Lorraine York, 301–34. Edmonton: University of Alberta Press, 2005.

———. *Defamiliarizing the Aboriginal: Cultural Practices and Decolonization in Canada*. Toronto: University of Toronto Press, 2007.

Fagin, N.B. *William Bartram: Interpreter of the American Landscape*. Baltimore, MD: Johns Hopkins Press, 1933.

Fischer, Diane P. *Paris 1900: The "American School" at the Universal Exposition*. New Brunswick, NJ: Rutgers University Press, 1999.

Foran, Jill. *Mary Schäffer: An Adventurous Woman's Exploits in the Canadian Rockies*. Canmore, AB: Altitude Publishing, 2003.

Francis, Daniel. *Copying People: Photographing British Columbia First Nations, 1860–1940*. Saskatoon, SK: Fifth House Publishers, 1996.

Franzen, Trisha. *Spinsters and Lesbians: Independent Womanhood in the United States*. New York: New York University Press, 1996.

Fry, Jacqueline. Untitled essay. Translated by Elizabeth Ritchie. In *The Distance Between Two Points Is Measured In Memories, Labrador 1988*, by Marlene Creates, 53–58. North Vancouver, BC: Presentation House Gallery, 1990. Exhibition catalogue.

Gadd, Ben. *Handbook of the Canadian Rockies: Geology, Plants, Animals, History and Recreation from Waterton/Glacier to the Yukon*, 2nd ed. Jasper, AB: Corax Press, 1995.

Gates, Barbara T. *Kindred Nature: Victorian and Edwardian Women Embrace the Living World*. Chicago: University of Chicago Press, 1998.

Gaudette, Marybeth. "Playing Fair with the Right to Privacy." *Archival Issues* 28, no. 1 (2003–2004): 21–34.

Gere, Anne Ruggles. *Intimate Practices: Literacy and Cultural Work in US Women's Clubs, 1880–1920*. Urbana: University of Illinois Press, 1997.

Gerson, Carole. *Canadian Women in Print, 1750–1918*. Waterloo, ON: Wilfrid Laurier University Press, 2011.

Gilbert, Michelle, and James Gillett. "Into the Mountains and Across the Country: Emergent Forms of Equine Adventure Leisure in Canada." *Loisir et Société/Society and Leisure* 37, no. 2 (2014): 313–25.

Gould, Stephen J. "A Web of Tales." *Natural History* 97 (October 1988): 16–23.

Gover, C. Jane. *The Positive Image: Women Photographers in Turn of the Century America*. Albany: State University of New York Press, 1988.

Gowan, Elsie Park. "Jasper's First Lady." *Heritage* 5, no. 4 (July/August 1977): 19–20.

———. "A Quaker in Buckskin," *Alberta Historical Review* 5 (Summer 1957): 1–6, 24–28.

Grand, Sarah. "The New Aspect of the Woman Question." *North American Review* 158, no. 3 (March 1984): 270–76.

Griffith, Bronwyn A.E. "'Dainty and Artistic or Strong and Forceful—Just as You Wish': American Women Photographers at the Universal Exposition of 1900." In *Ambassadors of Progress: American Women Photographers in Paris 1900–1901*, edited by Bronwyn A.E. Griffith, 12–23. Giverny, France: Musée d'Art Américain Giverny, 2001.

Griffith, Bronwyn A.E., ed. *Ambassadors of Progress: American Women Photographers in Paris 1900–1901*. Giverny, France: Musée d'Art Américain Giverny, 2001.

Hannum, Gillian Greenhill. "Frances Benjamin Johnston: Promoting Women Photographers in 'The Ladies' Home Journal.'" *Nineteenth Century* 24, no. 2 (Fall 2004): 22–29.

Hart, E.J. *Diamond Hitch: The Pioneer Guides and Outfitters of Banff and Jasper*. Banff, AB: Summerthought Ltd., 1979.

———. *Jimmy Simpson: Legend of the Rockies*. Canmore, AB: Altitude Publishing, 1991.

———. *The Selling of Canada: The CPR and the Beginnings of Canadian Tourism*, Banff, AB: Altitude Publishing, 1983.

———. "Yahe-Weha—Mountain Woman: The Life and Travels of Mary Schäffer Warren, 1861–1939." In *A Hunter of Peace: Mary T.S. Schäffer's Old Indian Trails of the Canadian Rockies*, introduction and edited by E.J. Hart, 1–14. Banff, AB: Whyte Museum of the Canadian Rockies, 1980.

———. "Yahe-Weha—Mountain Woman: The Life and Travels of Mary Schäffer Warren, 1861–1939." In *A Hunter of Peace: Mary T.S. Schäffer's Old Indian Trails of the Canadian Rockies*, 2nd ed., introduction and edited by E.J. Hart, 11–26, foreword by Jennifer Rutkair. Banff, AB: Whyte Museum of the Canadian Rockies, 2014.

Hastings, Sally A. "Travelling to Learn, Learning to Lead: Japanese Women as American College Students." In *Modern Girls on the Go: Gender, Mobility, and Labour in Japan*, edited by Alisa Freedman, Laura Miller, Christina Reiko Yano, 193–208. Stanford, CA: Stanford University Press, 2013.

Heilbrun, Carolyn G. *Reinventing Womanhood*. New York: W.W. Norton, 1979.

———. *Writing a Woman's Life*. New York: W.W. Norton, 1988.

Henson, Pamela M. "'Through Books to Nature': Anna Botsford Comstock and the Nature Study Movement." In *Natural Eloquence: Women Reinscribe Science*, edited by Barbara T. Gates and Ann B. Shteir, 116–43. Madison: University of Wisconsin Press, 1997.

Heron, Liz, and Val Williams, eds. *Illuminations: Women Writing on Photography from the 1850s to the Present*. London: I.B. Tauris, 1996.

"Homegrown Mountain Movie Maker." *Mountain* 3 (Fall 2000): 28.

Homer, William Innes. *Pictorial Photography in Philadelphia: The Pennsylvania Academy's Salons, 1898–1901*. Philadelphia: Pennsylvania Academy of the Fine Arts, 1984.

Howgego, Raymond John. "Benham, Gertrude Emily (1867–1938)." *Oxford Dictionary of National Biography*. Online ed. October 2008.

Huffman, Nikolas H. "Charting the Other Maps: Cartography and Visual Methods in Feminist Research." In *Thresholds in Feminist Geography: Difference, Methodology,*

Representation, edited by John Paul Jones III, Heidi J. Nast, and Susan M. Roberts, 255–83. Lanham, MD: Rowman & Littlefield Publishers, 1997.

Jacob, Christian. *The Sovereign Map: Theoretical Approaches in Cartography throughout History*. Translated by Tom Conley. Chicago: University of Chicago Press, 2006.

Jehlen, Myra. "Archimedes and the Paradox of Feminist Criticism." *Signs* 6, no. 4 (Summer 1981): 575–601.

Kawai, Michi. *My Lantern*. Ginza, Tokyo: Kyo Bun Kwan, 1939.

Kilgannon, Corey. "Family Rallies in Late Innings for a Pioneering Shortstop." *New York Times*, 23 September 2015, A21.

———. "Late Rally for Doc Adams, a Jeter Before There Were Mitts." *New York Times*, 23 September 2015, www.nytimes.com/2015/09/23/nyregion/late-rally-for-doc-adams-a-jeter-before-there-were-mitts.html?_r=0.

King, Thomas. *The Truth about Stories: A Native Narrative*. Toronto: House of Anansi Press, 2003.

Kingsland, Sharon E. *The Evolution of American Ecology, 1890–2000*. Baltimore, MD: Johns Hopkins University Press, 2005.

Kohlstedt, Sally Gregory. "In from the Periphery: American Women in Science, 1830–1880." *Signs* 4, no. 1 (Autumn 1978): 81–96.

Kropp, Phoebe. "Wilderness Wives and Dishwashing Husbands: Comfort and the Domestic Art of Camping in America, 1880–1910." *Journal of Social History* 43, no. 1 (2009): 5–30.

Krutak, Lars. "Tattooing among Japan's Ainu People." 2008. http://larskrutak.com/tattooing-among-japans-ainu-people/.

Lang, Michale. *An Adventurous Woman Abroad: The Selected Lantern Slides of Mary T.S. Schäffer*. Victoria, BC: Rocky Mountain Books, 2011.

Laviolette, Mary-Beth. *A Delicate Art: Artists, Wildflowers and Native Plants of the West*. Calgary, AB: Rocky Mountain Books, 2012.

Lepore, Jill. "Just the Facts, Ma'am." *The New Yorker* 84, no. 6 (24 March 2008): 79–83.

Lester, Geoffrey. *Atlas of Alberta Railways*. University of Alberta Press, 2005. http://railways.library.ualberta.ca.

Lippard, Lucy. Introduction to *Partial Recall: Photographs of Native North Americans*, edited by Lucy Lippard, 13–45. New York: The New Press, 1992.

MacFarlane, Lisa. "Mary Schäffer's 'Comprehending Equal Eyes.'" In *Trading Gazes: Euro-American Women Photographers and Native North Americans, 1880–1940*, by Susan Bernardin, Melody Gaulich, Lisa MacFarlane, and Nicole Tonkovich, 108–49. New Brunswick, NJ: Rutgers University Press, 2003.

MacLaren, I.S. "Cultured Wilderness in Jasper National Park." *Journal of Canadian Studies/Revue d'études canadiennes* 34, no. 3 (1999): 7–58.

———. Introduction to *Culturing Wilderness in Jasper National Park: Studies in Two Centuries of Human History in the Upper Athabasca Watershed*, edited by I.S. MacLaren, xv–xliii. Edmonton: University of Alberta Press, 2007.

McCowan, Dan. *Hill-Top Tales*. Toronto: Macmillan, 1948.

Mandell, Richard D. *Paris 1900: the Great World's Fair*. Toronto: University of Toronto Press, 1967.

Milliken, Katherine. "Quakers in Nature: The Vaux Family's Photographs of Mountains and Glaciers." Master's thesis, University of Alberta, 2005.

Minh-ha, Trinh T. *Woman, Native, Other: Writing Postcoloniality and Feminism*. Bloomington: Indiana University Press, 1989.

"Moberly Descendants Ignored in Totem Dispute." *The Fitzhugh* (Jasper, AB), 13 May 2010.

Morantz, Alan. *Where Is Here?: Canada's Maps and the Stories They Tell*. Toronto: Penguin Canada, 2002.

Morra, Linda M. *Unarrested Archives: Case Studies in Twentieth-Century Canadian Women's Authorship*. Toronto: University of Toronto Press, 2014.

Morra, Linda M., and Jessica Schagerl, eds. *Basements and Attics, Closets and Cyberspace: Explorations in Canadian Women's Archives*. Waterloo, ON: Wilfrid Laurier University Press, 2012.

Nelson, Lise, and Joni Seager, eds. *A Companion to Feminist Geography*. Oxford: Blackwell Publishing, 2005.

Newhall, Beaumont. *The History of Photography: From 1839 to the Present Day*. New York: Museum of Modern Art, 1964.

Ofgang, Erik. "Efforts Ramp Up to Get CT Legend Into Hall of Fame." *Connecticut Magazine* 6 March 2015, www.connecticutmag.com/Blog/History/March-2015/Efforts-Ramp-Up-to-Get-CT-Baseball-Legend-Into-Hall-of-Fame/.

Owens, Louis. *I Hear the Train: Reflection, Inventions, Refractions*. Norman: University of Oklahoma Press, 2001.

Panzer, Mary. *Philadelphia Naturalistic Photography 1865–1906*. New Haven, CT: Yale University Art Gallery, 1982. Exhibition catalogue.

Patterson, Martha H. *Beyond the Gibson Girl: Reimagining the American New Woman, 1895–1915*. Urbana: University of Illinois Press, 2005.

———. "Recovering the Work of American Clubwomen." *American Quarterly* 51, no. 1 (1999): 221–28.

Philips, Patricia. *The Scientific Lady: A Social History of Women's Scientific Interests, 1520–1918*. London: Weidenfeld and Nicolson, 1990.

Piper, Karen. *Cartographic Fictions: Maps, Race, and Identity*. New Brunswick, NJ: Rutgers University Press, 2002.

Piper, Liza, and Lisa Szabo-Jones, eds. *Sustaining the West: Cultural Responses to Canadian Environments*. Waterloo, ON: Wilfrid Laurier University Press, 2015.

Poivert, Michel. "A Taste of the Avant-Garde: The Reception of American Women Photographers in Paris (1900–1901)." In *Ambassadors of Progress: American Women Photographers in Paris 1900–1901*, edited by Bronwyn A.E. Griffith, 38–50. Giverny, France: Musée d'Art Américain Giverny, 2001.

Quitslund, Toby. "Her Feminine Colleagues: Photographs and Letters Collected by Frances Benjamin Johnston in 1900." In *Women Artists in Washington Collections*, edited by

Josephine Withers, 97–109. College Park, MD: University of Maryland Art Gallery and Women's Caucus for Art, 1979. Exhibition catalogue.

Rak, Julie. *Boom! Manufacturing Memoir for the Popular Market.* Waterloo, ON: Wilfrid Laurier University Press, 2013.

Reichwein, PearlAnn. *Climber's Paradise: Making Canada's Mountain Parks, 1906–1974.* Edmonton: University of Alberta Press, 2014.

Reichwein, PearlAnn, and Lisa McDermott. "Opening the Secret Garden: Mary Schäffer, Jasper Park Conservation, and the Survey of Maligne Lake, 1911." In *Culturing Wilderness in Jasper National Park: Studies in Two Centuries of Human History in the Upper Athabasca River Watershed*, edited by I.S. MacLaren, 155–98. Edmonton: University of Alberta Press, 2007.

Richie, Marlene. "Michi Kawai: An Inspiring Woman with a Mission." *Child Research Net*, 21 May 2010. www.childresearch.net/papers/new/2010_02.html.

Riegert, Paul W. "Fletcher, James." *Dictionary of Canadian Biography Online 1901–1910*, vol. 13. University of Toronto/Université Laval, 2003–. www.biographi.ca/en/bio/fletcher_james_13E.html.

Riley, Glenda. *Women and Nature: Saving the "Wild."* Lincoln: University of Nebraska Press, 1999.

Rix, Martyn. *The Golden Age of Botanical Art.* Chicago: University of Chicago Press, 2012.

Roberson, Susan L. "American Women and Travel Writing." In *The Cambridge Companion to American Travel Writing*, edited by Alfred Bendixen and Judith Hamera, 214–27. Cambridge: Cambridge University Press, 2009.

Rose, Barbara. *Tsuda Umeka and Women's Education in Japan.* New Haven, CT: Yale University Press, 1992.

Rosenblum, Naomi. *A History of Women Photographers.* New York: Abbeville Press, 1994.

Roth, Mark. "The Photographs and Travels of Mary Schaffer Warren." *The Beaver* 309, no. 3 (1978): 28–33.

Roy, Wendy. *Maps of Difference: Canada, Women, and Travel.* Montreal and Kingston: McGill-Queen's University Press, 2005.

Rutkair, Jennifer. "Adding Gender to the Archival Contextual Turn: the Rocky Mountain Photographic Records of Mary Schäffer Warren." Master's thesis, University of Manitoba, 2011.

Ryan, Mary P. *Mysteries of Sex: Tracing Women and Men through American History.* Chapel Hill: University of North Carolina Press, 2006.

———. *Womanhood in America: From Colonial Times to the Present.* 2nd ed. New York: New Viewpoints, 1979.

Rydell, Robert W. "Gateway to the 'American Century': The American Representation at the Paris Universal Exposition of 1900." In *Paris 1900: The "American School" at the Universal Exposition*, edited by Diane P. Fischer, 119–44. New Brunswick, NJ: Rutgers University Press, 1999.

Sandler, Martin W. *Against the Odds: Women Pioneers in the First Hundred Years of Photography*. New York: Rizzoli International Publications, 2002.

Sanford, R.W. *High Ideals: Canadian Pacific's Swiss Guides, 1899–1999*. Canmore, AB: Alpine Club of Canada, 1999.

Schäffer, Mary T.S. *Old Indian Trails of the Canadian Rockies*. 1911. Abr. ed. In *A Hunter of Peace: Mary T.S. Schäffer's Old Indian Trails of the Canadian Rockies*, introduction and edited by E.J. Hart. Banff, AB: Whyte Museum of the Canadian Rockies, 1980. (2nd ed. with foreword by Jennifer Rutkair, 2014).

———. *Old Indian Trails of the Canadian Rockies*. 1911. Abr. ed. Foreword by Janice Sanford Beck. Vancouver: Rocky Mountain Books, 2007. (Abr. 2nd ed., 2011).

Schwartz, Joan M. "Photographic Reflections: Nature, Landscape and Environment." *Environmental History* 12 (October 2007): 966–93.

Schwartz, Joan M., and James R. Ryan, eds. *Picturing Place: Photography and the Geographical Imagination*. London: I.B. Tauris, 2003.

Scott, Chic. *Mountain Romantics: The Whytes of Banff*. Banff, AB: Whyte Museum of the Canadian Rockies and Assiniboine Publishing, 2014.

———. *Pushing the Limits: The Story of Canadian Mountaineering*. Calgary, AB: Rocky Mountain Books, 2000.

Scott, Joan Wallach. *Feminism and History*. New York: Oxford University Press, 1996.

Shtier, Ann B. *Cultivating Women Cultivating Science: Flora's Daughters and Botany in England 1760 to 1860*. Baltimore, MD: Johns Hopkins University Press, 1996.

Skidmore, Colleen. "Imaging the West: Hugo Viewegar and the Autochrome in Canada." *History of Photography* 27 (Winter 2003): 342–48.

———. "Taking a Deep Interest: Métis and Aboriginal Women." In *This Wild Spirit: Women in the Rocky Mountains of Canada*, ed. Colleen Skidmore, 1–18. Edmonton: University of Alberta Press, 2006.

———. "'Touring An Other's Reality': Aboriginals, Immigrants, and Autochromes." *Ethnologies* 26, no. 1 (2004): 145–64.

———. "Women Workers in Notman's Studio: 'Young Ladies of the Printing Room.'" *History of Photography* 20, no. 2 (1996): 122–28.

Skidmore, Colleen, ed. *This Wild Spirit: Women in the Rocky Mountains of Canada*. Edmonton: University of Alberta Press, 2006.

Smith, Cyndi. *Off the Beaten Track: Women Adventurers and Mountaineers in Western Canada*. Calgary, AB: Coyote Books, 1989.

Smith-Rosenberg, Carroll. *Disorderly Conduct: Visions of Gender in Victorian America*. New York: Oxford University Press, 1985.

Snipes, Samuel M. "The Life of Japanese Quaker Inazo Nitobe." *Friends Journal*, 1 August 2011, www.friendsjournal.org/life-japanese-quaker-inazo-nitobe-1862-1933/.

Snow, John. *These Mountains Are Our Sacred Places: The Story of the Stoney People*. 2nd ed. Calgary, AB: Fifth House Publishers, 2005.

Sontag, Susan. *On Photography*. New York: Farrar, Straus and Giroux, 1977.

Spears, Betty. "Mary, Mary, Quite Contrary, Why Do Women Play?" *Canadian Journal of History of Sport* 18, no. 1 (1987): 67–75.

Stearns, Sharon. *Hunter of Peace*. Victoria, BC: Scirocco Drama, 1993.

Sterry, Lorraine. *Victorian Women Travellers in Meiji Japan: Discovering a "New" Land*. Kent, UK: Global Oriental Ltd., 2009.

Swanson, Darren. "A Place for the Dead—the Foreign Cemeteries of Kobe and Osaka 1867 to the Present Day." 2010. www.academia.edu/6123999/A_Place_for_the_Dead_The_Foreign_Cemeteries_of_Kobe_and_Osaka.

Thorn, John. *Baseball in the Garden of Eden: The Secret History of the Early Game*. New York: Simon & Schuster, 2011.

———. "The Father of Baseball? You Probably Never Heard of Him." *Elysian Fields Quarterly* 11, no. 1 (Winter 1992): 85–91.

Trachtenberg, Alan. *Reading American Photographs: Images as History, Mathew Brady to Walker Evans*. Toronto: Collins Publishers, 1989.

Treaty 7 Elders and Tribal Council with Walter Hildebrant, Dorothy First Rider, and Sarah Carter. *The True Spirit and Original Intent of Treaty 7*. Montreal and Kingston: McGill-Queen's University Press, 1996.

Tyson, Patricia Peterson. "Mary Sharples Schäffer: Explorer of The Canadian Rockies." *Frontiers: Annual of the Academy of Natural Sciences of Philadelphia* 3 (1981–82): 64–77.

Van den Hoonaard, Will C. *Map Worlds: A History of Women in Cartography*. Waterloo, ON: Wilfrid Laurier University Press, 2013.

Vaux, Henry, Jr. Personal correspondence (email), 25 October 2015.

Vicinus, Martha. *Independent Women: Work & Community for Single Women, 1850–1920*. Chicago: University of Chicago Press, 1985.

Vickers, George Edward. *Philadelphia: The Story of an American City*. Philadelphia: Dunlap Printing Co., 1893.

Voxall, Helen. "Privacy and Personal Papers." *Archives and Manuscripts* 12, no. 1 (May 1984): 38–44.

Wagner, Anton. "Elsie Park Gowan: Distinctively Canadian." *Theatre History in Canada* 8, no. 1 (Spring 1987): 68–82.

Waiser, W.A. "Macoun, John." In *Dictionary of Canadian Biography Online 1911–1920*, vol. 14. University of Toronto/Université Laval, 2003–. www.biographi.ca/en/bio/macoun_john_14E.html.

Walker, Doreen, ed. *Dear Nan: Letters of Emily Carr, Nan Cheney and Humphrey Toms*. Vancouver: University of British Columbia Press, 1990.

Wallace, W. Stewart, ed. *The Encyclopedia of Canada*, vol. 3. Toronto: University Associates of Canada, 1948.

Wexler, Laura. *Tender Violence: Domestic Visions in an Age of U.S. Imperialism*. Chapel Hill: University of North Carolina Press, 2000.

Wheeler, William. *Botanical Illustration*. Paris: L'Aventurine, 2003.

Whitfield, Paul. "Follow-Through Day of 1903 Was Much Like Any Other." *Investor's Business Daily*, 27 June 2014. http://education.investors.com/investors-corner/706592-how-to-identify-the-start-of-an-uptrend.htm.

Wilford, John Noble. *The Mapmakers*. Rev. ed. New York: Alfred A. Knopf, 2000.

Williams, M.B. *Jasper National Park: A Descriptive Guide*. Hamilton, Saskatoon, and Vancouver: Larson Publishing Company, 1949.

Williams, Roger L. *"A Region of Astonishing Beauty": The Botanical Exploration of the Rocky Mountains*. Lanham, MD: Roberts Rinehart Publishers, 2003.

Williams, Val. *The Other Observers: Women Photographers in Britain 1900 to the Present*. London: Virago Press, 1991.

Williamson, Steven. "Seven Ways to Compute the Relative Value of a US Dollar Amount, 1774 to Present." *MeasuringWorth*. www.measuringworth.com/uscompare/.

Withers, Josephine, ed. *Women Artists in Washington Collections*. College Park, MD: University of Maryland Art Gallery and Women's Caucus for Art, 1979. Exhibition catalogue.

Wolf, Edwin. *Philadelphia: Portrait of an American City*. Philadelphia: Stackpole Books, 1975.

Wood, Denis. "The Fine Line between Mapping and Mapmaking." *Cartographica* 30, no. 4 (Winter 1993): 50–60.

———. "Maps and Mapmaking." *Cartographica* 30, no. 1 (Spring 1993): 1–9.

———. "What Makes a Map?" *Cartographica* 30, no. 2 & 3 (Summer/Autumn 1993): 81–86.

Wood, Elizabeth A. "Memorial to Ida Helen Ogilvie (1874–1963)." *Geological Society of America Bulletin* 75, no. 2 (February 1964): 35–39.

Illustrations and Permissions

Whyte Museum of the Canadian Rockies

The Mary Schäffer fonds in the Archives and Library of the Whyte Museum of the Canadian Rockies, Banff, Alberta (WMCR) consist of manuscript (M79) and visual (V527) materials. Other fonds include Schäffer materials as well. Mary Schäffer produced and reproduced photographs in a variety of media; knowing the media and sites in which an image was viewed during Schäffer's lifetime illuminates circulation, audiences, and meanings that ensued. In the captions for these images in this book, the codes used by the WMCR following the (V) collection number indicate the medium in which each image was made and is preserved. Photograph albums (PD) contain monochromatic paper prints in a variety of sizes, which Mary Schäffer and Molly Adams gathered, arranged, and occasionally labelled for their private use. These are contact prints made from the original negatives exposed on glass (NG) until 1906 or film (NA) from 1907 onwards by Schäffer, Adams, and their colleagues. Schäffer also made positives on glass slides (PS) that she hand-tinted and exhibited in public lectures by means of a lantern slide projector. These slides are rarely titled or dated. One framed print (PC), inscribed to a friend, is also found in the Schäffer collection. All original forms in which an image is found in the archives are cited. Occasionally, only a negative, or a slide, or a print survives in the collection. The source for the reproduction in this book is the final collection number cited, and used with permission of the Whyte Museum of the Canadian Rockies.

Smithsonian Institution

The mounted, titled, and signed platinum print photographs that Mary Schäffer sent to Frances Benjamin Johnston for the 1900 Paris Exposition are preserved in the Mary Schäffer Photograph Collection, Division of Culture & the Arts at the National Museum of American History (NMAH), Smithsonian Institution, Washington, DC, and reproduced with permission.

Adams Family Collection

Reproductions of photographs and documents, and excerpts from diaries and letters written by Mary W. (Molly) Adams, in the Adams Family Collection are used with permission.

Wilson Family Collection

Excerpts from diaries and letters written by Henrietta L. Tuzo (Wilson) in the Wilson Family Collection are used with permission.

1 She Who Colored Slides

2 Philadelphia, Paris, and the Rocky Mountains of Canada, 1889–1903

3 The Rocky Mountains of Canada, 1904–1906

4 Maligne Lake, 1907–1911

5 Japan, 1908–1909, and Banff, 1909–1939

Index

Page numbers in italics refer to illustrations and maps. MS refers to Mary Schäffer; MA refers to Molly Adams; CS to Charles Schäffer; and WW to William Warren.

Other Titles from The University of Alberta Press

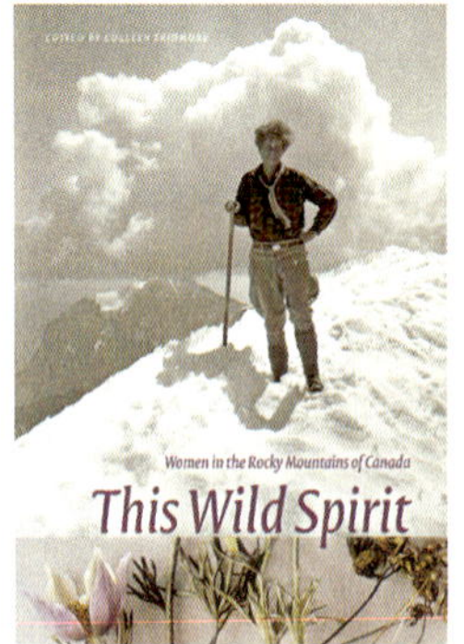

This Wild Spirit

Women in the Rocky Mountains of Canada

COLLEEN SKIDMORE, *Editor*

This popular book traces women's creative and cultural legacies in the Rocky Mountains of Canada.

Mountain Cairns: A series on the history and culture of the Canadian Rocky Mountains

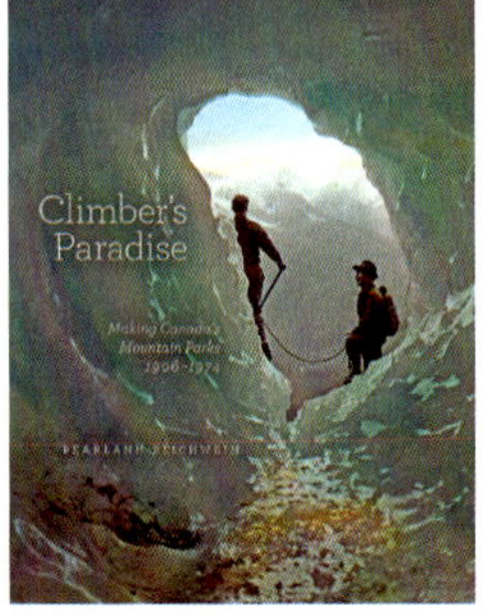

Climber's Paradise

Making Canada's Mountain Parks, 1906–1974

PEARLANN REICHWEIN

Tenacious activism of the Alpine Club of Canada leads to mountain recreation and conservation.

Mountain Cairns: A series on the history and culture of the Canadian Rocky Mountains

Culturing Wilderness in Jasper National Park

Studies in Two Centuries of Human History in the Upper Athabasca River Watershed

I.S. MACLAREN, *Editor*

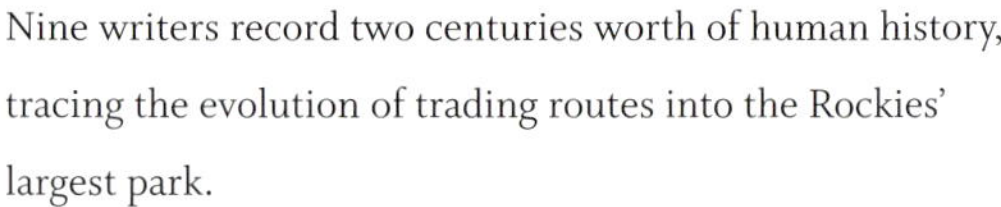

Nine writers record two centuries worth of human history, tracing the evolution of trading routes into the Rockies' largest park.

Mountain Cairns: A series on the history and culture of the Canadian Rocky Mountains

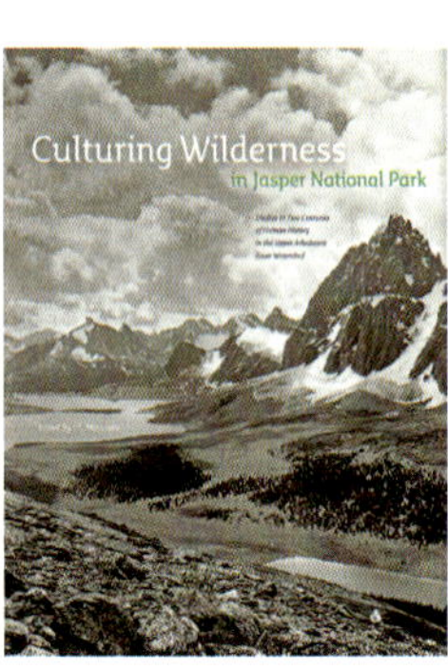

More information at www.uap.ualberta.ca